A CHORUS LINE

AND THE

MUSICALS

OF

MICHAEL

BENNETT

....

A CHORUS LINE

AND THE

MUSICALS

OF

MICHAEL

BENNETT

....

KEN MANDELBAUM

ST. MARTIN'S PRESS
NEW YORK

Design by Raquel Jaramillo

Library of Congress Cataloging-in-Publication Data

Mandelbaum, Ken.
    A Chorus Line and the musicals of Michael Bennett / Ken Mandelbaum.
        p. cm.
    ISBN 0–312–03061–4
    1. Bennett, Michael, 1943–1987   2. Theatrical producers and directors—United States—Biography.   3. Choreographers—United States—Biography.   I. Title.
PN2287.B4323M36   1989
782.81′092′4—dc19
    [B]   89-4067

First Edition
10 9 8 7 6 5 4 3 2 1

To
my
parents
and
grandparents,
who
took
me
to
musicals

CONTENTS

ACKNOWLEDGMENTS

I WOULD LIKE TO EXPRESS my enormous gratitude to those who took the time to share with me their personal reminiscences of Bennett and his work: Bob Avian, Ben Bagley, Kelly Bishop, Pamela Blair, Steve Boockvor, Candy Brown, Joe Calvan, Wayne Cilento, Marilyn Cooper, Graciela Daniele, Nicholas Dante, Merle Debuskey, Ron Dennis, Tom Eyen, Victor Griffin, Eivind Harum, Danny Herman, Bob Herr, Jennifer Holliday, Peter Howard, Bernard B. Jacobs, Robert Kamlot, Lainie Kazan, James Kirkwood, Howard Kissel, Marvin A. Krauss, Henry Krieger, Swoosie Kurtz, Jack Lenny, Fran Liebergall, Dorothy Loudon, Bob MacDonald, Donna McKechnie, Tharon Musser, Leland Palmer, Michon Peacock, Michael Peters, Don Pippin, Tom Porter, Trish Ramish, Ann Reinking, George Rose, Justin Ross, Sandra Roveta, Carole Schweid, John Sharpe, Treva Silverman, Alexis Smith, Stephen Sondheim, Tony Stevens, Jane Summerhays, Gerald M. Teijelo, Jr., Robert Thomas, Sada Thompson, Tommy Tune, Jonathan Tunick, Michael Vita, Robin Wagner, Jimmy Webb, Harold Wheeler, Janet Stewart White, Charles Willard, and Martin Zone.

For their help, support, and encouragement, I would like to thank the following: John Breglio, Bryan Brooks, Rex Bunnett, Steve Cole, Betty Corwin, Jillana Devine, Jeffrey Dunn, Roz Dunn, Carol Edwards, Mike Emyrs, Irene Gandy, Barbara Gelb, David Gersten, Kevin Grubb, Dan Jinks, Susan Lee, Larry Moore, Richard Norton, Lonny Price, Bob Schear, David Semonin, David Shine, Dennis Soens, Dorothy Swerdlove, Richard Traubner, and the entire staff of the Billy Rose Theatre Collection and the Theatre on Film and Tape Collection of the New York Public Library at Lincoln Center, especially Richard C. Lynch, Chris Karatnytsky, and Ed Sanger.

Special thanks to my mother, Helen Mandelbaum, my sister, Beth Mandelbaum, my brother-in-law, Richard Bernstein, and Arthur Mones for their constant support, loyalty, and love; to Ezio Petersen, for the use of his 1983 interviews with Marvin Hamlisch and Edward Kleban; to Don Shewey, for permission to use the transcript of his in-depth 1983 interview with Bennett; to Tim McGinnis, who gave me the opportunity to do the book but did not live to see it published; to my editor Michael Denneny, for his belief in the book and his marvelously incisive supervision of the manuscript; and to Ethan Mordden, without whom this book would not have been written, and whose constant generosity and assistance were crucial to its existence.

NOTE ON
QUOTATIONS

U NLESS A SPECIFIC SOURCE is noted, all quotations in the book are
from my personal interviews with the subjects, with the following excep-
tions:

Michael Bennett quotes, unless otherwise noted, are from the transcript of a 1983 interview with Bennett conducted by Don Shewey, from
tapes of Bennett in rehearsal, or from Bennett on television.

Marvin Hamlisch and Ed Kleban quotes are from radio interviews
conducted in 1983 by Ezio Petersen for WKCR. A couple of Hamlisch
quotes are from the memorial tribute to Kleban.

"Source" indicates that the subject did not wish his or her name to be
associated with the quote.

I would like you to say that I am a direct descendant of Terpsichore, and I don't have a mother and father, and I wasn't born in Buffalo, and all the boring things that are really true about where I come from. I wish I was born in a trunk in a basement of a Broadway theatre, and I crawled into the pit and looked up and there was Jule Styne conducting the overture to *Gypsy,* and I heard Ethel Merman sing, and the first moment of life was experiencing a Jerry Robbins musical. I can't think of anything more perfect.

—Michael Bennett, 1983

PROLOGUE

"NO SHOW

RUNS FOREVER"

ON SEPTEMBER 29, 1983, THE SHUBERT Theatre in New York was packed with an audience witnessing a unique theatrical event, one that many felt was the pinnacle of their theatregoing lives. It was the night of the 3,389th performance of *A Chorus Line,* and the man who conceived, directed, and choreographed the show, Michael Bennett, in an act of breathtaking creativity and prodigality, restaged the show for that one performance to celebrate its becoming the longest-running in Broadway history.

Exactly four years later, September 29, 1987, the Shubert was again packed, with many of the same people who had been present for that milestone occasion. But this time they were assembled for a memorial tribute to Bennett, who died on July 2, 1987. The tribute had originally been scheduled for July 27, but it was postponed. Bennett's longtime associate and friend Bob Avian was occupied choreographing the London premiere of *Follies* (his first assignment without Bennett at his side) for a July 21 opening, and he and John Breglio, Bennett's lawyer and executor, were at a loss as to how to do justice to Bennett without the uncanny theatrical instincts of Bennett himself to guide them.

But it was now 3 P.M. on September 29, time to pay tribute to Bennett, the theatrical wizard, and Bennett, the loyal, generous, unpredictable colleague and friend. Virtually everyone present was well aware that Bennett was the supreme conceptual artist of the musical theatre of his time, capable of creating moments that could send an audience into screaming ecstasy, and others that could bring audiences to a level of emotional identification rare in musical or nonmusical theatre.

But what came across most strongly on this occasion was the degree to which Bennett had touched the lives of those who knew him, and how important he was to those with whom he had worked. All who spoke expressed a sense of being lost without him. And, as "The Dreams" from *Dreamgirls* sang during the memorial, it was, for everyone, "Hard to Say Goodbye."

The tribute began with Marvin Hamlisch playing "What I Did for Love" on the piano, while films were projected of Bennett, first at age three, tap dancing at a wedding, then as a sixteen-year-old, striking *West Side Story* poses in the family driveway. When the screen was raised, eight black-and-white blowups of Bennett, looking alternately handsome, pensive, and pixieish, were lowered. The stage setting for the rest of the afternoon, until the finale, consisted of the photos, a piano, a standing microphone, and a white line, a fixture of the Shubert stage since 1975.

Avian, whose professional and personal collaboration with Bennett was unparalleled, spoke of meeting the seventeen-year-old Bennett on tour in *West Side Story,* of the four-flight walk-up they shared, and of "the honesty and love and respect for each other which would always overcome any problem." He related the ailing Bennett's response when he broached the offer he had received to choreograph *Follies* in London: "You've got to do it, especially the way things are now. It's time you went out and carved a career of your own."

Bennett's design team—Robin Wagner, Tharon Musser, and Theoni V. Aldredge—appeared next. Wagner, increasingly choked with emotion, spoke for the group: "He made everyone who knew him his own. We all felt singled out. Last January, he said that whatever happened, he didn't think he missed anything. It is certain that we'll never know the full extent of his loss as an artist, and his loss as a friend is inconsolable."

Marvin A. Krauss, general manager of Bennett's final productions, spoke of the interview his eleven-year-old son had had with Bennett for a school report. Krauss's son asked Bennett, "If for one day you could be anyone in the world and do anything you want, who would you be, and what would you like to do?" Without hesitation, Bennett replied, "I would be me, and I love what I'm doing."

Bennett's brother, Frank DiFilia, said, "He showed us deep truths about ourselves. He made us more aware of being alive, to use the words of one of his great collaborators. The Greeks, I think, call this a catharsis. Michael called it a Broadway musical."

Breglio expressed his feeling of being lost without Bennett, who "was in charge of everyone and everything around him." He remembered that when he first thought about planning a memorial, he had said to Avian, "How can you expect hundreds of people to come to the Shubert Theatre in memory and tribute to Michael Bennett, and not ask Michael what he wanted us to do?" Breglio surveyed the stage and said, "He's probably furious right now because the podium's in the wrong place, the lights are wrong, I'm saying the wrong things, and everyone's referring to him in the past tense." Shortly before Bennett died, Breglio had asked him whether there was anything he wanted done or said after he died. "He looked at me, and he gave me that incredible wry, enigmatic smile, and he said, 'Tell them no show runs forever.'"

Breglio concluded by relating the circumstances of the only time he had ever seen Bennett cry. It was in 1984 when Bennett played for Breglio one song from an advance copy of the original cast album of *Sunday in the Park with George*. Breglio then introduced the composer of that song, Stephen Sondheim, who muttered a few words through tears, sang "Move On," the lyric of which took on special significance on this occasion, and then choked back sobs as he said, "Goodbye, Michael."

Next, the supreme interpreter of Bennett's work, Donna McKechnie, took to the stage and began by reminding everyone that "Michael was a dancer, a wonderful dancer." She recalled how he had unselfishly helped her to outshine him when they were fellow dancers on television in the 1960s. She told of how Bennett had changed the ending of *A Chorus Line* during previews at the Public Theater, veering from the truth in order to give people hope. "He searched for the truth always, and he always remembered to give people hope. Truth and hope—that's what he's left us."

Bernard B. Jacobs, president of the Shubert Organization, recalled Bennett's practice of calling him and other colleagues in the middle of the night, and described Bennett as "sensitive, caring, compassionate, a wonderful human being." He also mentioned Bennett's willingness to help out shows in trouble, and his refusal to take any credit for doing this, so as not to diminish the reputations of the other creators.

Columnist Liz Smith said Bennett could have been a great general or military tactician, could have done anything, in fact, but "the theatre was his one and only love." She also reminded the audience, "There are an awful lot of people in the theatre today who've made a lot of money and are very famous, and they owe it all to Michael. I hope they're as loyal to him as he has been to them."

The final speaker was Joseph Papp, producer of *A Chorus Line,* who spoke of the need to do something about the plague of AIDS, and added, "He made every moment work. There was no such thing as wasted time. I think that's a marvelous lesson for all of us today."

Most present expected the memorial to conclude with a performance of the finale of *A Chorus Line*—"One"—and it did, but at the moment in the number when the mirrors usually revolve to reveal a sunburst, the mirrors revolved, but in place of the sun was an enormous photo of Bennett, grinning and with arms outstretched, as if to embrace the theatre and everyone in it.

As always, the lights dimmed on the dancers, kicking their way into musical comedy glory and oblivion, but the final image the audience applauded was the photo of Bennett, and the still-lit white line.

PART ONE

. . . .

THE TRADITION

FROM THE EARLIEST COLONIAL days, there were musical shows in America that danced. What changed in musicals over the years was the degree of importance given to dance, the uses to which dance was put, and the way in which dance functioned along with the other elements of the play.

The first theatrical choreographers were billed as "dance directors," and the dances they fashioned for musical shows during the first thirty years of this century were primarily story interruptions or respites from hectic, farcical plots. There were a few dance directors, however, who saw that choreography could function significantly in the action. Robert Alton, whose career on Broadway and in Hollywood spanned four decades, created dances that were an integral part of the story of the 1940 musical *Pal Joey*. Act I ended with "Joey Looks into the Future," a direct antecedent of Agnes de Mille's dream ballet in *Oklahoma!* three years later.

It was George Balanchine, however, who changed the idiom of Broadway dance for years to come and elevated professional but standard entertainments to glamorous cultural events through his contribution to them. A product of Diaghilev's Ballets Russe, Balanchine came to New York in 1934, where he was to found the School of American Ballet and the New York City Ballet Company, and become the foremost figure in dance of his generation. Balanchine established ballet as the mode of Broadway dance, made greater demands on the Broadway dancer, and, in so doing, gave that dancer a new importance. The 1936 musical *On Your Toes* was about dancers and a ballet company, so dance had a natural place in the show, and Balanchine's creations were a part of the action, even if they were only dimly related to the characters and situations of the book. In such other musicals as *I Married an Angel, Louisiana Purchase, Cabin in the Sky,* and *Where's Charley?* Balanchine gave dance a prestige and importance it had never before enjoyed in the musical theatre.

But while his ballet origins gave Broadway a new dance idiom it would continue to employ for decades, Balanchine's work still existed separately from the other elements of the musicals on which he worked. Because Balanchine was never given full control over the staging of his shows, earning co-director status on only two, his dances remained glorious but separate entities.

No one ever revolutionized Broadway dance to the extent that Agnes de Mille did. She gave dance a new integrity and a new theatrical significance, while creating perhaps the most personal dance vocabulary of any Broadway choreographer. De Mille set a pattern for dance in musicals that was to be copied by show after show from the 1940s through the 1960s. And she made the contribution of the choreographer as important as that of the book writer, composer, or lyricist.

De Mille's first New York triumph was not in a Broadway theatre, but at the Metropolitan Opera House, when she choreographed and danced the lead in *Rodeo* with the Ballets Russe de Monte Carlo. On the strength of her work in *Rodeo,* she was hired by the Theatre Guild to create the dances for the 1943 Broadway musical *Oklahoma!*

Oklahoma! is generally considered to be the first show that fully integrated book, score, and dance, but such musicals as *Show Boat, Pal Joey,* and *Lady in the Dark* had already taken major steps in that direction. What was genuinely revolutionary and innovative about *Oklahoma!* ultimately comes down to de Mille and her contribution.

In a program note, de Mille recalled how she assembled her *Oklahoma!* dancers: "I wanted a group of girls and men who were all dance soloists in their own right, but who could also act. A good dancer has to be a comedian, tragedian, pantomimist—everything. And we didn't want a chorus line. We wanted people."

De Mille's dancers were allowed to emerge as people, as characters in the story, and her dances were used to reveal the emotions and anxieties of the principal characters. The dances were not so much part of the plot as poetic metaphors of what was in the mind of the central characters. They enhanced the story as much as any of the songs, and explored the psychology of the characters as ballet had for centuries.

De Mille gave new importance to the dancer, making dancers principals in her productions and using many of them again and again in her shows. The formerly anonymous "ladies and gentlemen of the dancing chorus" were no more once de Mille's dancers took the stage. But more significant was her use of the dancer for emotional expression and of dance to reveal the inner conflicts, fears, and longings of the characters. De Mille's dancers were allowed the same depth of character, personality, and emotional complexity that had been the property of the actors, and sometimes the singers, in earlier musicals. Because of this, de Mille's work had to be viewed as equally important to that of the librettist, lyricist, composer, and director.

The dance style of *Oklahoma!* was not new; de Mille had used it before on the ballet stage. However, it was the first time Broadway audiences saw it, and, from then on, critics and public alike would not be satisfied with less than the artistry and expression de Mille brought with her from the ballet world.

While the dream ballet that concludes the first act of *Oklahoma!*, "Laurey Makes Up Her Mind," was not, as is often assumed, the first major dream ballet in a musical, de Mille took the concept and created a Freudian, psychological dance that summed up the heroine's psyche and foreshadowed her subsequent behavior, a ballet that arose directly out of the character's emotional state.

In *One Touch of Venus* the same year, de Mille gave notice that she was as adept at parodying urban angst and suburban conformity as she was at filling a stage with western Americana. Her "Civil War Ballet" for the 1944 musical *Bloomer Girl* was another high point in emotional Broadway dance. For *Carousel* in 1945, de Mille created a heartbreaking Act Two ballet that furthered the narrative, telling the audience all it needed to know of the unhappy first fifteen years of a girl's existence.

What makes the 1947 hit *Brigadoon* hold up particularly well when revived today is de Mille's contribution, her most significant to a single musical. As in *Oklahoma!* and *Carousel,* the dances were again extensions of the plot, but in *Brigadoon,* more of the show was given over to dance, and de Mille rose to the occasion by creating ballets worthy of being placed in the repertoires of dance companies. The dances were such an integral part of *Brigadoon* that the narrative would have been incomplete without them, and few musicals lose as much when revived without the original choreography.

De Mille directed three Broadway musicals but rarely achieved the degree of control that later director-choreographers would enjoy. But she took dancing as far as it could go in the conventional musical, which still insisted on equal time for the book and songs. No one before had made dance and dancers so vital a part of the musical theatre. It remained for Jerome Robbins and Michael Bennett to make a whole show dance.

"Book based on an idea by Jerome Robbins," ran a credit on the title page of the *Playbill* for *On the Town,* the 1944 musical that introduced Leonard Bernstein, Betty Comden, and Adolph Green, as well as Robbins, to Broadway. Never before had a choreographer been credited with the fundamental idea for a show, but Robbins was to make his contribution to the shows on which he worked as important as, and ultimately more important than, that of his collaborators.

Like Bennett, Robbins danced in the ensemble of several Broadway musicals, but Robbins soon joined Ballet Theatre. His acclaimed piece for that company, *Fancy Free,* became the basis for his first Broadway musical. *On the Town* seemed to audiences a giddy lightweight spree, but it was an extraordinarily sophisticated mixture of serious symphonic music and ballet, which, thanks to director George Abbott, was never permitted to become heavy or pretentious. But while the song, dance, and book elements were beautifully integrated and care was taken to avoid any hint of classical seriousness, even the casual theatregoer had to notice that no Broadway musical had ever emphasized dance as did *On the Town.*

De Mille had worked separately from the other creators of *Oklahoma!* In the case of *On the Town,* however, the scenarios for the ballets were written as part of the book, and Bernstein scored the ballets working side by side with Robbins as he invented the dances. Sono Osato, de Mille's lead dancer in *One Touch of Venus,* was elevated to stardom in *On the Town,* receiving top billing and playing a central role.

On the Town had a heavier dance program than any earlier musical, and all of Robbins's dances were a part of the action. More importantly, the dances, along with Bernstein's music, elevated the entire show, making what might have been a lightly touching but purely conventional musical into something richer, one of the most distinctive Broadway entertainments of the 1940s.

While de Mille's contribution to *Oklahoma!* was ultimately what made that show so innovative, it was not allowed to dominate the proceedings. In *On the Town,* the dance component of the show was given an amount of time and a relative importance to the book and songs that were unprecedented. The dances became as important as, or perhaps more important than, the book scenes and songs, and the show was choreographed from start to finish.

After *On the Town,* Robbins made significant and memorable contributions to such other shows as *High Button Shoes, Look Ma, I'm Dancin!,* and *The King and I.* In 1954, he became a co-director, on *The Pajama Game,* and a director-choreographer, on *Peter Pan.* His most significant contribution to the musical came three years later.

West Side Story, like *On the Town* and *Look Ma, I'm Dancin!,* was fundamentally Robbins's idea, although collaborators Arthur Laurents and Stephen Sondheim were responsible for the plot shift from religious differences to gang warfare. As Bennett would for *A Chorus Line,* Robbins assembled his collaborators and conceived, directed, and choreographed what was to become the most significant work of musical theatre of the 1950s.

In a program article for the 1968 Lincoln Center revival of *West Side Story,* Stephen Sondheim told Alan Rich, "I think that what the show was really about was style: how it approaches the telling of a story. The techniques are the revolutionary aspect, the milestone if you prefer, far more than the content." Because the techniques pioneered by Robbins in the show were commandeered by many others, most successfully by Bennett, what was shockingly innovative in 1957 may not seem unusual to today's audiences. So it is necessary to take a closer look at *West Side Story* to understand how revolutionary it was.

If earlier musicals such as *Oklahoma!* and *On the Town* integrated all the elements of musical theatre, *West Side Story* made it impossible to separate them. Robbins saw to it that everything was subsumed by movement, and, in so doing, made his the all-important contribution to the production, the one that unified all the other elements. *West Side Story* has one of the shortest books of any musical, because, while the show has a highly eventful plot, so much was musicalized and choreographed, and so much of the plot development and characterization was accomplished in the dances.

But Robbins's greatest contribution in *West Side Story* was his creation of a new race of performer, the dancer-singer-actor. In virtually all the earlier de Mille and Robbins musicals, a clear delineation was made in the program between the cast principals, who acted and sang roles, and the singing and dancing choruses. De Mille and Robbins had done everything they could to blur the distinction by giving the dancers parts or creating dancing "stars," but the separation remained. In the program for *West Side Story,* however, there was no chorus of singers or dancers, only a list of roles with the names of the actors who played them. The performers were required to act, sing, and dance, and Robbins rewarded the extra effort required by giving each performer a character to play and a personality to convey. This marked the end of an era; it was no longer enough to be just an actor or singer or dancer. After *West Side Story,* you had to be all three to work in the Broadway musical theatre.

De Mille continued the play's action and characterization in dance, but she was rarely allowed to introduce them through dance; Robbins did just that in the Prologue to *West Side Story.* Later, in the fifteen-minute sequence that begins as the dress shop set "fades" into the gym set, music, dance, and movement are continuous, and, through them, the main characters and conflicts are presented. The dances in *West Side Story* become scenes, and vice versa. No earlier director had ever managed to sustain a sequence as long or as fluid as the gym scene, and no one would again until Bennett. Robbins also experimented in this sequence and elsewhere with the kind of cinematic dissolves and scene changes that Bennett would later emphasize.

The 1959 musical *Gypsy,* Robbins's next show, was not a project to which he was able to make the kind of total contribution he had made to *West Side Story.* But *Gypsy* was the ultimate conventional musical, a work so perfect of its kind that important musical theatre talents such as Sondheim and Harold Prince may have felt that they could not take the conventional musical beyond where *Gypsy* had taken it. Its perfection led directly to experimentation in the Sixties, and the Sondheim, Prince, and Bennett musicals of the Seventies.

Robbins's next show was written as a conventional book musical, and could have been just that, but he saw to it that it became much more. Because of Robbins's contribution, *Fiddler on the Roof* combined the conventional book, song, and dance structure of *Gypsy* with the overall choreographic conception of *West Side Story,* and proved a more popular show than either one. While the book writer, composer, and lyricist of *Fiddler* made extremely strong contributions, Robbins was the auteur of the show in the sense that his hand could be felt everywhere, even though *Fiddler* was a musical without a great deal of dance.

Robbins's style unified his shows, but, unlike some later director-choreographers, his style was always at the service of the material. The techniques he introduced may occasionally be taken for granted now, but they can be seen to have been absorbed in much of today's musical theatre, and no one after Robbins used them with as much integrity until Bennett.

Although many of the shows to which Jack Cole contributed choreography and direction were failures, he is of enormous importance in the history of Broadway dance. Moving sharply away from the ballet mode favored by Balanchine, de Mille, and Robbins, Cole introduced a new jazz style that can be felt in almost every modern Broadway dance. Cole was the strongest influence on the career of an ultimately more famous Broadway director-choreographer, Bob Fosse. Cole trained both of Fosse's great dancing stars, Carol Haney and Gwen Verdon, and the latter assisted Cole on Broadway and in Hollywood.

In an interview with Clive Hirschhorn in *Plays and Players* magazine, Michael Bennett, comparing the techniques of various choreographers, commented: "Fosse tends to place his own particular stamp on whatever the subject may be, whether it's *Pippin* or *Charity* or *Chicago* or the movie of *Cabaret*. There's a very particular Fosse style, and you can always tell a Bob Fosse show."

Fosse changed the relationship of stager to writers, and that of staging to the other elements of a musical. Robbins sought total integration of all the elements through dance, but Fosse gradually reached a point where his staging was not just the unifying force of the show—it *was* the show. His staging assumed such importance that the work of the composer, lyricist, and librettist was sometimes curtailed or distorted to allow more time for the Fosse magic.

The actual steps in a Fosse show stood out more than in the work of de Mille and Robbins. He created the flashiest, sexiest, funniest theatre dances ever, dances that called attention to themselves and were calculated to bring down the house. Fosse had perhaps the most readily identifiable style of any Broadway choreographer, and he was criticized for using similar characteristics—pelvic movements, isolation of body parts, geometric patterns, derbies, white gloves—from show to show.

More than any other director-choreographer, Fosse succeeded in creating dancing stars, first with Haney, who went on to become a Broadway choreographer, then with Verdon, who became the only dancer in recent theatre history to achieve the level of musical-comedy stardom that was reached by such singer-actresses as Ethel Merman, Mary Martin, or Angela Lansbury.

In *The Pajama Game,* "Steam Heat" became the first classic statement of the Fosse style. In *Damn Yankees,* "Whatever Lola Wants" and "Who's Got the Pain" were pinnacles of comic dance on Broadway.

With *Redhead* in 1959, Fosse took on the direction as well as the choreography of a musical for the first time, and because it was the first show of which Fosse was in charge, it was also the first Fosse show where dance dominated all other aspects. *Redhead* is crucial in the Fosse career because it demonstrated that he had the power to make a show into a hit without relying on especially distinguished contributions from his collaborators. This would eventually lead Fosse, on his last two shows— *Dancin'* and *Big Deal*—to do away with collaborators altogether.

Sweet Charity in 1966 was, in a sense, Fosse's "de Mille show," for in it, he used dance to convey plot and character. More than any other element, it was the dances in *Charity* that developed the central character and her world, and her longings and fantasies were expressed more strongly in the choreography than in the book or songs. *Charity* demonstrated that light, comic Broadway dancing could be used to express the emotions of characters and paint background and color, and was a far more innovative production than it was thought to be when it first opened.

In *Pippin,* Fosse's staging was not simply at the service of the other elements—it became the whole show. His total conception and control were evident in every minute of the production, but an element of decadence began to creep into his work here, style becoming an end in itself. *Pippin* demonstrated how different the idea of total control was for Robbins and Fosse. While all was choreographed in *West Side Story* and Robbins's stamp was on every scene, the show was written in such a way as to allow his creative genius to unify all the elements. In *Pippin,* Fosse superimposed his brilliantly stylish work on the material. Robbins worked with his collaborators to create a completely organic work of art;

Fosse took the material of *Pippin* as if it were a mere sketch for a show, and made it into a hit because of what he applied to it.

Chicago, Fosse's last great contribution to the musical theatre, saw him co-author the book in addition to directing and choreographing. The stylistic mannerisms that were by now famous were to be seen throughout *Chicago,* but it was the last time they were used at the service of strong material, and the show, at least with its original cast, was one of the most striking musical productions of the last twenty-five years.

There were those who were never completely comfortable or happy with the innovations and the serious uses of dance favored by de Mille and Robbins. For them there was Gower Champion, who kept alive the old-fashioned tradition of bravura show-business extravaganzas. He did so, however, by mixing dazzling staging with subtly artistic craftsmanship, and, while not an innovator, brought the staging of conventional musicals (*Bye Bye Birdie, Hello, Dolly!*) to its highest peak.

Another major Broadway choreographer from the Forties through the Sixties was Michael Kidd, who, after choreographing and dancing the lead in Ballet Theatre's *On Stage,* a short ballet about a sympathetic stagehand and a nervous auditioner, made his Broadway debut with the choreography for *Finian's Rainbow* in 1947. Kidd's biggest hit was *Guys and Dolls,* in which his dance sequences were excitingly virile and energetic, adding much to the colorful "Runyonland" so beautifully captured in the dialogue and score. If Kidd did not become quite the theatrical legend de Mille, Robbins, Fosse, or Champion became, it cannot be denied that he created wonderfully vital dances and was among the top Broadway choreographers for more than two decades. It was Kidd's choreography that was danced by a young "gypsy" from Buffalo in his first two Broadway musicals.

PART TWO

. . . .

ENTER

MICHAEL BENNETT

1

···

"I LOVE 'USICALS"

O N THE LAST DAY of March 1943, Agnes de Mille's new conception
of theatre dance set New York on its ear when *Oklahoma!* opened on
Broadway. Eight days later, on April 8, 1943, Michael Bennett Di Figlia
was born in Buffalo to Helen Di Figlia, a secretary at Sears, and Salvatore
Di Figlia, a machinist in the local Chevrolet plant.

Russian-German-Jewish on his mother's side, Sicilian on his father's,
Bennett was throughout childhood and adolescence so totally immersed
in dance that there was never any question of the direction his life
would take. And it is significant that the decades in which he grew up
were dominated by such Broadway dance giants as de Mille, Robbins,
Fosse, and Kidd. There have always been, and will always be, young
people whose goal is to get to Broadway, but it is unlikely that the
particular drive that Bennett had as a child would have been as strong in
an earlier period. For Bennett didn't want to just dance or sing or even
star on Broadway; he wanted only to be something called a director-
choreographer.

Several characters in *A Chorus Line* talk of dancing around the house
to music at an early age, and Bennett began dancing to music on the radio

when he was two. An aunt noticed his ability and eagerness and she began taking him to weekly dance classes, where he would improvise his own steps. Bennett soon began earning money for his choreography, performing freestyle routines at weddings, bar mitzvahs, and on street corners. This money supplemented the family income.

Bennett was fortunate to have parents who encouraged his proclivities, and he was soon receiving additional training—in tap, ballet, jazz, and modern—for what came naturally to him. At the age of three, he was enrolled in Miss Betty Rogers's School of Dance, and by the time he was nine, he was one of Mrs. John Dunn's Little Stars of Tomorrow, trouping to veterans' hospitals, homes for crippled children, orphanages, and reformatories. Somehow, Bennett knew from childhood that dancing to other people's steps would not ultimately be his forte: "Even then, I wanted to choreograph. When I was just a little boy, I used to arrange marbles as dancers—people thought I was playing with marbles, but I was actually staging musicals. What I wanted to work at was putting on big shows . . . and I wanted to make these shows on other people, not on myself."*

Bennett's parents and relatives not only encouraged his training but took him to movies and the theatre. His mother recalled, "Before he was five years old, we were taking him to theatre and movies, and he would say, 'Let's go to a 'usical! I love 'usicals!' " He was taken to New York to see *Damn Yankees,* with Verdon dancing Fosse's wonderful routines.

One of Bennett's teachers had given him a subscription to *Dance Magazine* two years earlier, and by the time he actually saw the real thing, his walls were full of pictures of Fosse, Kidd, Robbins, and Verdon. Years later, *Dance Magazine* would do feature stories on Bennett and award him prizes; in his childhood, it taught him a tremendous amount about the musical theatre of the Fifties, an education that would stand him in good stead for the rest of his life. Kristine in *A Chorus Line* speaks of her almost religious devotion to "The Ed Sullivan Show," and the choreography and excerpts from Broadway musicals that Bennett watched every Sunday night on this program were another significant influence.

Bennett attended Hutchinson Central Technical High School for Boys, preparing for a career in architectural design as something to fall back upon; but there was not the slightest doubt in his mind that he wanted

. . . .

*To Olga Maynard, *"A Chorus Line:* A Gathering of Dancers," *After Dark,* August 1975.

to be the next Jerome Robbins, his idol then and throughout his career. He had already formed his own dance company and appeared on television in a local show called "TV Party Time." In high school, he staged and choreographed shows, while spending summers in New York studying with Aubrey Hitchins and Matt Mattox. He worked in summer stock and soon won the role of Baby John in one of the first stock productions of *West Side Story*. Jack Lenny, who was to become Bennett's lifelong agent, managed the Melody Fair chain at the time. He recalls: "Michael had been just an apprentice at the Melody Fair Theatre in Buffalo in 1959. He was supposed to be an apprentice again in 1960, but before the season started, he went to New York and auditioned for the tour of *West Side Story* that was to play the circuit. He got it, and because that tour was booked into Buffalo for a week, he came back a professional to the theatre where he had apprenticed.

"Michael said to me when he was an apprentice, 'I want to be a choreographer.' He was the most ambitious youngster I ever met. He asked me to be his agent, and I told him I would guide his career until the time I thought he was ready to be a choreographer."

Theoni V. Aldredge, who would design the costumes for *A Chorus Line,* did the clothes for the *West Side Story* stock production, and recalled, "This young man came in. Just looked up and said, 'Can I have a yellow sweatshirt?' I called Gerald Freedman, the director, who said, 'Give him anything, he's brilliant.' "*

Just as it was a key show in the development of musical-theatre staging, *West Side Story* became key in Bennett's career. Seeing it in New York confirmed his desire to be a director-choreographer, and it was the show in which he first appeared professionally. It was to change his life forever.

The company that brought *West Side Story* back to Broadway for a return engagement in 1960 was to embark on a one-year tour of Europe, and Bennett was again offered the role of Baby John on the tour. He dropped out of high school shortly before graduation to seize the opportunity. Bennett would later feel that his failure to finish high school rendered him inarticulate and illiterate, but there had been no avoiding the inevitable. The opportunity to dance Robbins's choreography and to study and dissect how Robbins had achieved the dazzling effects of *West Side Story* were diploma enough to cap years of dance training and obser-

. . . .
*"The Dream Team on Collaboration," *Theatre Crafts,* August/September 1982.

vation. Bennett was seventeen when he joined the tour, and he celebrated his eighteenth birthday in Paris.

It was on this tour, which traveled to Israel, France, Holland, Germany, and Italy, that Bennett met Bob Avian, who would work side by side with Bennett for most of the next twenty-five years.

AVIAN: "I toured in *West Side Story,* and that tour came back to Broadway. When it closed, they asked about half of us to go on a tour of Europe. We rehearsed in Israel, but first we had a couple of days in New York with Jerry Robbins, where he blended the new people in with the old, and picked out who would do which sections. That's where I first met Michael. He was the new kid in the room, a baby.

"During the two years I was with the show, I played almost every role, including Chino and Bernardo. It was like *A Chorus Line,* where dancers understudy several roles and get shifted around. It was a great first show to learn from.

"Michael and I instantly became best friends. He was four or five years younger than I, and he was going with a girl named Audrey Hays, who was my best friend in the show. Right away we hit it off. I thought he was very smart, talented and a very hard worker. He was very ambitious; that showed right away. I liked that, although some kids in the show didn't, and said, 'Who is this kid? He's awfully pushy.' But I respected him, and he looked upon me as an older brother, to guide him and be his ally in the company."

2

"WOW,

YOU DANCE ON BROADWAY!

YOU GOT SOMEWHERE!"

AFTER TOURING EUROPE, BENNETT settled in New York and began teaching a jazz dance class at the June Taylor Studios. It was there that he met Robert Thomas, who played drums for these classes and became Bennett's rehearsal drummer and later music coordinator of *A Chorus Line.* While Bennett was teaching, he was also auditioning, and jobs came rapidly.

The three Broadway musicals in which Michael Bennett danced fall into a category of Broadway musical all but nonexistent today. Each was a standard assembly-line Broadway product of mediocre achievement, the kind of "in-between" show that opened to less than ecstatic reviews but, because of the economics of Broadway in the 1960s, was able to run the season. Professionally put together, not disasters but not hits, the three musicals in which Bennett served his time as Broadway gypsy were outstanding in one department only, but that was sufficient to make them an education of enormous value.

Subways Are for Sleeping opened on Broadway two nights after Christmas 1961, and dealt with dropouts from urban society, those without fixed abodes and who lived by their wits. The darker, more unpleasant aspects of the material went unexplored in favor of conventional musical-comedy treatment with a happy ending for all.

Like most musicals of its day with marketable names on the marquee, *Subways* had enough theatre parties and advance ticket sales to keep it going in spite of sharply negative reviews, and it managed to stay afloat until the summer of 1962, closing after a run of 205 performances, which would be almost impossible today for a musical accorded a reception similar to that of *Subways*.

What was most vital about *Subways* was its dancing, for the show was directed and choreographed by Michael Kidd. John Sharpe, who danced in the show and was its "dance captain"—the dancer in charge of maintaining the dances during the show's run and teaching them to replacements—said: "There was a wonderful golden age in musicals when a brand new human being was born in the musical theatre called the director-choreographer, and Kidd was a giant in the profession. Kidd's background was ballet, and the key to his choreography was masculinity, virility, and a bombastic, athletic exercise of technique, all based on ballet technique.... Kidd never did anything without a reason, without an idea. The idea of doing a number, filling up bars of music with movement, was not what he was about; nor was de Mille or Robbins or Fosse or any of the great people."

Kidd had a reputation for letting dancers with whom he did not immediately feel comfortable go after a day or two of rehearsal. Union rules at the time allowed management to dismiss a performer within four or five days of the beginning of rehearsals, and it was through one of Kidd's chorus firings that Bennett got his first Broadway chance.

SHARPE: "Kidd let a dancer go, and the stage manager on *Subways*, Joe Calvan, had been stage manager on the *West Side Story* tour that Bennett had done. Joe said to Kidd, 'There's this young guy I worked with this summer—excellent dancer, really sharp. You should see him.' . . . Bennett came in on a lunch break, and I, as dance captain, taught him some steps. He got the show that day."

As were most conventional musicals of the period, *Subways* was constructed in such a way as to allow ample opportunity for dancing, and when it *was* dancing, *Subways* was a distinguished musical. There were dances for the stars ("Comes Once in a Lifetime" was a minuet performed by Carol Lawrence and Sydney Chaplin in the French wing of the Metropolitan Museum of Art), ensemble dances ("Ride Through the Night"), and one classic comic Broadway dance. John Chapman in the *Daily News* wrote of the "Be a Santa" number: "The show is at its best when director Michael Kidd turns his dancers loose. Kidd has staged a wonderfully joyous ballet in which a woeful assortment of Clauses breaks loose in a joyous and whooping riot."

Kidd's sense of humor was always apparent in his dances, and he hit upon the idea of spoofing the current hubbub about the Moiseyev Ballet, which Sol Hurok had imported.

SHARPE: "Kidd decided to treat a bunch of street-corner Santa Clauses as a bunch of nutty quasi-Russian ballet dancers. It was a very difficult number to perform."

Bennett was one of the Santas, but, in his first Broadway show, he was already stepping out of the ensemble.

SHARPE: "There were a lot of changes made in the show on the road, and when it came time to bolster the opening of the second act, they contrived a situation where Carol Lawrence was alone on the subway platform, and two teenagers came on. The number was called 'Subway Incident,' and the two teenagers were Bennett and myself. Marc Breaux and Dee Dee Wood assisted Kidd on *Subways,* and the three of them, plus Carol, Bennett and myself, put the new number together."

JOE CALVAN: "Michael helped a lot with the dancing . . . he was destined to be a choreographer. He worked very hard with Kidd, and a lot of his work went into the number that opened Act Two. That number was a breakthrough from the usual choreography of the period, which was ballet and conservative modern. That was the start of the type of dancing you see nowadays on Broadway. Kidd was not so familiar with that style, but it was Bennett's forte."

SANDRA ROVETA,* who danced with Bennett in his first two shows, remembers how Bennett's personal style was used in the number: "The twist was brand new then, and nobody could quite get it, but Michael had all those moves down. This was street dancing, contemporary dancing, and Michael could do all that new and modern movement, which was not the traditional kind of technique most dancers had. . . . He loved to go out after the show to the Peppermint Lounge."

The subway platform twist was singled out by *New York Times* critic Howard Taubman as one of the show's few pleasurable interludes. If none of the critics mentioned the names of the two dancers who per-

. . . .

*She would later play Cassie in the International Company of *A Chorus Line.*

formed the number with Lawrence, as they might today, given the post-*Chorus Line* respect for dancers, it is still remarkable that Bennett had been given a featured dance spot in his first Broadway show. Perhaps even more significant is that he was listed in *Playbill* not only as one of the two "Teenagers" but also as "A Delivery Boy," who, unlike most Broadway dancers of the period, was actually permitted a few spoken words.

Bennett's first musical was not a smash, but he was thrilled to be part of the world he had seen from a theatre seat and dreamed of as he pored over *Dance Magazine.*

SHARPE: "Bennett got along beautifully with the company; everyone liked him. As a young man in a New York show, he was meeting people and getting a decent salary. He loved the city, the freedom and the feeling of, 'Let's have a good time.' And he really stood out as a dancer. When I watched the 'Be a Santa' number from out front as dance captain, my eye went to Michael. You can look at a group of people doing the same identical step, all dressed the same, and one of them will stand out. There's something in the personality and the presentation that pulls your eye. It goes beyond any technical facility or ability. You looked at Michael."

Bennett, like so many of the other dancers listed in *Subways's Playbill* (one of whom was Valerie Harper), might have gone on to dance in many shows; the term *gypsy* was first applied to the Broadway dancer because he or she tended to travel from show to show. Bennett, however, was only to dance in two more musicals, and he would assist the choreographer of the last, as well as dance in it.

ROVETA: "I think Michael learned very early on that performing wasn't something that he really loved doing. He knew he wanted to be on the other creative end of it."

Bennett danced for Kidd again in *Here's Love,* which opened at the Shubert Theatre on October 3, 1963. Kidd was hired only for choreography this time, but when the show's original director, Norman Jewison, was fired, the producer, Stuart Ostrow, hired himself to direct, and Kidd wound up helping Ostrow with the direction. Once again, Sharpe and Roveta danced with Bennett in the show. Sharpe this time assisted Kidd on the choreography, and among the dancers was Baayork Lee.*

. . . .

*Lee would later create the role of Connie in *A Chorus Line.*

Here's Love followed the basic story line of its well-known source, the film *Miracle on 34th Street.* It saw Bennett once again toiling in a routine show, better received than *Subways* but vastly overshadowed by such other Broadway musicals as *Hello, Dolly!* and *Funny Girl,* which opened soon after.

As in *Subways,* Kidd was the show's lifesaver. There were two major dance sections in *Here's Love,* both in the first act. The show began with the astonishing "Big Clown Balloons" number, which transformed the stage into the Macy's Thanksgiving Day Parade as filtered through the imagination of a top Broadway choreographer. But the dance centerpiece of *Here's Love* was the ballet that ended the first act. As this was still the post–de Mille era, it was a dream ballet, in which a little girl imagined a fantasy birthday party at which all manner of doll pranced about, auditioning as possible new mates for her divorcée mother. Kidd's imagination and comic energy were at full tilt in the ballet, nowhere more so than in a floppy, Twyla Tharp–like pas de deux danced by a fireman—one of the candidates for new father—and a rag doll he was rescuing. Gene Kelton was the fireman, and Bennett the rag doll.

ROVETA: "Michael and Gene worked a lot on their dance and contributed a lot to the choreography. The style was very loose, and they worked together, creating lifts that were comfortable for them. Gene really threw Michael around in that, and I remember Michael got hurt a lot in it, pulling muscles."

SHARPE: "Bennett contributed to the choreography of his dance. The Raggedy Andy–type doll had to mesh with the fireman, who threw the doll around his shoulder and dropped him and picked him up. So they had to make a lot of it work for themselves, and Michael made a major contribution."

Kidd's inventive and ultraprofessional staging, and his ability to inject color and life into routine material, were logged in Bennett's mind, and while Bennett's choreographic style would not be similar to Kidd's, the experience could not help but inform Bennett's later work. One could see traces of Kidd's frenetic urban movement from the "Subway Rush" number of *Subways* in Bennett's "Grapes of Roth" sequence in *Promises, Promises.* The idea of having performers wear several layers of clothing at once so that they could make split-second costume changes, as in Kidd's "Big Clown Balloons" number in *Here's Love,* was used by Bennett in the lightning-fast costume changes in *Dreamgirls.*

In his last appearance as a Broadway gypsy, Bennett actually played a gypsy, in the 1964 Broadway musical *Bajour,* again at the Shubert Theatre and again a show of middling quality that ran about eight months.

But *Bajour*'s milieu—that of New York gypsy families and their store-front abodes—allowed for frequent interruptions of the book by exciting terpsichory of the intense Latin variety, and Peter Gennaro, who was Robbins's co-choreographer on *West Side Story,* created sensuous routines, led by Chita Rivera.

Leland Palmer, who later would be Bennett's assistant and lead dancer for his first official Broadway choreographic assignment, was also in *Bajour.* As in his two previous shows, Bennett was given a solo spot, billed as "A Young Music Lover," in a number called "Variations on a Theme by Bird." But when the number was cut on the road, Bennett's billing was reduced to that of "dancer," one of nineteen others.

Of particular importance is the fact that, while Bennett received no credit as such in the *Bajour* program, his later bios state that he was assistant to the choreographer of *Bajour.* Ever restless and ambitious, Bennett was systematically unable to remain one of the ensemble, however exciting were the routines he was given by a Kidd or a Gennaro. *Bajour* marked the end of Bennett's career as a Broadway dancer, but the importance of this period of his life to his later work is crucial. The man who would conceive and create the ultimate statement about Broadway dancers, *A Chorus Line,* could obviously not have done so without the experience of having been one himself. While Bennett was fortunate in working with choreographers who respected dancers and allowed them to participate in the choreographic process, he still could not have failed to notice that the Broadway dancer's lot was one of low pay, insecurity, and fierce competition. Dancing in shows taught Bennett the discipline and hard work necessary to sustain a run, as well as the monotony and injury that went along with that run. By dancing the work of Kidd and Gennaro, and being there as it was created, Bennett was able to see how top choreographers worked with dancers, how they developed ideas into sustained sequences, and how they were able to get the discipline and exhausting work they demanded from dancers. He learned that a good Broadway dance had to have an idea, a concept behind it, and that steps that filled up time and were about nothing were unacceptable. Above all, dancing in shows allowed him to see how the Broadway system worked. It was a lesson in where the real power on Broadway resided, and Bennett learned it quickly and well.

3

. . . .

THE CHOREOGRAPHER:

FOUR FLOPS, ONE HIT

STOCK, *NOWHERE TO GO BUT UP,* AND TV

BENNETT'S DRIVE TO CREATE the moves rather than execute them was too strong to be held in check for long. After he had danced in only one Broadway musical, *Subways Are for Sleeping,* he plunged headlong into choreography, first on the summer- and winter-stock circuits. His first professional staging job was that of assisting Donald Driver on sequences requiring movement in a 1962 Washington Shakespeare Festival production of *A Midsummer Night's Dream.*

JACK LENNY: "Then I put Michael in stock, choreographing many shows. Every director Michael worked with was so intimidated by his talent that they almost allowed him to take over the direction. Almost every time he got involved as choreographer, he was immediately into the direction."

LELAND PALMER: "I assisted Michael when he choreographed *West Side Story, The Pajama Game, How to Succeed* and others in stock. Michael wanted to be important, and was very driven. It was so important to him to make it. There was a freshness, an eagerness and innocence about him then, and that total, naked talent. He was so talented, and all he was saying was, 'Here I am. . . . Just give me a chance to show what I can do.' All he wanted was to be recognized and to express himself. His personal life often got pushed aside because of his need to express this tremendous talent."

Before Bennett returned to the chorus to dance in *Here's Love,* his name would appear, in the back credits of the *Playbill,* as assistant choreographer of a Broadway musical.

Nowhere to Go but Up, based on the colorful real-life story of 1920s Prohibition agents Izzy Einstein (Tom Bosley) and Moe Smith (Martin Balsam), had the shortest run of any show with which Bennett was ever associated; even in the days when musicals could survive a season on very mixed reviews, *Nowhere to Go but Up* opened at the Winter Garden Theatre on November 10, 1962, and closed after nine performances.

Nowhere to Go but Up was originally to have been directed by Ernie Kovacs and choreographed by Danny Daniels, but ultimately Sidney Lumet directed (the distinguished film director's one foray into musical theatre), and young Ronald Field was given his first chance to choreograph a Broadway show.

AVIAN: "I danced in the show. Michael had met Ron Field, and very aggressively asked him if he could assist. . . . Michael was originally second assistant to Ron, but when the first assistant pulled out because she wasn't comfortable with all the tap dancing in the show, Ron let Michael move up.

"I felt very comfortable having Michael there as assistant. We were comrades again, and he could cry on my shoulder and pour out his anxieties to me. He was still a baby.

"We all had a lot of affection for that show, because it was one of the few times where there was no singing chorus, just 24 dancers who also sang. We were on stage constantly, and rehearsals were a ball, all gypsies. Everything was great until we opened out of town, and from then on it was downhill."

Ron Field's choreography was well received, with Walter Kerr in the *Tribune* noting that it "is good enough for the show this ought to be," and Ernest Schier, reviewing the Philadelphia tryout, stating, "If the story line is uncertain, Ronald Field's choreography is quick to step in to cement the pieces."

SANDY ROVETA, who danced in the show: "Ronny did a wonderful job, and as it was his first Broadway show as a choreographer, the dancers felt real supportive of him because he was getting his chance. I'm not sure Michael enjoyed assisting, just as he had not enjoyed dancing in shows that much, because he still wasn't in the creative seat and in control. He just needed to do things a few times—dancing in a show, assisting—to know that that wasn't where to be for him. . . . But he learned a lot from assisting, and as Michael was a very good hoofer and the *Nowhere* choreography was all tapping, he was able to contribute a great deal to it, in pre-production and later.''

THARON MUSSER, who lit the show: "In those days we'd go in in the morning lots of times and light without the company there. It was before computer boards and it took a lot longer. During *Nowhere*, Michael was always sitting behind me, and I finally said, 'Why are you always here?' He said, 'I've got to find out what you do. I know it's a very contributing thing, and I've got to find out more about it.' ''

Bennett helped *Nowhere*'s leading lady, Dorothy Loudon, to win the only raves the show received, thus beginning a working relationship that would be rekindled sixteen years later.

LOUDON: "It was my first musical. The dancing was incredible, Ron Field at his best. Ron worked mostly with the leading men because they really couldn't dance. They assigned me to Michael, which was the best thing in the world. We were rehearsing at the Winter Garden because it was empty, and we'd go out on the fire escape or into the alley and dance. I had all these tap numbers, and he taught me all of them. He was very patient, which I thought was very unique in somebody so young. What I was singled out for in the show was what Michael had given me to do, like what to do with my hands when I sang, and the dances.''

Television variety was still a thriving genre in the Sixties, and Bennett choreographed numbers for "The Ed Sullivan Show," "The Kraft Music Hall," "The Hollywood Palace," "The Dean Martin Show," and others for about five years.

AVIAN: "When Michael began choreographing on television, he didn't use me as his assistant at first. His background was more jazz and tap oriented, and mine was ballet oriented. This became a plus when we later collaborated, but at that time, he was doing what we affectionately called 'shake your ass' choreography, disco-style dancing before the term disco existed. It was organic to Michael.''

The centerpiece of Bennett's TV years was "Hullabaloo," an NBC rock-and-roll series that ran almost two years, concluding in August 1966. The show featured a weekly guest host, and contemporary movement was supplied by the Hullabaloo Dancers, among whom were Donna McKechnie and Michael Bennett.

MCKECHNIE: "I met Michael in 1965 when we were dancing on 'Hullabaloo.' David Winters was the main choreographer, Jaime Rogers also did some, and the dancers would come in and do their own stuff. On one program, they allowed the Hullabaloo Dancers to choreograph their own number, and we each had to choreograph a solo of about 32 bars. I got stuck, and that was the first time Michael choreographed me. He helped me with my piece, which was done to drums, very hot. He gave me all the rhythm and structure and then I put in what I did well. It became the strongest piece of all the dancers, so they built the others around mine. He was so generous—he was competing with the rest of us, but was more interested in his choreographic work than in shining himself. . . . He saw something in my ability to take his work and go with it. . . . He knew immediately that I was right for his choreography; he would never tell me face to face, but I would get it from other people. Talent excited him, and it was more exciting for him to see his work and make somebody else look good and be the star, than for him to go out there and shine."

During his TV period, Bennett also found time to stage the very brief musical sequences of a nonmusical film, a light comedy called *What's So Bad About Feeling Good?*, which was directed by George Seaton for Universal Pictures and starred Mary Tyler Moore, George Peppard, and John McMartin.*

A JOYFUL NOISE

Bennett's first job as a full-fledged Broadway choreographer was for a dimly remembered 1966 Broadway musical called *A Joyful Noise*. A conventional and very weak show about a country singer (John Raitt) who falls in love with an innocent young girl (Susan Watson) in Macedonia, Tennessee, is driven out of town, and becomes a star in Nashville, *A Joyful Noise* chose an unconventional tryout path, eschewing Boston, New Haven, or Philadelphia to play the summer tent circuit.

LENNY: "When I first gave Michael the script to read, he said, 'This is terrible. I don't want to do it.' But I thought the chances for dancing were tremendous, and that he'd get attention."

. . . .
*Bennett directed McMartin in *Follies* in 1971.

Right from the start of its tour, the book and casting problems of the show were obvious, as was the one thing that *A Joyful Noise* had going for it—Michael Bennett. All the reviews during the tour singled out Bennett's work and the dancing of Leland Palmer, Bennett's lead dancer, assistant, and dance captain on *A Joyful Noise,* and Swen Swenson, who had stopped the show for Fosse in *Little Me.* Arnold Reisman in the *Quincy Patriot Ledger* said, "[Bennett's] exciting dances invigorate the play's function. He's adept at handling a revival-stomping beat or floating footwork, and the choreography dominates the show." Ardis Smith in the *Buffalo Evening News* hailed a native son and said, "Melody Fair's first book show of the season could be entitled, with equal relevance, *Joyful Dances.* Mr. Bennett has thought up some of the most beguiling, various and infectious patterns and steps seen on the tented stage since he began his career there a few seasons ago."

MARVIN A. KRAUSS: "I was in charge of production for Guber and Gross, in whose theatres the show was trying out. I met Michael in Cleveland after he'd just finished staging the Clog Dance. He ran up the aisle and said, 'Marvin, do you think I'll ever amount to anything?' I said, 'Michael, some day you're going to own Broadway.' I didn't realize how prophetic that statement was until Michael brought it up to me years later. But you could see his tremendous talent and lust for theatre . . . busting out in those days."

A Joyful Noise was a troubled show from the beginning, and the cast and creative team underwent severe shake-ups before the show reached Broadway. McKechnie was saddled with the nondancing ingenue lead on the summer tour, and was replaced for Broadway, and there were numerous other cast changes before New York. No one, particularly Raitt, was happy with producer Edward Padula's book, so Padula hired Dore Schary to replace the original director and to rewrite the book, Schary taking no credit for the latter. Close to opening night on Broadway, Schary withdrew, and producer-writer Padula added the directorial credit in the program to his others.

The New York reviews were unanimously negative, although all agreed that the dances were the evening's bright spots. George Oppenheimer in *Newsday* wrote, "The heroes and heroines of the evening are the dancers. They occupy the stage for a large portion of the time, and Mr. Bennett gives them three or four exciting routines." Jack Gaver, UPI, wrote "[Bennett] has turned out a number of rousing items with a fine corps of dancers, including Tommy Tune of Texas, who is the tallest hoofer I've ever seen in a line." The show closed on Christmas Eve, 1966, after twelve performances.

Many shows as weak as *A Joyful Noise* tend to drag all elements down with them. What, then, made Bennett's choreography so outstanding?

TOMMY TUNE, who danced for Bennett in *A Joyful Noise* and whose career would intersect in interesting ways with Bennett's from then on: "The dancing was fabulous, the rest of the show was lousy. What made the dancing so outstanding was that Michael was using dancing of the moment, very urban New York, even though the show took place in de Mille country. He combined the two styles. It was Westernized urban New York. After all, what did he know about the West? He was from Buffalo, and was very New York. So it was a strange and wonderful mix, and it was very exciting. The ensemble of dancers was incredible. I was the tallest, of course, and Baayork Lee was the smallest, and there was a lot of talent in between.

"I remember coming back after the first day of rehearsal . . . crippled. . . . We were using muscles we had never used before. . . . I think he crippled a lot of dancers permanently during his career, but I guess that's not supposed to be a choreographer's concern. A choreographer has to create, and never mind what happens to the animals he's creating on. It was lethal—but it was great.

"There was no question what a talent he was then . . . such high invention and high dynamics. He also had a way of making you feel that because you were working for him, you were in the 'A' group. . . . He also had that thing of making each of us feel that we were his favorites, which makes you work harder."

MCKECHNIE: "He was already working conceptually, with ideas, and it had to be more than one idea at work at the same time. He worked on different layers, one feeling against the other. And he knew how to build a number—he had a real talent for that. That was the commercial side of him, the showy side; he just knew what worked. But it always said something, too."

Many choreographers whose first Broadway show fails are never given the chance to do another one, and they either revert to dancing or to staging industrial shows and regional or stock productions. But when the Tony Award nominations were announced, Michael Bennett's choreography for *A Joyful Noise,* long since gone from Broadway, was nominated, and he was in the company of Lee Theodore, Danny Daniels, and Ron Field, his good friend whom he had assisted on *Nowhere to Go but Up* and who won for *Cabaret.*

Receiving a Tony nomination for his first Broadway choreography, and in an instant disaster at that, was an enormous accomplishment and served notice that Bennett's first Broadway show as choreographer would not be his last. But something even more significant had occurred before the show opened on Broadway. While Bennett's program credit for *A Joyful Noise* remained "Dances and Musical Numbers Staged by Michael Bennett," when Dore Schary withdrew as director, the press release issued stated that "the direction has been taken over by Mr. Padula and Michael Bennett, choreographer."

LENNY: "Michael's work was so strong on the show that the producer asked him to take over the direction. . . . I said to him, 'You'll get raves as a choreographer, but as the director, they'll blame the book on you.' I wouldn't let him take direction credit, although he had a lot to do with what direction there was."

Just as Bennett had become a contributor to the dances and an assistant to the choreographer while he was still a dancer, Bennett, while choreographing his first Broadway musical, had become a director. He was also now and forever a part of the Broadway system, and the day after *A Joyful Noise* opened, this overachieving twenty-three-year-old entered six years of analysis.

HENRY, SWEET HENRY AND *HOW NOW*

Had Bob Fosse had his way, Bennett would have choreographed another musical during the same season as *A Joyful Noise*.

BENNETT: "Fosse was very helpful to me when I was starting out. There was a show called *Walking Happy,* which Danny Daniels eventually choreographed, and they wanted me to do it. Fosse said he would guarantee me, which is when you say you'll back up this young choreographer should he not succeed."

The dancing was again the strongest element of Bennett's second Broadway show as choreographer, *Henry, Sweet Henry,* in 1967. *Henry* was based on a novel by Nora Johnson—*The World of Henry Orient*—which was made into a popular 1964 film, directed by George Roy Hill, who also directed *Henry, Sweet Henry.*

As is the case with many adaptations, the writers of *Henry, Sweet Henry* (book by Nunnally Johnson, father of the novel's author; music and lyrics by Bob Merrill) failed to flesh out and develop the characters and situations as appealingly and fully as in the film. *Henry* told the story of two adolescent girls and their infatuation with a musician, whose attempts at seduction they inadvertently yet repeatedly foil. After various complications, including the revelation of an affair between the mother of one of the girls and the musician, the two girls go off to their first dance, ready for maturity and boys their own age. The book was undistinguished, with the adult characters handled with particular ineptness, and the score was uneven, though it featured a few lovely songs ("Here I Am," "I Wonder How It Is to Dance with a Boy"). Nevertheless, *Henry, Sweet Henry* was vastly superior to *A Joyful Noise,* and it received good reviews on its Philadelphia tryout. Any chance for a good Broadway run was scuttled, however, when *Henry* got to New York and was one of the first musicals to be reviewed by Clive Barnes in his new post as drama critic of *The New York Times.* Barnes would insist throughout his first season that the music of Broadway musicals should reflect the contemporary sounds of rock music, and as *Henry* was strictly in the mold of conventional musicals of the Fifties and Sixties, it was curtly dismissed.

But even Barnes admitted that "the briskly modest dances by Michael Bennett proved the most original aspect of the show," while Walter Kerr in the Sunday *Times* said the songs were "pleasantly choreographed in a parade of production numbers that are easy to watch." Hobe Morrison in *Variety* saw more in Bennett's contribution than the others: "Hill and Bennett have apparently worked closely as director and choreographer, for the two naturally related elements seem to have blended almost as one. Thus, some of the non-production scenes are staged almost as if they were ballets, and the numerous production numbers contribute handsomely to characters, situations and story development."

Bennett's big set pieces in the show were the opening, in which he smoothly moved schoolgirls from a city street to a moving bus to the school locker room; "I Wonder How It Is to Dance with a Boy," which began in a luncheonette, the walls of which disappeared to make way for a fantasy of schoolgirl longing; and the opening of the second act, "Weary Near to Dyin'." The latter, a hippie happening set in Washington Square Park, had little to do with the plot. But Bennett, here and in such later shows as *Seesaw,* was able to take numbers that were not especially related to the story and stage them with so much invention and such a solid concept that it didn't matter. While other choreographers seemed to be filling time if their dances weren't integrated or plot-related, Bennett could create a world of his own in the dances, full of underlying ideas that made a seemingly mindless dance convey a great deal.

A Joyful Noise had closed on Christmas Eve, 1966, and *Henry, Sweet Henry* closed on New Year's Eve, 1967, after only eighty performances. However, once again Bennett received a Tony nomination for his choreography, this time in the company of Kevin Carlisle (whom Bennett had helped get the job of choreographer on TV's "Garry Moore Show"), Onna White, and Gower Champion, who won for *The Happy Time.*

The credits for *Henry, Sweet Henry* reveal a great many names with whom Bennett would be associated in later years. Bob Avian danced in the chorus in addition to receiving billing as "Second Assistant to the Choreographer." Three original cast members of *A Chorus Line,* Baayork Lee, Priscilla Lopez, and John Mineo, were also *Henry* dancers. The dance music was the work of William Goldenberg, who would write the score for Bennett's *Ballroom,* and Marvin Hamlisch, who would compose *A Chorus Line.*

It was during and just after *Henry, Sweet Henry* that the Bennett-Avian partnership solidified.

AVIAN: "We were best friends, and we'd sit next to each other. He'd ask, 'What do you think?' and I'd say, 'I like that. *That* I have trouble with. . . .' We both came to realize that my biggest talent with him was that of an editor. . . . He'd bounce things off me, and see things through my eyes. I wasn't afraid of him or worried about a job and having to please him. That was the basis for our whole relationship. I'd tell him whatever I thought, and it became a very strong alliance.

"Michael would always look for the opportunity to redesign the numbers he was given to do so as to take them one step further from what was required of him as choreographer, to make character points, to make book points in the dancing, and to do it with an unusual style or approach. He was really thinking like a director already.

"Sometimes when a show is failing, you just give up, or you coast with it, because you know nothing will save it. Michael never stopped striving to get the most out of his area that he could. . . . He was very aware that if a young choreographer gets his first crack and the show is a bomb, his career can be over. Michael ensured himself that if he was with a turkey, he would survive it.

"After *Henry* closed, he was hired to do a big production number for Carol Lawrence on the Sullivan show, 'I'd Rather Lead a Band.' He asked me to work on it with him. On *Henry,* he would have the idea for the number in his head, then he'd do it, then ask me how I liked it. On this TV number, we sat down together in a room and started tossing ideas back and forth to each other. We realized we flowed creatively, and that I didn't want to be him, and he didn't want to be me. I enjoyed being in the position of assistant. I could let him be the star; I liked that, and, of course, he liked it, too.

"I never stepped into the position of collaborator until he opened the door and asked me. Choreographers have egos, and you need your own juices to flow before you need an assistant to tell you whether they like it or not or contribute. When Michael was just a choreographer, I was just an assistant, never a co-choreographer.

"At that time, I was making up a lot of the steps. Steps are a dime a dozen, and what you need are concepts and ideas. After a while, we didn't know who made up the steps."

By the time of *Henry, Sweet Henry,* Bennett, who had yet to have a Broadway hit, was recognized in the business as a reliable and often brilliant young choreographer, one who seemed to go beyond the conventional when dealing with even the most pedestrian material. His services were much in demand, and those services were often called upon in the capacity of "doctor," one who could be called in to a production already rehearsing or playing a tryout and relied upon to take charge or at least to offer help. Bennett would continue to perform these functions throughout his career, even after his greatest successes. Before *Henry,* he had assisted on the 1967 Off-Broadway revival of Rodgers and Hart's *By Jupiter.* After *Henry,* he was paged to help out *Your Own Thing,* whose leading lady, Leland Palmer, and director's assistant, Jo Jo Smith, had been Bennett's assistant choreographers on *A Joyful Noise.*

PALMER: "Don Driver was a strong director, but needed Michael because he couldn't quite pull it together choreographically. He and Michael were good friends at the time, and he asked Michael to come in and help him after it was pretty much set. Michael's contribution was to integrate the choreography with the story, which he was so great at doing."

The 1968 Off-Broadway musical went on to become a major hit.

In between these two Off-Broadway doctoring assignments came one on Broadway, which was far more substantial. It is an indication of Bennett's rapid rise that, less than a month after the opening of *Henry,* he was hired by David Merrick to replace, without program credit, choreographer Gillian Lynne on his new musical *How Now, Dow Jones*, another troubled and ultimately unsuccessful show of the period. Max Shulman's original book, which told a thin tale of love and Wall Street, was probably the fundamental problem, but the bloodshed during the tryout extended to several departments. Merrick had already fired director Arthur Penn, and replaced him with that most legendary of theatrical "doctors," George Abbott, during the second week of *How Now*'s tryout. Neil Simon, who would figure in varied and interesting ways in at least five future Bennett shows, was briefly in Boston in an advisory capacity.

PETER HOWARD, *How Now*'s musical director and dance and vocal arranger: "Merrick would fire people at the drop of a pin. He wasn't happy with Gillian, who had already done *Roar of the Greasepaint* for him, but then everything was going wrong on this show. Merrick forced Gillian to remain because he had a contract with her, and she stayed around, sitting in the audience while Bennett re-did . . . most of the numbers. I don't think he wanted credit for it, though, because a lot of Gillian's stuff remained, and he didn't particularly want his name on another show that was not a hit."

As was always the case when Bennett took over a show, he brought a team with him, and part of that team was dancer Tommy Tune.

TUNE: "I joined the show in Boston on the night they fired Madeline Kahn, whose part was written out. . . . He did the damnedest thing on *Dow Jones*. There was one number in the show that was working on the road, 'Step to the Rear.' That was the first thing he attacked, and he made it work a hundred times better. That was a brave thing, because usually you just go where the hideousness lies, but he took the best number and made it better.

"Michael's idea was that Gillian would stay and help him and assist . . . but I think ego-wise she couldn't take that, and I think she quit. Although he wanted her to stay, he also wanted to rule over the whole thing.

"Michael and I were very, very close at that time. He was an odd dichotomy, a workaholic, who had to be pushed to get him started, and then he wouldn't stop. Part of my job on *Dow Jones* was getting him to the theater in the morning. It wasn't easy, because he would use all sorts of nefarious plans not to get there."

PALMER: "I assisted Michael on *Dow Jones*. The first time I got the sense that he was really interested in directing was when he took on the doctoring of that show. He was beginning to see how integral the dancing and the acting were. It was inevitable that his strong instincts would be articulated in directing as well as in choreography."

Gillian Lynne would go on, years later, to choreograph two of the most successful musicals in theatre history, *Cats* and *The Phantom of the Opera*, and Michael Bennett would now go on to his first hit.

PROMISES, PROMISES

Promises, Promises, which opened at the Shubert Theatre on December 1, 1968, was a show blessed in all departments, one of the last successful, crowd-pleasing, conventional musicals. Based on the hit film *The Apartment*—written by Billy Wilder and I.A.L. Diamond—*Promises* marked the first time Bennett was working with a strong team that included major Broadway names mixed with a couple of Broadway newcomers who had already had huge success in the field of pop music. David Merrick, for whom Bennett had danced his first steps on Broadway in *Subways Are for Sleeping,* was the producer; Neil Simon, who was already the most successful playwright of his day and had written two well-received musicals, *Little Me* and *Sweet Charity,* in addition to such blockbuster comedies as *Barefoot in the Park* and *The Odd Couple,* handled the book; the score was written by Burt Bacharach and Hal David, who had written numerous hit songs for Dionne Warwick, Herb Alpert, and others. The show's director, Robert Moore, had never staged a musical before but had had great success with *The Boys in the Band* a few months before *Promises.* The show's orchestrations were by Jonathan Tunick, one of the orchestrators of *A Chorus Line,* and the settings were by Robin Wagner.

Neil Simon's book, which told the story of a young executive (Jerry Orbach) lending his apartment to senior executives for dalliance, while in love with a young executive-dining-room waitress (Jill O'Hara) who turns out to be one of the girls taken to the apartment, could be relied on for a laugh every minute or two. But it also fleshed in the characters in confident strokes and used a clever device whereby the hero confided in the audience, explaining, justifying, and revealing things to it as if talking to a trusted friend. The score not only contained rhythmically infectious numbers and one obvious "hit" ("I'll Never Fall in Love Again") but it introduced a new sound to Broadway. While avoiding rock, the *Promises* score used contemporary styles, and brought to the theatre the "record" sound of the popular music of the period, for which Bacharach had been largely responsible. It is debatable whether or not this sound could have been used comfortably in many more musicals, and as Bacharach never contributed another score to Broadway, it was never heard again. But it influenced the sound of such later shows as *Company* and *A Chorus Line,* and hearing it for the first time in *Promises* was as bracing as the show's funny lines, poignant love story, and excellent songs.

Moore's work was superb, but, as this was his first musical, Bennett's job as musical stager took on additional importance. While *Promises* was not a heavy dance show, featuring in its final version just one all-out dance number and a couple of others more along the lines of choreographed movement, Bennett was able to make an enormous contribution to the show by weaving scene into scene, staging marvelous "crossovers," with secretaries spinning through revolving doors in stylized movements reminiscent of the "go-go" steps of "Hullabaloo." All the elements blended perfectly, and the show was Bennett's longest run until *A Chorus Line,* lasting 1,281 performances on Broadway; it was a hit in London as well.

AVIAN: "Michael very much wanted to be offered the show, and prayed that he would get it, because of the really top people involved. When the script came in, he was flying.

"It was not a dancing show; it was a very 'booky' show. So we grabbed every transition. We did everything we could to add dancing to the evening."

It was Bennett who decided to place four strong female vocalists in the orchestra pit to give Bacharach the kind of sound to which he was accustomed on recordings. In so doing, Bennett freed himself: By having extra vocal backing in the pit, he was able to hire a chorus made up entirely of dancers.

Promises also marked the beginning of Bennett's use of Donna McKechnie as the most expressive instrument of his vision. Not only did she lead the big dance and stand out in *Promises* but she seemed to embody all that Bennett was doing in his choreography, and became so essential to its energy and line that she was asked to open touring companies of *Promises* in America as well as the London company, even though her role in the show was relatively brief.

Bennett's work received generally strong critical reaction, but because *Promises* was strong in all departments, his contribution was not singled out as much as it had been in the reviews of *A Joyful Noise* and *Henry, Sweet Henry.* Even before Bennett's big dance number went in, Samuel Hirsch of the *Boston Herald Traveler* noted, "Something must be said about the dances invented by Michael Bennett. His crossovers are masterpieces of exultant movement and the way he captures the worm-like squirming of a 3rd Avenue bar on 2nd Avenue is that exquisite blend of comic attitudes and pulsing motion you've come to expect from this talented choreographer." Walter Kerr in the Sunday *Times* wrote, "Michael Bennett's choreography knows just where to stop. Instead of beating you to death with book, [the show] catches its breath and plucks a dance step out of nowhere. Then, having investigated just how far hip and arms can be swung with a discreet, unhysterical, *tight* abandon, the dance cuts off, like lights in an electrical storm, like a poem with a short last line."

Bennett made his mark in *Promises* with two sequences. In the hands of another choreographer, both could have been extractable interludes only distantly related to the central story. But because of the ideas underlying them and the way in which Bennett developed them, they became much more, and audiences felt a charge whenever the *Promises* dancers (including Baayork Lee and Carole Bishop) started moving.

The first sequence was a brief scene of choreographed movement portraying the frenzy of an afterwork singles bar called "The Grapes of Roth." Graciela Daniele, a dancer who worked for Bennett for the first time in *Promises* and who would go on to choreograph such Broadway shows as *The Pirates of Penzance, The Mystery of Edwin Drood,* and *Zorba,* and breakthrough as a director-choreographer with *Tango Apasionado* in 1987, remembers the development of the number.

DANIELE: " 'Grapes of Roth' was a little jewel. You can't imagine the time it took him to create that bunch of people just moving together. It wasn't really dancing, but it was a scene with nothing but movement. . . . We were this mass in a Sixties singles bar, but there was a scene going on in the clump. It was all interrelated, but we all had our own little stories to play. That you might not see from the audience, but do you know what it meant to the dancers to have that? . . . We all knew who we were in that scene, and knew what we were doing. That's the difference between jazz choreography and a choreographer who directs when he choreographs, and I learned that from him."

MCKECHNIE: "The show was representative of its time, and the moves were contemporary, show dancing with a contemporary feel. You could see moves like 'Grapes of Roth' at a real bar, but Michael heightened those moves and gave them form. It was a perfect integration of those new styles."

AVIAN: "Michael knew exactly what to do with that number right away. He had certain images in his mind, and it was the first thing we did and our best work in the show. People didn't perceive it as a production number or a dance number, but it used such stylish movement, creating an environment on stage, utilizing the characters and setting the tone of the evening."

The number remembered as the show's big dance was "Turkey Lurkey Time," at the end of the first act. It replaced another number that wasn't working during the tryout.

AVIAN: "There was originally a big office party sequence at the end of Act One, and Michael had constructed an eight-minute sequence, not a dance number but an office party staged to music. You had dirty old men coming on to secretaries, guys getting drunk and getting into drag. It was incredible, but when we opened in Boston, it didn't pay off like we hoped it would. . . . We threw the whole sequence out and created this fast production number. It was all because of the dynamics of the show. In a musical, you can feel what needs to happen when, where the hills and the valleys belong. We knew that in order to make it more of a musical, we had to land dance-wise at that point. It was three minutes and bang."

HAROLD WHEELER, the show's dance arranger and musical director: "Michael said, 'I want them to start applauding before the number is over.' So we built an ending, with the dancers dancing dangerously on table tops, and with repetition of steps and music, and it was so infectious, you had to applaud. In everything Michael and I did together in later years, he would always say, 'This number is going to be the "Turkey Lurkey" number of the show.' It was very special to him. He even asked for that in vocals. For Jennifer Holliday's big number in *Dreamgirls,* Michael said, 'The ending has to be like "Turkey Lurkey." Remember how we made them applaud before it was over?'"

BENNETT: "I wanted to do with it what I later did with *Company.* I wanted the psychology of all the participants in a wild Christmas party to come through. But out of town, the audiences felt let down. They wanted a big dance number, without each office boy, secretary and company official emerging as individuals. I realized the way things were going, *Promises* would be conventional. I shifted gears and gave them a big number."*

. . . .

*To Robert Wahls, "A Tony for Bennett?" *Daily News,* April 23, 1972.

If the number became more about stopping the show than about anything else, it was one of the most dynamic dances of its period. The "Turkey Lurkey" number was performed on the 1968 Tony Awards, and when seen today, the steps are clearly of their period, but the imagination underneath is Bennett's.

MCKECHNIE: "He would always work with an image, an idea, or a comment. His image for the secretaries in the final version of 'Turkey Lurkey' was that they had seen a few Betty Grable movies. So they moved like Grable in the movies. People in the audience may not have seen that they were trying to act like Grable, but that concept made it personal for us. We weren't three dancers, we were three secretaries doing a show for the people we work with every day, and they're laughing at us and enjoying it. It was a dance number that built because every moment led to the next for a reason. Each moment was born out of the one before. At the end, when everybody was doing the repetitive kicking, there was a reason, because now they were joining in. It was great fun, but it had form and it made a comment. It was also exhausting to do, but it brought down the house."

DANIELE: *"Promises* was where I really started learning about the theatre, watching Michael. He always seemed so young, so dynamic, so energetic, so wild. . . . He had this incredible personality that goes with all great leaders; everybody fell in love with him. Men and women, young and old, we were all in love with him. Dancers have that more than singers; for dancers, their choreographer is like God. He was gorgeous, and could do everything better than anybody else.

"From the very beginning, he used the individual in a way I had never seen before. In the ballet world, you are more a tool to express the choreographer's vision. With Michael, we were that, but he used our personality and made every single person very much an individual. In the Act Two opening, 'A Fact Can Be a Beautiful Thing,' we were all characters, different from the ones we were in 'Turkey Lurkey.'

"In *Promises,* Michael was already going beyond the conventional Broadway style; he was never conventional. Even when he used a conventional formula, it was to achieve something greater. Look at the *Chorus Line* finale: The kick line could be taken as conventional, but what it means makes you cry.

"It was the complexity rather than the amount of time he took staging a number. To teach a combination of 16 bars doesn't take that long. But to create these moving scenes takes forever, because you have to tell stories for each person. It's not about the steps. It's about something much deeper, much more organic to the show."

Avian, assistant choreographer of *Promises,* was already established as Bennett's indispensable "other eyes." The important new association of *Promises* for Bennett was with Robin Wagner. It was on this show that Bennett began to work closely with this brilliant designer.

WAGNER: "Right from the start, Michael had the desire to have continuous action, to never have a curtain come down. You just keep going, in a kind of cinematic technique. In *Promises,* there was pure cinematic motion: they danced in, they danced out, they danced into the next scene. Nothing ever stopped. And Michael asked that the scenery 'dance' too.

"He loved to stage the scenery going on and off. When the scene moved to the executive dining room, he had the dancers dance on with the little dining room pieces, then get out from behind them and become people in the dining room. He loved objects that he could play with and that the dancers could dance on and off.

"Michael always loved mirrors, and they were there in *Promises.* The set was made of sepia-tinted glass panels with brass edges, and lots of mirrors, particularly in the bar scenes."

KELLY BISHOP: "The final audition for *Promises* was seven hours, an epic. I think he might have used it as part of the concept of *A Chorus Line,* the idea of the endless audition. I was angry when I got the job. I thought, 'Isn't this wonderful? I'm going to make $150 a week, and I've just given them $5,000 worth of training.' But I remember during *Promises* that Michael said dancers really could act."

THE MILLIKEN BREAKFAST SHOWS

A week after *Promises* opened, NBC's "Hallmark Hall of Fame" telecast a new musical version of *Pinocchio,* which boasted dances and musical numbers staged by Bennett. The book was by Ernest Kinoy, and the music and lyrics by Walter Marks, both of whom had written *Bajour,* in which Bennett had danced four years earlier. The leads were Peter Noone, Burl Ives, and Anita Gillette, and several Bennett regulars were in the ensemble, including Tommy Tune, Baayork Lee, and Bob Avian. Bennett's work included a ballet about ghostly "runaways," dropouts from the world, who were clothed and made up in black and white, exactly as the ghosts in *Follies* would be three years later.

Two of the most elaborate and expensive musical productions choreographed by Bennett ran only thirteen performances each and were not open to the theatregoing public. These were the two Milliken Breakfast Shows on which he worked, one in the spring of 1968, shortly before *Promises,* and the other the following spring, with *Promises* running as an established hit.

Created in 1953, the Milliken Breakfast Shows were the most celebrated and elaborate industrial shows in America, each costing up to $2 million and running for two and a half weeks every spring. They were performed in the grand ballroom of the Waldorf-Astoria Hotel, with room for 1,500 at each performance. Shows began at 7:50 A.M., just after breakfast service, with several additional afternoon performances. Milliken and Co., a large textile manufacturer, sponsored these shows to introduce their new line of fabrics to garment-manufacturer buyers, who eagerly attended the annual event. The shows were elaborate book musicals, using original lyrics with as many references to Milliken products as possible, sung to well-known melodies. There were large production numbers that invariably demonstrated how the new fabrics looked by placing them on the lovely "Milliken Girls" who graced every show. Because the Milliken Shows paid the cast extremely well, and gave cast members a bonus and limousine service to and from the Waldorf, they were able, over the years, to attract such stars as Gwen Verdon, Ginger Rogers, Angela Lansbury, Dorothy Loudon, Ann Miller, Alexis Smith, Nancy Walker, Chita Rivera, Ray Bolger, Bert Lahr, and Donald O'Connor. The dancers supporting the stars were drawn from Broadway's best; for Broadway gypsies, the Milliken Show was the dream job, offering prestige and top pay.

Bennett's 1968 Milliken Show starred Molly Picon, John McGiver, Anthony Roberts (of *How Now, Dow Jones*), and Leland Palmer. Among "The Girls" were Donna McKechnie, Priscilla Lopez, Sandy Roveta, Carolyn Kirsch, and Barbara Monte,* as well as Neva Small, who had played one of the leads in *Henry, Sweet Henry.* Among the male chorus was Robert Avian, who was also one of two assistant choreographers.

By the time of the 1969 show, Bennett's billing changed from choreog-

. . . .
*All five women figured in *A Chorus Line.*

rapher to "Musical Numbers Conceived, Staged and Choreographed by Michael Bennett." As *Promises* was now playing, Donna McKechnie rose to the level of leading player. The stars this time were a trio of comics, David Burns, Lou Jacobi, and Phil Leeds, and among "The Girls" were Carole Bishop, Graciela Daniele, Mary Jane Houdina, Carolyn Kirsch, and Barbara Monte. Avian did not perform this time but was again assistant choreographer. Both of Bennett's Milliken Shows had book and lyrics by Arnold Horwitt and direction by Stanley Prager.

PETER HOWARD, the musical director and dance arranger of numerous Milliken Shows: "Byron Sanft, the producer of the shows, was the first to recognize how brilliant Michael was. . . . While there was always a separate book director, Michael did everything. In later years, Michael would come and offer advice and assistance on the Milliken Shows at Byron's request."

AVIAN: "Michael changed the face of the Milliken Show. It was the prestige trade show to get, and the first year he got it, he did it their way, which was the conventional book-style musical. They loved the work he did on it, because he brought it to new heights. He used wonderful gimmicks, like having doves flying from the back of the ballroom to the stage.

"The following year, they asked him to do it again. He said, 'I'd like to do it, but I want to change it. I'd like to make it more like a revue, with only a thread of book.' No one had ever been allowed to change the Milliken Show before. We added lights around the stage, runways into the auditorium, and made it a spectacular revue. Michael added a full line of boys, and put the band on stage. From that show on, Michael's formula stuck."

4

NEW CONCEPTS

COCO

*P*ROMISES, WHILE NOT A heavy dance show and still very much centered on a solid book, was key in Bennett's career simply because it ran, and people were able to enjoy his work without having to sit through an otherwise uninspired production. It was material with which he felt an affinity, but it did not show off his range. He selected his next project mainly to avoid being typed or pigeonholed.

Coco, a musical based on the life of Coco Chanel starring Katharine Hepburn, opened on Broadway on December 18, 1969, and was not well received by critics. Audiences, however, flocked to *Coco* to witness the spectacle of a beloved nonsinging star tackling her first (and only) musical role, and while almost everyone loved Hepburn's typically feisty, sharp-angled performance and the many comic ripostes librettist Alan Jay Lerner had given her, most dismissed the rest of the production as a fashion parade, hardly a musical at all.

While the idea of a musical based on Chanel's life was not a particularly good one, especially when its creators were limited by the age of their star to Chanel's later years, *Coco* did have a characteristically witty book from Lerner, an often-pretty Hollywood-style score by Andre Previn (his only Broadway musical), and lavish sets and costumes by Cecil Beaton. Hepburn's star performance (which improved vastly during the run) was immensely entertaining, even if she remained her Yankee self and made little attempt to become Chanel.

But the most underrated aspect of *Coco* was Bennett's work on it. If *Coco* had little actual "dancing," it had an enormous amount of choreographed movement, and Bennett somehow managed to turn the fashion parades required by the story into dances. Bennett's hand was visible throughout the show, but there were three sequences that stood out. In "The Money Rings Out Like Freedom," Chanel pored over a scrapbook with her new assistant, while highlights of her celebrated career came to life, with the dancers appearing in stunning tableaux, moving about with often astonishing gestures and poses. In "Ohrbach's, Bloomingdale's, Best & Saks," a celebration of Coco's success in selling her collection to American buyers, Bennett came up with a can-can that even managed to get Hepburn dancing. The finale, "Always Mademoiselle," in which Coco came to an understanding of how her career had taken the place of love and family in her life, featured gorgeous women in dazzling shades of red pouring down a mirrored staircase (mirrors were by now a Bennett trademark), with more ladies floating on a revolving double staircase that moved across the stage as Hepburn strutted in front of it.

The critics did not entirely fail to notice the quality of Bennett's work. John Simon wrote in *New York* magazine, "Michael Bennett has again come up with wonderfully sculptural and suggestive movements for the dances and fashion sequences. His choreography is mostly the heightenings of the tempos of everyday goings-on, the embellished groupings of social intercourse, but the telling details add up to the perfect orthography of evocation and delight." Catherine Hughes in *Plays and Players* felt that, "The one really good thing about the show is Michael Bennett's staging of the musical numbers and fashion sequences. Somehow, Bennett has given the all-too-numerous fashion parades a variety and style that *Coco* itself so painfully lacks."

Coco was also the show where Bennett began to experiment with cinematic staging, a device that would soon become his signature. Using mannequins that revolved offstage on one side to reappear in a new outfit on the other, he was starting to stage sequences using a montage effect, with things overlapping or wiping away others.

ANN REINKING, a dancer in *Coco:* "Fosse had already introduced the idea of the cinematic segue in *Charity,* and Michael used the turntable in

Coco for cinematic segues, like a 'bleed' in film. It helped to take the bumps out of a musical. He was an advocate of this smooth, 'all-one' technique, a truly graceful segue."

In addition to Bennett's cinematic style, *Coco* employed actual filmed sequences featuring Coco's father and former lovers.

AVIAN: "Before rehearsals began, Michael almost pulled out of the show. Lerner had conceived these 'living screen' things that were film, and the dancers would come through the film and become live. Michael didn't want to make this a 'movie for the stage.' He found the whole concept too binding, as he would have been stuck with filmed numbers that might not work. Because Lerner wanted Michael to do the show, they rethought the use of film."

Bennett was never entirely happy with the brief filmed sequences that remained, as he was already finding ways to create genuinely cinematic effects without the use of actual film.*

Once again, Graciela Daniele worked closely with Bennett on the production. She said, "Michael was not happy during *Coco,* but his work on it was unbelievable. . . . It really was not a great show, but we had two fantastic things going for us, Kate's charisma, and the genius of Michael, creating a world that never stopped flowing.

"In 'The Money Rings Out Like Freedom,' he had a very clear vision of the women looking like pictures in magazines in movement. We weren't exactly playing characters as in *Promises,* it was more the manne-quin, but he still allowed that kind of freedom, talking about who you were. Even if you didn't talk about it, you always felt you were a character with Michael, probably because he treated us that way, like actors, as opposed to just dancers. He got everything out of us because he was so seductive.

"From a feminine standpoint, it was a beautiful show to be in because of the way he had us behave and look; we all felt like top fashion models, even though we weren't. 'The Money Rings Out Like Freedom' was about Coco's liberation. It started with pictures and poses, and Michael figured out how to go from one movement to the next, and make move-ment that created dance. We were literally walking, but you never felt it. . . . Michael was great at unconventional design, and it was never just lines and circles and squares. He was a great admirer of Busby Berkeley,

. . . .

*One of the on-film characters was reshot during previews, and it was Bob Avian who was ultimately seen (but not heard) on film as Grand Duke Alexandrovitch every night in *Coco.*

and I think he was influenced by Berkeley a lot in *Coco*. When I watched *Coco* as dance captain, that number was literally an army of gorgeous women in black, attacking and swivelling, but it was dancing."

GEORGE ROSE, who played his first sophisticated Broadway role in *Coco:* "Lerner was very happy with Michael. He seemed to know exactly what he wanted. Only when he made Kate a bit too mobile or got her to dance more than she thought she could do was there any friction. . . . He was always very sweet to me. I was not a dancer, but I always felt that . . . he respected and liked my work. He was infinitely patient. He knew we were actors and needed a lot of time. Kate wasn't a great mover, and we looked pretty clumsy alongside that chorus.

"The staging of the finale to the first act was a miracle, all done to music cues, with Kate rushing around on the revolving stages going in different directions, ripping a piece of chiffon off one girl, pinning something on another, all done to music.

"Bennett's contribution to the show was immeasurable. He was just a strange little genius. One looked at those parades, and the girls seemed to be not doing very much, but when you saw it in performance in the clothes, it was stunning. He used the revolves wonderfully, a little like *Les Misérables.*"

Coco proved to be more than just another staging assignment for Bennett; it became a double lesson in power and control. Michael Benthall, the show's director, had directed Hepburn in Shaw's *The Millionairess* and Shakespeare's *As You Like It* on Broadway, and he was a great favorite of the star's. But he was not a director of musicals, and suffered from a drinking problem. It became evident in rehearsal and during the first week of previews that Benthall would be unable to pull together a huge production such as *Coco*. While Hepburn remained loyal to him, and he continued to work on book scenes, the show became Bennett's unofficial directorial debut.

DANIELE: "Michael assumed most of the staging during early previews. Although Benthall was still around, I would say Michael directed most of the show. I think Benthall was mostly there because of his relationship with Kate, and he did work on the scenes. But the flow of the show and all the staging was Michael."

AVIAN: "Benthall was frightened by it all. Hepburn was basically guiding the show through him, but he had a hard time handling anything with more than two or three people in a scene. So all of a sudden, instead of working on our sequences, Michael had to go in and stage scenes, including dialogue, that had more than four people in them. And most of the scenes had twenty people in them! Benthall was thrilled to step aside and let Michael take over."

REINKING: "*Coco* was when Michael realized he could direct. I heard him say, 'This is what I want to do. I belong here,' when he was directing. Benthall did contribute, but as he got sicker, there was very little choice, and it was a good opportunity for Michael. He took over in a graceful way, and while he was under the watchful eye of Benthall, Beaton, Lerner and Hepburn, he got through. They started relying on him more and more, probably because of the difficulty of the turntable set. The actual structure of the set was Michael's greatest ally."

Bennett was in no way intimidated by taking the reins of a major Broadway musical, and the month he had spent in Paris watching Chanel work gave him a very specific vision of what he wanted. But the eminently capable Bennett faced a greater challenge in *Coco* than the full responsibility for staging a large show: that of directing the show's star. Hepburn and Bennett clashed on numerous occasions, and, as both were strong-willed and stubborn, neither gave in easily.

ROSE: "Hepburn is always bossy. If she has an idea in her head, you can't get rid of it, and there are certain things she won't do. I remember times when she wouldn't do things Bennett wanted her to do. And of course, her word was law."

DANIELE: "I adored Kate. Michael had difficulties with her. It was two very strong people, two leaders, two great people together. It was a love-hate relationship. She adored him, and told me so. And I know he admired her, too. But they fought. Sometimes I would see Michael leaving her dressing room with an agonized expression. . . . Kate is brilliant, and she knew perfectly well that Michael knew what he was doing. She respected him very much. But they were both stubborn and very opinionated."

AVIAN: "Hepburn was not a musical performer, so we couldn't use her as the center of the production numbers. She had to be pretty still, and we had to create all the numbers around her.

"It was tough for her, never having done a musical before. She was very vulnerable, and kept on questioning her ability to do one. She would stop and say, 'Why am I doing this?' but she knew she had to plow ahead. She was great to the company, and they loved her, but she was difficult too, because she's very opinionated and sees things from her point of view. You tended to be nervous when you were working with her. She tended to be contrary, and it took her a while to trust Michael, but they worked it out and she came to have great respect for him."

REINKING: "They fought, and she tested him. They were strong wills, but they did listen to each other and help each other, and they both profited. She needed help in the musical aspects of the part, and finally she said to Michael, 'Help me.' After that, it went very well. And she was crazy about Bob Avian."

HAROLD WHEELER, who did the dance-music continuity for *Coco:* "I remember Hepburn saying, 'And a child shall lead them.' Most of the people on that show were veterans, and Michael's youth gave the show the spark she wanted. She trusted him, to the point where, after Previn and Lerner would tell her she sounded wonderful in a song, she would turn to Michael and say, 'How do I sound?' And he would answer, 'It's getting there.' Never 'You're wonderful, darling.' Always 'It's going to get better. Just remember you're an actress, and put that into your singing. Don't try to become a wonderful singer.' "

LENNY: "Hepburn kept coming in late for rehearsal. One day she came in about two hours late for a ten o'clock rehearsal. At three o'clock, Michael picked himself up and started to leave. She said, 'Where are you going?' He said, 'I did my day's work.' He left, and she went crazy. Michael was never in awe of a star."

Working on *Coco* was one of the more remarkable interludes of Bennett's career as a choreographer, but it took its toll on him, and as soon as it opened, he flew off to London to collapse. It was not an experience that he would later place among his favorites.

AVIAN: "It was not really a good show; it lacked tension and was hard to buy. . . . He didn't get to the last week of rehearsals during previews because he was so upset with the show, not with his work, but with the fact that the show was not good. He wanted it to be this huge, *My Fair Lady* musical, but it wound up being this beige nightmare. He wanted mystery and magic, but Beaton created this beige set which you couldn't light. Beaton said, 'This is your design, these are the clothes,' and there were no 'buts.' And Michael and Lerner spoke different languages. Lerner was a gentleman's gentleman, Michael was a street kid.

"We hated previewing in New York without a tryout. At the first preview, every major person in the industry was there, which was a killer.

"Michael and I used to refer to *Coco* as our 'smash flop.' While Hepburn was in it, the grosses were enormous, and the checks poured in. After we finally got a hit show with *Promises*, *Coco* was a great disappointment, and a very difficult show to do. But it was some of the greatest work we ever did."

Bennett hit on perhaps the most important aspect of the experience when he said, "The best thing I can say about *Coco* is that it helped me do better on *Follies*."*

COMPANY AND THE CONCEPT MUSICAL

Bennett had by this time secured a reputation for imaginative, content-based dances far superior to the standard work of many Broadway choreographers. Thus far, however, his work had been seen in productions that followed conventional musical-theatre patterns of realistic book scene, song, and dance, even if his work had occasionally been able to go beyond those conventions. He was now to become involved in one of the most original and unconventional productions in musical theatre, one that would make its own rules as boldly as did *Oklahoma!* or *West Side Story* in earlier eras. Two earlier musical productions are helpful to an understanding of Bennett's next show, *Company*.

In 1948, a highly unconventional musical called *Love Life* opened on Broadway and played for eight months. Written by Alan Jay Lerner and Kurt Weill, *Love Life* was directed by Elia Kazan and choreographed by Michael Kidd. It told the story of a troubled marriage, but each scene in the first act was set in a different era, moving from Colonial days to the present. While the leading characters (played by Nanette Fabray and Ray Middleton) never aged, the story of their marital problems moved from period to period, and reflected the changes in American society of each period.

What was most daring about *Love Life* was its structure and the way it used musical numbers. *Love Life*, as Fosse's *Chicago* years later, was billed as "a vaudeville," and in between the book scenes, which were "realistic" except for the fact that they took place thirty or forty years apart in time, numbers were performed that did not continue the action of the play but that commented upon it in sometimes obscure ways. A group of eight "go-getters" sang ironically of "Progress," and a black quartet dealt with

. . . .

*To Clive Hirschhorn, "Leader of the Dance," *Plays and Players*, August 1976.

the incompatibility of "Economics" and romance. A hobo appeared between scenes set in the 1890s and the 1920s to sing a plaintive song about what true love should be, a song he finds ignored as he drifts through the country. *Love Life* featured circus acts (the heroine is sawed in half in the opening, to represent her divided self) and culminated in a minstrel show, in which an interlocutor took the leading couple through a series of numbers offering possible solutions to their personal impasse. This final sequence, which ends with the leads walking a tightrope toward each other, functioned in much the same way as the final sequence of *Follies*.

Love Life could be considered the first "concept musical," a musical in which a theme or idea—in this case marriage and the increasing difficulty of relationships in modern society—takes the place of a progressive, realistically developed plot. *Love Life* also broke every rule of the Rodgers and Hammerstein school of musical, which was firmly entrenched when it appeared, and was the most daringly innovative musical of its day.

Harold Prince had been involved as a producer of such important musical productions as *West Side Story, The Pajama Game,* and *Fiddler on the Roof.* But in the early Sixties, he began to direct musicals, and his years of working with Abbott and Robbins helped him to create the most ground-breaking musicals of the Sixties and Seventies.

Cabaret, which Prince directed in 1966 (and again in revival in 1987), is a key production in the history of musical theatre, for it was the only show that managed to be both a conventional, realistic, book-centered musical in the mold of the Forties, Fifties, and Sixties, with a clearly structured plot and conventional songs, as well as a completely new, daring, concept musical. While it provided audiences with the pleasures of the Rodgers and Hammerstein tradition, it featured stunning new ways to use songs and musical sequences, which would lead directly to the musicals of Prince and Sondheim, two of which would also be Bennett musicals.

Cabaret had the traditional main plot and subplot, but Prince had a daring conception that took *Cabaret* well beyond any other musical of its period. Its realistic scenes were punctuated by numbers featuring the "Master of Ceremonies" (Joel Grey), but, while this emcee was to be seen in the realistic scenes in the Kit Kat Klub—where the heroine, Sally Bowles, worked—the numbers he performed in *Cabaret* were not meant to be numbers in that club. They were performed in limbo, and became commentary on or ironic counterpoint to the book scenes, in a manner similar to the vaudeville songs of *Love Life.*

Cabaret broke with realistic staging and writing, but, unlike several later innovative musicals, it achieved wide popularity and a four-year run on Broadway, probably because it offered the best of both worlds—conceptual ingenuity with old-fashioned love stories and a solid plot. This would not be the case in Prince's next shows, and it would not be until *A Chorus Line* that another musical as innovative as *Cabaret* would be a large-scale financial success.

With Robbins inactive, Prince was now the most original and conceptual director working in musicals, but, unlike Robbins, he was not a director-choreographer, and he would require the services of a choreographer capable of work as bold as his. It was not very long before Prince would need to call upon the services of Bennett.

Coco opened in late 1969, and just a few months later, Bennett was at work on *Company,* directed by Prince, with a score by Stephen Sondheim and a book by George Furth, which opened at the Alvin Theatre on April 26, 1970.

AVIAN: "Hal was impressed with Michael and his work and had been trying to get Michael to do a show with him. When Michael was offered *Company,* he said, 'There's not much in here for me.' Hal said, 'Well, I'll hire Donna McKechnie,' and Michael said, 'Okay.' And that team was so attractive to Michael. We had been busy with *Promises* and *Coco,* in London and on the road, so they had done much of the work on *Company* before we even got there. I would listen at the meetings, and it was like a new animal, requiring a total brain readjustment."

Like *Love Life, Company* was a musical about marriage, in this case five marriages, as a reflection of the environment, in this case "New York City—NOW," as stated in the program. Also like *Love Life,* it had no real plot, the characters and scenes linked by the central idea. Similar to *Love Life* and *Cabaret,* it used songs and musical sequences in totally new ways. Yet *Company* would go further than any earlier musical had in its use of nonlinear storytelling, innovative structure, and unconventional use of song.

Company was about a bachelor named Robert, his three girlfriends, and the married couples in his life. It was about the need for commitment, the difficulty of maintaining relationships in urban society, and the struggle to coexist with other people. But it also sought to use New York City as an embodiment of these themes, and nowhere was this more evident than in Boris Aronson's scenic design. The set, awash with projections, was a steel jungle gym of levels, platforms, and elevators, an abstract embodiment of the isolation and coldness of city life that rendered relationships so difficult.

In *Company*, Bennett also hit upon a concept that reflected Robbins's work in *West Side Story* and foreshadowed *A Chorus Line*. In *West Side Story*, Robbins had eliminated the anonymous chorus by making all the dancers characters with names, thus individualizing each to a degree. In *Company*, Bennett eliminated the chorus entirely, having the show's fourteen actors function as principal characters and also as a singing and dancing ensemble.

SONDHEIM: "We wanted to have a small cast. Hal's idea was to have them living on stage all the time, which didn't work out. It was Michael's idea to use them as a kind of P.T.A. group when it came to company numbers such as 'Side by Side.' They would be treated not only as people who were each other's company, but they would be a company of semi-amateur singers and dancers. That was the impression he wanted to give, and we even had a little ballet in the first act, which was staged and rehearsed but not performed, in the 'Have I Got a Girl for You' song. Michael knew that we were not going to get fourteen people who could sing, dance and act with equal facility. So he decided to make a virtue out of necessity, and give them the feeling of talented amateurs when they would dance."

Both acts of *Company* opened and closed at birthday parties, but unlike the office party of *Promises*, the parties in *Company* were nonrealistic. It was impossible to tell just where the parties were supposed to be occurring, or how many different parties there were. The ambiguity made the parties, like the reunion in *Follies* the following season, into psychological landscapes, points in Robert's life when he could no longer avoid a confrontation with commitment.

As in *Love Life*, *Company* used songs in a variety of nonrealistic ways. They could be comments on the action of a scene sung by those not involved in the scene (seven actors suddenly appearing in the living room of one couple and on the upper levels of the stage to perform "The Little Things You Do Together") or inner monologues ("Someone Is Waiting," "The Ladies Who Lunch") revealing the subtext of scenes. They could be intercut with dialogue and recur throughout a scene ("Another Hundred People"), they could use pastiche to comment on the action ("You Could Drive a Person Crazy"), or they could even *be* scenes ("Barcelona").

Bennett's staging of these songs, like Aronson's set, was a perfect embodiment of the jarring neuroticism of city life, in which people zip madly about without quite connecting. It achieved a nervous, electric dynamism that was capable of giving way to passionate lyricism. While there were only a couple of "dance" numbers, all was choreographed, the movement always a correlative of the show's themes and concept.

In "You Could Drive a Person Crazy," a number performed by the three girlfriends, the stylized movement never ceased, combining the Andrews Sisters-style of the song with typical Bennett heightening for theatrical effect. In the opening of Act Two, "Side by Side by Side" and "What Would We Do Without You," Bennett used the hoariest, hokiest steps, from vaudeville buck and wing, to kick-lines, tap, soft shoe, top hats and canes, but all to fresh and surprising effect. In Donna McKechnie's solo dance, "Tick Tock," Bennett created passionately expressive movement, like that of Cassie's dance in *A Chorus Line*, and, as in Cassie's dance, only McKechnie could do full justice to it.

Prince was not slow to realize that he had found in Bennett a partner capable of extending what he was doing in his staging and enhancing it.

PRINCE: "While I'd be working scenes, he'd come and look over my shoulder and perhaps I'd say, 'Take it for a minute and move them somewhere.' He works very much from character and isn't interested in steps per se. What does interest him is the actor, the character he's playing, the shape of his body and how he uses it. In this way, he gets the physical qualities that come from character into his dances and so eliminates that awful wrench when you go from a scene to a song and dance."*

Prince was also quick to notice Bennett's tendency toward cinematic staging, a technique that was of great interest to Prince and that both he and Bennett would develop further in their next project together.

PRINCE: "When Elaine Stritch stands there and looks down and says, 'It's the little things,' what you've done is you've brought a camera in to a lady, and quick cut to her face. If you read *Company,* you'll see that it uses close-ups, cross fades, dissolves—all the techniques of film and none of the techniques of the stage."†

AVIAN: "Trying not to let the show stop was basically what he wanted, not to have dead air when going from one spot to the next. There were times when I thought I was watching a movie."

. . . .

*To John Kane, *"Company:* A New Landmark?," *Plays and Players,* February 1972.
†To Robert Waterhouse, "Direction and Design: The Partners," *Plays and Players,* March 1972.

Company was Bennett's first involvement with a musical in which all the elements—book, songs, musical staging, and direction—were deployed in a truly integrated fashion and at the service of an overriding metaphor, the city as an embodiment of modern relationships. Because of the need to integrate all the elements, Bennett could not stage his dances in separate rooms while the director worked on the scenes, as he had in *Coco* or *Promises,* because the dancers *were* the actors and singers, and the movement ran through the scenes, intercutting and bisecting them. While he would not officially become a director until his next show, his work, like that of Robbins in *West Side Story,* was now inseparable from that of the other creators.

CHARLES WILLARD, company manager of *Company* on Broadway and on tour: "Everybody realized that Michael's contribution to *Company* had been very significant, that he really made it a musical theatre piece, with a real edge, when it might have been academic, over-intellectualized and serious. I heard that Michael had a lot to do with the re-shaping of the show when it was in Boston, taking out some of the darker colors.

"Michael was not an intellectual. I think he was basically a very warm and intuitive artist who used a vocabulary of show business idioms with which he was very familiar to translate the impulses of his time into musical theatre. . . . I don't think he ever stood back and intellectualized it, or had discussions about concept musicals. Because he was very alive to his time, he was very aware that expressing things in a fragmented, non-linear way was of his time, and so that's how he did it. It just came out that way. He didn't intellectually reject doing an old-time, linear show. He just didn't feel it that way, so it didn't come out that way. But he never lost that kind of Irving Berlin sense of show business either."

Most of the raves for *Company* went to Sondheim, Prince, and Aronson, and Bennett received only brief mentions in many of the original reviews. But his contribution cannot be overestimated: Most of the show seemed to move and "dance," and it was in agitated patterns that reflected the book, music, and setting. A few critics did take notice. John Simon in *New York* magazine felt that Bennett deserved more credit than Prince, stating, "Mr. Bennett has the gift of making old things look new, simple things look prodigiously difficult, and dance look like inspired sculpture in motion rather than, as usual nowadays, just sculpture in disintegration."

If Bennett's work was largely unsung by the press, those involved in the production realized how important his contribution was:

SONDHEIM: "When I was writing the opening number, Boris Aronson had already designed the set. The first thing Hal does on a show is get the set designer to sketch or make models of the set. I got photographs of models and I asked Boris how long it would take the elevators to work, to go down from the upper level to the lower, stage level, and Michael and I discussed the staging of it, and how the climax of the number should be with everybody getting down to the floor level, after they'd been all over the set. I worked it out so that he wouldn't be stuck and made the long note on the word 'love,' which was timed out to just enough seconds to get them all down on the stage. Hal said the opening number has to introduce all the characters to the audience and their relationship to Bobby, and the title of the show. It was a large assignment. I worked it out myself, and Michael felt that the ending was not strong enough, and asked me to figure out how to extend the ending so they would say 'Company' three times.

"I had one difference of opinion with Michael, on 'Side by Side'; I didn't like the tug of war and he did, but the tug of war stayed in.

"Michael was very much involved in 'Being Alive.' I wrote the song without having the notion of having the lines interrupted. I wanted a change of tone between the two choruses, the first chorus being a statement and the second a prayer. But it was Michael's idea to have the lines not finish."

WILLARD: "Whenever Bennett and Avian were at the theatre, rehearsing or auditioning, I remember the whole theatre was very quiet and intense; everybody in the company not only had such respect for Michael as an artist, but also they were so fond of him, so grateful for the way he worked because he always worked with them very quietly and very intimately and very paternally . . . no shouting or carrying on, with none of the tension that accompanied Hal's rehearsals. . . . It was intense, because people were working hard, but there was always that kind of communal camaraderie about it.

"Michael's big concern . . . that came up at all his rehearsals was the energy of the show, because he knew he was dealing with non-dancers, with the exception of Donna. . . . He had to work very hard to get those actors to perform as dancers in terms of putting out, really delivering. He would say, 'You can't just do this once a week. If the number's going to work, you've got to do it as a dancer, and you've got to think like that, you've got to put your body into it, all your energy, or it's not going to work.' . . . Sometimes they resisted, because they felt they were being pushed to do something that they really weren't trained to do. But they were all so fond of him and had such respect for him that they wanted to score.

"Michael was always very concerned about the 'Tick Tock' dance because he considered that his pièce de résistance in the show, the one set piece of choreography that was unmistakably his, and because it had been conceived for Donna, there was always the problem of who else could do it. It had been so specifically built for her, there was always the issue of, 'Can someone else do it?' . . . It was the same problem as the Cassie dance, also built on Donna, and no one else could ever quite do it. With both dances, Bob and Michael made adjustments to accommodate other performers, but never really re-did the dance for another body."

AVIAN: "The opening was wonderful. It took forever to stage, because none of them could dance. Michael would say, 'Well, this is what I want. Bobby, you teach them.' I staged most of 'You Could Drive a Person Crazy,' because that was more my bag. Usually when we worked, it was like a mirror, and I would follow him. When we hit that number, he followed me. We each had our thing, and he was very good about it. We never said, 'I did this. I did that.' It wasn't about that."

Although Donna McKechnie had been noticed in *Promises,* it was *Company* in which she became the embodiment of Bennett's choreographic impulse and style, and in which she first emerged as a dancing star. It led to a principal role the following season in Ron Field's revival of *On the Town,* after which she would try her luck in California.*

MCKECHNIE: "By the time of *Company,* Hal knew that Michael loved working with me and had success with me, and that I had been very important to him in *Promises.* I don't know if Hal did this on purpose, but he called me in and told me he was trying to get Michael, and I think he used me as bait a little bit. . . . Michael at that time had started to feel that he didn't want to work just as a choreographer. . . . I made it more appealing, but he still had to be talked into doing it just as a choreographer, because his way of working was already so conceptual. He was doing most of the director's work, and coming off shows better than the director. But he felt that with me, he would at least have one number of pure choreography.

. . . .

*That period was later reflected in McKechnie's *A Chorus Line* character.

"Hal Prince staged the scenes, but I think Michael had a lot of input without credit. I never saw Michael take over at rehearsals, but in their meetings, I think he had a great sense of how to make it more like a movie, with editing. I remember the karate scene was all Michael's and Bob's. Michael was evolving as a theater creator, and people who worked with him, like Hal, respected him, and knew he had something to say.

"As Bob Fosse said, 'The hardest thing to come up with when you begin creating a dance is the first step.' I remember coming into an empty room with him and Bob to create 'Tick Tock.' Michael would start with an idea. He said, 'I want to say something about loneliness, about adult sexuality, about how you can be in bed with someone but alone.' . . . He would say, 'When you're making love, you're really alone. I want to find that lonely moment. Maybe you're with someone, and you're supposed to be involved, and all you can hear is the clock ticking.' That's why you heard the ticking in the number. The 'Tick Tock' dance was like an impressionistic or modern painting. The audience doesn't have to figure it out or analyze it, but the impact of it should take you to a certain place or stimulate your imagination. . . . He was trying to locate that idea and make it come across subliminally without really saying it. . . . The character of Robert had a great need for intimacy, but was also terrified of it, and we reflected that in the number.

"I was really shy then. Michael came up to me in rehearsal and said, 'You know, I really want to do something different here. How do you feel about dancing topless?' I could do all that stuff with my clothes on, but not without. I tried not to blush, and said, 'Michael, yeah, how interesting, but I really think we'd be disturbing the mystery of the piece. I think we should create the feeling and the idea, and let the audience use its imagination.' Maybe he realized he was asking the wrong person, but he never brought it up again.

"At first, Wally Harper, who did wonderful work on the show as dance arranger, did an arrangement for the dance that was too one-dimensional, like a rock number. . . . It was too obvious, and it didn't move you. It was about fucking, not the need for love, and it was close to vulgar. There was a need for anger and frustration in it, but it needed a sense of yearning. . . . There was a need for another arrangement, and Wally was very upset when David Shire came in to do it."

SONDHEIM: "Michael felt that Wally Harper's music wasn't what he wanted, so when we were in Boston we had David Shire come in to do the music for that. He was a friend of mine, and somebody who I'd been helping in his career with Dick Maltby. I was trying to do for him what Oscar Hammerstein had done for me."

MCKECHNIE: "The thing that separated [Michael] from other people, and that allowed him to grow and get better and better, was that he never disallowed things. He would allow himself the luxury of making mistakes, or saying something that people might laugh at later. He was more interested in finding the best way, and the way to do that was to put all the ways out there."

Company is today looked back on by those who were involved as one of the most thrilling experiences of their career.

AVIAN: "It was so impressive to watch Michael and Hal work on it. I used to sit at those rehearsals with my mouth open, seeing what would come up, and watching them save the gold. . . . It taught us a lot. Working with sensibilities like Hal and Steve, and the idea of a new kind of musical, was fabulously interesting."

Company was the first great Sondheim-Prince collaboration and one of the landmarks in the modern musical theatre. If Bennett's contribution was overlooked by some at the time, it was clear to those who saw the show again and again that Bennett had had a great deal to do with everything that was daring, innovative, and new in it.

Bennett's rise was steady, and his work seemed to become more confident with each show. In four years, he had gone from contributing exciting dance numbers to forgettable shows to making a major contribution to one of the most original and important shows in musical theatre history. It was obvious to all that he had to take the next step and take on the direction of a musical. It was equally obvious to Prince that he needed Bennett for his next project, a musical on which Sondheim and James Goldman had been working for several years.

5

. . . .

THE DIRECTOR:

MUSICAL DESPAIR

AND STRAIGHT PLAYS

FOLLIES

*F*OLLIES, WHICH REUNITED BENNETT with *Company* creators Prince, Sondheim, and Aronson, opened on Broadway in April 1971. If Bennett had been ready to direct as early as *Coco* and *Company,* he was by this time frustrated at being unable to exercise his talent for integrating all the forces of a production.

BENNETT: "The true facts are that *Company* was going to be my last show as a choreographer, so (Prince) really let me co-direct *Follies* just to keep me. I loved Stephen Sondheim and Hal so much that he kept me on by making me a co-director."*

AVIAN: "Becoming a director was a natural progression for him. . . . The experience in *Company* had been so good that when *Follies* came along, he knew he had to do it. But he wanted to be co-director. Hal went along with it, which to this day amazes me."

Follies was to be Bennett's first and last show as co-director, and, when it was all over, Bennett would tell Jack Lenny, "I don't ever want to do another show with Hal." But their collaboration produced one of the most

. . . .

*To David Galligan, "*Dream* Merchant Michael Bennett," *Drama-Logue,* March 31–April 6, 1983.

· 66 ·

breathtaking examples of total theatre ever seen on the American stage.

Follies depicted a reunion of former Follies showgirls and their mates, centering on two unhappy marriages. Although James Goldman's book seemed to have more story than *Company, Follies* was again an essentially plotless musical, whose story, songs, design, and staging were all unified by a theme.

As SONDHEIM told *New York* magazine, "In the thirty years since they've seen each other, their lives have fallen apart, just as the Follies have, just as the country has. What was hopeful and promising and naive and innocent back there is now cynical and lost and bitter."

The "Follies" of the title had multiple meanings. They were literally the series of annual revues produced in America throughout most of the first half of the twentieth century, shows that glorified girls and beauty and that were all fantasy, dreams, and glitter. They were the follies of youth, mistakes made that could never be undone, roads not taken, loyalties betrayed. The guests at the reunion were often guilty of the folly of still holding on to youthful dreams of romance, success, and happiness that were never to be, and that tenacity led at least one character into another kind of "folly," madness.

Tying all these definitions together was the metaphor of show business. The Follies were presented in a time when American life was less complex and the spirit of the nation more hopeful. *Follies* showed how the tinsel, glamour, and gaiety of show business past provided a false set of standards, which resulted in a disillusioned postwar America. In its way, *Follies* addressed the idea of the American dream as strongly as Arthur Miller's *Death of a Salesman.*

The way in which *Follies* used show business to convey its themes resulted in the most passionate and frightening musical Broadway has ever seen. Sondheim, a master at both pastiche of musical styles of the past and lyrical, intensely personal interior monologue in song, created a score that echoed the works of songwriters of the Follies' period, such as Irving Berlin and Jerome Kern. But these sounds of the past were filtered through Sondheim's lifelong sense of ambiguity, setting up a tension between the simple joys of old and present-day neuroticism that runs throughout the score. Designer Boris Aronson once again produced a set that was the embodiment of everything the show was about. He created an empty theatre already partially demolished, with scaffolding, disorienting levels, numerous raked playing areas, and rubble and exposed brick strewn about.

The staging by Prince and Bennett was again a reflection of the show's setting and themes. Like the birthday parties in *Company,* the reunion of showgirls in *Follies* was a deliberately ambiguous occasion. While *Playbill* stated that the audience was at "a party on the stage of the Weismann Theatre, tonight," it was not a realistically depicted event. The leading characters had not simply arrived at a reunion, but rather had wandered onto the psychological landscape of their lives, where they would have to confront both their younger selves and their present unhappy state, amidst the remains of a theatre with a gaping hole in it. The raked stage and the various levels were used to heighten the surrealistic atmosphere, and giant showgirls glided around silently in black-and-white makeup and costumes.

Sondheim and Goldman had been stuck while working on *Follies*—originally known as *The Girls Upstairs*—and it was Prince who came up with the concept of having the past collide with the present onstage by using "ghosts," the younger selves of the aging characters, made up and clothed in black and white. The ghosts were shown in scenes from the past, stood next to their older incarnations during scenes, or were seen performing their old numbers next to their aging selves doing the same number. Beauty, despair, and terror were palpable on the Winter Garden stage.

Follies, an enormous, expensive production with a cast of fifty and over 140 costumes, offered Bennett his greatest opportunities thus far to conceive or stage rich, complex numbers. Because Bennett was always a showman and a "Broadway Baby," he used his razzle-dazzle tendencies to make several of these complex numbers into showstoppers. In *Follies,* however, he also used show-biz razzle-dazzle to convey the psychology of the characters.

The opening, showing the guests (and their younger selves as ghosts) arriving for the reunion, was an extraordinarily rich sequence, which was redone several times before the show came to New York.

SONDHEIM: "We had all worked out the original opening according to a scenario that Jim and I had written. It was an avant-garde collage of old records, sound effects from the street, a clock ticking, and people arriving, and it actually had Michael's voice-over through the loudspeakers. We opened with it in Boston, and it didn't work. We sat down and Michael . . . started to outline a scenario, Jim and I took it up, and then I went off with Michael in the theatre. He said, 'We need music to tie this together. Play all the stuff you've cut out of the show,' and I did. He liked a song called 'All Things Bright and Beautiful,' so that's the music that was used under the opening to hold it together."

GRACIELA DANIELE, a dancer in the "Bolero d'Amour" number, and also Bennett's assistant on the show: "We had so many versions of the opening; it felt like fourteen. In Boston, we would finish the show, take off our makeup, and go onstage and try another version that night. . . . At three o'clock in the morning, my phone would ring, and it would be Michael with his new idea for the opening. But that prologue was one of the most incredible things I've ever seen in my life; he had ideas nobody had ever used before. In the prologue, nobody was dancing to the music heard by the audience; we were all dancing to our own rhythms, the rhythm of the song of the character we represented. Michael Misita and myself, who played the young version of the bolero dancers, were moving not to the music of the prologue, but to the music of the bolero, which we hummed quietly, from the beginning of the show until the 'Beautiful Girls' number. The "chicken girls," in white with feathers, were mouthing and moving in slow motion to the mirror number. Mary Jane Houdina, who was Young Hattie, was doing 'Broadway Baby' during the opening. It was so rich, and put together with great effort."

The most celebrated number in *Follies* was "Who's That Woman?" often referred to as "the mirror number." "Who's That Woman?" was as brilliantly staged as any musical number in Broadway history. It took Bennett weeks to create, and its conception showed him at the top of his form. While the decrepit middle-aged women recreated their old dance downstage, their younger "ghosts," in mirror-laden costumes, performed a perfect mirror image of the number upstage, past and present merging in a circle at the number's climax. It was both an all-out showstopper, a reflection of the show's theme of self-confrontation, and another scary reminder of the ravagement of time.

SONDHEIM: "The mirror number was very much Michael's conception. I had conceived it as a number for six women, one of whom was dead. They would go through their routine, but there would be this hole in the line all the time. Michael decided that that would not work because there weren't enough women to show the hole in the pattern. He said if there were 36, it would make sense, but with six it didn't. When I went down to the rehearsal studio to see what he had done, and saw the mirror number for the first time, I was very upset, because he hadn't followed my scenario, but when he explained why the scenario wouldn't work, and then showed me the number he had done, I was stunned and thought that it was wonderful, and I still do. The mirror number in *Follies* and the opening of *Company* are two of the best numbers I ever saw in my life."

The most complex sequence, in terms of both writing and staging, was the climactic "Loveland." The two couples reached an impasse and suddenly, in a total break with reality, they were transported to a lace-bordered world where "everybody lives to love." The four principal characters became figures in Follies-style numbers that simultaneously explored the character's psyche and gave the audience at *Follies* the dazzle and glamour they had come to see.

Each of the numbers was set in a different part of Loveland, and each was simultaneously a pastiche number using an old musical form, and a psychological exposé of the character performing it. "The God-Why-Don't-You-Love-Me Blues" was a comic patter song placing Buddy Plummer in a miniature car, driving down a thoroughfare that was his muddled life. In a boudoir setting, Sally performed a Helen Morgan-type torch song. (This number, "Losing My Mind," was staged by Bob Avian.) In "The Story of Lucy and Jessie," Bennett, as in the Act Two opening of *Company,* used traditional patterns, in this case honky-tonk or burlesque gyrations, but stylized them to reflect the song's message. Ben's Folly, "Live, Laugh, Love," surrounded him with a kick-line similar to that of the *Chorus Line* finale, but it culminated in a terrifying breakdown in which the "performer" of the number was unable to complete it, just as Ben was unable to resolve his feelings of despair.

SONDHEIM: "We did not decide on the approach to the 'Loveland' sequence until the second week of rehearsal. I had only planned on three numbers in the sequence. I was afraid of having four in a row, and I thought if I had one man's number, a number for the two women, then another man's number, it would be enough. I'd written 'Losing My Mind' for both Phyllis and Sally to sing. Alexis Smith said that she would prefer to have her own number because she knew she couldn't sing very well, and she wanted something where she could strut and dance. She felt 'Losing My Mind' should be a solo number for Dorothy Collins, and she was dead right about it. But that left me one number behind. I wrote the entire sequence while we were in rehearsal. The number for Alexis was originally called 'Uptown, Downtown,' and I wrote it just before we went to Boston. I left it for last because Ben's number was more important, and I had to figure out how to have the breakdown and what followed. Once that had been solved, I went on to Phyllis's number, which I only handed to Michael the day before we went to Boston. He had to rush it up on the stage because he had no time, and therefore turned against it and asked me to write another number in Boston, which I did, 'Lucy and Jessie.' I don't think there's really any difference between the numbers, but because he had more time to think about it, I think he liked it better."

BENNETT: "We went into rehearsal, Steve hadn't finished the last part of the show, and I was ordering the clothes for numbers I'd never heard. We staged many of the sequences just before we left for Boston. I think it was really *Follies* more than any other show where I realized that you just need more time. Everybody else didn't need more time, but I did."

"Loveland" culminated in an unlisted sequence, known as "Chaos," in which platforms moved and the whole company, on various levels, performed their earlier numbers simultaneously. It produced a terrifying cacophony that was the culmination of the leading characters' outpouring of emotion in their solo numbers.

SONDHEIM: "The big problem with the 'Loveland' sequence was to figure out how to get out of it, which I did in the third week of rehearsal. None of us could figure out how to get out of the Follies and back to reality. . . . Michael decided in Boston that he couldn't stage the 'Chaos' sequence which led out of 'Loveland' until we got all the scenery working, and I remember him saying, 'Just give me an afternoon and don't come in and look at it until I'm through.' And he and Bob went off to the Bradford Hotel and staged the whole thing in one afternoon."

The opening, "Who's That Woman?" and "Loveland" were but the centerpieces of the musical staging. There was a flashy, athletic yet lyrical dance tailored to Gene Nelson's style in "The Right Girl," which sent Nelson spinning in neurotic patterns up and down stairs and platforms. (Bennett later admitted that he only created this dance because the audience expected Nelson to have one showy number.) There was the beautiful "Bolero d'Amour," with the older dance couple shadowed by several more couples on upper platforms, all choreographed in a style Bennett would use again in *Ballroom.* There was the touching gallantry of the women descending the staircase in the show's first song, "Beautiful Girls," a song written at Bennett's request.

SONDHEIM: "When Michael joined the show, I had already written the opening song, called 'Bring on the Girls.' Michael asked me to change that, and I couldn't figure out why he wanted me to, and every time I would try to pin him down on it, he couldn't quite state it. So I wrote another number, called 'Beautiful Girls.' I think it really was because he didn't want old material. He wanted to feel that he was starting something new. I think that was psychological, because there's really no difference between the two numbers in feeling."

Bennett's work on *Follies* was so expansive, so prodigal in its imagination and lavishness, and yet so organically tied to the show's story, score, and ideas, that there could no longer be any doubt that no comparable talent existed on Broadway at the moment. Because he shared credit with Prince for direction, Bennett received less space in the reviews, as critics seemed unsure of how to assess his contribution. But some were aware of his achievement. John Simon in *New York* magazine wrote, "Michael Bennett, as always, turns the simplest dance routines, by sheer alchemy, into provocative terpsichorean tracery"; and Martin Gottfried, in a Sunday *Times* answer to the negative reviews of *Follies* that Clive Barnes and Walter Kerr had filed earlier in that paper, said, "Michael Bennett's dazzling dance memories and perpetually musical staging are as seamlessly woven into [Sondheim's musical] personality as they are into Prince's immensely creative general direction."

Bennett had been nominated for a Tony Award for *A Joyful Noise, Henry, Sweet Henry, Promises, Promises, Coco,* and *Company,* but he was to win his first Tonys—for choreography and co-direction—for *Follies.* Accepting the award he had coveted for years, he told the audience, "I don't have to go and play with Ron Field's Tonys anymore. And I finally made it to the stage."

If critics and award-givers recognized Bennett's work, it was probably those closest to the production that best appreciated it.

SONDHEIM: "*Follies* allowed Michael to use all his show-biz instincts. *Company* was more restrictive, and you could see Michael go when he got something like 'Side by Side,' a vaudeville routine with a sense of tradition. . . . Whenever it had to do with his roots, he loved to let go, so *Follies* offered him a lot of opportunities to do all that traditional musical stuff for dramatic purposes, as it did me, too."

DANIELE: "We all knew what we had in *Follies* was unique. From the first moment when that seven-foot Amazon ghost turned and looked at the audience with that music underneath, you knew you were in the hands of masters, you felt it, and it just kept going.

"The casting was incredible and frightening because the characters were so close to the people playing them. 'I'm Still Here' was Yvonne De Carlo telling her own life.

"That show was spooky. During *Follies,* I said to Michael, 'I don't know if I want to continue performing.' You saw yourself and what you were going to become if you continued to be just a dancer. It was nerve-wracking to see yourself thirty or forty years from now. . . . That show was about surviving, about letting go of dreams that make you live in the past, and just going on with life without trying to hold on to the past. It made me realize that I'd better not stay in a world of illusions."

Tharon Musser, who would light *A Chorus Line* and become part of the Bennett team, did remarkable work on *Follies,* contributing enormously to the show's atmosphere and emotional power.

MUSSER: "*Follies* was Hal and Steve and everybody at their best, and one of my favorites. The acclaim I got for it, well, that was Michael. There was something about him when he was sitting next to you and talking about a show. I can't explain it, but it caused juices to flow. Boris Aronson was a genius, you know, and he was one of the first people I know who said to me, 'That boy is a genius,' talking about Michael.

"There are times when I'm too conservative and worry about going too far; certain people in the business get scared if you do something too drastic. The marvelous thing about anything I did with Michael was, he always said, 'Go for it.' You could just do anything that came into your head, and if it didn't work, you'd say, 'What the hell, we tried.' Anything theatrical was *it* for him. With Michael, you could just fly.

"We used light in *Follies* to create moods and separate the past from the present. . . . We knew early on that those figures of the past had to be handled separately. I used side follow-spots from the boxes, which was not done much then. It was almost like a movie, and there were parts in it where you felt it was a movie double-screen."

Prince and Bennett shared a similar vision in *Follies* and the dialogue scenes blended effortlessly into musical numbers.

DANIELE: "Hal respected Michael very much. The scenes were mostly directed by Hal, but they worked together a lot, and if they disagreed, it didn't show in rehearsals or on stage. Hal has a great eye for musicals, and the collaboration with Michael was one of his best. . . . It just flew."

But if the end product of the Prince–Bennett collaboration was a model of integration, the collaboration itself was not altogether smooth.

SONDHEIM: "Because Michael had so many non-book numbers to stage, Hal was taking over the book numbers, and Michael was upset at that. Michael wanted to stage a book number, so Hal gave Michael 'Could I Leave You?' to stage, which Michael did. But it really was so overwrought that we decided it should be restaged, and Hal restaged it. That was the only book number that Michael ever staged, because he had his hands full with all the other numbers."

Many critics felt that Goldman's book was the weak link in *Follies,* and that it contained unpleasant characters difficult to care about and action that was hard to follow. These critics were only echoing Bennett's sentiments throughout the tryout.

AVIAN: "Co-directing is a difficult situation. . . . There was a lot of tension between Hal and Michael. Michael was not happy with the book and wanted to do something about it. Hal was pretty satisfied with it, or felt that, at that point, as much as could be done had been done with it, and to do anything drastic to it would . . . create a mess."

SOURCE*: "The book was not to Michael's liking. Michael got Neil Simon to say he would come in, and he also asked George Furth to help. He went out and bought Jim Goldman a joke book. One night, Hal grabbed Michael and said, 'Michael, trust me. We are in Boston. This is not New York, and the audience is not as sophisticated. The reaction will be very different in New York.' Michael, who had never finished high school, told me that because they had degrees, he felt they must know something he didn't, and he decided to trust them. At a late preview, Hal took him out to the lobby and said, 'We just got our first review. It's incredible. We're a smash. Of course, she didn't like the book, but we always knew that was a problem.' Michael said Hal went on talking, but he never heard another word."

LENNY: "Hal and Michael broke on *Follies*. Michael felt the book wouldn't work, and he wanted rewrites. . . . Michael and Hal were very close friends, but Hal didn't want to let loose of things on which he and Michael didn't see eye to eye. And Michael was never one to sit back; he said exactly what he felt."

The show's critical reception seemed to bear out Bennett's complaint, and *Follies* closed after a year and a half at a loss of its entire investment. While Bennett acknowledged how extraordinary was much of his and Prince's achievement in *Follies,* his reservations about the book and his failure to get anything done about it made *Follies* less than his favorite show in later years.

AVIAN: "We were so proud of so many elements of the production, but the audience did not like it, and the disappointment was enormous. The sophisticated audience, those who knew what had been achieved, liked it. But my mother hated it! She didn't understand the poetry of the piece. The good reviews treated the show like a work of living art, but the audience really did not like it."

. . . .

*"Source" indicates that the subject did not wish his or her name to be associated with the quote.

BENNETT: "In *Follies,* the idea and the visual metaphor became stronger than the material, or more interesting. That's why it was not successful."

But the reasons for the financial failure of *Follies* went deeper than that. Audiences didn't want to hear the message of it, and didn't want to face its portrayal of ferocious relationships and of foolish illusions destroying lives. It was not that audiences couldn't follow the book; they were unwilling to listen to the unpleasant things *Follies* was saying.

Nor was it the surreal, complex techniques that caused the show to fail. *A Chorus Line* would break just as decisively from realistic staging, using all the cinematic, fluid techniques Bennett employed in *Follies.* In *A Chorus Line,* however, they would be at the service of material that, while still questioning the myth of show business and Broadway itself, would be more acceptable and moving to audiences.

TWIGS

In November 1971, Bennett made his debut as the director of a nonmusical play; it was also his debut as a solo director, and it is curious that he chose a straight play as his first solo directorial vehicle. Did Bennett, like Zach in *A Chorus Line,* choose to direct *Twigs* so that he would not be "stuck making up dance steps"? More likely, he was eager to direct on his own and to demonstrate his versatility. He wanted to show that he could do even more than create thrilling musical staging, and he needed to be in complete control. He was also attracted to the property.

AVIAN: "I was stunned when Michael decided to do the play, especially after *Follies.* I asked him why; I liked it, but it seemed like such a small evening for him. He said, 'I understand it. I know what it's about.' "

Twigs marked a double debut for Bennett. The top-line producer was Frederick Brisson, for whom Bennett had worked on *Coco,* but the next line read "in association with Plum Productions, Inc." While the program offered no explanation of Plum Productions, it was actually Bennett's newly formed production company, the same company that would be associated with Joseph Papp in the production of *A Chorus Line.* Bennett was at once a solo director and a producer with *Twigs.*

AVIAN: "It was always about control, so we co-produced *Twigs.* At that time, Michael didn't want to use his name as producer, because he felt it was too soon. He had this real instinct for timing."

Although he had stepped into alien territory, he was careful to surround himself with several familiar faces. Bob Avian was listed as production assistant. To compose the play's incidental music and one brief song, "Hollywood and Vine," Bennett acquired the services of no less than Stephen Sondheim, and, although Sondheim had had his first Broadway success as lyricist to other composers' music, "Hollywood and Vine" marked one of the rare occasions in his career when he composed a melody to someone else's words, those of George Furth, author of *Twigs.*

Twigs was actually an offshoot of Furth's *Company. Company* had originally been conceived by Furth as a series of playlets with one actress playing all the parts, and at one time Kim Stanley was announced to star in it. When Harold Prince saw the material, he encouraged Furth to musicalize it. But not all of the material fitted into *Company*'s urban ambience, and at least one of the four plays in *Twigs,* the "Dorothy" sequence, was a castoff from *Company.* Both *Company* and *Twigs* shifted from household to household, but in *Twigs* the households were linked by the fact that the ladies of all four households were related, the lady of the last scene being the mother of the other three leading female characters. (There were originally four daughters.)

SOURCE: "The reason Furth wanted Michael to direct is that he had four one-act plays, and he wanted Michael's choreographic sense to link them all together. George envisioned magical transformations, both of the set and the actress as she changed characters, and wanted lots of links between the plays. But Michael wanted to be taken seriously as a director, so the moment he took it on, he took out all the links, changed the set design concept, and made it strictly curtain up, curtain down for each play."

Sada Thompson had had a huge success Off-Broadway in *The Effect of Gamma Rays on Man-in-the-Moon Marigolds* the previous year, and she had been doing wonderful work in repertory companies and regional theatres before that breakthrough. She was involved in *Twigs* several years before Bennett entered the project.

THOMPSON: "I had a funny history with the work. George Furth had written this series of one-act plays, and many people were interested in them. Some of them were used in *Company,* but before *Company,* I did several readings of these plays with a lot of other actors. At that time, the concept was not to have one actress in all of them. The one scene that

I always read was what turned out to be the 'Dorothy' scene, the third scene in *Twigs,* which was based on George's parents.

"Then, George wrote *Twigs* and Michael became involved. Michael and Bob Avian came to a reading at which I had been asked by George to read Dorothy. When Michael, who had just seen *Marigolds,* heard that, he said, 'Oh, that's not a good idea. She wouldn't be right for the part.' George said, 'She's done a lot of readings of this play, and I really can't disappoint her and tell her no. Please let her come to the reading.' I went to the reading, read the scene, and Michael later told me that that's when he said, 'She should play them all.' "

Thompson had one of the greatest personal triumphs of the decade in *Twigs,* and, although other actresses tried the role on television and around the country, anyone who saw Thompson do it would find it difficult to enjoy any other performer in the tour-de-force series of roles.

But, while Thompson garnered most of the raves, *Twigs* was an impressive directorial debut, and there is no doubt that Bennett helped Thompson achieve the performance she produced. Bennett's critical notices were excellent, but no one appreciated Bennett's contribution more than the show's star.

THOMPSON: "Michael was not at all nervous about directing his first play. He claimed to be, a little. I think what he really wanted to do was to experience every kind of discipline in the theatre in order to fulfill the larger vision of the musical theatre that he had. And he wanted very much to work with actors and to work on dialogue.

"He made some wonderful suggestions to George, and was an absolute joy to work with, always very creative, an electric person, giving you such attention. His mind always seemed to be on it, yet at the same time he was also a sponge, just eating up any of your impressions or your feelings or little ideas.

"During the tryout, there were a lot of changes. In fact, I finally had to have a little piece of paper, that both George and Michael signed, saying 'There will be no more changes,' because there had been changes every night, and I thought I would lose my mind. They tried placing the plays in different order. At one time, two of the male characters appeared in more than one play.

"The way in which Michael worked with Bob is beyond words, extraordinary. They just seemed like one person. Michael was very much the leader as a personality, but ideas just spilled out of both of them, and in all the time we worked together, I never heard either of them say,

'That was my idea,' or 'Was that your idea?' That was of no interest to them. There was a free flow of ideas between them with no thought of who deserved credit.

"Michael gave me a feeling of very great trust in my own ideas and abilities, and I leaned on him tremendously. I had the feeling I was in good hands, incomparable hands, and I'm only sorry that we didn't ever get to do anything else together. I look back on *Twigs* with gratefulness and tremendous affection, and on Michael—well, he's just one of the two or three great people you meet in a lifetime."

At the 1972 Tony Awards, Thompson was named Best Actress for *Twigs,* but, while Bennett picked up two awards that night for *Follies,* his work on *Twigs* was not nominated. The play ran eight months on Broadway, closing as a financial failure. But it was a distinguished credit for Bennett, who now seemed at home in all genres, able to do anything.

When Bennett was hired as director of *Twigs,* the play went by a different name. Bennett told Furth he disliked the title and asked him to change it. Furth came up with *Twigs,* a title he never liked as much as his original title—*A Chorus Line.*

GOD'S FAVORITE

In 1973, Bennett had stepped in to give an uncredited assist to director A. J. Antoon on Neil Simon's *The Good Doctor.* Bennett had already worked with Simon on *Promises, Promises,* and *The Good Doctor* led directly to the second and last full-length nonmusical Bennett was to direct, Neil Simon's *God's Favorite,* which ran for only three months during the 1974–75 Broadway season. *God's Favorite* was a reworking of the Job story. Set in Long Island, it told of wealthy Joe Benjamin and a messenger from God who appeared to inform Joe that he was to be severely tested. The leading man was Vincent Gardenia, who would be Bennett's lead again in *Ballroom,* and Avian was assistant director this time.

One of Simon's weakest plays, *God's Favorite* received mixed to negative reviews, while Bennett came off decently, as it was the script that was criticized and not the staging. It is hard to say whether *God's Favorite* caused Bennett to lose interest in directing plays, or if the right opportunity never again arose. In any event, Bennett had little time to concern himself with the failure of *God's Favorite,* because three weeks after it closed, *A Chorus Line* played its first public performance.

6

. . . .

TOTAL CONTROL

WITHIN THE SYSTEM

SEESAW

IN BETWEEN THE TWO straight plays directed by Bennett came one
more musical prior to *A Chorus Line, Seesaw,* which opened at the Uris
(now the Gershwin) Theatre on March 18, 1973. *Seesaw* was a show that
contained none of the brilliance of *Company* or *Follies,* nor was it a surefire
smash like *Promises, Promises.* Artistically, it was one of Bennett's lesser
shows, but it would prove to be crucial in the Bennett career, which it
altered forever.

If on his previous musical, *Follies,* Bennett had been overruled by
Prince when he asked for book changes, Bennett now took on a project
that would put him in total control. *Seesaw* was, for Bennett, not about
putting a show together, but rather about power, and how it can and must
be exerted on a seriously troubled show. *Seesaw* represented Bennett's
ascent to the position he would retain for the remainder of his career. It
marked a radical change in his status, and, to some, created a new Bennett
with whom they were less than happy.

If one looks at the program for *Seesaw* when it opened its tryout
engagement at Detroit's Fisher Theatre on January 16, 1973, one will
search in vain for the name Michael Bennett. Bennett had by this time

earned a strong reputation as doctor, but while he did help several earlier musicals, he had never officially taken over a show for which he had not been hired by the time rehearsals started. And in the case of Bennett and *Seesaw,* "taking over" would mean more than it ever had in the history of the American musical theatre.

Based on William Gibson's hit comedy-drama *Two for the Seesaw,* which had originally starred Henry Fonda and Anne Bancroft on Broadway, *Seesaw* told the story of Gittel Mosca, an ulcer-ridden, insecure aspiring dancer, and her affair with Omaha WASP lawyer Jerry Ryan, who was in the process of getting a divorce. When it opened in Detroit, *Seesaw* seemed a hopeless disaster. The slight, bittersweet love story was lost in an overblown production, with forty-eight different roles listed in the program, at least six of which were principal parts. Almost nothing seemed to be working, and the show's principal producers, Joseph Kipness and Lawrence Kasha, realized immediately that help was needed.

As usual, Bennett was at the top of the list of those to call at such a time, and he was asked to go to Detroit, see the show, and act as artistic adviser to the show's director, Edwin Sherin, and choreographer, Grover Dale (with whom Bennett had danced across Europe in *West Side Story*). Bennett saw the show, and at first refused to become involved in any capacity.

AVIAN: *"Seesaw* was not the kind of show Michael wanted to do at that point in his career. We were offered it originally, and Michael turned it down. We went to Detroit as a favor to Joe Kipness and Larry Kasha. We liked the love story, but decided not to do it, because there were so many difficulties, so many elements that were not working or were not in our style.

"But 'Crying Joe' Kipness carried on, and said, 'We'll do anything you want. We'll spend all the money in the world. We've got a show here, and you can fix it.' We got roped into it, because it was so hard to say no to Joe."

But it was not only Kipness's tears that won Bennett over to the project. He was able to see through the miasma onstage at the Fisher Theatre to what had made Gibson's original play a success.

TOMMY TUNE, whose career would be transformed by his work as performer and associate choreographer in *Seesaw:* "We always felt like we were wasting our creative energies doctoring shows. So many shows would be in trouble, and they would call Michael, and we would go and help, and it would be an unfulfilling experience for him, because he was there cleaning up other people's messy work. I said, 'I'm going to embroi-

der a sampler to hang over your bed saying, "Thou shalt not doctor." '
But he would need money, so he would do it.

"Michael called me to come to Detroit. I saw the show and thought
it was awful, and I said to Michael, 'Why do you want to do this?' He
said, 'There's that love story, and the love story works.' He had peered
into this disastrous show and seen that love story between those two
people. He knew the rest of it was fixable . . . if he could just clarify it
and bring it to the front."

But Bennett did not simply agree to take over the direction from
Sherin or the choreography from Dale. He insisted on absolute artistic
control of the production, as it was his feeling that a fresh start was
needed. Bennett would have less than eight weeks to do with *Seesaw* what
he sometimes had a year to do on other shows, and he was aware that
radical changes were in order.

DON PIPPIN, the show's musical director and vocal arranger: "We
were all amazed that he would take on the show, because it was a mess.
It had the wrong cast—everything about it was wrong. It took a lot of
courage to take it over, but he brought in his complete 'army,' Avian,
Tune, Baayork Lee, Thommie Walsh and others.

"He made it absolutely clear to management that he had total, dictato-
rial control. No one could question him; neither Cy Coleman nor Dorothy Fields, who wrote the score, had to approve anything he did. As
young as he was, Michael knew one thing: You can't work if your hands
are tied and you have to go through a lot of protocol to get approval."

Bennett decided to consider the show that was playing in Detroit a lost
cause, and he left it alone during the remainder of its run, putting no
changes in, while creating an entirely new *Seesaw* during the day.

Never in the history of postwar musicals did a show's credits change
as much as those of *Seesaw* from tryout to opening night on Broadway.
Sherin was gone immediately. Dale's name became one of four choreographers listed by the time the show opened in New York, and only one
of his original numbers remained.

MICHON PEACOCK, a dancer in *Seesaw* from the beginning, later a key
figure in the making of *A Chorus Line:* "Grover Dale retained his credit
because he choreographed the best number in the show, the opening,
'My City' . . . He was kept around to watch from the audience. Even in
the opening number, Michael actually directed us, helping us find characters out of the physicality that Grover had given us."

While Tune and Avian were ultimately listed as associate choreographers, and Dale as co-choreographer, Bennett was ultimately listed as choreographer, although he functioned largely in an advisory capacity.

TUNE: "He didn't get around to choreographing too much of that show because he was so busy. He had to make the *show* work, never mind the numbers. And he could always come in and play with the end of a number and make it work. So he concentrated on making the whole show."

PEACOCK: "Michael pulled everything together. He directed more than he choreographed."

TUNE: "When Michael called me to come to Detroit, he only wanted me to choreograph two numbers, for $500 each. I choreographed the Balloon number, 'It's Not Where You Start,' and the 'Salt' number, 'Chapter 54, Number 1909.' Those were completely mine, except for the ending on the Balloon number. I had put a small ending on it; it all built, then dwindled down to where I swept Baayork Lee off. Michael wanted a big ending, then the sweeping. He was right; he wanted it to stop the show, and it did. Michael did *great* endings. It was like sex—he knew how to make a number 'come' better than anybody.

"Michael liked the numbers I choreographed, but before we left Detroit, Michael decided I should *do* the two numbers I had choreographed for Bill Starr. Bill was a friend of mine and of Michael's, but something had gone wrong between him and Michael, and once something went wrong with Michael, it could never be repaired. So I think he harbored a feeling toward Billy and couldn't wait to get him out of there. I was very, very upset, and Michael said, 'Darling, it has nothing to do with you. It's my choice.' I said, 'But Billy is my friend.' Michael said, 'I won't have him. I want you to do it.' I remember Billy ran from the theatre in tears, and I sat up all night, wrote a letter, and took it over in the wee hours of the night, in the snow, to the hotel where Billy was staying. I never got the $500 per number I was originally offered, but I never asked because he gave me so much more by giving me the role, which launched my career."

Tune won a Tony in the part of David, and Bill Starr, a gypsy who had danced in *Nowhere to Go but Up* and many other musicals, lost his chance to play a featured role and speak lines onstage. But Starr was only one of four featured performers who lost their roles. Richard Ryder was out; Joshie Jo Armstead remained for a while but was fired during previews in New York; and Christine Wilzak lost her role but remained in the show's chorus.

Those involved with the show began to lose count as the firings continued. Fourteen dancers were let go in all, and not always in the kindest way.

SOURCE: "He handled all the firings horribly. He wouldn't speak to anyone or see anyone. Grover Dale had to tell the dancers before each performance that they had been fired. Some of them were so incensed that they did not feel like continuing in the show for the final weeks of the tryout. Sometimes they were informed during intermission that they would not be going to Broadway."

When Bennett saw Anita Morris assisting Dale on the revisions he asked for in the opening number, he demanded that Morris be put into the number. Her presence sparked the opening, and Tommy Tune would later take advantage of the acrobatic style she demonstrated in *Seesaw* in his own production of *Nine.*

Bennett fired Hugh Forrester, who was the arranger of dance music in Detroit, and those arrangements were ultimately the work of four men, two of whom were the show's composer, Cy Coleman, and Marvin Hamlisch.

But none of these firings was as humiliating and widely publicized as that of the show's leading lady. Lainie Kazan got her first attention as Barbra Streisand's understudy in *Funny Girl,* and had gone on to a career as a nightclub and recording artist. But she knew Gibson's play and had dreamed of playing Gittel for years, feeling that she *was* that awkward passionate girl, and she sought an audition for the role as soon as she heard about *Seesaw.* She was granted one after first-choice Liza Minnelli turned down the part.

KAZAN: "When I auditioned, they asked if I would lose some weight. I had been very ill before this, and I had gained. So I lost about 20 pounds.

"Ed Sherin and I hit it off great. This was my second chance at life, and I was back in great mental health. I was ready to take on the test of starring in a Broadway show.

"When we opened in Detroit, the acting was fine. The book worked, and it was a very heart-felt piece. But someone was needed to blend the dancing with the play, and give it an overall integration.

"The producers got concerned about the reviews. Ed's direction was brilliant, but he didn't understand the musical idiom that well. He wasn't in charge of that whole vision that's needed in a musical, and Grover was just the choreographer. Cy, Dorothy Fields, and Michael Stewart, the original writer, started to panic and think about getting a new director.

"Then we heard that a couple of people had turned the play down, such as Gower Champion, and that Michael Bennett was coming in. What I didn't know when he joined was that his stipulation for taking over was that he would be able to bring in his own leading lady. So I went on singing and dancing and doing the show. The first inkling of trouble was that when Michael started working on the numbers, he never talked to me or spent any time working with me. He didn't want to see any of *my* numbers, just the chorus numbers.

"I went to Larry Kasha and said, 'I think something is wrong. Doesn't Michael like me?' He said, 'No, no, everything's fine.' The next day, I got a call early in the morning at my hotel from my manager. He said, 'Lainie, they're replacing you in the show. You can be a real lady and stay with the play until it closes in Detroit, or you can leave right now.' I agreed to stay, and I had to play the show for two or three more weeks, which was probably the most painful thing I've ever done in my life.

"I asked for a meeting with Michael. I said, 'I'm not somebody you can just discard like this. I have to find out what the problem is.' But he would not see me. He ignored me. Every night he watched me in the show, but he would not talk to me in any way.

"Michael finally came to see me one night. He walked in and said he only had a couple of minutes. He was not very kind or very compassionate. I said to him, 'If you're not happy with the way I'm doing this, I'm a flexible actress and could play it differently.' He said, 'We're hiring a dancer.' I knew Michele Lee had already been hired, and that she wasn't a dancer per se; I danced as well as she did. I also thought that Gittel was a loser, and if she was a little heavy or a little unkempt, that was part of her vulnerability. But Michael said, 'The die is cast.' I said, 'What goes around comes around, and I'm sure we'll meet again. I'm sorry you didn't give me a chance, and I hope you have a success.'

"Then the management sued me, because they didn't want to pay me a run-of-the-play salary. They said I hadn't lost the weight which I had promised to lose, which was a lie, and that I wasn't on time, which was also a lie. They accused me of not knowing my lines. I'm an improvisational actress, and in rehearsal I would improvise and do unorthodox things, but I knew my lines on stage. There was eventually a settlement, but it was many months before I saw any money, and they never paid me all they owed me.

"I was tormented by the experience when I returned to New York. I decided to stay in New York because, in some dark recess of my mind, I really thought they'd find out they had made this horrible mistake, and call me to come and save them. That never happened. I was not a very healthy person for a long time, and couldn't get a job because of the reputation the firing had given me. It took me years to build my courage, my confidence and my reputation.

"Years later, when I was nominated for an Oscar, I ran into Michael when he was drunk and stoned at a disco in New York. He said, 'Lainie, I'm so happy to see you're doing so well.' I said, 'I'd like to thank you for my career as an actress. I think if what happened hadn't happened, my career wouldn't have taken this turn.'

"That was the last time I ever saw him. I thought he was brilliant, and I have great respect for his talent. But I didn't respect the way he handled people and his life. He hurt me very much."

TUNE: "Michael had to fire Lainie. You couldn't believe that she was a dancer. I love her and she's a friend of mine, but the show as written and conceived was really beyond her. I don't think she'll ever understand why she was fired, but she just wasn't right; it wasn't working."

No other leading lady was ever fired so dramatically from such a juicy role, and Kazan was so devastated that she leapt headlong into a Broadway-bound revival of Clare Booth Luce's *The Women,* accepting a role she was far less suited to than Gittel. She was out of that production within weeks of her *Seesaw* dismissal. This was not to be the last time that Bennett would fire a leading performer, nor would it be the last time he would be accused of doing so in a cruel or insensitive manner.

The most amazing change in the *Seesaw* credits from Detroit to New York occurred gradually. In Detroit and during New York previews, the book was attributed to Michael Stewart, award-winning librettist of such hits as *Hello, Dolly!, Carnival!* and *Bye Bye Birdie.* Bennett's initial credit in New York read "Entire Production Directed and Choreographed by Michael Bennett." But the program given to Broadway first-nighters bore the startling credit, "Written, Directed and Choreographed by Michael Bennett," and Stewart's name was gone.

Did Michael Bennett, who had no previous writing experience, actually write the book of *Seesaw?* With so many conflicting reports issued to the press, and with such tumult and overhauling occurring daily, it was ultimately difficult for even those involved with the show to figure out who had finally written what. A fair amount of the dialogue in Stewart's original book came from Gibson's play, and much of it was retained in the final script. Four days before the opening, *Variety* reported, "At the moment, [Neil Simon] is concentrating on rewriting the book of *Seesaw.* Michael Stewart, who wrote the initial adaptation and is billed as the librettist, is understood to have withdrawn and agreed to allow Simon to revise the script. According to those close to the production, Simon has made substantial changes, chiefly strengthening the comedy element in the story. Simon will not receive billing and the financial terms for his stint have not been disclosed."

But members of the production would soon deny that Simon was actually rewriting. It was later reported that Simon had only edited out about thirty minutes of the original dialogue. Bennett himself claimed that everyone—from Fields to his leads, Michele Lee and Ken Howard— was participating in the rewrites.

AVIAN: "Michael Stewart said, 'I can't continue. I don't believe in what you're doing. I think it's all wrong. We had a show here, and I don't like what you've done to it.' He quit, and no one would take writing credit, so Michael did."

PIPPIN: "Michael Stewart tended to throw tantrums. All Michael Bennett had done was make *Seesaw* into a show that had style and was working and made sense. Neil Simon came in as a favor and wrote some one-liners. Michael did not write the book in any way. But you couldn't open a show with no one getting credit for the book, so after Dorothy Fields declined, Michael said, 'What the fuck—put my name on it.' "

Thus was born Bennett the author-director-choreographer-conceiver, and it was this Bennett who would create *A Chorus Line* and the shows that followed.

A comparison of the Detroit script and the final version reveals one of the most radical revisions any show has ever undergone. In Detroit, Act One began with a scene and song for Jerry, "Pick Up the Pieces," both of which were eliminated, and the song "My City," which in the final version came at the top of the show, was performed later. Gittel's first number in Detroit, "Big Fat Heart," was replaced by "Nobody Does It Like Me." The "In Tune" number originally featured more than the two leads. Gittel's next song, "Highly Emotional State," was replaced by "Welcome to Holiday Inn." A scene in a dentist's office was dropped. Larry, the character played by Bill Starr (changed to David for Tommy Tune), and Gittel had a number called "Tutu and Tights," about Gittel's need to dance, which was cut. There was no "Lovable Lunatic" song, no "He's Good for Me," and "Ride Out the Storm" was in Act Two in Detroit. The last scene in the original Act One ended with a song sung by Jerry, called "More People Like You," which was also cut.

In the original second act, Jerry's estranged wife paid Gittel a visit in person (the character only communicated by phone on Broadway);

"Ride Out the Storm" was a book number performed by Gittel's friend; and Gittel's final number was only a third as long as it later became.

Bennett managed to strip away the multitude of unnecessary subplots and undeveloped characters, and emphasize what had attracted him to the show in the first place, the appealingly mismatched lovers. The show became clearer, cleaner, and more entertaining.

The changes in *Seesaw* went beyond even the text, cast, and creative team, for Bennett brought a new concept to *Seesaw*.

PEACOCK: "It went from the reality of the Spanish ghetto to the slick and the abstract, the story presented against New York and utilizing as much of slick New York as possible. We were street people in Detroit, and there was nothing slick about the show at all. It was all meant to be real gutsy, with no touch of New York chic, which was what Michael wanted to do. He wanted to make the three principal characters real, and everybody else a reflection of the New York environment—abstract 'pictures.' It was the same with the star. Lainie was very earthy, gutsy, where Michele was sophisticated, slick and quick."

Like Robbins's *On the Town, Seesaw* became a love letter to New York, and the city became a character of equal importance to the principals, as it was in *Company.* Bennett by this time had realized that designers could be as important to his shows as writers, and he began to work with Robin Wagner—as he would in all his future musicals—to make the set design blend with his overall conception.

WAGNER: "Michael kept the basic scenic context, but instead of just having projections on the scenery, he started making the scenery dance, as it had in *Promises.* Suddenly, screens were moving in and out, and we reinvented each of the scenic pieces so that he could deliver them through movement. He created a new environment, and choreographed every aspect of the production, not just the dancers, but the scenery, too."

Bennett was also interested in *Seesaw* in exploring the cinematic technique he had already used in *Company* and *Follies,* and he created a show that moved with enormous fluidity and assurance.

With all of these complex and profound changes, how good was *Seesaw* by opening night on Broadway? The show contained several showstopping numbers, with eye-popping and imaginative staging, particularly the two staged by Tune, and "My City," the work of Dale, Bennett, and others. But these showstoppers were never satisfyingly integrated into what was essentially an intimate love story, now played on the enormous stage of the Uris Theatre and interrupted by huge Radio City Music Hall-style production numbers. The show's strengths were ultimately its fine score by Coleman and Fields, its very appealing leads (Lee was a shrewd choice, even if she looked far too attractive and "together" to ever be totally believable as the loser she was playing), and Gibson's original love story. While no one could deny that Bennett had pulled a sprawling unfocused show together, supervised some wonderful musical staging, and saw to it that *Seesaw* was as professional and slick as any other show around, the fact remained that a touching two-character play had been unnecessarily blown up for the musical stage, gaining little in the process.

LENNY: "Michael did a herculean job, and I'm sure if he could have had one more week of previews and working on the show, it would have been a big hit. When I went to Kipness and asked him to postpone the opening, he cried on my shoulder, saying he had no more money and had to open. Michael was never able to finish and do all the work he wanted to do on *Seesaw*."

AVIAN: "When the money ran out, we had to fix what we had, even though tons more changes were needed. Michael put in some money of his own to get certain things he wanted."

The reviews were mixed but generally good; all loved Lee, Howard, Tune, the scenic projections, and the dancing, but many could not entirely overlook the inevitably pieced-together quality of the show. Douglas Watt in the *Daily News* stated, "In *Seesaw*, an intimate, bittersweet comedy and a big, brassy musical seem to exist side by side, independent of one another. Both shows have great points in their favor, but they never truly become one."

In spite of decent reviews, the closing notice went up for *Seesaw* the day after the opening, as the box office response was not immediately strong and the show had by now cost over a million dollars. To help the show, Bennett magnanimously refused his director's fee, and two events occurred the following week that stimulated ticket sales: Mayor Lindsay, supposed look-alike of leading man Howard, went onstage during "My City" and played straight man to the gyrating female dancers, and Walter Kerr gave the show a rave in the Sunday *Times*, a far stronger notice than Clive Barnes's in the daily *Times*. *Seesaw* remained open for ten months but closed on Broadway at a loss of its entire investment.

Seesaw opened too late for the 1973 Tonys but was remembered after its departure in the 1974 race. Tune won his first Tony for his performance, and Bennett won for his choreography. The show was sent on a national tour, with a cast headed by Lucie Arnaz, John Gavin (who replaced Howard on Broadway), and Tune. As Bennett had never had the time to do everything he wanted to do with the show during the frenetic period that preceded the Broadway opening, he made several major changes in the show for the tour, including a new Act One Finale— "The Party's on Me"—for Gittel and the entire company.

TUNE: "That was the last song Dorothy Fields ever wrote. During rehearsals, Dorothy wrote the song, went home and died. The national tour was better than the original. Michael got rid of 'Ride Out The Storm,' and 'Spanglish' was eventually dropped when Giancarlo Esposito, who was the only reason for that number, left the show."

AVIAN: "The road version was very different and much better. It moved well, the story was stronger, and the audience cried at the end."

The reviews were more positive on the road than they had been in New York, and Bennett won the Los Angeles Drama Critics Award, this time for direction.

In retrospect, *Seesaw* cannot be counted among Bennett's finest productions, but it was a highly significant one in his development. It brought Bennett together with a group of people who would be significant in his next project: Broadway *Seesaw*-ers Wayne Cilento, Mitzi Hamilton, Loida Iglesias, Baayork Lee, Michon Peacock, Michael Reed, Thomas Walsh, and Chris Wilzak, and touring *Seesaw*-ers Sammy Williams, Brandt Edwards, and Nancy Lane, would all figure importantly in *A Chorus Line.* More significantly, *Seesaw* was the first musical of which Bennett took total, some thought ruthless, control. He would exercise the same degree of control and involvement in all of his forthcoming musical projects. What made his all-encompassing vision more successful in later shows was that every element of them would be filtered through his original conception. Vastly different as *Seesaw* was on Broadway compared to its Detroit days, the show was still not completely Bennett's in the way his later musicals would be. This was because he had inherited a plot and characters that he was obliged to use, albeit in drastically altered fashion. *Seesaw* still had a fundamental conventionality that even Bennett's transformation could not transcend. He had gone beyond the conventional in *Company* and *Follies,* but *Seesaw* marked a temporary return to it. It would be the last time Bennett ever worked on a conventional musical, and the last time he ever worked within the conventional Broadway system.

Bennett began work on two new projects.

AVIAN: "We worked on a show called *Space,* written by John Phillips of The Mamas and the Papas, and produced by Michael Butler. It was to star Phillips's wife, Genevieve Waite. Michael was going to have Peter Larkin design it as a giant circus. It was going to be a huge spectacle, to open at the Aquarius Theatre in Los Angeles. The plot was silly, but we liked the score. We worked on it for months and months, but it got out of hand. The people involved were spacey, and Butler wasn't there, so there was no one in control. There was not enough cohesiveness, so we pulled out of it."

The show was later produced on Broadway in 1975 by Andy Warhol, under the title *Man on the Moon,* and lasted five performances.

In the spring of 1973, another Bennett musical project was announced. First, *Variety* told its readers, *"Pin-Ups,* a musical with book by Leonard Gershe and songs by John Kander and Fred Ebb, is to be produced on Broadway next fall by Michael Bennett, who will also do the staging and choreography. No one is set for the cast." A month later, *The New York Times* offered details on the show, some of which had already changed from *Variety*'s data: "Bennett will produce and direct *Pin-Ups,* a revue. . . . [It] will have music by Cy Coleman and lyrics by Dorothy Fields, who were also involved with *Seesaw,* and, although the show will have a revue format, it will have a book written by Leonard Gershe. The story is set in 1942, during World War II when, Bennett says, 'We were more innocent and believed in ourselves.' The plot, which will involve spies and such and 'be real scary,' stems from a four-part magazine serial, 'The Man With the Miracle Mind,' written in the early twenties by Samri Finkel. Actually a play within a play, *Pin-Ups* will be developed in five sequences, each devoted to a decade. Bennett says it will be a history of pin-ups, roughly from the time advertisers began using girls as sex symbols."

Pin-Ups was budgeted at $1.5 million, and Bennett had already invested $60,000 of his own money in the show when he abandoned it. *Pin-Ups* would have been developed in the traditional time-honored fashion of most Broadway musicals, and Bennett had begun to sense that that way was now outmoded. The Broadway where Bennett had danced, the Broadway where he had had his first choreographic successes, no longer functioned effectively. Bennett, always very attuned to his times, realized that it was necessary to do things in a new way. To do something utterly new, he would have to go back to his roots.

PART THREE

· ·

A CHORUS LINE

Martha Swope

1

. . . .

THE INSPIRATION

I T IS VIRTUALLY IMPOSSIBLE to pinpoint the moment Bennett first had the idea of doing the show that became *A Chorus Line.* As with any major creative project, the motivations for it were many, and the ideas that inspired it gestated within Bennett for several years.

After the show opened, he often proclaimed that it was the Watergate Hearings of 1973 that led him to do it. After watching hours of falsehood, cover-up, and deceit on television, Bennett became disgusted. He yearned to see truth on the stage and to say something positive about a country whose values had been called into question and whose self-esteem had suffered a severe blow.

Yet this reaction to the Watergate hearings would not have sufficed to motivate Bennett, had it not been for a deep personal malaise. The Broadway about which Bennett had fantasized as a child and in which he had danced as a teenager had changed. Economics dictated that musicals could not be produced with the frequency or size of the 1960s, and, with the exception of the musicals of Sondheim and Prince, the 1970s had produced few musicals of real distinction and, with the exception of Fosse's *Pippin,* fewer that could truly be deemed "dance musicals." With

all that Bennett had achieved thus far, he had yet to direct and choreograph a musical by himself from its inception, nor had he been able to
conceive a show in terms of dance along the lines of his idol, Robbins.
Bennett had turned thirty, increasingly isolated himself, gained weight,
and was unsure of the next step.

He was not alone in his sense of despair. Close friends such as Avian
and McKechnie shared this feeling of uncertainty and helplessness, and
McKechnie and Bennett actually considered a drastic step.

MCKECHNIE: *"A Chorus Line* was born out of the frustration of many
dancers, myself included. I had gone to California, and when that didn't
work out, I was thinking of quitting show business yet again. I had heard
that it was possible to get 10,000 acres of land in New Zealand for
practically nothing. I told Michael and others that we could farm it, grow
things, raise animals and live off the land. Then we'd create a theatre and
film colony, and bring over all our frustrated friends. That was my brilliant brainstorm, and while I don't think any of us would really have gone
to New Zealand, the idea stimulated us to do something together, to go
somewhere together."

The most profound impetus for *A Chorus Line,* however, came not from
Watergate, a personal crossroad, or the state of Broadway in general.
Bennett was, first, last, and always, a dancer, and the complex vision he
had of what that meant was the real inspiration for the show. He had long
had in mind the idea of doing a show centered on dancers. But suddenly
the Broadway dancer became for him the perfect embodiment of the state
of Broadway, the exact opposite of the dishonesty of Watergate, and the
reflection of his personal uncertainty.

The dancer is of necessity a creature of honesty. The mirror into which
the dancer spends his life looking does not lie, and the effort involved
in expressing oneself through body movement cannot be faked. No one
had been affected more than the dancer by the changes in the economics
of musical theatre. Gone were the days of sizable singing and dancing
choruses. By the 1970s, the Broadway dancer had to sing and act as well
as dance, for there was often only one chorus, which often consisted of
no more than ten performers.

But it was more than just the shrinking job market that Bennett wished
to address. It was the position of the dancer in musical theatre that had
become so frustrating to him and many of the dancers with whom he
worked. The primary function of the dancer at the time seemed to be to
remain in the background, making nondancing stars look good, and this
was no longer acceptable to the low-paid, highly trained, and skilled

performers who were vastly overqualified for the assignments for which they fought. It was generally the singers rather than the dancers who were given small speaking parts, for it was perceived that dancers were not sufficiently intelligent or able to speak lines onstage. And just to get the often humiliating jobs they were seeking, dancers had to undergo the demoralizing audition process that had been in effect for decades. As early as 1972, Bennett was telling close associates of his intent to use the dissatisfaction of dancers as the basis for a show.

BERNARD B. JACOBS, president of the Shubert Organization: "At the opening night party for *Follies* when it opened in Los Angeles in 1972, Michael pulled me aside and started telling me that he wanted to do this musical based upon the so-called 'cattle call,' the chorus audition for a musical."

LENNY: "In 1973, he told me he had an idea about dancers. He said, 'Dancers kill themselves in a show. They're always the low man on the totem pole. They work like dogs, they get less money than anybody else, and they don't get any real credit. I want to do a show where the dancers are the stars.'"

AVIAN: "All the time when he was doing shows, Michael kept on saying, 'I'd love to do a show just with dancers, about dancers, and make that an evening.' He knew he wanted to do that, but he didn't know what that was."

Throughout his career, Bennett believed in paying debts and giving back to the theatre everything it had given him. A show that would put dancers with whom he had worked for years front and center, that would actually be about them and their plight, that would allow them to talk and reveal all the aspects of their talent would give Bennett the opportunity to give something back to the people with whom he had danced and who had worked so hard for him. He could give them the dignity that he felt had been so long denied them, and he could use the wonderful humanity, indomitableness, and humor he saw in them as a reflection of something larger.

Bennett also felt that it was time for him to allow himself to indulge his dream of picking up where Robbins had left off and develop a musical that would not only be about dance and based on dance but one in which dance would unify all the other elements of the production and that would be conceived choreographically. But it was some time before he envisioned the vehicle that would allow him to do this.

MCKECHNIE: "I remember him talking about it, especially after *Company.* He wanted to do a show with a lot of dancing in it, and in the early

'70's, he had the idea of creating a dance/theatre piece with music. It would begin in a rehearsal room with one dancer at the barre, then another would join, and it would show the privacy of the dancer and the feeling between dancers. Class would start, and a sense of each dancer's condition would be conveyed without it being stated."

Whatever form this idea would take, Bennett knew from the start that he wished to pay tribute to a very unique species of performer, and in so doing pay tribute to his roots, to himself. Bennett disliked the term *gypsy,* feeling that it robbed the Broadway dancer of dignity; the word *gypsy* would never be uttered in *A Chorus Line,* but the Broadway "gypsy," traveling from chorus line to chorus line, was precisely what Bennett was, and to what he now felt obliged to pay tribute.

Rarely was much attention paid to the "gypsy" prior to *A Chorus Line.* There was a passage in George Abbott's autobiography—*Mister Abbott,* written in 1963—in which he described rehearsals for *The Pajama Game* and noticed the special communication between dancers: "I had been rehearsing with Carol Haney for two weeks before Robbins joined our group. I felt that I was on easy terms with her and that I knew her fairly well, but I could not help observing that within an hour or so after Jerry began to work, she was more relaxed with him than with me. It made me conscious again of something I had often observed: the clannishness of dancers. They live in their own world. They talk to the rest of us, they sometimes marry us, but at the same time they shut us out. We can never learn to speak their language unless we become one of them. We call them gypsies—and they call themselves that."

Having spent too many years working with performers in such shows as *Company* and *Follies* who moved well but were not dancers, Bennett was now ready and eager to work with the finest dancers around and at the same time call attention to the insular, valiant, and heartbreaking world of the show dancer.

MCKECHNIE: "Michael was trying to recreate the period of time in his life when he was happiest, and that was when he was a chorus boy. He was longing for the innocence, the pure expression of just going in there and working, backing up the star, dishing with the guys, having flirtations, standing in the back and saying, 'God, I'm better than that director.' It was a time of innocence for him, before he had the responsibility of the whole show. He had gotten to a place where he was well-known, where he was wheeling and dealing, yet he was growing away from the fundamental idea of what a dancer's life is. He was wondering . . . 'Where am I in relation to dance and the theatre?' He was happy to be where he was, but he was also lonely. . . . Sometimes when you move ahead, instead of feeling like *you're* leaving people, you feel like you've been abandoned by them. All of a sudden his pals were looking up to him as the big boss and the big director, and he was feeling a sense of alienation."

Among the many ironies in theatre history is the fact that one of the most catastrophic musicals ever to get to Broadway provided the motivation for the most triumphant of all Broadway musicals.

Rachael Lily Rosenbloom—And Don't You Ever Forget It! was a musical spoof that began previews at the Broadhurst Theatre on Monday, November 26, 1973, and shuttered forever on Saturday, December 1, 1973, without an official opening. A wild, vulgar camp spoof of Hollywood and show business in general, the show followed its eponymous heroine from her humble beginnings among the garbage cans of Brooklyn—where she sang an ode to her idol and inspiration, "Dear Miss Streisand"—to her becoming the maid of glamorous, mean movie star Stella Starfuckoff, to her winning an Academy Award. While there was much that was bizarrely amusing in *Rachael,* the show was woefully out of place on Broadway and suffered from the beginning from the lack of a strong hand. Originally the work of Paul Jabara solely, Tom Eyen* was brought in to work on the book and replace the original director, Ron Link. The property had been written for Bette Midler, who expressed interest, but when Midler requested changes in the material, she was refused and her talent was lost to the project. Midler was replaced by Ellen Greene, who would later have success in *Little Shop of Horrors.* Grover Dale, who had been replaced by Bennett on *Seesaw,* was brought in to redo some of original choreographer Tony Stevens's work.†

The history of Broadway musicals is strewn with disasters as bad as, or worse than, *Rachael Lily Rosenbloom,* but this show proved to be a particularly frustrating and humiliating experience for its dancers.

TONY STEVENS: "*Rachael* was my first show as solo choreographer, and

. . . .

*Eyen would later write the libretto and lyrics for Bennett's *Dreamgirls.*
†The show featured an ensemble of the most skilled dancers around, several of whom had danced for Bennett in *Seesaw,* and several of whom (Thomas Walsh, Carole Bishop, Wayne Cilento, Michon Peacock, Jane Robertson) would be involved in *A Chorus Line,* as would Stevens and *Rachael*'s set designer, Robin Wagner.

it was a nightmare. . . . I used to sit in the back and pray that it would close. I tried to turn people away at the door, but they kept coming because they'd heard it was so crazy. When Stephen Sondheim entered the theatre, I said to him, 'Please don't come in,' but he said, 'Oh, no, I hear it's a hoot.' A lot of the kids in the show had taken a chance by coming with me to support me in my first show."

MICHON PEACOCK: "It was a horror story, with stars and writers doped up and freaked out. The two directors treated people terribly, and were actually nasty, particularly to the dancers. Whatever their knowledge of their craft, it was certainly hidden by the way they handled things. They used the dancers mainly as scenery, and felt that dancers didn't know how to sing or talk, and had no minds. Everybody was very unhappy—it was a real personal insult considering the talent in that company. Tony and I used to scotch it up every night after rehearsals, saying, 'What are we going to do?' We were all relieved when it closed."

Stevens and Peacock were so strongly affected by the personal affront of this debacle that they were unable to shake it off and go on to the next chorus line.

STEVENS: "Michon and I sat down and said, 'We can do it better. The people in control don't know how to put a Broadway show together.' We had worked on hits and flops, but we knew how to put a show together, and we felt we were being victimized by the people in power. There was a point of view lacking, and it was the point of view of dancers. We knew dancers who directed, wrote, designed and did lighting, who had grown and now approached work differently from a singer or an actor. Dancers just get up and do it, and physicalize it, and find the truth of it that way. That's what a dancer knows that nobody who isn't a dancer can understand."

PEACOCK: "Tony and I started hashing through what we could do about the conditions that dancers had to deal with on a regular basis. . . . Our goal was to begin to create a company of dancers who could do everything and come up with our own show in which the dancers did everything. We wanted to show the many aspects of dancers, and to show what dancers could offer, instead of just being scenery on stage. . . . But we didn't know how to get started or how to make it seem legitimate."

As noted, Bennett had toyed with the idea of a show about dancers for years, and it has been generally understood that *A Chorus Line* was solely Bennett's inspiration, the embodiment of his views on dancers and humanity in general. It might never have come into being, however, if

Peacock and Stevens hadn't turned to Bennett as 1974 began. They had both danced for Bennett in *Seesaw* the same year as they had experienced the *Rachael Lily Rosenbloom* calamity, and they were both aware not only of his talent but of his ability to take control and make things happen.

PEACOCK: "When we didn't know how to take the first step, I called Michael. He said he had had some kind of a germ of an idea in his mind for many, many years along this line, but never quite knew the timing, when to start getting something going."

STEVENS: "As far as we were concerned, Michael was the new Jerry Robbins. We thought he'd be into this, because he loved dancers, and his head and talent were where we wanted to be. He was the perfect symbol of what we wanted the company to be."

Equally little known is the role Buddhism played in *A Chorus Line*'s development from its inception to the present day. At least a dozen cast members over the years have embraced Buddhism, and it was the Buddhism of Peacock and her friend Nicholas Dante that led her to do something positive after the *Rachael* humiliation.

DANTE: "Part of the organization of the particular sect of Buddhists, N.S.A., that Michon and I were involved in used the idea of 'creating value in your life and in the society.' We believed that a human being is only truly in trouble if they don't feel valuable. Michon was learning this theory of not waiting for life to happen to you, but rather trying to create value yourself. . . . Michon decided to create value and do something special for dancers that would feed the society."

Peacock, Stevens, and Bennett now had in common a passionate desire to do something by, for, and with dancers, and they decided to meet with other dancers and explore the possibilities. They knew that an attempt needed to be made to unify the experience of dancers, and to explore where they came from, what it meant to be a dancer, why they danced, and where they were going as dancers.

PEACOCK: "The three of us drew up a list of people to invite, and all names were cleared through Michael. I did most of the calling. I asked Michael if Nicholas Dante could come. Michael didn't know him, except from auditions. I knew Nicholas had never worked with Michael, but I knew he was not only a dancer but a writer, and I wanted him to be there as a writer and to share his experience. I had been his friend since 1968, had introduced him to chanting in 1972, and by now I had heard his life story a thousand times."

DANTE: "Michael specifically did not want just *his* dancers to attend, because he didn't feel they would all open up to him. The dancers who were invited were those we thought would be interested, people who would open up and feel this was important.''

STEVENS: "We invited people we had worked with, people with a cross-section of experience about being a dancer, young, old, straight and gay, those who had had small or featured parts and those who hadn't. We wanted the biggest cross-section possible so that we could try to find what the common experience was. And Michael wanted some enemies in the room, so there were rivals there, people who had histories that were not so great.''

The reactions to the invitation varied widely, and many were reluctant to go or refused outright. Several dancers who were to become very important in the history of *A Chorus Line* declined to attend, while others were reluctant.

STEVENS: "Baayork Lee said, 'No, I don't want to sit around and talk about my life.'. . . Baayork was slightly older than us, and . . . there was a Sixties sensibility about a community of dancers getting together and talking about your life and evolving something out of that.''

WAYNE CILENTO: "I was excited but terrified. Thommie Walsh, Sammy Williams and myself made a deal that we'd each go if the other two did; if one didn't, the others wouldn't.''

At midnight on Saturday, January 18, 1974, Bennett and eighteen dancers, some of whom came directly from dancing in shows, arrived at the Nickolaus Exercise Center on East Twenty-third Street in Manhattan. The space for the event, consisting of two large rooms, had been donated for the occasion because N.S.A. Buddhists were involved in the owner- ship of the studio. The dancers who were present that night were, in alphabetical order: Steve Anthony, Renee Baughman, Carole Bishop, Steve Boockvor, Candy Brown, Chris Chadman, Wayne Cilento, Nicho- las Dante, sisters Jackie Garland and Tricia Garland, Mitzi Hamilton, Priscilla Lopez, Donna McKechnie, Michon Peacock, Denise Pence (wife of Boockvor), Tony Stevens, Thommie Walsh, and Sammy Wil- liams.* Bill Thompson, who owned the studio, joined in the event peri- pherally. It was a collection of friends, enemies, and strangers whose lives would be altered during the next twelve hours.

There is no doubt that Bennett, as much as anyone else, was there to

. . . .

*Only eight of these dancers would be in the original cast of *A Chorus Line,* but they would all be closely involved in the show in some respect.

explore why he had started dancing, and to try to recapture something he had lost along his way. It is harder to determine whether or not Bennett had a show in mind when he arrived at the studio that night.

DANTE: "Michael was a bit devious, and though it wasn't about a show at the time, knowing how much Michael wanted to do a show about dancers, I now see how this played right into his hand. He said going in, 'We don't know if there's anything here at all. It may come to nothing, maybe a play, we don't know.' The understanding was that it was just about the event. If anything came from it, great, but it was completely exploratory."

BOOCKVOR: "I didn't think that what we were saying that night was going to be the basis for a show, but I think Michael did. That was the difference between Michael and the rest of the world. He was light years ahead of all of us, and always saw things in terms of what he could do with it on a stage."

AVIAN (who had declined Bennett's invitation to attend the event): "Michael said, 'Do you mind if we tape the evening?' Tony and Michon thought it was fine. The taping was Michael's idea. He was always thinking."

ROBIN WAGNER: "I remember having dinner with Michael one night at his apartment about two weeks before the event. He said he wanted to do a show that would put all his friends to work. . . . He told me he was going to make these tapes, and that he was going to do a show for all his dancers."

Shortly after arriving at midnight, all assembled took a dance class from Tony Stevens, thus beginning the event by doing that which, above all, gave these people their identity. It relieved many of those in attendance to dance first, and then all repaired to the adjoining room for food and drink—in a huge mound on the floor—paid for by Bennett.

Returning to the first room, everyone sat down in a circle. Bennett began by telling the group that they were there to explore where they had come from, where they had been, and where they were going. He was interested in their childhood and family background, what made them start dancing, what attracted them to a career in show business—their life stories. The questions had been prepared by Bennett, Peacock, and Stevens, and, exactly as in *A Chorus Line,* everyone was first asked to give his or her name, stage name if different, and place and date of birth. Next, Bennett asked each to tell about his/her childhood and how they first became interested in dancing. Bennett spoke first, then each member of the circle contributed, and it became less and less necessary to toss out questions.

STEVENS: "We used my big, old Sony reel-to-reel tape recorder to record it on. We started by discussing why or how we started dancing, and by the time we got a quarter of the way around the room, we realized we were getting into deep stuff, and that people wanted to divulge a lot. We talked for about five hours, got up and stretched, then continued until about noon the next day."

Not everyone was able to open up easily. Nick Dante, whose life would be changed because of the story he told that night, recalled: "Just like Paul in *A Chorus Line,* I kept asking myself all night long if I would be able to tell my story. I was really concerned about having to reveal it, but . . . I didn't really have a choice. Not even for my own good, but for the good of whatever was to come out of that evening, I had to."

What did those assembled have in their childhoods and early lives that could possibly be the basis for a play? A surprising number of broken homes and alcoholic parents, an array of sexual hang-ups and confusions, feelings of isolation, loneliness, and being different from others—all poured out with astonishing force. Dante's harrowing personal experiences issued forth in a remarkably lucid fashion while others fumbled, but all managed to express how dancing had transformed their lives, giving them a sense of belonging or making them feel beautiful.

Long-held feelings of guilt were released in a manner similar to a group therapy session, but, more important, those present realized for the first time how similar their experiences had been, and that realization formed a bond between them. They discovered that which *A Chorus Line* would reveal, that dancers with whom they had worked were individuals, people who could talk with wit and humor and who were above all painfully human. It became a process of self-discovery, for as each dancer listened, things said by others triggered off recollections of that dancer's own personal experience.

STEVENS: "While that room contained rivals and friends, lovers and ex-lovers, people with terrible childhoods and people who had had it easy, that group encounter thing happened. The affection and the common experience of what we all understood as the dance experience, along with the joy of doing it, couched everything and gave you the bravery to speak your deepest feelings that maybe you had never voiced. When we held hands at the end and the Angelus started ringing outside, we opened our eyes, looked at each other and everybody started crying.

. . . We shared so much in those twelve hours, and the common knowledge that, no matter what, we were dancers, made it amazing."

DANTE: "All walls came down, everything, and we were just a group of people together. It was very funny and terribly human."

MCKECHNIE, who had experienced eight years of therapy herself by this time, was initially the observer but became just as involved as the others: "What was so profound to me was that this group of people would sit down and collaborate in this way and give of their personal lives. . . . It struck me that, 'Here we are, told we could never speak, and we're speaking.' And they were not only speaking but speaking poignantly, with a dancer's humor. . . . Even people who didn't like each other were drawn together. . . . The thing that made it unusual was what happened to this particular group of people, who weren't group oriented, weren't verbal and weren't used to taking a look inside and bringing it out."

BOOCKVOR: "I was initially more interested in eating than in dancing or talking. But sitting on a mat on the floor, I heard stories from people I didn't care for but who I started to love and understand that night, because of all the wonderful, funny and awful stuff they revealed. I realized that some of the people I had thought were pompous were actually terrific. Michael was always more accepting of people than I was, and always saw the talent behind the problem."

It is interesting to speculate about how the event might have been different had Bennett not been there to guide it. While Bennett still considered himself a gypsy, he was no longer on a par with those assembled. He was now a Tony Award-winning director-choreographer, sought after for most new musicals that went into production. While he was as involved and committed as the others, and learned as much about himself as did anyone, there can be little doubt that his presence changed the nature of the event.

AVIAN: "Because Michael was a working director-choreographer, it meant that all of a sudden you had a father figure in the room. It was meant to be equal, but with Michael there, it wasn't. A lot of these kids were Buddhists at that time and were into sharing their experience. Introducing a father figure made them talk to him specifically, so it changed the tone of what they had been going for. They purged themselves, and Michael became the motivator, just like Zach in *A Chorus Line*."

So intense and important had this experience been for all assembled that it was immediately decided to do it again, so on February 8, 1974, almost all of the same people reassembled, joined by one or two other new recruits.

STEVENS: "Because we had only gotten up to arriving in New York at the first tape session, we had to do it again. This time Wayne Cilento taught class, the new people spoke first, and then we all continued, winding up with another twelve hours. A different method of questioning was used. At the first, a question was answered by going around in a circle. This time, a question was thrown out, and anyone could respond."

DANTE: "The second tape session was just not the same. It was repetitious, and not as focused, and I almost don't remember it."

At this point, no one involved was at all clear about what the next step would be, or to what purpose these twenty-four hours of tape would be put. There was no simple way to condense this outpouring of emotion into a play, nor was anyone yet convinced there was even the basis of a play in it. What is so extraordinary in retrospect is the fact that not only was *A Chorus Line* able to synthesize the stories spoken on that occasion but that the show managed to convey to its audience exactly the same feelings that everyone present at the tape sessions experienced. The impulse to share, the feeling that, in spite of all the suffering exposed, one was not alone but was part of the human race—all this would be conveyed theatrically and form the bedrock of emotion that would make *A Chorus Line* so powerful. The midnight dancers of January 1974 were already "One," and it would not be long before theatregoers would join them.

2

··

BEGINNINGS

G IVEN THE IMPACT OF the tape sessions on all involved, it is natural to assume that Bennett now felt he had found the basis for his long-pondered show for dancers and would rush headlong into this dream project. Yet Bennett was initially reluctant to commit himself to anything.

PEACOCK: "After the second tape session, Tony, Nick and I met with Michael in the office in his apartment on 55th Street. Michael said, 'I don't know. It could be anything. It could be a book.' I said to myself, 'A book? All this life?' He said, 'Let's see what happens,' and we walked out of there stone silent. We decided, 'We can't stop. That's not it.'"

DANTE: "Michael told us there was no show there, maybe a book. I'm sure this was completely manipulative on his part. He said he didn't know what to do with the material and that he didn't have any strong ideas. When we left, I said, 'No show there? Who's he kidding, no show? I'll write a show. He can keep the tapes.'"

What was Bennett's real motivation behind this delaying tactic? The simplest explanation is that Bennett had already committed to directing a new comedy and would be unable to deal with the other project immediately. He also needed time to decide just what his involvement in all this would be, and how many of those involved in the project thus far he wished to continue working with. As a major "name" director, he had to carefully think through the sensitive issues involved in a project that he himself had long considered but that now had developed into a collaborative effort.

The comedy Bennett went off to direct in March 1974, was *Thieves* by Herb Gardner, and there is no doubt that what ensued further soured Bennett on the commercial Broadway system.

MERLE DEBUSKEY, press representative for *Thieves:* "Michael cast *Thieves* and directed it. When it opened in New Haven, Gardner refused to make alterations in the script. Michael decided the leading lady, Valerie Harper, was not right, and she was out by the time we got to Boston. Then Michael quit, then the original producers, Eugene V. Wolsk and Emanuel Azenberg, quit."

When Bennett withdrew in Boston, he told the press that he had reached a point where he didn't know what to do with the show, and, having replaced stagers on other projects, felt it was best to let someone else take over. Charles Grodin succeeded Bennett as director, and Marlo Thomas, girlfriend of Gardner at the time, eventually took over as leading lady. This kind of chaotic, unpleasant theatrical situation was exactly the kind of thing that would motivate Bennett to proceed with the project that was to become *A Chorus Line.*

Interestingly, Bennett expressed interest in several other projects at the time of his departure from *Thieves,* none of which had anything to do with chorus dancers. He told *Variety* that he was about to begin work on two film projects, a movie version of *Promises, Promises* and a mystery-musical, *Pin-Ups,* which had suddenly become a film.

AVIAN: "We asked Steve Sondheim and Tony Perkins to write a synopsis for a film version of *Pin-Ups,* which we were calling *The Chorus Girl Murder Case.* The plot was now about girls getting murdered in the middle of huge production numbers. Their treatment was so complicated we could hardly figure it out."

A source witnessed the following saga of the beginning of another Bennett project at this time, one that relates significantly to *A Chorus Line.*

SOURCE: "Michael had worked with George Furth on *Company* and *Twigs,* and George was now working on a set of lyrics about a woman who had had an unhappy love affair, going into a recording studio in the middle of the night. It was going to be a one-woman show, and Marvin Hamlisch was writing the music. Marvin played the songs for Michael one night, and Michael became very interested, liked the idea of doing a show in terms of a night-club act, and flew George to New York. George was just about to write a book around these songs. Michael wanted to do the show, but it all fell apart over a contract. Michael insisted on producing, directing and choreographing it, and it also had to say 'conceived by,' which George couldn't accept as he'd already conceived it. . . . He knew he'd have no power if he accepted that billing. Michael said, 'But Jerry Robbins gets it, Gower gets it.' George said that he knew he would regret it later if he went along with it, and Michael said, 'Then we're not going to do it.' . . . George flew back to L.A. and waited for Marvin to return, but Marvin stayed and began working on *A Chorus Line.* * Michael later told George, 'It really wasn't the contract. We weren't ready to work together again yet. It was too soon.' "

If Bennett was unclear in the spring of 1974 about what his next move should be, Peacock, Stevens, and Dante had not wavered in their determination to see their goals fulfilled. The tapes were now in Stevens's possession, and because the three dancers could not be sure of Bennett's future interest or participation, they decided to create their own company. Twenty-two dancers, including many of those who had been at the tapings, met in March and formed a "Broadway Creative Commune," with Stevens as Communal Director and Dante and Peacock as assistants. Their goal was to form a repertory company in which members would create projects for themselves and others in the group, feeding off each other and using each other's skills. One week a member might direct a scene, the next perform in one, the next write.

Broadway Creative Commune soon gave way to an even more elaborate structure, "Ensemble Theatre, Inc." A lawyer was contacted about incorporating and grants were sought. In the charter drawn up by Ensemble Theatre, Inc., the group is defined as follows:

> The Ensemble Theatre, Inc., is a company of professional dancers formed to further develop their theatrical talents such as choreography, direction, design, writing, acting, singing, etc., by creating and performing new theatrical pieces originating from and composed of members of the company. The qualities particular to the

. . . .
*Furth's show, then called *Personal Appearance,* became *The Act* three years later.

company will in turn provide a source for original theatrical forms and entertainments to support and foster the growth of the American theatre.

Stevens was president, Dante vice-president, and Peacock secretary, and the Board of Artistic Advisors was to include Bennett, Gwen Verdon, Martin Charnin, Harvey Evans, Peter Gennaro, Cy Coleman, David Chapman, Alan Johnson, Joe Masteroff, Robert Morse, Martin Aronstein, and Gretchen Wyler.

Among the proposed projects on which the company was about to begin work was a piece entitled "Third Girl on the Left in Green" or "Especially the Girl on the Left." It was to focus on a chorus line, particularly one girl's experience of being on a line. Dante was writing vignettes for it and Stevens had begun to develop choreographic ideas. Donna McKechnie was contemplating pieces on Dorothy Parker and Emily Dickinson. At the same time, the group had not abandoned hope of working on a piece with Bennett based on the real lives of dancers, and they continued to conduct interviews with members of the company who had not been at the tape sessions.

PEACOCK: "As we continued in the next couple of months, and had three or four more meetings, it became very clear that one person was going to have to be at the helm of this, and none of the three of us wanted to be that person. We were all getting busy again . . . and Michael returned before we had resolved anything."

STEVENS: "It was a noble idea . . . but ultimately, it's about making a living, and how much time can you give up for a great idea and turn down a show? We realized it was going to take a lot of time to organize it, and that Michon and I would have to drop out of our careers to do it. . . . We were really torn, because we realized how worthy this was. We were still floundering, not knowing what to do, when Michael came back. He said, 'Joe Papp wants me to do something at the Public Theater. And I think there's something in those tapes that's me. I don't know what it is, I don't know if it's a book, a theatre piece, a play, or a Broadway musical. But there's something in all this stuff we did.' Finally, he said, 'Why don't you sell me the tapes?' Michon, Nick and I discussed what we should do, and whether or not we should give it up at this point. I was concerned about Nick, because I felt it would provide a chance for him to write something, and I didn't know what his involvement would be if Michael took over. . . . We decided we had to give it up. We signed contracts with

Michael, selling him the tapes and our stories. Each person sold his story for a dollar, in the good faith that if something came of this, we'd share a part of it.

"People often ask me if I'm angry because I ultimately wasn't a part of the show but had been in a way responsible for creating it. I always say, 'No, it's Michael's show. He fashioned it and it's his.' Michon and I were the impulse that got the show on. We were literally the sperm that led to the birth of the show. I celebrate that that happened in my life, and one of these days I figure somebody's going to come to me and I'll be able to do the same—take their idea and fashion it into something great."

Probably the most unforgettable tale told at the first tape session was that delivered by thirty-three-year-old aspiring writer Nicholas Dante. It was a harrowing account of the early years of a New York-born Puerto Rican whose real name was Conrado Morales. Dante had experienced the pain and humiliation of a difficult childhood, growing up a sexual misfit in the Fifties, and dancing in tawdry drag shows. Perhaps because of his writing ability, he was able on that night to recount it all in a lucid, hilarious, devastating, and deeply moving fashion. It would go into *A Chorus Line* almost exactly as delivered at the first tape session.

DANTE: "Most people now know that the story Paul tells in *A Chorus Line* is mine. I was a drag queen until my late teens, then I studied dancing for about four or five years. When I started dancing at the Jewel Box, I was not really a trained dancer, just gifted in that area.

"I got my first summer stock job in 1965, and my first Broadway show, *I'm Solomon,* in 1968. I was in *Ambassador* and *Applause.* On *Applause,* it was between me and another boy to be picked for the last slot in the chorus. They took me and made him a swing. That other boy was Sammy Williams, who wound up playing me in *A Chorus Line.*

"I had always wanted to write. I wrote when I was very little and I wanted to major in journalism, but I quit school in 1955 because people made such terrible fun of me. When I was growing up, gay wasn't the thing to be, it was a thing to hide, so as a kid I wrote fantasy things. When I quit school, I decided that you couldn't write without an education, so I wrote nothing for ten years. I went back to writing in 1965, because I thought I could write material as good or better than most of the shows we had done in stock that summer. I wrote an original musical with a friend called *The Orphanage,* then a musical version of *Dr. Jekyll and Mr. Hyde.* I showed them to a few people but they never got done. Writing was becoming very painful and hard for me, but I thought, 'I'm an aging dancer, so what am I going to do?'

"Michael and I had a 'nodding across the room' acquaintance. He knew I was a dancer. I had even sent *The Orphanage* to him, and he sent back a rejection letter of one sentence written on a huge piece of paper. . . . I always felt I had a destiny with Michael of some sort, and had this fantasy relationship going with him.

"After we had had several meetings of our Ensemble Theatre plan, I got a call from Michael. He said, 'I think there is a show here, and I would like you to help me write it if you're interested. If we can't pull it off, we'll get another writer and another until we get it right. . . . Would you like to try?' I said, 'Are you kidding, of course I would.' Michael really didn't know whether or not I could write, and I realized years later that he wanted me because he wanted my story. I think he felt he wouldn't be able to use that story otherwise. He knew I wanted to be a writer, and he must have thought that I wouldn't give him my story if there was no stake in it for me. I think Michael was that shrewd."

These words of Bennett's to Dante may come as a surprise, as Bennett's name does not appear as a writer on *A Chorus Line.* But Bennett had already taken the writing credit for *Seesaw,* even though the size of his contribution was open to question, and it was Bennett and Dante who began to tackle the material.

The form that *A Chorus Line* eventually took, that of an audition, would seem to have been the natural, logical one to contain and transmit the life stories from the tapes, but this was not immediately evident. It was not until the tapes were replayed again and again, and Bennett and Avian conducted additional interviews with such other dancers as Pam Blair, that the concept suggested itself.

AVIAN: "Michael realized that these kids sitting around telling him stories were actually auditioning their lives for him, saying 'Love me' and talking to a parent. It then came to us to use an audition situation. Michael was very attracted to Nick's story and the way Nick had told it, and he said, 'That's the center of my evening. We start with an audition, and the end will be who gets the job.' So we now had the beginning, the middle and the end, which is a lot to have."

The tapes were transcribed, and Bennett, Avian, and Dante began working with the stories, selecting chunks from some, combining others, and putting some actual characters down on paper. There was an enormous amount of material from which to choose, but eventually a crude script evolved, the title page of which read "by Nick Dante," but "copyright Plum Productions."

It was at this point that Bennett took his most radical step. Bennett and Dante and perhaps another writer could have continued to work on the script, honing, shaping, and developing it, while a composer and lyricist might have been hired to begin writing a score. However, none of this was to happen. *A Chorus Line* would be cast and put into rehearsal before it was written, and musicals would never be the same.

Joseph Papp first began a "Shakespeare Workshop" in a church on the Lower East Side of Manhattan in 1954, then moved up to the East River Amphitheater for the first summer of free Shakespeare in the Park in 1956. By 1962, Papp had gotten the city to build a permanent theatre in Central Park, the Delacorte, for his annual Shakespeare productions. In 1966, the New York Shakespeare Festival, as it had come to be called, purchased the about-to-be-demolished Astor Library building on Lafayette Street and in 1967 reopened it as the Public Theater, dedicated to the production of new plays by American writers. The rock musical *Hair* was the first presentation at the Public. In 1973, the Shakespeare Festival took over the Vivian Beaumont Theater in Lincoln Center, and when Papp's first two seasons of new plays did not go down well with the conservative Lincoln Center audience, he switched to classics and brought in such stars as Liv Ullmann.

By this time, several New York Shakespeare Festival productions, including *Sticks and Bones, That Championship Season, Two Gentlemen of Verona,* and *Much Ado About Nothing,* had moved to Broadway, winning awards and a degree of commercial success for this nonprofit organization. It is still one of the theatre's great ironies, however, that the most commercially successful production in Broadway history up to the Eighties was produced by a noncommercial organization.

Papp was aware of the talents of this hot young director and was interested in hiring Bennett for a project he had in mind for his Vivian Beaumont season—a revival of the 1938 Kurt Weill–Maxwell Anderson Broadway musical *Knickerbocker Holiday.*

BENNETT: "Now I'm just perfect to do *Knickerbocker Holiday*—wouldn't you think of me first, too? It's just the opposite of what I do. It's doing an old-fashioned revival, and I don't believe in revivals. But I had this crazy idea for a musical, and I told Joe about it. I had the tapes, Nicholas and I were working on the book, and in my head I had most of the cast. I said, 'I want to do this musical, and all you have to do is pay everybody $100 a week or something. I want to hire the cast first because I can only do this musical if I do it on the people.' I hadn't thought of Joe Papp because I never work Off-Broadway or in non-commercial theater."

Papp listened to excerpts from the tapes and decided to proceed, but a strong force in Papp's decision to take on the project was his associate producer, Bernard Gersten, now Executive Producer of Lincoln Center Theater.

MERLE DEBUSKEY: "Bernie had an understanding and appreciation of Michael's idea, and knew who Michael was. He was very interested in and very knowledgeable about dance. Although Joe had produced such musicals as *Hair* and *Two Gentlemen of Verona,* he was not very knowledgeable about Broadway musicals at the time, and I don't think Joe really knew that much about Michael."

While Papp would be less actively involved in the development of the show than would Gersten, there is no doubt that Papp's decision to give Bennett space at his Public Theater to develop the show made an incalculable difference to the end result. Bennett was nearly broke at this time, and he and his company would be earning just one hundred dollars a week for the next nine months, but Papp gave Bennett something he could never have obtained from any of the commercial managements with whom he had worked in the past: time. Away from the commercial pressures of a Broadway production, Bennett would have the time to develop the material on which he was already at work by using a method that had never before been tried on a musical. He now had a place to explore, a place to try things, and a place to fail.

BENNETT: "Joe Papp was wonderful. I don't think he always understood what we were doing, but he always understood that we were passionate about what we were doing, and he kept writing the checks."

3

....

THE WORKSHOPS

F OR DECADES, MUSICALS HAD been put together in more or less the same way. Writers worked on a book and score, sometimes at the behest of a producer, sometimes with the hope of interesting a producer in a draft of the material. The dialogue and songs were written: Sometimes they were created simultaneously but separately and later integrated, while on other occasions the songs would be added to an already existing book. When a satisfactory script consisting of dialogue and songs existed, and a producer had the financing, the show was put into rehearsal. By this time, a choreographer had been hired and had done some preproduction work, but most of the dancing and musical staging had to be created with the dancers during the rehearsal period of five weeks. During those five weeks, the writers could continue to write new material and refine what already existed, but there was rarely time to rehearse the changes and additions they would make during that time. Sets and costumes were designed during the rehearsal period for characters, songs, and sequences that would change or be eliminated altogether during the following few weeks. At the end of the five-week rehearsal period, the show would travel to Boston or Philadelphia or New Haven to play a tryout of about three weeks, often stopping in more than one city. The show would be reviewed by critics, and rehearsals would take place daily, during which old material would be revised and new material added, almost everything changing to some degree. The show would then move on to a couple of weeks of New York previews, during which time more changes would be made, now under severe restrictions of time and money. At last, the New York opening. In recent years, some musicals, including Bennett's *Coco,* had done away with the out-of-town tryout in favor of a longer preview period of about a month in New York. Either way, the entire process, from first rehearsal to Broadway opening, lasted about eleven weeks. Only a certain amount of money could be spent during this period, no matter how radically the show needed to be revised. No musical had been changed more dramatically than *Seesaw,* yet Bennett had never had the time or money to do with it all he would have liked.

Bennett had twenty-four hours of taped life stories and had begun to fashion them into a very rough script, yet he sensed that, even in collaboration with other writers, he could not continue the writing before working on the dance element of the show; and he could not begin working on that dance element until he had a full company of dancers in a rehearsal hall.

BENNETT: "When I did *A Chorus Line,* I had done sixteen Broadway shows. I was used to having five weeks of rehearsal, four days of tech, two weeks out-of-town, you move to New York, have previews and open. . . . All I was doing was looking at the clock and thinking, 'Do I dare try this? What if I'm wrong? I've just wasted three days of rehearsal. . . .' Also, because shows were costing so much money, I was feeling the pressure of money. I just thought, there's got to be another way to do this. This is all fine, the unions have said it should be like this, but there's not enough time anymore to be ambitious, to be agressive, to try and do some new things.

"In the case of *A Chorus Line,* you could not talk to writers about dramatizing a rehearsal scene, or dramatizing what a dancer goes through, working very hard to look like every other dancer in the room. . . . I had to 'dummy' chunks of the show on people before the writers could write it."

In addition to giving Bennett freedom from the pressures of Broadway, the "workshop" system gave him the total control he had been unable to exercise on earlier productions. While Joseph Papp and the Shakespeare Festival were co-producers with Bennett's Plum Productions, Papp wisely did not attempt to exercise much authority during the workshop period, trusting Bennett to develop the material and only dropping in occasionally to sample. Bennett was conceiving the show himself, co-writing it, hiring all the talent involved, and supervising all the creative elements.

ROBERT THOMAS, Bennett's rehearsal drummer: "Michael and I thought that *Promises, Promises* was about as good as we could do under the Broadway system. He always used to talk about having the freedom to put together all the ideas he had. So often the producer or director wound up cutting half of the stuff we worked on in rehearsals. One day, he called and said, 'I'm doing a show.' I wasn't sure if I wanted to go through that kind of stuff anymore. He said, 'This one's going to be different. I'm the director, the choreographer, and I'm the producer, along with the Shakespeare Festival.' I said, 'Fine. Now who do we have to answer to?' He said, slow and drawn out, 'Nobody.' "

Was the workshop process a Michael Bennett invention? While it had never before been used to develop a full-scale Broadway musical, plays had been worked on in workshop situations for years. Bennett's workshop concept was actually closest to techniques from the Off Off-Broadway scene, such as Joseph Chaikin's Open Theatre, in which plays were not written but developed through improvisation with a company of actors. Writers would fashion the material into a script during the rehearsal period; occasionally, no writer would actually be credited with the piece when it opened to the public.

Bennett's team already consisted of Dante, co-choreographer Avian, and producers Papp and Gersten. It was time to hire people to write a score and to design the production.

By the time Marvin Hamlisch was hired to compose the music, he had won four Grammy Awards and made Hollywood history by winning three Academy Awards in one night. Yet he had never written a musical before, and he would now be asked to create a score in a thoroughly unorthodox fashion.

Born in Manhattan, Hamlisch auditioned for the Juilliard School of Music at the age of seven, and later graduated from it. At sixteen, he wrote a hit song for Lesley Gore, and then became a rehearsal pianist on television, assistant vocal arranger of the Broadway musical *Funny Girl* (in which Bob Avian danced), and, most significantly, dance arranger for Bennett's *Henry, Sweet Henry* choreography. After working on Las Vegas club acts, he began scoring films, winning Oscars for his work on *The Way We Were* and *The Sting.*

HAMLISCH: "When Michael called me about *A Chorus Line,* he was already pretty well into the idea of the project. He brought me in, and I listened to some of the tapes of dancers talking about their lives. He asked me whether I thought that out of all this there would be a musical. . . . I said I thought it could be, and he began telling me about a lyricist he was very high on. Michael was going with people who had never done a musical before but had aspirations to do one."

BENNETT: "Although Marvin was not a dancer like Nick and myself, he was a dance arranger. He and I started out together, and we'd known each other since we were 20 or 21. He did dance arrangements for me when I was doing "The Ed Sullivan Show," and we became very friendly. He knows more about dancing than almost any other composer in the musical theatre, so he was quite the ideal choice for this."

There was one stumbling block before Hamlisch accepted the assignment. As a multi-award winner and now-famous name, Hamlisch, and particularly Hamlisch's agent, found it difficult to accept the proposition of working for one hundred dollars a week for months on an experimental, exploratory project that might never develop into a show. Hamlisch found the prospect too tantalizing to resist, however, and persuaded his agent that this was the correct career move.

Unlike Hamlisch, the man Bennett chose as lyricist of *A Chorus Line* was totally unknown to the public. Ed Kleban was a red-haired, stocky graduate of New York's High School of Music and Art, where he was sports editor of the newspaper—not because of any knowledge of the field but because he lived near Yankee Stadium. After graduating from Columbia University, he became a successful executive with Columbia Records, yet in 1968 gave up that lucrative position to do what he loved, write songs. After devising revue material for Café La Mama and the Manhattan Theatre Club, Kleban worked on two musicals, one of which, *Gallery,* would become a lifetime project. *Gallery* was an evening of songs, each of which was created around an art object in a museum, and it was first presented publicly in Manhattan in May 1972, as one of three works-in-progress by the Broadcast Music Incorporated (BMI)'s Musical Theatre Workshop, under the direction of Lehman Engel. It was favorably reviewed, and Sheldon Harnick worked with Kleban on arranging a full-scale production of the piece. Also in the early Seventies, Kleban had composed the score for a musical, with book by Peter Stone, called *Subject to Change.* It concerned Kleban's own divorce, and marriage in general; work on it was interrupted by *A Chorus Line.*

Kleban was both a composer and a lyricist, but, like Stephen Sondheim on his first two Broadway musicals, he was asked to contribute only lyrics to Bennett's project.

HAMLISCH: "The first time I saw the name Ed Kleban . . . I was playing for Barbra Streisand when she was going to give a live concert for Daniel Ellsberg in California. She brought out a song called 'Better,' and it was incredible. A year or so later, when Michael was telling me about his idea for the show, he said, 'I've found the greatest lyricist, incredible. His name is Ed Kleban.' I was totally intimidated, and said, 'I've heard a song he wrote and it's great. Why would he possibly want to write just lyrics? He's better than me.' Michael said, 'Just meet this guy.' Michael brought us together. He was the rabbi, he made the marriage. We met on the West Side at the home of my parents—neutral ground. Ed was very concerned about me, because I had had some success. I was very concerned about him because of what I had heard of his work. When we started writing, because he was a musician, he willingly gave ideas all the time."

KLEBAN: "In June, 1974, Michael called me. He had heard my work only once when I auditioned a score for him a year before. Michael was looking for someone to work with Marvin and he thought of me. I'm a composer as well, and Michael said, 'I'm offering you half of what you usually do. Would you be interested?' I'd never met Marvin, and Michael said, 'Marvin's a lot more Jewish than you are, but it'll work out.' He introduced us, left the room, and Marvin and I spent six weeks kicking each other in the stomach a lot, as you do in the beginning of a collaboration. There was no reason for me to believe that he could write theatre songs, and there was no reason for him to believe that I could write theatre songs. But after about six weeks and about three really lousy numbers, all openings as I recall, we finally came up with a good number that everybody seemed to like. Then we came up with another one, and once you have two that not only both of you like and can get behind, but everybody else can too, you begin to sit still for each other, to feel safe together.

"What we began with was the tapes and transcripts from the tape sessions. Most of it was intensely boring, the same nonsense over and over again. . . . Except that every twenty or twenty-five pages, there would be something interesting to the outsider and not just to a chorus gypsy. Suddenly you discovered something like the realization that 'I can do that,' that that young man could excel and have a special life if he danced. There was a song."

The importance of Kleban's involvement in the BMI workshop created by Lehman Engel cannot be overestimated. Kleban had already learned how to develop material in a workshop situation that involved sensitivity to others and a strong commitment to collaboration, and this experience stood him in excellent stead for the somewhat parallel process Bennett was about to employ.

Although Bennett knew that no designs of any kind were necessary until well into the workshop process, he immediately asked Robin Wagner to be set designer. Their work together on *Promises, Promises* and especially *Seesaw* had demonstrated to Bennett that Wagner could be very much a part of the creative process and was very flexible in adjusting his designs to the concepts underlying Bennett's staging. Theoni V. Aldredge was the resident costume designer for the New York Shakespeare Festival, and that fact, plus Bennett's awareness of her talent, made her the obvious choice for the clothes. The key choice, however, was selecting Tharon Musser for the lighting, and for two reasons. First, the choice of Musser was crucial because Musser had spent years working in the dance world.

MUSSER: "Working in modern dance was great preparation for the theatre. . . . In modern dance, you really collaborate, and you're really in on what they're trying to say. There's next to no scenery, so it's just costumes and lights that help . . . say what they're trying to say."

In addition to that background, the fact that Musser was not just a lighting designer but a true theatrical artist and painter with light made her important to the new project. Throughout the Thirties and Forties, there was often no lighting designer listed in the program of a musical, and it was frequently the director and stage manager, working with electricians, who plotted the show's lighting. But just as the art of musical theatre had developed into something far more complex and expressive, theatrical lighting had now become an art form as well, thanks to the work of such pioneers as Jean Rosenthal and Peggy Clark. Musser had apprenticed with Rosenthal and was now supreme in her field, and her contribution to *A Chorus Line* would be equal to that of the writers and even to that of Bennett himself.

None of these three talents individually would be as important as what happened between them and Bennett during the workshops. Before Bennett discussed ideas for the set, costumes, and lighting, he discussed the material, the show itself, with them and allowed them to contribute ideas freely, knowing that that would help them create designs that would be truly integral to the other elements of the show. Each was present during most of the workshop rehearsals, and, while they waited months before beginning to design, they talked to each other, with the other collaborators, and with Bennett, all the while hearing the life stories of dancers and experiencing a new method of creating a show.

Now that Bennett had his team, it was time to get the bodies on which he would make the show. Those who arrived to audition for the first workshop were aware that it would last four or five weeks and that it would pay one hundred dollars a week, but no one could guarantee there would be a second workshop, let alone a show at the end of it all. Most of the dancers who did audition had worked with Bennett and were aware that he was one of the most distinctive talents in his field. However, it may have been more the unfortunate state of Broadway at the time than a desire to work with Bennett that caused so many to audition for the *Chorus Line* workshop.

BENNETT: "The thing is, in 1974, there wasn't other work. If there'd been work, they wouldn't have been at the Shakespeare Festival for $100 a week. No one's that noble. Not much was running at the time. I think that was the beginning of the revival. Museum theater, one of my faves."

It may come as a surprise that auditions for the workshop were held at all. At the tape sessions, Bennett had shared intimacies with about twenty excellent dancers, and one might have assumed that those dancers would automatically become the performers of the workshop, with one or two added or subtracted where necessary. Bennett insisted, however, that everyone, whether present at the tape sessions or not, audition for the workshop. Of course, there were certain individuals—notably Donna McKechnie, Carole Bishop, and Priscilla Lopez—whom Bennett already knew he had to have; yet even they auditioned.

MCKECHNIE: "Even though Michael knew everybody, everyone had to audition, to see how they presented themselves on stage, and to allow the writers to see the people. It was funny to some people when they were given their own life, transcribed, to read as their audition."

CILENTO: "Those of us who had been at the tapes were really pissed off. . . . When I walked into the Public, Michael handed me a sheet of paper which contained a story I had told on the tapes, typed up. He said, 'Go out there and do this monologue.' There was no way I could *read* what I had said on the tapes. I said to Michael, 'I can't read this.' He said, 'Well, put the damn paper down and just tell me the story again.'"

There was only room for a limited number of dancers in the workshop, and several of those at the tapes came close to not getting hired, while others were rejected outright.

DANTE: "My dear friend Rene Baughman didn't sing that well, and I had to tell her that she might not get hired for the workshop, after she had told her story at the tapes. She said, 'You can't do this to me! That's my life, you cannot give my life away!' "

PEACOCK: "The auditions for the workshop of *A Chorus Line* coincided with those for *Chicago.* I had a magical audition for Fosse, then did an audition, really for myself, for *A Chorus Line,* and they weren't interested."

BOOCKVOR: "My wife went to the midwest to act in plays. I auditioned for the workshop but didn't get it, mostly because of Marvin Hamlisch, who I don't think was too crazy about me."

DANTE: "Although my life story was definitely going to be in the show, I knew I was never going to be playing it. I don't think Michael ever wanted me to do it. He wanted Sammy Williams from the start."

Ultimately, the group that began the first workshop in August 1974, working fourteen hours a day for five weeks at the Public's Newman Theater and other spaces at the Public and at the American Theatre Lab on West Nineteenth Street, included Renee Baughman, Carole Bishop, Candy Brown, Chris Chadman, Wayne Cilento, Trish Garland, Baayork Lee, Priscilla Lopez, Robert LuPone, Cameron Mason, Donna McKechnie, Michael Misita—who dropped out and was replaced by Tony Stevens—Jane Robertson, Michel Stuart, Thommie Walsh, and Sammy Williams. Some of the people who had offered their lives at the tapes proved unsuitable to play them, and were hurt by what they considered a betrayal. Some, such as Mitzi Hamilton, would later get to play the role partly based on her story—after the show had opened on Broadway.

MCKECHNIE: "When someone didn't get hired to play his or her own life story, it wasn't so much because they weren't good. It had more to do with picking very specific individual types. Although Michael knew he wasn't working with a lot of experienced actors, he had confidence in his ability to direct anybody, so it wasn't that people weren't hired because they couldn't act or sing as well as someone else. He wanted very distinct personalities, and they couldn't be too similar. He knew he wanted to work with Carole Bishop, for example, so he couldn't hire someone who was going to compete with her. . . . Not everybody hired was the best actor or best singer he could find, but there was something very specific and unique that he saw in each person he hired."

By the time the workshop began, there existed a one-and-a-half-hour, incomplete play, which soon grew to about four hours.

DANTE: "We went into rehearsal with no music and no lyrics, and ¾ of a script. There was no ending, and the script was mainly the material from the tapes somehow slogged down from 24 hours into monologues and chunks. Initially, it was this very surrealistic piece where dancers came in this back door and talked to a God-like, unseen voice that asked questions. The surrealistic concept made Michael see it as a straight play with dancing."

MCKECHNIE: "At this point, the show had no design. It was basically one monologue after another, interesting but not real theatre. . . . One after another of these stories robbed the piece of a sense of drama; you knew the next person was going to get up and do another monologue. There was no humor or surprise, and it tended to hit you over the head."

The script changed constantly, and side scenes were added in which the characters, in groups of two or three, interracted and had conversations, in between scenes with the full group. But the script at this point was secondary to the other aspects of the workshop, and most of the time was taken up with the beginnings of the creation of musical sequences.

Robert Thomas, the drummer whose beat Bennett had depended on over the years to stimulate his choreographic invention in the rehearsal hall, became even more crucial to *A Chorus Line.* In conventional musicals such as *Henry, Sweet Henry* and *Promises, Promises,* the songs had been written prior to rehearsals, but Bennett needed Thomas to provide rhythms as he created the dance sequences, the music for which often came later. With *A Chorus Line,* the rhythms came before any music and lyrics whatsoever.

THOMAS: "I would beat out rhythms, Michael would invent to them, and Marvin would later create something with that concept. Some of the rhythmic things Michael used came from things we had done in dance class fourteen years earlier."

CILENTO: "The first workshop was all dancing. . . . Michael got to know how all of us danced, and how strong we were. We worked on a number for Donna, but at that time there were four boys in it. . . . There was no song yet; it was all done to drums and percussion. Some of the steps in the final version were there, but very few."

BENNETT: "It wasn't improvising, it was sketching out. I staged an opening number without the music and without the lyric that is currently in the show. It was an idea, a rough form of the number that now exists.

The dancing in this particular musical needed to come first, because the dancing was the plot of the musical; it wasn't something that could be done after the fact."

Throughout this process of "dummying" dances, Hamlisch and Kleban were in attendance, observing the choreographic patterns, interviewing dancers during breaks, and simply absorbing the atmosphere of the dancer's world. They were also beginning to compose songs, tailor-making them for the personalities at hand, although none of these would be rehearsed until the second workshop. Bennett's original concept of a play with incidental music and dancing was giving way to a full-fledged musical.

HAMLISCH: "We wrote the songs as we rehearsed and watched things. . . . We wrote 'One,' 'At the Ballet' and an opening number which we later changed. What we were finding out was that we could musicalize even more, that in fact the play wanted to be musicalized."

WAGNER: "Marvin and Ed watched what Michael was doing. He sent them away with ideas for songs. He already had scenes, and those scenes became their songs. . . . 'One,' 'Sing' and 'Nothing' soon developed."

BENNETT: "When they found 'At the Ballet,' they found the style to write the show in. 'Ballet' set the tone for the whole score."

AVIAN: "During the first workshop, we spent weeks on the opening number. The first number Marvin and Ed worked on was for the opening. It was originally a big number called 'Resume,' about all the shows they had all been in. We started staging it, but Ed Kleban felt we needed a traditional musical theatre 'I want' song to establish up front what the characters wanted, like 'Wouldn't It Be Lovely?' in *My Fair Lady.* So that number eventually came to be about the need they had, as opposed to just exposition as in the first workshop."

Several interesting concepts were tried for the number which would become "One."

STEVENS: "Originally for the finale, Michael wanted to bring somebody up out of the audience and we would back them up and make them a star. He said Sammy, Wayne and I would lead this person around, but we couldn't understand how this could work."

CANDY BROWN: "We were working on this 'big star number without the star.' At that time, it was just a chorus dancing around and focusing on a spotlight, as if a star were dancing and singing in it."

Throughout, the same exploration of childhood experience and the reasons why people dance that took place at the tape sessions was continuing. Bennett would ask again about why they started dancing; Avian would ask people what they would do if they couldn't dance anymore; and Kleban would ask for greater elaboration of phrases from the tapes that had captured his imagination. Not only were the numbers being created on these dancers, but these dancers were involved in the creation of the material, the "book," as well. Few stars had ever been given the opportunity to contribute to the material in the way these chorus dancers were now doing.

Near the very end of the first workshop, Bennett employed a startling method of obtaining a "real" reaction from his cast.

AVIAN: "Michael told myself and the production stage manager that he was going to fake having an accident. He said, 'I want to do this scene, but I don't want to spend weeks rehearsing it.' Michael was rehearsing 'One,' tap dancing with the kids, and all of a sudden he fell—bang! The strong kids all came running to see what they could do. The more frightened ones pulled away. And the confused ones just sort of hung where they were. Some began crying hysterically. Michael maintained this for about 4 or 5 minutes, while I pretended to call our doctor. All of a sudden, Michael looked up and said, 'Does everybody remember exactly what they did?' Half of them were furious. Baayork Lee was hysterical; she started sobbing, and was terribly angry at him for doing this and manipulating them like that. He immediately staged the scene, and everybody knew exactly where they had gone and what they did and what their reaction was, which made it totally real. . . . Much of the dialogue in Paul's accident scene was later written, but their reaction was all real."

STEVENS recalls another manipulative device Bennett employed to enhance the reality of the acting: "Every time we'd rehearse the final scene, somebody else would be eliminated, and you would never know if you were going to get picked or not. You were always upset when you weren't, and it made you go through the feeling of an actual audition, which Michael wanted to maintain at all times."

Bennett needed privacy and a complete absence of the standard Broadway pressures in order to work in the manner he had established, and Papp understood this.

MCKECHNIE: "Michael kept Joe out of the situation in the early stages, and with good reason, because he wanted to have carte blanche. He wanted Joe to see it only after he had a certain amount done so Joe could give him objective feedback."

BENNETT: "At the end of about five weeks, I had like two scenes to show Joe, and a couple of stylistic techniques I was playing around with. I thought, 'God, this isn't an awful lot to show for five weeks' work.' But Joe looked and said, 'Well, this is interesting. Keep working.' "

The company then took a break of about twelve weeks before beginning the next workshop, and it was during this break that Bennett began to feel the need for another writer, who could take a fresh look at the material. Bennett would later say of his writing talents: "I do write, but then I'm rewritten by some of the best writers in the business. . . . I structure and I will do first versions of things, then I will get people to do it better. I'm really surprised I can write at all, because I can't spell."

However well the collaboration between Bennett and Dante had been working up to this point, Bennett now felt the material needed a writer of more proven ability.

Bennett called a halt to the first workshop in September, and it was not only because of the need everyone involved felt to take a break, examine, revise, and focus what already existed, and invent new material, all of which would be necessary before returning to the rehearsal halls. Bennett had a more practical reason: He was committed to directing Neil Simon's new play, *God's Favorite,* which opened on December 11.

By the time Bennett began the second workshop at the very end of 1974, he was aware that the amount of time he would need to devote to the staging would allow him virtually no time to further assist with the writing. It was at a Broadway preview of *God's Favorite* that Bennett made contact with the writer he was seeking to join Dante.

By 1974, James Kirkwood was an acclaimed novelist, but he had only reached that stage after a colorful life and career on both sides of the footlights. The son of silent-screen stars Lila Lee and James Kirkwood, Sr., Kirkwood had survived an unstable childhood; the high school from which he graduated was the eighteenth he attended. He performed in clubs and on Broadway with a partner, the late Lee Goodman, and acted extensively in summer stock and in New York. When he left New York for Hollywood and found it difficult to get work, he turned his attention to writing, and soon finished *There Must Be a Pony,* a semi-autobiographical novel. Later novels include *Good Times/Bad Times* and *Some Kind of Hero,* both of which garnered fine reviews and had a cult following. For the theatre, Kirkwood had dramatized *There Must Be a Pony* (Myrna Loy toured in it on the summer circuit but it did not come to New York) and co-written *UTBU: Unhealthy to Be Unpleasant,* a bizarre comedy that ran

seven performances on Broadway in 1966. He was working on a dramati-
zation of his novel *P.S. Your Cat Is Dead* at the moment his path crossed
that of Bennett.

KIRKWOOD: "Michael had toyed with directing *P.S. Your Cat Is Dead*
about a year or two before. I sent it to him because everybody said, 'This
guy is really talented. He's not just a choreographer. He's a real director,
too.' He was intrigued with it, and we had six or seven meetings about
it. He was a little afraid of the subject matter, and he wasn't quite sure
he was up to it. He vacillated, then decided he was more comfortable
doing *Seesaw.* I was very annoyed with him; it had been like a tease. The
night I went to see *God's Favorite,* Jack Lenny, for whom I had worked
in summer stock, came over to me and said, 'Michael's over there.' I said,
'Say hello to the little bastard for me.'. . . Michael ran over and said, 'My
God, I've been trying to get a hold of you for weeks. I have an idea for
a musical. Have you ever thought of doing one?' I said, 'Yes, but I don't
know how.' He said, 'Who does? If everybody knew how, there'd be all
these musicals. I have an idea, and because you were a performer, I think
it might be right for you.'

"The minute he said it was about auditions and competitions, I was
hooked. The worst thing I ever experienced as an actor was auditioning
for musicals. You had no one to react to. When you read for a play, you
read with someone, but for a musical you're singing a love ballad to
David Merrick sitting in the twelfth row smoking a cigar. . . . When
Michael told me about the show, I sensed right away that it was something
close to me.

"I loved the idea of a show about an audition, which had never been
done before. Michael wasn't sure at the time if it was going to be one
audition or a series of auditions, but it was going to be about chorus
people, not stars, and why they went through the humiliation.

"Now Michael was the great manipulator of all time. After I said I
wanted to do it, he then dropped on me the fact that I would have a
collaborator. Michael said of Nick, 'He's wanted to be a writer for years,
and now he's starting. We worked together and I wanted to write it, but
I'm not really a writer.' And Michael wasn't—his attention span was too
short. I was now having second thoughts . . . but Michael said, 'Listen,
you'll like Nicholas.' Michael introduced us in the lobby of his building
and Nick said to me, 'You wrote my all-time favorite book, *Good Times/
Bad Times.*' I turned to Michael and said, 'There will be no problem
here.' "

DANTE: "When Michael told me he was calling Jimmy in, he didn't do it in a very nice way. He called me on the phone, told me, and hung up. I freaked, because Michael had said he didn't want his name on the script, and I was expecting to get sole writing credit.

"The main reason Jimmy came in was because Michael felt the relationship between Cassie and Zach that we were developing for the second workshop script wasn't working, and he didn't think we could pull it off together. At the time Jimmy came in, I was beginning to panic and was under great stress. When they brought Jimmy in, I was relieved and thought, 'Oh, he'll get all the blame.' Actually, he got all the credit. But it freed me up to keep having fun, although I was now doing a lot of writing from a strange place, from behind."

KIRKWOOD: "I never listened to the tapes. Instead, I met with several of the dancers Michael was using, and I talked with them about auditions, and why people went into the theatre. When I received transcripts of the tapes, I found them almost impossible to read. But one night in bed, I came across a line that killed me, when one of the boys said, 'I realized I was a homosexual and I got so depressed because I thought I'd never be able to wear nice clothes.' I wondered why anyone would think that, and not the opposite."

Both Dante and Kirkwood agree that their collaboration over the next six months was a happy one.

KIRKWOOD: "It was the happiest I've ever been involved in. There were very few fights, and Michael was a firm captain of the ship and saw to it that, whatever the problem, we would never leave of an evening with bad feelings. . . . Michael was constantly around while we were writing, always there when we had a new scene. Nick and I worked separately and together. Sometimes he would do a draft and I would go over it. Sometimes the two of us would sit in a room, and one would pace, the other type, then we'd reverse positions. We played 'What if?' a lot: what if Cassie and Zach had had an affair? The only arguments we ever had were about punctuation."

DANTE: "I know that Marvin and Ed had their difficult moments, but Jimmy and I never did. . . . We had this idea that something great has to be suffered, but since we'd all suffered our lives, we realized we didn't need to suffer the art, so we just had a wonderful time. We rarely worked with Marvin and Ed. It was usually Jimmy and me, and Marvin and Ed. Michael wanted it that way."

Kirkwood was the last one to come in on the show, and perhaps for that reason he was the first to sense that it would be a hit.

KIRKWOOD: "I turned down a very lucrative book offer to work on the show because I was convinced it was going to be a big success. Because of that, I asked for a bigger percentage when the show paid off, but they wouldn't give it to me . . . I think the pie was all split up by the time I got there. Then I tried to put money in the show and Michael said, 'You can't. I can't.' . . . But that's how much I believed in it."

It is interesting to contrast the fate of *A Chorus Line* with that of Kirkwood's play *P.S. Your Cat Is Dead,* which opened on Broadway one month before *A Chorus Line* opened at the Public Theater. It closed after sixteen performances. (It was later revived with greater success). The element of homosexual fantasy in the plot, which featured a sequence in which an attractive heterosexual leading man tied up a half-nude punk burglar, may have been one of the reasons why the play proved unpopular with Broadway audiences. In *A Chorus Line,* the gay element of the script, with at least three characters overtly or presumably homosexual, became far more palatable to general audiences, probably because of the correspondence between the show's themes and the gay experience. By making the gay element an integral part of the action, rather than using it subtextually as in *P.S., A Chorus Line* made the subject acceptable to a broad public, probably for the first time.

The material—book, music, lyrics, and staging concepts—changed daily throughout the second workshop. It was during this seven-week period that the show became structured and focused. The key to this was the invention of the character of Zach. In the first workshop, there had been an amorphous God-like figure billed only as "Voice." There was now an actual director character leading the audition, one who would soon be given a past involving one of the other characters. Ways were then found to vary the action, and much of the time was spent integrating the monologues with the staging ideas that had already been worked on and with the songs that greeted the actors on their return.

The character of Cassie, partially based on the actress who would play it—Donna McKechnie—gave the collaborators particular difficulty. In the first workshop, she was called Maggie and was not allowed to stand out from the stream of consciousness of that version. When the second workshop began, Cassie had a star entrance.

MCKECHNIE: "I remember going across the street with Michael and saying, 'I know you're trying to give me an entrance and make me a star here, but you're killing me with kindness.' "

DANTE: "You had sixteen people come out at the beginning and milk your heart, and then she came on, and she was this cunt in furs. He wanted to show she was a star and different from the others, but it didn't work."

The role of Cassie would go through further changes in the next months, but it had now become central to the structure.

MCKECHNIE: "Michael was using the character as a catalyst, the one connection with the director that would involve him in the play without his being part of the play. She would be the mirror to Zach. To him, there was something very threatening about her being there, as she was his reflection."

During the first workshop, only a limited amount of time had been spent rehearsing dialogue scenes, and actors had not been guaranteed roles or lines, although certain parts were clearly tailored to certain performers. At the beginning of the second workshop, all the existing monologues and side scenes were read aloud by the company, and roles were definitively cast.

Having the performers who were to play the roles *there* as the writing continued led to constant changes to make the parts closer to the actors playing them, and to help the performers achieve more honest, "real" performances. Words that one dancer had uttered at the tape sessions might be taken away from that dancer and given to another performer to speak in the show. Everyone contributed to the final text because it was their lives that were being dramatized.

It gradually became clear during the second workshop that simpler was better, and several of the plot elements were phased out in favor of a sparer, leaner text. A fight scene between Al and Greg, a rebellion scene in which the dancers imitated and "interviewed" Zach, a long monologue for Cassie about a breakdown she suffered in California—all were tried and eventually eliminated. Prime considerations throughout were to avoid excessive melodrama and any monologue that would detract from Paul's, the Nick Dante story, which was intended to stand alone as the evening's climax.

At one point during the workshop, three separate eliminations, one at the beginning, one midway, and one at the curtain, were tried. At another point, the accident scene that Bennett had tricked the cast into staging at the end of the first workshop was tried with a female character sustaining the injury.

DANTE: "I was annoyed that it had to be the gay character who also had the accident. I thought, 'Why does it always have to be the poor fucking gay character?' But we found out it had to be Paul. If it was a lesser character, you didn't feel as much."

By the time the first workshop ended, two or three songs had been written, but now that Hamlisch and Kleban were confident that the material could be musicalized, virtually all the songs would change or be newly written during the second workshop.

Hamlisch and Kleban would often work in one room at the Public Theater or at the Nineteenth Street rehearsal hall, while Bennett, Avian, and the company would work on the staging in an adjacent room. Kleban could stop by and question one of the dancers about something he or she had said on the tapes, and Bennett could drop by the other room to hear what Hamlisch and Kleban had just come up with. Having the luxury of time to experiment and the opportunity to be with the people about whom they were fashioning songs made the collaboration between Hamlisch and Kleban an exciting, if volatile, one.

HAMLISCH: "Ed had a wonderful technique of talking to each of the people who were in the show before we even wrote any of the songs, to get their thoughts. He would take those thoughts and incorporate them in the lyrics. He believed in a lot of research into anything before he wrote a lyric.

"We usually wrote together in a room. I would start playing the greatest melody in the history of mankind, and, after I'd killed myself, Ed would say, 'No, that won't work.' When Ed said, 'It won't work,' that was it. When he finally heard a melody that he liked, I would give him a tape and he would go off and write a lyric. Sometimes, as with 'One,' he came up with the idea for the number, I went off and wrote the melody, then he wrote the lyrics.

"When, after we'd gone through 97 versions, a number was finally written, I had to make a tape of the piano part. Why? Because Friday afternoons at four, Ed would take the song to be assessed by the B.M.I. Workshop. I said to him, 'We've just done 97 versions. I love it, you love it. Are you going to tell me that a class is going to tell you what's funny and not funny?' He said, 'Yes.' Knowing the way I felt about this, he never invited me. If the workshop turned thumbs down on a song, we'd lost another song."

The musical number to which the greatest amount of time was devoted during the second workshop was the "montage" sequence, originally titled "Goodbye Twelve, Goodbye Thirteen, Hello Love," later changed to "Hello Twelve, Hello Thirteen, Hello Love." The development of this sequence demonstrates how inseparable were the contributions of *A Chorus Line*'s collaborators.

DANTE: "Michael said to me, 'I wish there were a way we could interview everybody, but we don't have time.' I said, 'Remember at the tapes, how when somebody would start talking, it would trigger you off on a whole train of thought? Suppose we have a scene where people are talking, then we go into pantomime as others start associating.' "

KIRKWOOD: "Marvin and Ed had a lot of trouble writing this musical number about adolescence that Michael wanted. So Michael, Marvin and Ed came to Nicholas and me, and said, 'Why don't you two write a little one-act play that encapsulates everything you can think of about being an adolescent.' Michael, Marvin and Ed said they would then 'raid' it and make it into a musical number. Nick and I wrote everything down that we could imagine, free associating. That's why so many of the lines in that sequence are separate and don't rhyme, like 'Tits—when am I gonna grow tits?' 'You're father went through life with an open fly'—that was a line my mother said to me about my father."

DANTE: "When I gave the scene to Michael, I said, 'This is all about lighting. If the lighting in this sequence does not work, it will not work.' What Tharon did with the lights and what Michael did with it was extraordinary."

Don Pippin, who joined the show during the second workshop as musical director and vocal arranger, remembers further refinements of the number.

PIPPIN: " 'Hello Twelve' originally had a ragtime, Dixieland, Charleston melody, to basically the same lyric. . . . One day, Michael said, 'Why isn't this number more contemporary sounding? Why are these young people doing this ragtime thing?' Marvin winged the new melody on the spot."

The combined talents of Dante, Kirkwood, Hamlisch, Kleban, Bennett, Avian, Musser, Pippin, and the entire company eventually made the "Hello Twelve" sequence into one of the musical theatre's prime examples of integration.

Multiple versions of several songs were tried: Cassie's "The Music and the Mirror" was once a song called "Inside the Music," and at least four other versions of the number were tested and eliminated. The new character, Richie, played by Ron Dennis, was given a duet with Connie called "Confidence," in which the two "token minority" figures on the line— the black boy and the Oriental girl—sang of the confidence instilled in them by the knowledge that the director of the show could not really do without them, no matter what he thought of their talents.

RON DENNIS: "The song was about how we were always the only

minorities in all-white casts. It was cleverly and subtly written. . . . When it was cut, Baayork and I sat around for weeks not knowing how they were going to use us. They came up with the '4 foot 10' section of the montage for her, but I didn't get my song until just before we started previews, because they really didn't know what to do with me. Finally, Michael and Bobby Thomas came up with the 'Gimme the ball' theme, which I went home and embellished."

One of the show's best songs, "Nothing," was almost cut during the second workshop.

KLEBAN: "At the tapes, Priscilla Lopez told of her experiences at the High School of Performing Arts, and when someone else informed her the teacher who had given her such a hard time had died, she said, 'Good.' I loved the fact that she got away with that remark in a room full of strangers, and no one said, 'How can you say that about another human being?' . . . She was a truth teller and I wanted to go with that story, even though it wasn't an obvious idea for a song, and there were other things in her transcript that other people would have preferred to see as her song, such as when she wowed her first audience. I felt, 'We're not doing *42nd Street.* We are doing the truth.' The truth is that these people's lives were full of people who did damage to them.

"We wrote the song, and first it was working fine, and then it wasn't. I had played it for my workshop and they loved it, so when the number got into trouble during rehearsal and suddenly 39 people wanted it to go, I was confident that this was one of the best songs we had done. I said to Michael, 'Give me Priscilla alone for a half hour in the next room.' . . . She had gotten away from the simple truth of the story, which was basically her own. . . . I said to her, 'Let's get back to the simple truth of it. No Las Vegas plastic performing tricks which somebody has added on.' When she did it again for the others, it was back to stay."

The song "And," originally performed as a self-contained unit, was merged with Bobby's monologue. The character Mike, played by Wayne Cilento, was supposed to have a song about what a performer goes through at an audition—based on Cilento's experience auditioning for *Seesaw*—but that song was never written and Cilento eventually inherited "I Can Do That." This was to have been done by Michael Misita, who dropped out. When Kleban, after having tried several openings, needed inspiration for the lyrics for "I Hope I Get It," the dancers were asked to come up with a list of things that made them feel insecure at an audition. And at the end of a day's rehearsal, Bennett, Avian, Hamlisch,

Kleban, and Fran Liebergall (who had been hired as rehearsal pianist for the second workshop and who eventually became the show's musical supervisor and one of its dance arrangers) would gather at the apartment of Bennett or Hamlisch, where much of the actual integration of music, lyrics, and dialogue was worked out.

While the score was being written, vocal and dance arrangements were begun.

PIPPIN: "As vocal arranger, I had to construct for people who were not really singers. You couldn't write the same for dancers, because they had to move when they sing. I learned that the simplest arrangement is often the most effective."

LIEBERGALL: "I was both vocal and dance arranger. Bobby Thomas and I did most of the dance arrangements, but it was all very collaborative. Michael would sing what he wanted, too. He *felt* the music so much that you could tell by watching him what he wanted. He inspired the arrangements just by being there and demonstrating. No one else performed the Cassie dance or 'Tits and Ass' as well as he did."

Bennett continued to work endless hours with the company on his staging of the big sequences, which by now were clearly defined as the opening, the montage, Cassie's dance (which was still not a solo and involved several male dancers), and "One." For the first occurrence of the latter, Bennett hit upon the brilliant device of integrating the dancers' rehearsal of the number with a confrontation between Zach and Cassie, which enhanced both the number and the dialogue scene. The only major dance sequence that was not worked on until after the workshops was the finale.

What is particularly noteworthy about Bennett's work with the dancers throughout the workshops was his willingness to take from them, and his reliance on their individual skills and personalities.

MCKECHNIE: "We improvised constantly. Michael did a lot of homework, but as he watched us he would get more and more ideas. While he always had definite ideas when he came in, he didn't know how to execute them without our bodies being there, and everyone contributed a lot to the staging."

DENNIS: "Once he had the final group of bodies there, much of the choreography changed. He would put us in groups of three or four to mutually choreograph sections, then he'd select the best. We'd work on steps for different parts of the montage, then he would look at it, pick certain things, and add his own stuff. It was a very collaborative effort, even though he tended to choose the work of the people he liked best or who he thought were better dancers."

CILENTO: "Bob Avian, Baayork Lee, Thommie Walsh, Sammy Williams, Donna and myself went into rooms and came up with steps. Michael came in with the whole vision in mind, cut, edited and put things together. He would come in and say, 'Let's do Thommie's step and Wayne's step, repeat that twice, then do Sammy's crossover.' . . . The choreography of the whole *show*, not just numbers, was what he was a genius at."

STEVENS: "For the montage, I was choreographing my group of four, Donna hers, and Baayork hers. He was not afraid to let *you* do it, in the style he dictated. He fashioned it, and he was the greatest editor ever."

To an outsider, the workshop was a fascinating example of art reflecting life, as director-choreographer Bennett put the dancers through the paces of a play about dancers being put through their paces by a director-choreographer.

PIPPIN: "The first day I walked into the workshop, I saw this maze of bodies doing what later became the opening number. There was no melody, and there were no lyrics yet; they were improvising words, chanting, 'I hope I get this show, I hope I get this show.' I didn't recognize the actor playing Zach who was in charge in the number, and my impression was that Michael, who was up on a high platform, was the director and this guy was the choreographer. I didn't realize they were running a number already rehearsed; it looked like it was just being set. I turned to Michael and said, 'I thought you were choreographing the show.' Michael was delighted that I was confused, and that I thought I had been watching the real process rather than a choreographed piece."

Bennett's designers were watching all the time, and during the latter part of the second workshop, they began to finalize their design ideas, abandoning earlier concepts for something much simpler and more organic to the play's content.

Several scenic concepts had been discussed throughout the workshops by Wagner and Bennett. One was to do the show on a bare stage, with only a white line across the floor, using the actual environment of the theatre in which the show was being performed. The other was an elaborate concept in which ideas in the songs were to have materialized, such as the miming of a toboggan trip during "Nothing." Wagner and Bennett also discussed a lavish four-part Ziegfeld finale with a huge staircase appearing. These concepts were abandoned in favor of an environment that reflected the show's subject.

WAGNER: "One day, when he was working in the mirrored studio on 19th Street, Michael said, 'I have to have mirrors.' He loved mirrors, from *Promises* to *Seesaw* to *Ballroom.* And it was a dance stage, so we knew it had to be black. Then it became apparent that we had to have a finale of some kind, and he decided he would dress them all up.

"That's when I came up with the old Greek device called a periaktoid, which is about two thousand years old. It's a three-sided device with a different scene on each side, and as you turn it, different vistas appear. We put eight sixteen-foot periaktoids on stage. Side A of each was black velour, side B was mirrors, and Side C, which we did not reveal until the finale, formed a deco sunburst.

"The set was conceived with the essential elements of the dancer's world in mind. The dance studio is surrounded by mirrors. The natural dance stage is a 'black box,' as Michael used to call it. And there is some form of backdrop. These are the three essential elements in the world of a dancer in Michael's vision of it. The periaktoid allowed him to add or subtract any of these elements instantaneously, and change the configuration constantly, so it was the perfect solution to the problem.

"The one other scenic element, the line, was there from day one. When he was auditioning dancers, he always put a line down.

"The mirrors were made out of a special light-weight mylar called Mirrex, which we found in the space program in Alabama . . . they've only been replaced twice in thirteen years; the velour has been replaced every three or four years.

"With Michael, everything was always an option, and we never settled on anything until around the time when you had to build it. When that time came with *A Chorus Line,* the idea of the periaktoid erased all others. It was a stripping away of options. It could have been a much bigger, lusher, heavier show. Instead, it became like a line drawing."

The options for the costume designer were not as great, as what was needed was obviously rehearsal clothes up until the finale, when the dancers quick-change into identical beige satin tuxedos and top hats. Yet the task of designing believable audition garb was not as easy as it might seem, for Aldredge, being a perfectionist like every member of Bennett's team, was interested in individualizing the characters through their attire.

ALDREDGE: "It is much more difficult to do a rehearsal garment than it is to do a beaded dress. To find a character in each dancer took us six months. I was in rehearsal every day with my Polaroid, and I watched the kids because they brought their own personalities, and I just borrowed from what they brought. . . . I took it as a compliment if people thought, 'Well, they're wearing their own clothes.' That is what it should look like.''*

Tharon Musser could have used the "real," hard light of a stage work light to create the aura of an audition, but it would not have blended with Wagner's visual embodiment of a dancer's existence, or with Aldredge's individualized, heightened designs. Musser was too much the artist to even consider reality when she could create a psychological lighting plot.

MUSSER: "We went through many ideas—at one point we were going to have the line lit under the floor. Michael was working on the whole 'inner thoughts' concept in his staging, and he said, 'We need something to help the audience know when we're in their head and when we're back to real life.' I said, 'We'll do it with color, and it won't be blue.' We used a deep lavender that has since been adopted by many other shows. Each character, with the exception of Bobby, had to have his or her own 'inner thoughts' light, and I decided to use 'down' lights instead of 'face' lights, to create off-colors.

"Lighting designers cannot show the director a model or sketches like the set and costumes designers can, so I showed Michael art books, saying, 'This is the kind of texture, the kind of color.' I decided to use a Mondrian pattern on the floor, and wherever the person happened to be, that became their special light."

WAGNER: "Michael wanted to keep the stage open for the lighting. He always thought in terms of light. He would do whole numbers for a lighting angle or sequence. In his imagination, the movement of light was as important as any other movement on stage, including the choreographic patterns. He choreographed lights, and was very concerned about their colors."

MUSSER: "What I remember about the workshops was the clarity, the simplification that occurred. . . . Less was better. Simple was better."

The changes in the lighting—from "work" lights, to "inner" lights, to a stage floor of stained-glass-like squares of color, to lighting that made the figures in line look like sculpture, to black—paralleled the constant

. . . .

*To Sheryl Flatow, *Playbill,* June 1982.

movement of Bennett's staging, and guided the audience into and out of the minds of the characters.

Although it was evident that the show was developing into a daring and original piece of work, it was not possible to avoid two crises—one occuring midway through the second workshop, the other at its end—that almost ended the relationship between *A Chorus Line* and the New York Shakespeare Festival.

MERLE DEBUSKEY, press representative for the Shakespeare Festival and later for *A Chorus Line* on Broadway: "There was a point where the show was almost aborted. . . . Joe had decided he didn't want to put any more money in it and extend the workshops any further. Joe had already spent perhaps the largest sum of money for a project that was not yet ready to go on. He said, 'Either put it on, or do whatever you want to do with it. I can't put in any more money.' Michael and Jack Lenny felt they had a number of producers who would have taken it on at that point. They had other avenues, but they really wanted to do it with Joe and the Shakespeare Festival. Bernie and I were very strong in our recommendation that the Festival continue with it. . . . We had a great emotional involvement in the show. We felt, given Michael's creative force and the originality of form the show was taking, it was almost obligatory to conclude it. In those days, Joe was willing to listen, then make up his mind based on what other people were telling him, and he changed his stance and decided to go on."

After doing the workshops at the Public Theater, Bennett was naturally prepared to open the show there, but he was almost prevented from doing so.

LENNY: "Near the end of the second workshop, Joe Papp went to Michael and said, 'I haven't any more money for the Newman Theater. I've used up that budget. I would like you to do *A Chorus Line* at the Vivian Beaumont. Michael said no. He felt it was not a show for the round or three-quarter stage, and that it would not work there. Michael called me and said, 'It looks like Joe's going to bow out of the show. Will you set up an audition for the Shuberts? Marvin, Ed and myself will go up and audition the show.' "

BERNARD B. JACOBS, president of the Shubert Organization: "They came up and played the score for us. You had the feeling that this was something that was important, although you really weren't quite sure what it was going to be. Michael had an idea about my producing it independently with him, which would mean leaving my job with the

Shubert Organization, which was absurd. But Michael, as always, was very intent upon what he was doing."

SOURCE: "Papp had told Bennett that he would have to come up with $100,000 to be able to do the show at the Newman. Papp persuaded the Shuberts to put up only half that amount after the audition. Bennett then called the Shuberts' rival, James M. Nederlander, who promised to put up the other half, even though Bennett had to inform him that Papp was going to move the show to a Shubert house if it went to Broadway. When this was reported to the Shuberts, they decided to put up all the necessary money, in the form of a grant to the Shakespeare Festival."

Throughout the second workshop, new cast members arrived while others departed; even late in the second workshop, no one was sure whether the show would go on to production immediately, and there was always the necessity of making a living. The workshop technique of development was so new that, to many, it didn't feel like an actual job.

BENNETT: "I had to keep motivating people, even though there really were no deadlines or opening dates. I had to make sure people didn't jump ship. There were a few people who did jump ship, and I thought, 'Good. Maybe it's right,' because it was a hard process for people to go through."

Jane Robertson, who was playing Bebe, left to do a leading role in an Off-Broadway musical that lasted one night, and she was replaced by Nancy Lane, who had been hired as an understudy. Tony Stevens withdrew to assist Fosse with the choreography of *Chicago,* a move that was to prove beneficial, as he was more interested in developing his career as a choreographer than as a performer. Clive Clerk joined the company to replace Stevens as Larry. Candy Brown, who was playing Angel, left to dance in *Chicago,* and her friend Ron Dennis took over her character, whose name was changed to Richie. Even Carole Bishop, who was one of Bennett's first casting choices, took other work between workshops, signing a six-month contract to tour in a featured role in *Irene.* Bennett had to buy out her *Irene* contract to get her back where she belonged. Don Percassi came in to play Al, because the actor who had been playing Al throughout the workshops, Robert LuPone, was suddenly called upon to move up to a pivotal role.

When the role of Zach was created for the second workshop, Bennett hired a rising actor named Barry Bostwick to play it. Bostwick would later become a Tony Award-winning stage performer and a much-sought-after television actor. However, Bostwick had two major problems with the part of Zach, and they would result in his dismissal by the end of the second workshop.

KIRKWOOD: "Barry, who is very talented, seemed to take on the hurt and the angst of the auditionees, and showed too much compassion. He emotionally joined their level, especially toward the end, and Michael kept saying, 'You can't do that. If you do, there are no opposites anymore. You've got to remain aloof and cold. . . . ' But Barry kept on going over that edge.

"He also wanted a musical number. As the lead male, it was understandable.

"After Michael let Barry go, Chris Sarandon was up to replace him. He came very close, and we all liked him. But he wasn't enough of a dancer, and Michael decided to up Bob LuPone."

DANTE: "Barry was let go because he was unable not to go for sympathy. He just couldn't be the villain, he couldn't be cold. He wanted to be liked."

PIPPIN: "Barry was very good. I think Michael was not totally comfortable with a person who has strong ideas about how they want to do something. He liked people who weren't quite that developed, who he could mold and manipulate."

Finally, at the end of the second workshop, *A Chorus Line* had its first run-through, open only to Papp and members of the company. On the basis of the run-through, Papp would have to decide whether or not to put the show into immediate production.

KIRKWOOD: "Our first run-through was about 4 hours and 20 minutes. We were exhausted watching; imagine how the dancers felt. We were all very disheartened. Michael said, 'We have twice the show we need.' "

LIEBERGALL: "When we did our first run-through, the show was known as 'War and Peace.' Everyone still had a Paul monologue, a traumatic sob story, and wound up crying. That was the kind of stuff that Michael made them use in their acting later, but it didn't have to be expressed on stage."

STEVENS: "The run-through was long and depressing. It had the catharsis that had happened at the talk sessions without anything entertaining added. It was like all these dancers throwing up. It was great to go through, but then you thought, 'Who's going to buy a ticket for this?' I don't think even Michael knew at that point what was going to make it work."

BENNETT: "We had a disastrous 4 and ½ hour run-through. It was a disaster in that every single character, every single actor, decided to make himself the tragic character of the piece. . . . You've never seen so much self-pity in your life as there was in that run-through. Of course, two-thirds of that was cut."

Somehow, the excitement of what had been occurring in the workshops in the past weeks managed to convey itself to the powers that be, and A Chorus Line was placed in rehearsal for immediate production. The first public performance was only six weeks away.

While the workshop technique employed for A Chorus Line now seems the inevitable way to have shaped the material at hand, it was not such an obvious choice in 1974. Jerome Robbins had given up working in the commercial theatre because he recognized that it was impossible to achieve his goals with five weeks of rehearsal and four weeks out of town. He attempted to develop musicals at his American Theatre Lab, but no production ever emerged, so it was difficult to gauge how successful this earlier attempt at a musical workshop situation had been.

What were the particular advantages offered by the workshop system that made it ideal for the development of A Chorus Line?

First, the cast was available to the writers at all times. They were able to get to know the actors, and to use this familiarity to create characters that would later allow the actors to give performances of remarkable verisimilitude.

Allowing the cast to be in on every aspect of the show as it was being developed—from staging to writing—gave the dancers, who now realized they were actors who could talk, a feeling of belonging that made the experience unique. The development process actually helped the actors when it came time to repeating their performances again and again.

MCKECHNIE: "The process was the most important thing, and because of the way the show was created, we were able to keep it spontaneous later. If you do the right kind of work in rehearsal, it'll never let you down in performance. . . . We were able to take the time to work the right way, allowing all the possibilities, not narrowing it down to the literal or the obvious, not limiting our options."

Another great advantage offered by the workshop process is that decisions on sets, costumes, lighting, orchestrations, and arrangements do not have to be made prior to or near the commencement of rehearsals, as they usually are. As the material developed, the requirements gradually became evident, and this saved a tremendous amount of money.

Above all, it was the luxury of time—time to try anything, to fail—and the lack of commercial pressure that made the workshop period so special for all involved.

KIRKWOOD: "Suppose we had opened in Boston with the show running over three hours. Everybody would have said, 'It's too long. Cut that and that, change that.' There would have been panic. I remember Michael being very calm the night of the endless run-through, even though he said, 'Look. We really have major surgery to do.'"

DANTE: "The workshops gave us time to find it, as opposed to having to just do it. . . . Michael could have workshopped the show and refined further and further. I said to him, 'When are you going to stop already?'"

HAMLISCH: "The beautiful thing about workshop is you try something out, it fails, and you don't have to shoot yourself. You just know that tomorrow you'll try something else out. If you try something out in Philadelphia and it fails, you're in a lot of trouble."

MCKECHNIE: "We had the luxury and the time to do all the wrong things. Michael's vision and his way of evaluating made the show, but in order for him to really see what was there, he had to see everything, what was going on underneath, the subtext. Too often, people don't have the time or the money to do that."

BENNETT: "The luxury of *A Chorus Line* is illustrated by what I was able to do with the 20-minute montage. . . . We spent six weeks on it, finished it, and decided we hated the song, which was the basis of the whole 20 minutes. So they wrote a better song, which meant that every single thing that was done had to be re-done, and it took us four weeks to fix something we had worked on for six weeks. But in a workshop, it was not a disaster."

Finding out one could do shows in a workshop situation changed Bennett's career and his entire outlook on the theatre.

AVIAN: "The show could have been done without workshops. . . . But when Michael heard from Joe about these workshops, his eyes went, 'Blink, blink, blink.' Michael loved to rehearse more than anybody in the world. He would never open if he didn't have to."

4

. . . .

A CHORUS LINE

GOES PUBLIC

FORMAL REHEARSALS BEGAN IN March, with an actual first preview and opening date in sight. By this time, Bennett had been so close to the material for so long that he began to worry about its believability. He took the opportunity offered by an audition for understudies to check the veracity of his vision.

DANTE: "Michael was afraid people would accuse him or the show of being unbelievable, not like a real audition. He thought people would question how far we were going in the revelations. So he decided to act out what happens in the show. He sat back at understudy auditions and did Zach's opening speech: 'I'm doing a show, I want you to tell me about yourselves.' As each talked, each revealed a little more, and by the time he got to the tenth person, that person was discussing his nervous breakdown. Michael was satisfied that the show was not far-fetched, and that dancers would reveal themselves for a job."

While Bennett was in no way prepared to stop working on the show, he realized that the company was beginning to need the feedback that only an audience could offer.

KIRKWOOD: "Michael noticed one day after rehearsal how dead the cast was getting. I said, 'All they've got to look at is you and me and Marvin and Ed. We're not laughing at the funny lines anymore. I think it's time to throw them to the lions.' So on a Sunday afternoon in early April, about two weeks before public previews were to begin, we did a run-through at the Newman Theater before an invited group of about 50 people. It was done with just piano and drums, there were no mirrors, and it went incredibly.''

It was now time to stage the finale, a section of the staging that had been largely ignored throughout the workshops.

AVIAN:. "The finale was the last thing we staged, just before we began previews. . . . For the finale, we knew we'd start with the bows, then build to 'One.' For the big V formation, we used the wedge from a number called 'Blaze On' which we'd done in a Milliken Breakfast Show. . . . We staged it in four hours, and never had to change it. It took as long to stage as it took them to learn it, because we had it in our heads.''

Bennett was still far from satisfied with many aspects of the show, and intended to try many different versions of scenes and numbers in the coming weeks. But he was aware that he had produced an extraordinary piece of work, and that he was in need of only one element to help him with the final shaping of the show: an audience. It was time to let them in.

CAROLE SCHWEID, understudy for the roles of Diana and Bebe, recalls: "Up until the first preview, Michael wanted everybody not to make a big fuss. He said, 'Let's not hype this thing up so that people will come expecting. Let's keep it a surprise.' There was going to be an invited audience the night before the first preview. The morning of that night, Michael said we could all invite two or three people. The friends I invited couldn't believe what they were seeing. People were devastated.''

The first formal public preview took place April 16, 1975, and the reaction was immediate and explosive, with reverberations that quickly traveled throughout the city.

LENNY: "After the first preview, Marvin, Ed, Michael and I went for a drink. I said, 'I don't know whether you guys know it or not, but you're sitting on a once-in-a-lifetime thing.' ''

DEBUSKEY: "The theatre is a small community, a tightly interwoven society, and there are virtually no secrets. The word spread like crazy, and by the time performances began, there was enormous anticipation in the little world of the theatre. It became bedlam in terms of people trying to get in.''

Packed celebrity-filled audiences were the rule throughout previews, which lasted through May 20. The show became the hottest preview ticket in New York history, with many lining up for cancellations, which were unlikely to occur in the 299-seat Newman Theater. Folding chairs were put in for some VIPs, while Liza Minnelli and others were content to sit on the steps. Many made numerous repeat visits before the opening.

TUNE: "I saw *A Chorus Line* during previews over and over and over. It was the story of our lives, and I was brokenhearted that I wasn't in it. But I had become too well-known by then and I would have thrown off the balance."

The morning after the second preview, producers Cy Feuer and Ernest Martin offered to buy an option on the movie rights for $150,000 and were turned down. Ironically, it would be Feuer and Martin who would produce the film version years later, after many others had tried and failed.

The near-hysterical fervor with which the show was greeted every night during previews was not lost on the cast, but they were too exhausted from rehearsing all day to fully enjoy it. And some began to question the response.

MCKECHNIE: "The word was out that it was hot, and people were flying in from the west coast and London. I thought it was just a trendy thing, and I didn't appreciate the magnitude of it. It was wonderful to realize that our work was paying off, but it was still playing to a very show-biz crowd, a very insular group."

A Chorus Line was now in a unique position: It was a hit before it opened. In recent years, such musicals as *Cats, Les Misérables,* and *The Phantom of the Opera* have arrived on Broadway as certified hits, but they had already won acclaim in London and involved names that guaranteed box-office success. Bennett had gone out of his way to keep the workshops out of the public eye, the show contained no star names, and, of the writers, only Hamlisch was known to the public, and not for writing shows. Even Bennett, although an award-winning director-choreographer who had earned the highest respect of his peers, was not the kind of directorial "name," as Champion, Fosse, and Prince, that sold tickets. It was the public that made *A Chorus Line* into a must-see hit before it opened anywhere, and that was unprecedented.

Some of those who kept returning to *A Chorus Line* during previews went back to watch Bennett, the master editor, change, refine, focus, and fine tune an already superb show. And, in spite of the tumultuous reaction, there were changes aplenty throughout the five weeks of previews.

There was still indecision about how to introduce the Cassie character, and a late, "star" entrance was tried at several previews, then abandoned. Ultimately, it was determined that subtle hints about Cassie within the introductory sequence would tell the audience more than singling her out, and she became part of the line when it first formed.

There were many changes in the musical numbers, most notably the late addition during previews of a new song for Mike (Wayne Cilento) that was heard only once.

CILENTO: "The number I had been doing in previews, 'I Can Do That,' was the first number Michael choreographed, and he had become dissatisfied with it because of the way the rest of the show had turned out. 'I Can Do That' was now the only male solo in the show, and very different in style from everything else. . . . So they wrote 'Joanne,' about how a little girl I had a crush on in school got me to go to my first dance class. It was staged MGM-style, very Gene Kelly. I did it once and Michael said, 'It's not right for the show.' I said, 'Give me another chance. I only did it once.' He said no. I now had to convince myself that 'I Can Do That,' which went back in, was a good number after he had told me that it was wrong for the show."

"The Music and the Mirror" had finally been settled on as the song for Cassie's big solo spot, but its staging and dance arrangement were to change during previews.

MCKECHNIE: "At one point during previews, I was doing 'Music and the Mirror' with four boys. It was a show about chorus dancers behind stars. . . . The boys came on in black outfits, moved the mirrors out from the wings, then danced the whole final section with me. It was exciting, but the statement wasn't as clear and powerful as Cassie dancing alone. The number was really about her isolation, her relationship with Zach and her identity with the mirrors."

No one was happy with the music accompanying Cassie's dance during early previews.

THOMAS: "We were losing the lines of that body. She was jerking all over the place. I asked Marvin to simplify the music. Finally, I arranged a meeting between Harold Wheeler and Michael."

WHEELER: "Having worked on *Promises,* I knew Donna inside out. . . . Michael asked me to see the show, and I loved it and agreed to do the number. . . . We worked for two or three days with Donna. I went home, wrote and orchestrated it, and it went into the show and worked. I declined Michael's offer of billing, because by that point in my career I didn't want to share credit with other orchestrators."

One arrangement that was scheduled to be added during previews proved unnecessary.

PIPPIN: "Michael had me write a big, show-bizzy, Vegas-style vocal arrangement for the 'One' finale. The kids worked very hard to learn it, but by the time previews started, Michael had only had time to throw together a temporary finale without this arrangement. But that finale turned out to be so fabulous that we never had to put this other one in, which would have been an even bigger number, with a spotlight indicating the missing star referred to."

The title "Dance: Ten, Looks: One" was changed to "Dance: Ten, Looks: Three," and the number was shortened, a section in which Val recreated a strip routine eliminated. "Nothing" came close to being jettisoned yet again.

PIPPIN: "When previews began, it was a much longer number, with other people on stage miming bobsleds, the cathedral, etc. There was even one chorus in Spanish. Michael didn't think the number worked, but I said, 'You don't need all those people on stage.' Suddenly, 'Nothing' was Priscilla alone, and shortened."

The most serious bone of contention among the musical numbers was the big "eleven o'clock" ballad, "What I Did for Love." Most of the songs in the score were specifically about dancers and their life experiences, and Hamlisch felt that the show needed to have at least one number that could easily be extracted and sung on radio and television. Kleban detested it and Papp suggested it be cut, but Hamlisch prevailed and it remained. Hamlisch later admitted that it did stick out from the rest of the score, but felt vindicated when the song became the only one in the score to achieve popularity outside of the show.

Throughout previews, Bennett continued to maintain the atmosphere of an audition by not letting the cast know which performers would be "hired" at the conclusion of each performance. While everyone had by now been contracted and the suspense was no longer as real as it had been in the workshops, this device kept the cast from becoming complacent. It soon had to be abandoned, however, as it wreaked havoc in the wardrobe department. The performers must do a very quick change into the finale costumes, and the boys who appear on stage first in the finale are those who are cut at the end. Wardrobe was far more comfortable when it knew in advance which characters would be cut and would be coming offstage first, so the eight characters selected soon became fixed.

With most of the characters, getting chosen at the end didn't seem to make a substantial difference, but a brouhaha developed over whether or not Cassie should be picked at the conclusion. The Cassie character was begging for a chance to start over, and audiences became upset at preview performances in which Zach rejected her at the conclusion. While Cassie was obviously overqualified for the job and a threat to Zach, audiences could not accept her being denied a second chance.

MCKECHNIE: "You can't put your life on the line and not get it. Cassie was saying that you have to face yourself and declare, 'This is what I want to do, no matter what others think. I deserve the right to make my life the way I want it. . . .' You couldn't then say, 'You can't have it.' Michael believed that she would not get it in real life, and he always tried doing things realistically first before taking license."

KIRKWOOD: "Michael thought it was more poignant when she didn't get it. He said, 'She's overqualified.' I said, 'But she wants to do it. And if she's that good, you can't not pick the one who's best.' "

DANTE: "I had a big fight with Michael about Cassie getting picked at the end. I was really annoyed when they ultimately gave her the job. I really believed that Zach wouldn't hire her. Zach was Michael—I was writing it as Michael. Michael would not have hired her, he would have been afraid of her. With Michael, you were out the door if you were a threat. . . . I told Michael he was selling out when he gave her the job. But I think Michael was ultimately correct."

Ultimately, the decision to hire Cassie at the end was due more to the campaigning of actress Marsha Mason, who became an early fan of the show and an observer, than to the desires of any of the show's creative staff.

MCKECHNIE: "Marsha was helpful by following the throughline of the character as it was developing in previews. Marsha was there to follow me and the character . . . to see what made sense and what didn't."

KIRKWOOD: "Marsha Mason was the one who really grabbed Michael by the throat and said, 'You've got to give her the job.' "

Mason's unshakable belief that everyone was entitled to go back and get a second chance carried the day. But Mason's involvement in the show was actually due to the sudden, largely sub-rosa involvement of her then-husband, Neil Simon.

Bennett began his "gypsy" years on Broadway with *Subways Are for Sleeping* in 1961. Above, he is extreme right at a rehearsal (lead Sydney Chaplin is center). [Billy Rose Theatre Collection, The New York Public Library at Lincoln Center, Astor, Lenox and Tilden Foundations] Below, he is the third Santa from the right, executing the exciting Michael Kidd choreography. [Billy Rose Theatre Collection]

A little girl's fantasy birthday party as a Michael Kidd dream ballet in *Here's Love,* 1963. Bennett is the rag doll being rescued by Gene Kelton's fireman, as leading lady Janis Paige looks on. [Billy Rose Theatre Collection]

In *Bajour* (1964), Bennett (above, extreme right) was an extra in the Guggenheim Museum scene, and an actual gypsy (below, third man from the left at top) otherwise. *Bajour* marked Bennett's last appearance on Broadway. [Both courtesy of Billy Rose Theatre Collection]

Bennett choreographed extensively in summer and winter stock in the Sixties. Here are Bennett and his assistant Leland Palmer dancing Bennett's version of "Steam Heat" in *The Pajama Game,* Phoenix Star Theatre, 1965. [Both courtesy of Leland Palmer]

Bennett became a Broadway choreographer in 1966 with the short-lived *A Joyful Noise.* Top, he rehearses John Raitt, Leland Palmer, and company. [Billy Rose Theatre Collection] Right, Palmer stands on Tommy Tune's head [Billy Rose Theatre Collection], and bottom, Tune stands out in one of Bennett's production numbers. [Billy Rose Theatre Collection]

Henry, Sweet Henry (1967) was another routine musical choreographed by Bennett, but again Bennett's work stood out and earned him his second Tony nomination. Above, the young ladies of Norton School in the opening [Billy Rose Theatre Collection]; below, the Act II hippie ballet. [Billy Rose Theatre Collection]

Promises, Promises (1968), the first Bennett hit. While the show was still conventional, Bennett's work went beyond convention, and every dancer at "The Grapes of Roth" (rehearsed above, Bob Avian center [Billy Rose Theatre Collection]) or at Clancy's Lounge (below) was given a character to play. [Billy Rose Theatre Collection]

Coco Chanel (Katharine Hepburn) opens her scrapbook to show Noelle (Gale Dixon) highlights of the rebellion she launched in women's clothes, and the past came magically to life in the "Money Rings Out Like Freedom" sequence. *Coco*, 1969. [Billy Rose Theatre Collection]

Hepburn and Bennett clashed, but she ultimately came to trust him. He managed to get his nondancing star aloft (above, in "Orbach's, Bloomingdale's, Best & Saks"), and center stage in the red-dress parade finale, "Always Mademoiselle" (below). [Billy Rose Theatre Collection]

Choreographing nerve ends: the opening/title number of the landmark Sondheim-Prince musical *Company*, 1970, above. At left, Donna McKechnie embodies isolation during intimacy in "Tick-Tock," in Act II. (McKechnie's costume was altered to a one-piece nightgown by the time the show reached Broadway.) [Martha Swope]

"Side by Side by Side" and "What Would We Do Without You ?," the opening of *Company*'s second act, with Bennett using vaudeville hokum for dramatic purposes. [Martha Swope]

Past and present collide in the passionate, terrifying *Follies,* 1971. Above, Vincent and Vanessa (right, Victor Griffin and Jayne Turner) go into their old routine as Young Vincent and Young Vanessa (Michael Misita and Graciela Daniele) materialize in "Bolero d'Amour." Below, "Live, Laugh, Love": the chorus line goes on hoofing as Ben has a nervous breakdown in "a supper club in Loveland." [Martha Swope]

"Lord, Lord, Lord, that woman is me!": The past mirrored by the present, in *Follies*'s "Who's That Woman?," arguably the best number in Broadway history. [Martha Swope]

Harold Prince and Bennett co-directing *Follies*. Prince made Bennett co-director to keep him, but Bennett was ready to create on his own. [Martha Swope]

Bennett directs his first nonmusical, *Twigs* (1971), with the dazzling Sada Thompson. Stephen Sondheim and George Furth provided one ditty, "Hollywood and Vine," performed by Thompson as the tragic Celia. Below, Thompson and Bennett form a mutual admiration society. [Martha Swope]

Tommy Tune triumphed in the "balloon number," "It's Not Where You Start," in *Seesaw*, 1973. [Mike Roberts] But not before Bennett saw fit to fire Bill Starr and leading lady Lainie Kazan and remove most of original choreographer Grover Dale's material. (Starr, Kazan, and Dale above at rehearsal.) [Bert Andrews]

DANTE: "One night during previews, Jimmy and I went to the theatre and there were about eight new lines in the show, wonderfully funny ones. We assumed Michael had written them—even though he wasn't really a writer, we thought he got inspired. . . . It wasn't until about nine years later that Michael told us that Neil had written those lines, which really annoyed me. Neil's lines were mostly in Sheila's monologue, like 'Sometimes I'm agressive,' or 'The other months better watch out.' And I think Morales's line about the Bronx, 'It's uptown and to the right,' was his. But eight lines does not a doctor make, and it disturbed me that Neil allowed that rumor to take hold. Perhaps his lines plus Marsha's involvement in the ending made him feel he was a doctor to the show."

Other parties involved indicate that Simon's involvement in the final text was more substantial than Dante or Kirkwood were permitted to know.

AVIAN: "Neil punched up the comedy. He contributed to Bobby's monologue, the lines about astro-turf on the patio and rearranging furniture. But this was a big secret. Michael had these lines on the floor between his feet, and would say in rehearsal, 'Thommie, why don't you try saying this?' "

CAROLE (later Kelly) BISHOP: "Neil wrote the dialogue into 'Tits and Ass.' He wrote a new monologue for Sheila, which I performed one night during previews. It made me a tough, mean, tacky bitch. When the performance ended . . . I said I would never do that again, and if Michael liked it, another actress could do it. . . . Michael admitted it was a mistake."

Some felt Bennett was crazy to make so many changes in a show that was receiving wild ovations and perhaps the strongest word-of-mouth in the history of the theatre, but he was a perfectionist. Don Pippin was witness to an incident late in previews that illuminates both Bennett's perfectionism and his ability to manipulate a company.

PIPPIN: "Just before opening night, he needed the company to waive an Equity rule so he could have an extra rehearsal to put a change in. It was a happy family, but the vote was no. Michael gathered the company on stage, and addressed them with tears in his eyes. He said how disappointed he was in them, how he intended to make stars of all of them when the show went uptown, and that as far as he was concerned, *A Chorus Line* had ended at that moment. He said he was sorry he had ever gotten involved in the show, and that he had never been so let down in his life. He walked offstage, and the cast was stunned. As he exited, he came face to face with me, his back to the cast, and as he passed me, he said, 'How was I?' with a twinkle in his eye. It was the most calculated thing. And five minutes later the company came to him and he got his rehearsal."

Just before opening night, many were confident, but no one could have expected the full magnitude of the success they were about to have.

KLEBAN: "The week before we opened, I had been paid between $500 and $1000 for the whole year's work, and I had no idea whether I'd ever be paid another dime. I didn't regret it; I had had fun, and I'd taken it for the experience. But whether the hysteria going on down at the New-man was just a bunch of cognoscenti and we'd run three weeks to the in-crowd of New York, or whether we'd sweep the world—I had no idea."

HAMLISCH: "I remember a conversation I had with Michael the day before we got reviewed. I said to him, 'We all know that we love this show. We made all the changes we felt were important, everything is ready to go. What happens if this show is a bomb?' He looked at me and asked, 'Did you like working on it?' I said I loved it. He asked, 'Do you think you did your best work?' I said, 'I sure did.' He said, 'Do you think you wasted any time?' I said no. He said, 'That's all you can do.' "

While it was difficult for Bennett to "freeze" the show, to give such a dynamic piece permanent form, it was now out of his hands. On open-ing night, May 21, 1975, Papp sent Bennett a note that read, "Michael, please come and fail at the Newman Theater anytime you want."

The response of the opening-night audience was tumultuous, but the reviews were the real surprise. By now, all concerned had every reason to believe they would be good, even excellent. But the original reviews *A Chorus Line* received amount to one of the most perceptive sets of critical notices a musical has ever gotten. Themes were clearly per-ceived, the emotional impact registered, the complex staging tech-niques were at least noticed, the performances appreciated, the design lauded, and the underlying honesty of the show understood. Other landmark shows such as *West Side Story, Gypsy,* and *Company,* while well received, had not been nearly as fortunate at the hands of the critics the first time around.

Clive Barnes, *The New York Times:* "The conservative word for *A Chorus Line* might be tremendous, or perhaps terrific . . . the reception was so shattering that it is surprising if, by the time you read this, the New

York Shakespeare Festival has got a Newman Theater still standing. . . . It is a show that must dance, jog and whirl its way into the history of the musical theater."

Walter Kerr, *The New York Times:* " . . . the sense of . . . an entire show being born on the spot, taking shape as we watch. Mr. Bennett *has* actually developed *A Chorus Line* out of six month's improvisation, teasing its myriad pieces into an ultimately miraculous pattern. The accomplishment is brilliant."

Martin Gottfried, *New York Post:* "It is a major event in the development of the American musical theater. . . . With this show, Bennett steps out on his own as a star director-choreographer . . . one whose staging wizardry and theatrical muscle are deepened by a swelling humanity. He is now a major creative force and *A Chorus Line* is purely and simply magnificent, capturing the very soul of our musical theater."

Jack Kroll, *Newsweek:* "What seals things tight is the heart-gripping sincerity of the performers and the rare intensity of the entire show, which builds to an overpowering emotional climax."

John Simon, *New York* magazine: "So authentic, interesting and, finally, innovative . . . *A Chorus Line* is something new and historic in musical comedy, the first musical-verité . . . what the show captures admirably is the curious duality that makes this underbelly of show business at once exceedingly soft and hard as nails. . . . You can find faults in *A Chorus Line,* even incontrovertible and not inconsiderable ones. But, in the last analysis, they don't matter."

The sole dissenter, William Glover in the Associated Press, sounded a note that would soon become a matter of concern: "For members of the profession and ardent buffs, *A Chorus Line* appears a cinch triumph. For civilians less involved, the mundane tribulations which form so much of the show could be a severe handicap to bounding delight."

Ticket prices were immediately raised after opening night, and the ticket demand became intense. The cast was now making two hundred dollars a week, the celebrities, from Margot Fonteyn to Ingrid Bergman, continued to pour in, and the show became the most talked-about in years. The run at the Public was marred only by much cast illness, the result of months of exhausting effort.

CILENTO: "We were all deathly sick at the Newman. I remember vaporizers and B-12 and C shots before shows. But we went on anyway."

LIEBERGALL: "One night at the Public Theatre, Donna McKechnie and Carole Bishop were out, and there was only one understudy for both, so they cut the role of Sheila for two shows. Bebe did some of Sheila's dialogue in the interview section, and 'At the Ballet' became a duet. Some of Sheila's best lines were given to Greg and other characters with attitude. After that happened, there were emergency sheets created about what happens if a certain performer cannot finish a show, and at what point other actors inherit that performer's lines."

Bennett was fond of saying during this period that he would like to keep the show at the Public Theater forever. But there was no use pretending that this was even a possibility. Even at sell-out level and higher ticket prices, *A Chorus Line* was losing more than one thousand dollars a week, owing to the size of the cast and orchestra. It was clearly the salvation of the Shakespeare Festival, which had capped a lackluster season at the Beaumont and the Public with the biggest musical hit in a decade. Audiences were clamoring to get in, and the show had the size and feel of a Broadway smash even at the Newman Theater. During previews, Papp and Bennett had discussed moving to Broadway. By the time it opened at the Public, they had decided to move it uptown, and as quickly as possible.

5

....

BOOK, MUSIC, AND LYRICS

THE BOOK

IT IS VIRTUALLY IMPOSSIBLE to separate the book, score, and staging components of *A Chorus Line* and discuss them as distinct elements. Not only are they totally integrated in the play, but because of the material's development in workshop, they were all created together and became inextricable. Nevertheless, an analysis of each component will indicate the achievement, and why the show had such an immediate and staggering effect on audiences.

A Chorus Line is not actually about a chorus line until the end, when the final choices are made. Until then, it's about trying to get into a chorus line and the painful but necessary process of auditioning. It is fundamentally a documentary, dealing with a real-life situation that every original cast member had undergone countless times.

Of course, the authors used this audition metaphorically, so *A Chorus Line* is also about putting oneself on the line, offering oneself up and facing rejection. Everyone has had an interview for a job or position at some time in his or her life, and the experience of the dancers in *A Chorus Line* is thus a universal one.

The show is about feelings of pain, isolation, and sexual awakening, about family problems and leaving home, about childhood, youth, adolescence, and maturity—experiences revealed by the dancers at the tape sessions, which, brought to vivid theatrical life, became experiences that struck profound chords in every observer.

A Chorus Line examines the fierce discipline, hard work, and devotion that is required to wind up "only" in the chorus, backing a star but never becoming one. Like Tom Stoppard's *Rosencrantz and Guildenstern Are Dead, A Chorus Line* probes the existence of the invisible "little" people, ignoring the stars. It examines that which drives people into the theatre, and is also about dance itself—what it means to those who do it and what it costs them to do it well.

On another level, *A Chorus Line* is about the changes in the musical theatre that have taken place during the past thirty-five years. With the combination of singing and dancing choruses and the shrinking of both due to economics, performers in the chorus of musicals were forced to become increasingly skilled and versatile, while their opportunities to demonstrate these skills had become fewer and fewer.

A Chorus Line was also a backstage musical, and thus part of a lineage that includes *Kiss Me, Kate, Funny Girl, Me and Juliet, Follies,* the film *42nd Street,* and *Applause.* It is worth pausing to examine the latter, a Broadway hit of 1970.

Applause, based on the film *All About Eve* and the story by Mary Orr, was a solidly constructed, thoroughly conventional musical, but it was also the only musical prior to *A Chorus Line* to devote its attention, at least in part, to the Broadway gypsy, the chorus dancers who, in *Applause,* faded away when the star (Lauren Bacall) and her up-and-coming young rival fought it out center stage, but who appeared in between plot scenes in numbers paying tribute to the indomitability of the gypsy. The show's title number was about that which made all the hard work, lessons, low pay, and injury worthwhile—applause. In "What I Did for Love," the *Chorus Line* gypsies tell us that love is what they do it all for. But "applause" was translated in the title song of the earlier musical as "the sound that says love," so it's not terribly dissimilar.

However, *Applause* chose to deal with the hard realities of the gypsy life in a light, tongue-in-cheek fashion, washing away all the hardship with the sound of an audience clapping. It remained for *A Chorus Line* to portray the reality and raise it to a universal statement. Interestingly, the cast of *Applause* on Broadway included Nicholas Dante, Sammy Williams, Carol Petri (who later changed her name to Mitzi Hamilton), and Renee Baughman.

Bennett asked George Furth whether he could steal the original title of *Twigs* for his new musical, and Furth replied, "You can have anything you want from me." Bennett especially liked the fact that it was A *Chorus Line,* rather than The *Chorus Line,* the former offering more metaphoric resonance.

The achievement of Dante, Kirkwood, and Bennett in the book can best be understood if one examines how the text developed from first workshop to second to final script.

FIRST WORKSHOP SCRIPT

In this script, there are no songs yet, although there are indications of where a couple of them might later appear. Here, the play begins with a steel door upstage opening to admit a group of dancers to a "fourth callback"; in the final version, we don't know how many times the dancers have been there, only that it's the final audition.

The interrogator is called only "Voice," there are no characters named Cassie or Bebe, but there are characters named Steve and Angel, who are not in the final version. Maggie, like Cassie later, has had a relationship with the "Voice," Angel rather than Richie is black, and Val makes a late entrance. After the characters are introduced, an unwritten number called "Resume" was to be performed.

The stories told by the auditioners contain some of the same material as in later versions, much that was cut, and a good deal that was later musicalized or given to other characters. Maggie, the Cassie character at this stage, tells of her traumatic childhood and running away from home to dance. Al is athletic and tells about the advances made to him by a gay student when he attended the High School of Performing Arts, which leads to the dredging up of a fight between Al and Greg. Paul's monologue, though similar to the final version, contains additional incidents later eliminated, and Val offers an amusing and lengthy account of her dance training, with only a brief reference to the plastic surgery that would later become the focus of her story.

While the basic interview structure is already there, what is radically different in the original script is the use of side conversations between pairs of characters. These conversations perform a function similar to the "inner thoughts" that are revealed musically in the final version, a far smoother and subtler means of filling in character detail. In the first workshop, the characters' spoken stories were frequently interrupted by pairs of dancers renewing old acquaintances, catching up on recent history, and revealing past relationships that bear on the present situation. We learn that Al has never gotten along with the "Voice," that Connie expects to be assistant to the "Voice," and that Maggie lived with the "Voice" for a time. These side scenes are overtly expository in a way that is carefully avoided in the final version. There is no trace of the montage sequence about adolescence and sexual awakening, and the kids sit on the line until chairs are brought out for them.

SECOND WORKSHOP SCRIPT

While the authors had come a long way by the second workshop script, jarring changes of mood, excessive melodrama, and choppy structure are still in evidence. This version also contains several beautifully written passages dropped by the time the show opened.

We are at a "third callback" this time, and Cassie (formerly Maggie) does not arrive until the introductions scene has begun. She is not in rehearsal clothes, asks for money to pay the cab driver she has left waiting, and then departs. She is discussed by the others: We learn she's been great in a couple of shows, she knows Zach, and she's suffered a nervous breakdown. How much less effective this is than the final version, wherein a few nervous remarks indicate the tension between her and Zach, left unexplained until midway through the evening. At the end of the introductions sequence, Diana sings "Resume."

Again, there are numerous differences in the stories told. Bobby reveals a far more pathological history of setting fires and enjoying electrical storms; Kristine tells about how she felt leaving home; Diana, an old friend of Zach's, recalls childhood dance recitals; and Don tells how his mother, a dance teacher, urged him against his will to study dance. He grew to like it, but when he went on the road at fifteen in *Hello, Dolly!*, his mother, accompanying him as chaperone, drowned at a San Diego beach. Val's story contains sordid descriptions of the strip joints in which she played after her operation. After Al tells of beating up a homosexual who made advances toward him during a *West Side Story* tour, Greg reminds Al that he also attacked him when Greg playfully swatted him on the behind once. Al and Greg get into a fight and have to be separated by others.

Cassie is given two distinct scenes. In the first, she tells a story omitted in the final version, about how, when fifteen, she got a call to tour the South. When her parents refused to give her the money to go, she raised it by putting on a private show for the local boys in which she exposed her body. Her father followed her and took her back and into juvenile court. In her second scene, in striking contrast to the Cassie of the final version, Cassie begins by accusing Zach of humiliating her by putting her through a chorus audition and treating her like the others. The stories of her needing a job and of the relationship between Zach and her follow, but are far less effective without the insistent "One" routine behind them, as in the final version. Cassie's scene is capped by a superbly written description of her nervous breakdown—which Zach missed—which began when she attempted to vacuum her cat into oblivion.

The side scenes in this version include conversations between Don and Sheila, in which Don talks of his impending divorce; Cassie and Sheila, who comment on Diana's verbosity and commiserate about what they're going through; and Kristine and Diana.

After Cassie's scene, Al appears to apologize to Zach for his behavior, and Zach lets Al know that his personality has already cost him the job. Zach goes off to take a phone call, and there follows a scene of rebellion involving all the dancers, making mock of the experience they're enduring. Greg pretends to be Zach, satirizing Zach's questions and making amusing comments about Zach's authoritarian instincts. Zach returns, overhears some of this, but lets them off the hook by revealing his human side, which is developed far more subtly in the final version. This earlier version also contains ten pages of lines that were later used as the basis of the "Hello Twelve" montage, without any structure or unifying device as of yet.

THE FINAL SCRIPT

The final script, of course, reflects the total integration of song and musical sequence that is the outstanding characteristic of *A Chorus Line*. For that reason, it is difficult to discuss this version solely as a text, apart from the musical numbers and staging one would experience with it in the theatre.

The final version can be roughly divided into eight sections of unequal length. In the opening sequence, which culminates in the first elimination, there are numerous subtle touches of characterization, such as Judy forgetting her number, or Sheila deliberately forgetting the combination when asked to demonstrate it upstage.

This is followed by the introductions sequence, filled with amusing and charming moments. The brief exchange between Cassie and Zach is the only jarring element, establishing a tension and setting her apart from the others.

Zach explains that he needs four girls and four boys to form the chorus of a new musical but adds that he wants to hear them talk about their lives and get to know them. This device, upon which the rest of the show depends, is open to criticism and has received a certain amount over the years. At a real audition, a director would rarely have the time or interest to listen to seventeen dancers relate their life stories; nor would it be particularly relevant to the task at hand.

Yet the device, a trick that enables the rest of the show to function, must be deemed pardonable. It was necessary to find a way to allow the characters to emerge as individuals, and the manner chosen is the best solution. If the audition in *A Chorus Line* strays from a strictly realistic portrayal, it still manages to include a sufficient number of the mundane aspects of a real audition.

The fourth sequence takes up most of the show's running time. The seventeen dancers tell their stories, and they are told through a mixture of spoken word, song, dance, interior monologue, inner thought, and stream of consciousness. Some of the stories are self-contained, some are interrupted by others, and some start and are continued later.

Some members of the audience may have been concerned at this point that they were about to hear seventeen different stories, all about characters whose lives overlap strikingly. But the director and writers of the show were able to vary the method of storytelling, so that one is constantly surprised. Some stories are told almost entirely in song (Diana, Kristine), some are related almost completely in a monologue (Paul, Bobby), and some mix song and dance in equal parts (Val, Sheila). Some are expressed most clearly in dance; while Cassie has a substantial scene of dialogue first, her big dance conveys her emotional state more powerfully than her words do. Maggie and Bebe are developed along with Sheila in "At the Ballet," while some characters (Richie, Al, Judy) are just sketched in.

The people on the line, roughly in order of revelation, are:

MIKE: Like Bennett, Mike is Italian, and was first exposed to dance when he tagged along to his sister's dance class. He soon realized he could do what he saw his sister doing, and do it even better.

BOBBY: As a child, Bobby gave strange recitals in his garage and broke into people's homes to rearrange the furniture. He was unable to live up to his father's expectations that he would be an athlete. He is zestful, funny, attractive, and, like Bennett, from Buffalo.

SHEILA: Sheila's mother wanted to be a ballerina, and when she was thwarted in her ambitions by her husband, she took it upon herself to make her daughter what she had wanted to be. Sheila saw *The Red Shoes* and wanted to dance, but she also used dance as a means to escape her unpleasant family situation. Strong, agressive but troubled, she is nearing thirty, and is full of sharp ripostes that mask an awareness that she may not be able to continue dancing in the chorus much longer.

BEBE: From Boston, Bebe was told by her mother that she was "different" looking, and she looked to the ballet to make her beautiful.

MAGGIE: Like Sheila, Maggie hails from a troubled home, and fantasized about a father figure, an Indian chief with whom she danced around the house.

KRISTINE: Like Bennett, Kristine danced as a child whenever the radio was on at home. Her one career obstacle is her inability to sing well, and she tends toward hysteria.

AL: Al is Kristine's husband, far more relaxed than his wife, and no longer the complex, uptight, and difficult figure of earlier versions.

MARK: Mark shares his memories of adolescent sexual awakening, in particular his recollection of misinterpreting a wet dream as gonorrhea, which was one of Bennett's tales on the tapes.

CONNIE: Usually but not invariably played by an Oriental actress, Connie never grew tall enough to be a ballerina, but she has no problem getting work in shows because of her ability to play parts several years her junior.

DIANA: Diana is a Puerto Rican who attended the High School of Performing Arts, where she encountered a teacher who advised her that she would never make it in show business. Near the end, she stands up for the excitement and glory of dancing on Broadway despite all the hardships.

DON: Like Michael Bennett, he worked in strip joints before dancing in shows, and he tells of an affair he had with an older stripper.

JUDY: Judy made her father laugh when she danced around the living room, and she is now ready for Broadway.

GREG: Greg, who describes himself as "very East Side," realized as a teenager that he was homosexual. He thought that meant that he would have to live a life of degeneracy, without nice clothes.

RICHIE: Richie announces to all that he is black. He won a basketball scholarship to college, almost became a kindergarten teacher, but decided to channel his obvious energies into dance.

VAL: Val dreamed of being a Rockette, but when she came to New York, her looks prevented her from getting work in spite of considerable dance skills. She then purchased that which her Creator had failed to provide.

CASSIE: A talented, stand-out dancer who had acquired a reputation in featured roles in two Broadway shows, Cassie now needs a job. She went out to California, did bit roles, and nothing happened for her. She now wants to start over again and be given the chance to do the only thing that means anything to her. Zach tells her she is incapable of dancing like everybody else, but she insists on putting herself on his line. Her personal relationship with him is filled in in the next sequence.

PAUL: Cassie is given the longest solo dance in the show, but Paul has the longest and most detailed monologue, largely the story Dante related at the first tape session. After early sexual experiences with strangers in Forty-second Street movie palaces, Paul quit school because his effeminacy caused others to mock him. He found work in a cheap drag revue, concealing the nature of his job from his parents. When they discovered the truth, they were somehow able to accept him for what he was. Paul is shy, suffers from the indignities of his past, and was recently operated on for torn cartilage in his knee. Some audience members have noted the subtlest hint of a homosexual attraction on the part of Zach for Paul, because of the special attention he devotes to this sensitive figure.

In the fifth sequence, Zach tells the dancers, who have been learning the lyrics to "One" offstage during Paul's revelations, of his need for perfect unison dancing in this number, which must not take the focus away from the star who will front it. Zach calls attention to the differences in Cassie's dancing, and this leads to the confrontation between Zach and Cassie. It is during this that the character of Zach is most strongly developed. We find out that Cassie left Zach because of his total absorption in the theatre and his career. Cassie felt Zach expected her to move up with him and become a star, but she detests that kind of competitive climbing, wishing only to do what she loves—dance.

In the sixth sequence, the dancers rehearse a tap combination in groups, which is cut short by Paul falling and reactivating his knee problem. He is carried out and the "alternatives" scene follows, triggered by Zach asking those assembled what they would do if they could no longer dance. The dancers discuss the lack of work in today's theatre, the problems of aging, the inescapable desire to be a star, and the possible options open to the retired gypsy. When Zach asks them how they would feel if this was the day they had to stop dancing, they respond with the song "What I Did for Love."

The seventh sequence is brief and heartbreaking. Zach separates the dancers into two lines; there is a terrifying moment when Diana is first asked to step forward, then told to step back in line. The front line is dismissed, leaving Mike, Bobby, Cassie, Mark, Judy, Richie, Val, and Diana to silently express their emotion as Zach gives them the standard information on rehearsal and tryout dates. The audience senses both the triumph of having survived and won and the pain the victors feel for those who are now departed.

There are two subtextual unifying devices in the *Chorus Line* script, rarely noticed by audiences but important to an understanding of what the authors were attempting. Much of the material that was jettisoned from the first and second workshops forms a subtext that Bennett taught his original cast and some casts thereafter. Unlike audience members, actors in the show are aware of their characters' relationship to every other character onstage, and each has his or her own "interior monologue" never heard by the audience. For example, the actor portraying Greg is supposed to be aware that he is the oldest on line—older than Sheila, who talks openly about aging—and this gives him a special rapport with Sheila throughout the evening. The relationship between Sheila and the two characters next to her on line, Cassie and Bobby, was based on the real-life relationships of the actors who created the roles. While the audience is unaware of this, the subtextual action that Bennett drilled into his players helped them to create rich, complex characterizations. These are characters who seem to have a life offstage, and this is because of the information underlying what the characters say and do.

AVIAN: "It's a composite evening about the life of a dancer, which most people don't realize. The first story is about a four-year-old, the next about an eight-year-old, the next is about an eleven-year-old, the next is about adolescence, and so on, getting older and older. That's how Michael found the construction for it, and how he knew which story should come next. But he didn't want people to be aware of it."

This statement proves to be quite true upon closer examination. "I Can Do That" is about childhood; "At the Ballet" is about the ballet school period; Bobby tells of youthful antics; "Hello Twelve" is about adolescence; "Dance: Ten, Looks: Three" is about the beginning of one's career; Cassie's story is about the development and maturation of a career and a life; the alternatives scene plunges into the future as the dancers ponder what lies ahead. The stories thus cover the entire span of a gypsy's life. Only Paul's accident exists in "real time," happening on the spot and precipitating the alternatives scene.

Charles Willard, company manager of *A Chorus Line* on tour, believes that Bennett could have focused on the life of one gypsy but instead chose to splinter the experience.

WILLARD: "Even in the Seventies, the conventional way to celebrate the icon of the Broadway gypsy would have been to do a show called *Cassie,* in which you would follow one gypsy to the audition and see the whole thing from her point of view. But, because Bennett was an intuitive artist, he thought, 'I want to do a show about a gypsy, but a star vehicle is old hat. Let me smash it into 17 pieces and do it in mosaic.' All the experiences related by the dancers could have happened to one dancer, and that dancer would probably be female, would have grown up in the Fifties, would probably come from a middle-class, mid-Western city, and would probably be an outsider. Whether Michael knew it or not, when he was making decisions about what to keep in or take out, he was guided by this one central character, somewhat similar to Donna. In the finale, all the pieces literally become "one," and the finale tells the audience that this is the story of one person.

"Had it been done as *Cassie,* it might have succeeded, but it never would have been the phenomenon without that trendy, non-linear, splintered sensibility. The Zach-Cassie relationship is almost a leftover from the *Cassie* kind of show. . . . What's innovative about *A Chorus Line* is Bennett's realization that, to make the show contemporary, he couldn't handle the story in a traditional mode. Having done *Company* and *Follies,* he saw that the story had to be told in this splintered way."

THE SCORE

The initial critical reaction to the show tended to downplay the importance of the contribution of Hamlisch and Kleban; indeed, the score of *A Chorus Line* has remained the show's least appreciated element, probably because Hamlisch and Kleban were trying for something very different from the standard Broadway collection of songs.

Bennett had asked them for an "opera-ballet," a work in which the music, like the movement, almost never stops and cannot be separated from the dialogue. The *Chorus Line* score is so thoroughly integrated into the overall production that it has tended to be overshadowed by the staging and thematic content.

Hamlisch was accused by some critics of demonstrating no distinctive musical personality of his own in the score, but he deliberately chose to compose music in a variety of styles and sounds—classical, rock, ballet, jazz, Broadway, period fifties and sixties—that would reflect the characters singing the songs as well as the different stages of life represented by different songs. Each character was unique because each song had a different sound.

The songs in *A Chorus Line* tend to weave in and out of scenes of movement and dialogue. Only "I Can Do That," "What I Did for Love," and "Nothing" are sung straight through without interruption by spoken word, and "Nothing" is performed in the middle of the "Hello Twelve" montage. The latter, a fifteen-minute interweaving of stream of consciousness, snatches of song, dialogue, and eruptions into movement, is a free-form dance-opera, and an example of musical theatre writing at its most ambitious.

Above all, the score was created to serve the production.

HAMLISCH: "We tried to make the music energetic, kind of angular, and very rhythmic. The idea of dancers who are hungry and need a job in the Seventies evokes a certain style. I tried to capture the rhythm of that. Only 'What I Did for Love' and 'One' came out of the show, because the rest are songs meant solely to be used in the show."

And as the show's book was based on the lives of those interviewed on the tapes, most of the songs borrowed heavily from those life histories.

KLEBAN: "I think right off I realized the thing they all had in common was that they all came from desperately unhappy homes. . . . Some of the tales of abuse and misery were far too strong to put on the stage in a musical number. 'At the Ballet' contains sort of a distilled cleaning up of some of the ravaged tales on those tapes. Even though the audience is not being told chapter and verse of how bad it was, the audience is moved by the song and knows the rest, the emotional truth of what those fathers and mothers must have been like, even if we didn't tell them every last miserable detail."

Only Walter Kerr in *The New York Times* recognized how successfully the score's rhythms capture the world of these dancers. He said, "Marvin Hamlisch's score is, for the entertainment's purposes, perfect. It summarizes, from the opening stock vamp, the entire lives of youngsters trained in dance halls, kept waiting in the wings. . . . Their ears become ours, relentlessly, elatedly." As original-cast-recording producer Goddard Lieberson stated in his notes for the recording, "It is somewhat difficult to recognize the quality of the music at first hearing because it is music about itself, that is to say, music about music in the theater."

Perhaps the most unconventional and most overlooked aspect of the score is the almost continuous underscoring. The sixteen-piece orchestra of *A Chorus Line* plays for more than ninety minutes of the show's two-hour running time, even though the show does not contain a large number of songs. This is because of the almost nonstop music in the pit, which underscores the dialogue, accompanies the dances, and is as responsible for the show's emotional pull as the spoken words and songs. Only three times during the evening does the music stop, and only for an extended period of time during Paul's monologue, the emotional content of which was so strong that no music was necessary to strengthen it.

PIPPIN: "Only a person with Marvin's background could have written that kind of score. As a film composer, he understood the importance of background music, of creating an emotional aura, and the underscoring is truly very good music. I know of no other show that was scored like a film, that used real emotional scoring, the way *A Chorus Line* did. The visuals were so brilliant that the score was overshadowed, but the music has made the show live."

Not many songs from *A Chorus Line* have ever been sung outside the context of the show, and so they have never become as well known as the songs from *My Fair Lady, West Side Story,* or *Fiddler on the Roof.* But they are a distinctive, sophisticated group of songs, and it is worth mentioning the history of a few.

"I HOPE I GET IT"

KLEBAN: "Marvin had been so burned in the film world with directors who would stick the music he had written for a love scene under a chase that he was determined, now that he was in the theatre, to have control over his material. Therefore, he wanted to write it chronologically, beginning with the opening. But we were writing an opening to a show that didn't exist when we began. . . . We took a hundred resumes and distilled them into this one classic gypsy resume, and that was the opening. It was like living sociology, but it was not right."

HAMLISCH: "We decided to change the opening to a number about needing this job. When you have a lot of people waiting to get a job, it has within it its own frenetic pace. We tried to get that freneticism, that desperation, into the opening number. It was one of the easiest numbers to write, having written the whole show."

"ONE"

KLEBAN: " 'One' was a craft-technique challenge, in that it was a song that was supposed to have been 'written' by somebody. It's not someone singing their true feelings. It's something that some songwriter—the composer of the score of the show for which they're auditioning—has written, and yet it has to have a subtext about other things in the play. To get all specific meaning out of it so that it can seem to have all kinds of other meanings is one of the harder tasks. You have to prune out any possible specificity, keep it very plain, like it's almost a Jerry Herman song, but it isn't quite, or an Alan Jay Lerner patter lyric in the middle section. . . . To say nothing is always harder than to say something."

"AT THE BALLET"

KLEBAN: "It was comparatively easy to write 'Ballet' because it was from the gut. We were writing a great deal of genuine emotion and feeling. It's my favorite lyric in the show, and as a song, it brought out the best of both Marvin and myself. It's at the center of the score, and I think it's a wonderful theatre song."

"WHAT I DID FOR LOVE"

HAMLISCH: "This song was a compromise on all of our parts. We all felt we wanted a song that could come out of the show, and I told Michael that, at that point, we didn't have one. 'What I Did for Love' was not as pointedly about the subject as the other songs, and we used the word 'love' as opposed to 'what I did for my dancing life.' . . . Two weeks before we opened, there was discussion of cutting the song because, stylistically, it's the least 'pointy' of all the songs, it's the one that pushes the plot ahead least and that's least about dancers. But I felt it was important, and I think Michael did too, to get a song that had a life of its own.''

KLEBAN: ''I think it's a dreadful song. I wanted another song entirely. I think it should have been in the tone of the rest of the songs in the show—'I did it for money, for this, for that, but basically for love.' But Marvin had this tune he liked, that he was sure was a standard. . . . I don't think of it as my best work, I don't think of it as a successful conclusion to the show, and I don't think of it as a particularly distinguished standard either. But you don't always win, and you have to be able to make certain compromises.''

Bennett wanted nothing to come between the audience and the atmosphere of a real audition, so he made the orchestra invisible, off stage right at the Newman. Because of this, many over the years have thought that the orchestra of *A Chorus Line* is prerecorded and piped in over the sound system.

Bennett also asked for a device based on the pit singers of *Promises, Promises* and *Company,* the use of hidden backup singers to augment the sound coming off the stage. The performers who are eliminated during the opening number are not able to go home after the opening, even though they do not get a bow at the end.

LIEBERGALL: ''They sing from the wings at the end of the opening after they're cut. Thereafter, they sing in a little booth off stage left, wearing headsets, during the montage . . . then in the two big choruses of 'One,' in 'What I Did for Love' when the full company joins in, and in the finale.''

Much of the crispness and distinctive sound of the score of *A Chorus Line* is due to the work of the show's orchestrators. The program lists Bill Byers, Hershy Kay, and Jonathan Tunick as orchestrators, but there were others who did not take billing. Harold Wheeler orchestrated ''The Music and the Mirror''; Philip J. Lang did ''Dance: Ten, Looks: Three''; and Hamlisch sought out Ralph Burns to do the finale but was only able to get him to do the last forty bars of it. Larry Wilcox and several others also had a hand in the orchestration. Reportedly, ''Nothing'' and ''At the

Ballet" were the work of Tunick, while "What I Did for Love" was orchestrated separately by Tunick, Byers, and Kay, and pieces of all three orchestrations were used.

Why were so many different orchestrators needed?

TUNICK: "Nobody dreamed that this show was going to be a hit. There were very few people that wanted to take it on, and most of us were busy with other things. It was difficult to get musicians, too, because it was Off-Broadway and it paid scale. Michael offered me the whole show, which I was unable to do, then asked me if I'd do a few numbers, which I did."

It is remarkable that the score, written in many different styles and orchestrated by many different hands, has a unified, homogeneous sound, a sound unlike that of any other Broadway musical.

6

BENNETT'S ACHIEVEMENT

E VEN IF BOB FOSSE'S name had not been on *Pippin* and *Chicago,* it would not have taken a theatregoer who had seen earlier Fosse musicals very long to figure out that those shows were the work of Fosse; all the trademarks were there. But throughout his career, Bennett always sought a total melding of style to content, and the staging of *A Chorus Line* did not resemble his work in *Seesaw, Coco,* or *Promises, Promises.* If it continued and elaborated on ideas he had developed in *Company* and *Follies,* Bennett was not repeating himself here but, rather, was seeking to find the essence of theatrical dance through a total choreographic conception.

Some dance critics who wrote about the show shortly after the opening felt that Bennett's big choreographic set pieces in the show were letdowns. But the choreography of individual numbers was never as important to Bennett as the overall staging of musical sequences and the concepts underlying the staging of these sequences. Other choreographers might have been able to come up with the steps for Cassie's dance or "Hello Twelve," but only Bennett, the master conceptual artist, could have conceived the show and assembled it from thousands of bits and pieces. It was a staging that could only have been created during months and months of rehearsal time, and the end result demonstrates that Bennett took full advantage of the creative opportunities offered by the time at his disposal.

Because of the manner in which the show was developed, an air of improvisation hangs over the staging. Even after repeated viewings, one can forget which combination comes next in the opening, or what moment is coming next in the montage. Yet *A Chorus Line* is staged within an inch of its life, and cast members maintain that if you walk a few inches downstage of where you're supposed to be, you have broken the line and look of the moment.

At the center of Bennett's staging is his use of the line of dancers, ever shifting, disappearing and reappearing, shooting off in tangents, and returning to stillness. Frank Rich in *The New York Times* wrote, "When one recalls the show, one thinks of the exhilarating movement of performers through the depth of an empty stage. Mr. Bennett's chorus line was less inclined to dance than to splinter and reconstitute itself constantly." It was just this "movement of performers through depth" that made *A Chorus Line* all but impossible to transfer to the medium of film. The staging of the show exists, triumphantly, only onstage, where what took months to create seems to be happening spontaneously, so organic is every movement.

Bennett told the *New York Post*'s Jerry Tallmer, "In a sense, I'm exposing musical comedy devices as nakedly as those kids expose their souls." From the moment the lights go up on the opening sequence to the final kick-line, *A Chorus Line* employs virtually every kind of dance ever seen in the history of Broadway. While Bennett was breaking new ground in staging, he was deliberately creating a virtual encyclopedia of every old routine—from vaudeville to the Rockettes—but always heightening the old steps to make them more expressive. He conceived such numbers as "I Can Do That" and "Dance: Ten" in the "in one" style used in vaudeville, where a performer did a number in front of a curtain while the scene was being changed behind it. In the case of *A Chorus Line,* the white line on the floor was analagous to the vaudeville drop curtain.

Bennett reached a new plateau in fluidity of staging in his *Chorus Line* work. There are none of the jarring "bumps" of conventional musicals, wherein one feels the gears shifting from dialogue to song to dance. In *A Chorus Line,* all three are often in use simultaneously, so that the audience is occasionally unaware that a performer has stopped singing and is now talking. This fluidity was particularly helpful in the frequent shifts from realism—in which the audience feels it is watching actual dancers at an audition—to the nonrealistic or surreal moments, such as when the audience is suddenly inside the mind of a character singing ("Hello Twelve") or dancing ("The Music and the Mirror").

The paradox of Bennett's staging of *A Chorus Line* is that its complexity required months of experimentation, yet the key to the final result is its utter simplicity. Without any of the trappings of recent musical spectacles, *A Chorus Line,* using only space, movement, the human body, and words—spoken and sung—was able to bring audiences to a level of emotional involvement as no other musical ever had before.

A Chorus Line also represents perhaps the most seamless blending of all the elements of musical theatre yet achieved by a theatre artist. While Bennett was clearly carrying on Robbins's work in *A Chorus Line,* no one had ever managed to create a continuous theatre piece in which dance, staging, book, music, lyrics, design, and performance were so completely of a piece. It is possible to discuss the score of *West Side Story* or the book of *Oklahoma!* as isolated elements. With *A Chorus Line,* it is ultimately futile to discuss the score apart from its staging, or the staging apart from the set and lighting design, and Bennett would continue this achievement and take it a step further in *Dreamgirls.*

Another staging device Bennett had already employed in *Company* and *Follies* that would reach its apotheosis in *Dreamgirls* was his use of cinematic staging. There is constant "jump cutting" in *A Chorus Line* as the audience's attention is shifted abruptly from one figure to another, and Bennett's ability to bring things into sudden, startling focus as in film is what makes so many *Chorus Line* moments spine-tingling. It was Bennett's special gift to be able to work cinematically while still creating the ultimate in theatricality.

It is only when *A Chorus Line* is over that one may notice that this most famous of "dance musicals" does not contain an abundance of dancing per se, certainly far less than audiences were given in *West Side Story,· Sweet Charity, My One and Only,* or *42nd Street.* But it was its deployment of musical staging that went beyond that of other musicals, giving it the uncanny feeling of something that just *happens* spontaneously onstage, a constantly changing, ever-shifting, always dynamic black box.

SEQUENCES

A Chorus Line starts with one of the most exciting openings in all musical theatre, one which could have unbalanced a lesser work. It begins in the dark with a six-note, standard vamp, but when the lights come up, the audience is immediately plunged into the midst of the action, and the show's first word, "Again," indicates that an audition is already in progress. It is a visceral opening that establishes a level of tension that never lets up. The steps of the opening combinations are the first examples of Bennett's heightening of conventional routines, the stage becoming a flutter of arms and legs, with groups vanishing, only to suddenly reappear. Bennett deliberately choreographed the opening combinations in such a way as to make them too difficult to execute perfectly. Zach demonstrates but does not have to dance everything, and only the last group of boys is meant to approach perfection.

The opening concludes with an epiphanic moment. The lights dim, the mirrors revolve to black, and the actors move downstage. When the lights come up, the seventeen dancers remaining have formed the line for the first time, holding their eight-by-ten-inch head shots in front of their faces, a perfect metaphor for their position at this moment, not yet individuals, still just faces at an audition. This moment—one of the show's most celebrated—represents the perfect blend of theme, staging concept, musical underscoring, lighting, and set design that marks the entire evening.

"At the Ballet" begins as if it might be a solo for Sheila, but Bebe soon emerges from the darkness and Maggie is then added. The lighting gives us a glimpse of figures performing barre exercises which quickly vanishes. As Maggie continues her story and reaches her climactic note, the upstage area is bathed in dim light that reveals a world of ballet steps, lasting about ten seconds, leaving the three ladies to conclude the song and return to the line as it re-forms. This is gorgeous staging, utterly simple and a subtle embodiment of a strong emotional song.

The "Hello Twelve" montage is Bennett at his best, a perfect example of the seamless blending of book, score, and design in the entire piece. The individual steps may be undistinguised or derivative here and there (Bennett quotes his own staging from the *Company* opening at one point), but that is of little significance. This is a constantly surprising, ever-changing, and alive sequence that also serves a thematic purpose: By blending together so many stories and thoughts, the idea that these people all share similar feelings and experiences, those of every member of the audience, is reinforced.

Cassie's "The Music and the Mirror" song becomes probably the longest solo dance in a musical, a vivid, abstract, and emotional outpouring that allows the dancer performing it to contribute her own dance personality within the parameters of the choreography.

MCKECHNIE: "The dance is about the need to rediscover the thing that makes you happiest. It's about the fundamentals, and trying to remember *why* you did what you did. . . . She's saying in the dance, 'I'm fighting for my life. Give me a chance to get my life back. Let me find myself so that I can go on. I don't care what anybody thinks, this is what I really love, this is what I do.'

"It's also about narcissism, about someone who has no identity without the mirror. There are three ideas that are choreographed literally: her relationship to the mirror, to the line, and to Zach. What the dancer does with it creates those relationships.

"This girl is making up the dance in her own mind as she goes along, so it shouldn't be too clever or fancy or sophisticated. It should be simple. . . . Michael used to tell me, 'Don't work so hard. You don't have to do too much with each step.' "

The confrontation between Zach and Cassie is another example of form reflecting meaning. By setting this personal argument against the rehearsal of a routine, unstoppable production number, Bennett brings out Zach's complete immersion in work, which led to the rift between him and Cassie, as well as Cassie's isolation in front of the mindless dance into which she is unable to blend. What was originally written as just a dialogue scene was combined by Bennett with a musical number, thereby giving both extra resonance and symbolic significance.

THE FINALE

Just when he was beginning to work on *A Chorus Line,* Bennett told a friend about a concept he had for it. "You're going to get to know all these dancers as individuals and care about each one. Then, at the very end of the play, they're all going to come out in tuxedos and top hats, and you're not going to be able to tell one from another. They're going to blend. They're going to do everything you've ever seen anyone in a chorus line do. It's going to be the most horrifying moment you will ever experience in a theatre. I have a vision of them forming a V and marching with frozen smiles, like in *Metropolis*. If I do this right, you will never see another chorus line in a theatre. Everybody will reevaluate what it is they're watching."

But was Bennett able to fulfill this early vision?

The finale of *A Chorus Line* is Bennett's masterstroke of bravura and irony, one which works on several levels simultaneously. It is the finale to the show called *A Chorus Line* that the audience has been witnessing for two uninterrupted hours; it is the finale to the show for which this audition has been held; it is a celebration of what these dancers have endured; and it is a fantasy, set in some musical comedy heaven wherein every hokey production number ever dreamed up is repeated eternally.

It begins with bows for all nineteen protagonists, boys first, and one notices immediately that as each comes on, it is difficult to distinguish one from another until each doffs his or her hat. These dancers, each an individual and a "star" for the last two hours, are now anonymous members of the ensemble once more. The number proceeds to offer the flashiest choreography of the evening, along with bright scenery and costumes after an evening of stark lighting, mirrors, and rehearsal clothes. The choreography is deliberately banal but goose-bump-inducing nonetheless.

MCKECHNIE: "He wanted it to be what everyone does with a hat, a cane and tails in a Las Vegas show. As we created it, we pretended Ann-Margret was in front of us, and we did the steps you would do in a Vegas floor show."

SONDHEIM: "Michael always used traditional things. The finale is right out of the end of *Follies,* but that was right out of the traditional, Ziegfeld-style line in top hat and tails. It's also close to the Rockettes, which, I suppose, comes from the Ziegfeld tradition. Michael used the Rockettes tradition for the last two numbers in *Follies,* Phyllis and Ben's numbers, and he used that again in the finale of *A Chorus Line.*"

As the dancers form a wedge and a circle, to the accompaniment of spontaneous applause from the audience, the number becomes a celebration of the mindless glitz and excitement of Broadway musicals, but there is the underlying irony that the individuals we have come to know and care about are once more part of the line, backing an invisible star. Finally, the dancers form a straight kick-line, and the show literally never ends, the lights fading on the still-kicking line, the music continuing as the houselights come up. Just as Broadway can never completely cease to exist, these dancers will never stop kicking. But the sad irony is that these dancers who we now know are special are kicking their way into musical-comedy oblivion. Bennett thus sums it all up by giving the audience the big all-out rouser for which it has waited, but he undercuts it by once again depriving the cast of their hard-earned individuality. They are all "one" again.

Bennett wanted the audience to be so upset by this final vision that they would never be able to see a chorus the same way again. He told *Dance Magazine*'s Richard Philp, "I want the audience to walk out of the theater saying, 'Those kids shouldn't be in a chorus!' And I want the people in that audience to go to other shows and think about what's really gone into making that chorus. I want them to ask, 'Who's behind the star? Who else is on stage?' " He told George Perry of the London *Times Sunday Supplement,* "That finale is so sad. The craft is wonderful, but you ask, did they go through all that, just to be anonymous? That finale says everything the show says. And it fades with them kicking. That's it. That's the end of the show. There are no bows. I don't believe in bows, just the fade-out. That's what a dancer's life is."

These bitter ironies are lost on many members of the audience, who are delighted to see a big all-out finale, which they accept purely as happy show-biz extravaganza. Some see it as a celebration of the perfect unity they have achieved. It can be argued that, in his final staging, Bennett chose to gloss over the more frightening aspects of what is occurring, letting the audience off the hook by turning on the razzle-dazzle, but most thoughtful viewers have at least felt some of the irony intended, which becomes more evident on repeated viewings.

GETTING THE PERFORMANCE

All directors have their own particular method of getting what they want from their cast, and it is worth examining the particular methods Bennett used to get the performances he wanted from his original company and from the many *Chorus Line* companies that were to follow.

LIEBERGALL: "Michael tended not to make general announcements. He gave a lot of personal direction. A word or phrase from him could all of a sudden change someone's performance or line reading. Only later in life, when he didn't have time, did he start giving people line readings. Before that, he really took his time to work with the individual and deal with that person's background. He always made each one feel like they were the only person in the room."

SCHWEID: "Michael was very specific in his direction, and worked differently with everyone. There were people with whom he knew how to work, and people he didn't. For example, Kelly Bishop was already a very good actress and he knew that she would be able to do what he told her to do, to take it and go with it. Priscilla Lopez, too. With some of the others, he would change a line, rather than give them a line reading when they weren't getting it."

BISHOP: "Michael left me alone, and I liked that. I was one of the few in the original company who had acted. But I saw his work with the others, and as far as I was concerned, there were 18 directors in that place, one for each person."

Bennett was dealing with many inexperienced actors in all the companies of *A Chorus Line,* but he did not want "performances"; he wanted the actors to be themselves. He referred to this as the "nonacting style of acting." He sought to find the special qualities of the individual actor and to apply the personality of each actor to the role that actor was playing. When new people joined the cast, he warned them about "playing" the parts; he wanted, instead, for them to apply themselves to the parts.

In order to achieve these goals, Bennett and Avian would conduct interviews with new cast members very similar to Zach's. Not only did this give the actor an experience he could remember and recreate in the show but it allowed Bennett to discover the individuality of each performer, so that he could then encourage the actor to use the special traits revealed in the interview when performing. If Bennett detected nervousness in the interview subject, he would ask the actor and the others watching to remember that feeling and use it in the show. He wanted the actors to observe the behavior of the others as they told their own stories: what happened to their voices, how their gestures were affected by nerves, how they looked as they tried to recollect things. He would ask someone to tell a joke, and when he heard the reaction of the group, he would tell them to use that reaction when Bobby or Greg tell their stories in the play.

Bennett didn't want the cast to "pretend" to listen, or to act out listening; he wanted them to just listen. He told the cast, "It's very important in this play that you *just talk*. Don't do funny things with words." He was concerned when performers began to sing too well rather than act the intention of the lyrics. "The lyric is just like dialogue, and you must get the point of it across, and not treat it like a song. The audience will stop listening to the story if you hold notes too long. I'm not saying you shouldn't sing well, but the biography is what's important."

Bennett insisted on maintaining the tension of a final audition. Often in performance, particularly around the time of the "One" rehearsal, the show began to take on the look of a rehearsal rather than an audition, and he fought hard to avoid this. He would tell his company, "At a final audition for Fosse or Champion or Kidd, the tension can be cut with a knife."

Always, Bennett reminded the cast that this was an audition, and that there was no audience. They were to remember that they were being watched by Zach, but they were not to play to the spectators in their seats. He told one company in rehearsal, "This play is not a musical comedy. It's a musical, a drama. You will have audiences for the first two or three months who will be intellectuals and buffs, and they'll understand it and find the real laughs. But later those laughs are going to stop. You're going to start pushing, and you will become forced. I don't care about the laughs. I care about the reality. If the audience has been at a Neil Simon comedy for the first half, by the time they get to Cassie and Zach and Paul, they won't be able to make that transition, and it will come out a musical comedy and a soap opera, and that's not it. It has to be one piece."

Bennett would act out the roles in rehearsal, beautifully connecting the thoughts from line to line. He insisted that the actors find the truth in the lines, and hear and find the right rhythms. He would not permit any variation from the exact words in the script, believing that the comedy depended on the rhythms of the lines and that an extra unwritten syllable threw it off.

PAM BLAIR: "What was great about Michael was he would first make you look great, and then you just got better. You'd find the part and the subtext over the months. There was no way you could be bad with him."

7

THE STATEMENT

Broadway had seen many smash hits before, but *A Chorus Line*'s trump card was not its score, its book, or even its staging, but its ability to leave audiences emotionally devastated. Many still remember vividly the first time they saw the show, not because of the theatrical techniques but because of how they wept at the end. *A Chorus Line* led people to go home and talk, not about the show but about their own lives. The miracle of *A Chorus Line* was that a show so specifically about a narrow insular community, so totally about dancers and Broadway, came to be about life.

On the most fundamental level, audiences identified with the plight of the dancers because the show is about getting work, and everyone at some time has been up for a job or position of some sort and has had to put themselves "on the line" to get it.

More than work, the show talks about teamwork. If these dancers will never become stars and make the impact as individuals in the theatre that they make during the show's audition, they are powerful collectively, as the finale demonstrates. The show deals with the work ethic itself, demonstrating the importance of work to the characters' lives.

When Zach questions Cassie's desire to rejoin the chorus, she answers by telling him that each of the dancers in that line is special, and *A Chorus Line* tells its audiences that each person is special, with feelings that must be expressed, goals that must be attempted, and an intrinsic value that must be respected.

It also explores the success ethic of American society itself, the competitiveness and the desire to be a "star" in any field.

KIRKWOOD: "We're taught in this country to compete, to be the best, to get the best grades, to rise in your company. When you present that to an audience, they see the parallels in their lives. There's a part of everybody that wants to be a star, and I think *A Chorus Line* scratches that feeling. Michael felt if we didn't glitz it up or fake it, if we told it as close to the truth as possible, people would understand."

A Chorus Line says that success isn't ultimately what's important; it is doing what you love that gives meaning to your life. For that reason, no one has a right to judge others, and everyone has the right to measure success or failure on his own terms.

MCKECHNIE: "It's about human dignity and compassion, compassion for oneself. It's about judging and being judged. The thing I really love about it is when you're in the audience, in the beginning, you're going, 'Oh, I hate that person, look at what she's wearing. . . .' You're in Zach's position, and you're there picking and choosing and judging with him. But soon you say, 'Oh, I wish he wouldn't treat her like that. Oh, that poor guy, what he went through.' By the end of the play, you come away feeling, 'Maybe I shouldn't judge people so quickly.' "

If *A Chorus Line* is about being part of a team, that team is ultimately the human race. It says that we are all "one," all human beings with a similar need for love and acceptance, and thus it is one of the few musicals to address the human condition itself.

BENNETT: "The show is really about the experience of growing up. It's a group biography, and I think that people in the audience have a subjective experience when they watch the show. They watch the dancers talking about their lives, and they go through experiences of their own lives, so that they're not only watching the play, they're reliving their whole growing up. And it's just nice to know that you're not alone. I think it makes people feel happier about being part of the human race. It makes you feel closer. The metaphor is a chorus line, being part of a great team. And being part of the human race is very nice. I don't think it would be fun to be the only human being around."

There were those observers who expressed doubt that the experiences of gypsies would speak to everyone, but they were proved wrong the moment the show got before an audience.

WILLARD: "*A Chorus Line* managed to find an uncanny kind of universality in the specificity of that white line. Dealing with the very specific milieu and ambience of chorus dancers, it somehow spoke to everyone, and from the very beginning, it cut across the gypsy story. Because of that, it's often forgotten that it was intended to be a show that celebrated a subculture."

8

THE ORIGINAL CAST

The ORIGINAL PROGRAM OF *A Chorus Line* contained a complete list of all the musicals in which the cast had danced, as well as a note that stated, "Collectively they have had 612 years of dance training. . . . While appearing in the shows mentioned above, they have sustained 30 back, 26 knee and 36 ankle injuries." What the audience was looking at was the real thing, actual gypsies who had been on that line again and again and had known the tension and fear of rejection their characters were experiencing. And, to enhance the feeling that this was a show not only about but also created by gypsies, Bennett's bio in the original *Playbill* listed only the three Broadway musicals in which he had danced (this was later changed to a standard bio, containing all his major credits).

But what created a special frisson in the audience, especially among those in the know, was the idea that the actors onstage in the original company were actually playing themselves and were taking the courageous step of exposing themselves and their lives as those at the tape sessions that inspired the material had done.

But were the members of the original cast actually playing themselves? Was Donna McKechnie really Cassie, and was Priscilla Lopez Diana

Morales? The roles in the final text of *A Chorus Line,* with the exception of Paul, are composites. Some are based predominantly on one dancer, while others combine two or three. All are fictionalized to a degree, and aspects of one dancer's life were often distributed among as many as six different characters.

It is possible, however, to go down the line and indicate the real-life sources of each role. The character of Don was based on Bennett (the affair with the stripper), Wayne Cilento, and Andy Bew, the latter two, like Don, married men supporting families in the precarious world of the theatre. Maggie was largely McKechnie, who, at the age of three, actually danced around her living room fantasizing about an Indian chief who would invite her to dance. Mike's "I Can Do That" story was Sammy Williams's, while his relationship with Zach was that of Cilento's (who played Mike) with Bennett. Connie is very close to the actress who created her, Baayork Lee, who, like her character, was in *The King and I* as a child and was still able to play young roles because of her height. Greg is some of Michel Stuart, who created it, some of Bob Avian, and some of others.

The closest parallels between McKechnie and Cassie are that both had stopped two shows in featured parts (in McKechnie's case, *Promises* and *Company*), and both had gone out to California with hopes of stardom and found only small film parts and little interest. McKechnie had known the need of a job earlier in her career, but, by the time of *A Chorus Line,* she would never have auditioned for a chorus position. The relationship between Zach and Cassie is partly based on that of Bennett and Leland Palmer, who assisted him during the early years of stock and Broadway choreography and became his dancing lead in *A Joyful Noise.*

PALMER: "In order to grow, I needed to cut the umbilical cord. He had a strong need to succeed, and I don't think my need to succeed expressed itself in the same way. He was genius, and with genius, it's a gift and a curse at the same time. It was almost like he was competing with himself. He couldn't totally enjoy the beauty and the power and the gift of what he created."

The overqualification of Cassie was based on dancer Judy West, whom Bennett was forced to reject for a chorus job in a Milliken Breakfast Show because she had already done parts in two films.

Sheila is clearly derived from the personality and life history of Kelly Bishop, who created the part, but it also includes elements of McKechnie (*The Red Shoes,* the desire to be a ballerina) and Charlene Ryan, who danced for Bennett in *Coco* and played Sheila in the Los Angeles company. Bobby is a good deal of Thommie Walsh, who played him, with some of Bennett as well. Bebe was mostly Bishop, who asked her mother whether she'd be pretty when she grew up and was told she'd only be "different," and partly Michon Peacock. Judy Turner was a composite of the creator of the role, Trish Garland, McKechnie (who had cut off her sister's hair and practiced kissing with girls like Judy), and others. Richie was mostly Candy Brown, a tomboy as a kid, who had planned to be a kindergarten teacher but left school when she realized that no one was going to give her a scholarship to life. Al and Kristine have their foundation in Steve Boockvor and Denise Pence, the only married couple at the tape sessions. But during the show's development, Al became less specifically Boockvor, and Kristine became more specifically Renee Baughman, who played her and had in common with her role a tendency toward hysteria and an uncertainty about her singing abilities. Val was based on Mitzi Hamilton, who actually underwent surgery to enhance her figure, and Pam Blair, who created it, and whose mixture of angelic appearance and ribald tongue entertained Bennett enormously. All of Val's story, with the exception of the surgery, was Blair's. The gonorrhea story Mark tells was Bennett's. Diana was extremely close to Priscilla Lopez's life, especially her experiences at the High School of Performing Arts.

Paul is, of course, Nicholas Dante, and in the final script it was the least embellished of all the original taped stories. Dante himself was later disturbed by the fact that so many of the original cast felt that they had "written" the play because they were playing aspects of themselves.

DANTE: "They so dismissed the work that was done to shape the characters. While the show could not have been done without their stories, what people did with that material was what made the piece work."

AVIAN: "Ultimately it was all written. A lot of the kids think they wrote their sections, but thinking that helped them play it. They contributed to the material, but less than they think."

The original cast of *A Chorus Line* became the toast of New York within months of the opening, and they were invited to a multitude of functions and social occasions. It made them special in a way they had never been before in their careers.

PIPPIN: "The show opened doors for them. Anyone who had any aggression at all about his career was getting commercials. They were the hottest things in show business, and just saying you were in it opened any door."

But this was to be only temporary. *A Chorus Line* changed the life of every member of the original cast, but for many it would ultimately prove a disorienting, traumatic experience, leaving some with deep-seated problems that took years to overcome. When asked to speak about the show for this book, several members of the original cast declined, saying that they had spent years in analysis rehashing their *Chorus Line* experience in an attempt to deal with it, and that they did not wish to dredge it up again. Some said they felt they had given away their lives to the show, been exploited or used by it, and were left feeling uncertain of themselves and their careers when they left the show. Some felt abandoned by Bennett after *A Chorus Line,* and deeply resentful and hurt.

Being in the show placed each cast member in an awkward position. Most had never had a speaking part in a show before and had never in any way stood out from the ensemble. *A Chorus Line* made each seem so special that it became very difficult for them to return to being anonymous chorus dancers thereafter. Returning to the chorus was also perceived as a downward career move. Cast members hesitated to leave the show, wondering whether they would ever get another chance to show off their personalities, acting skills, and singing voices. The expectations set up by going from chorus dancer to principal player in *A Chorus Line* were, in many cases, never fulfilled.

PIPPIN: "That show destroyed people, because Michael created a totally false fantasy which they lived out. Michael so uniquely used what they could do that he made them stars for a day. That later gave those people a lot of emotional problems."

SCHWEID: "Everyone involved in the show at the beginning is somehow haunted by it. It was wonderful, but it was terrible. . . . The show cost everybody a lot—and that's why it was so good. That was on the stage."

One of the great ironies of *A Chorus Line,* however, is that, while the show celebrated and glorified the chorus dancer, those who played in the original cast, now that they had been allowed to act and sing onstage for the first time, became dissatisfied with being only a chorus dancer. The show made each of them feel like a "total performer" for the first time and made them realize that they could no longer feel "special," as Cassie says they all are, just dancing behind a star again.

Above all, it was Bennett's manipulation of these raw talents that left many of them bewildered and upset in later years. Avian, who was able to witness this without being the victim of it, addresses this issue cogently.

"For the original cast, there's a lot of tension and churning when it comes to the show. They often don't even know why. It's because of a love-hate relationship between them and Michael. He turned them into other people, and there was no follow-up to it. He made some of them potential stars and got their career going, and then it didn't happen. Or he seduced them with words and manipulated them to get them to do what he wanted, and it caused great anxiety later. Of course, the nature of the show is very purging, and it cost them emotionally and they were unable to resolve that, too. Some left the show because they were unable to do it anymore, and nothing good happened for them later. But it all goes back to Michael, and his way of getting them to do what he wanted. I spent most of my time with the original company taking care of them, being liaison and babying them. Michael would create tension for a reason, when he was going for results, and you had to let it happen. He would have been furious if you broke it. It was his way of getting results, his choice, whether you approved of it or not. But then you had hysterical people on your hands, and I spent much of the time just calming them down and taking care of them so they could keep functioning.

"Because they were not experienced actors, they didn't understand what he was doing and took everything personally. But it wasn't really personal. Michael loved to mind-fuck. They needed that, or wanted it. I worked with Michael for 20 years, watching all of it go down, and I never had that problem with him, because I had a different relationship with him. As best friends, closer than brothers, he knew that I would not allow myself to be manipulated, and I had a control over him to a degree. I really wasn't working for him, I was there because we were pals. But these performers were in a different position, they were working for him. Also, I was older and knew Michael's history, every moment in his life, and so I knew exactly why he was behaving the way he was. I knew his sense of morality and amorality, and I knew the reason for it. But none of the performers knew that, and they couldn't understand why he would have to do things to get to the place he had to get to."

BISHOP: "He got caught in his own trap with the manipulation thing. He would get people where he wanted them, get the performance out of them he wanted, and then he wanted to get away, and they wouldn't let go. This had a tendency to make him sever, and just push aside, for his own freedom."

RON DENNIS: "He knew how to intimidate people to get the performance he wanted out of them. He would say certain things to key members of the cast to really get them angry and up for their character. But he would do it as Michael to them, one to one, and they wouldn't know he was playing these psychological games to get a performance. On big nights, he would come in and say terrible things to Sammy Williams, just to get him in the right state for Paul. I don't think you get a better performance that way. You just make a person a nervous basket-case, and it took Sammy and others years to realize that what he was saying was not directed at them personally."

BLAIR: "I remember him going up to Sammy Williams opening night in L.A. and saying, 'I want to see real tears out there tonight. Just think of how much I really hate you.' Michael thought that by doing that, he'd make him so unhappy that he'd be able to do it. He was treating him like he really wasn't an actor, but Sammy *could* act. It seemed awfully cruel, but maybe in some cases he had to do things like that to get the performance."

WAYNE CILENTO recalls the pressures the original cast experienced: "Michael did a lot of head trips, and we were mad at him a lot, through the whole thing. He was playing around with our lives. He took my story away from me and gave it to another actor. I felt, 'Don't take my story away because you think the audience won't believe that I'm married and have a kid and a house, then tell me that a tap dance will fit my character more. I'm me. I'm married. I have children.'

"Emotionally, the show was very difficult to perform. It didn't work when you got comfortable with it and tried to 'act' it. It was basically us on raw nerves, and that energy made the show work. The uniqueness of the show was us, who we were, and when we were trying to act, the powers that be came down on us, and we were under constant pressure."

Ron Dennis recalls Bennett telling the cast that they were all going to be stars, his stars. But in 1983, Bennett told *People* magazine, "There was no one in the show with star quality. There wasn't meant to be." It is no secret that not a single member of the original cast of *A Chorus Line* has had a major career as a performer in the years since. The disparate career paths taken by these actors are a paradigm of the difficulties of maintaining a career in today's theatre.

No actress ever played Sheila with quite the combination of ripe physicality, acerbic wit, and underlying pathos that its originator, Carole Bishop, brought to it. Carole Bishop, who became Kelly during the first year of the show's run when she joined the Screen Actors Guild, had played featured roles before, but *A Chorus Line* was her real Broadway acting debut, and it was an extraordinary one, earning her a Tony Award. Bishop left the show before any other original cast member when Bennett refused to give her a raise; she soon appeared in a featured role in the film *An Unmarried Woman.* But in spite of numerous stage *(Piano Bar, Night of the Iguana,* understudy to Judith Ivey in *Precious Sons),* film *(Dirty Dancing),* and television ("The Thorns") credits, she has yet to find a role to take full advantage of her skills, and has admitted that she expected her *Chorus Line* Tony to do more for her than it did. She returned to the cast of *A Chorus Line* on two occasions.

Priscilla Lopez brought a combination of vocal strength and personal warmth and appeal to the role of Diana Morales that has never been equaled. Having taken over roles in such musicals as *Your Own Thing, Pippin,* and *Company* (McKechnie's original role) prior to *A Chorus Line,* she was a more experienced performer than most of those on the original line. She seemed likeliest of the original company to become a major star, and, soon after leaving the show, was leading lady in a television series called "In the Beginning." She won a Tony Award for her performance in the 1980 hit *A Day in Hollywood/A Night in the Ukraine.* She went on to nonmusical roles in *Key Exchange, Extremities,* and *Edmond,* and was later involved in Bennett's *Scandal.* She was also special assistant to Tommy Tune on *Nine,* and replaced the vacationing Liliane Montevecchi in that show. Lopez is an abundantly talented performer who, as of this writing, also awaits a new role that will properly display her considerable abilities.

Sammy Williams won a Tony Award for his unforgettable creation of Paul San Marco, but it was his acting debut, and winning that award placed him on a new plateau. As did many of the original cast, he went out to Hollywood to try his luck and did a few television guest shots. He has never played another major role on the Broadway stage. He returned to the role of Paul on Broadway in 1983, but, at this writing, is in the business of creating floral arrangements.

Robert LuPone, originally Al in the workshops, gave a memorable performance as Zach, a role to which he returned in 1985 and again in 1988. After *A Chorus Line,* he did a great deal of repertory theatre, returning to musicals to play the leads in two disasters, *Nefertiti,* which closed on the road, and *Late Nite Comic.*

Pamela Blair, the irresistibly comic and adorable Val of the original company, had done principal acting roles on Broadway prior to *A Chorus Line.* She went on to *The Best Little Whorehouse in Texas* (in which she lost her big song to the show's leading lady during previews), the ingenue lead in the musical *King of Hearts,* and *The Nerd* on Broadway, but none of these has given her the recognition she received in *A Chorus Line.* She, too, went out to Hollywood, and discovered that being in *A Chorus Line* didn't mean a great deal to the powers that be at television and film studios.

Several original performers chose paths other than performing and reaped far greater rewards. Thommie Walsh, the original Bobby, won two Tony Awards, as co-choreographer with Tommy Tune on *A Day in Hollywood* and co-stager and choreographer with Tune on *My One and Only.* In 1988, he directed the musical *Lucky Stiff* at Playwrights Horizons. Baayork Lee spent most of the next decade re-creating Bennett's staging and choreography of *A Chorus Line* in productions around the world, many of which she also cast. In 1983, she was associate choreographer of *My One and Only,* and in 1988, she created the choreography for *Let 'Em Rot* in Florida and *The Cocoanuts* at the Arena Stage in Washington. Kay Cole, the original Maggie, won featured spots on the "Carol Burnett Show" after *A Chorus Line* and later returned to the show as Diana. She then went into choreography, staging the dances for the London production of *Snoopy,* and later appeared in the Los Angeles company of *Les Misérables.*

Wayne Cilento has had one of the more interesting careers of the original cast members. Well aware of the awkward position in which chorus dancers had been placed by *A Chorus Line,* he left the show to dance behind Liza Minnelli in *The Act.* Although he received good notices for his work, he realized he was back in the chorus. Bob Fosse's *Dancin'* came along soon after, and that show made dancers "stars," although not in the way *A Chorus Line* had. He had a featured dancing role in Fosse's last show, *Big Deal,* but by that time he had done the musical staging for *Baby* and the choreography for *Jerry's Girls* on Broadway. Cilento admits that he feels trapped, still wanting to perform as well as choreograph but unable to find satisfying roles.

Don Percassi, the original Al, stayed with *A Chorus Line* longer than any other performer, then went into the ensemble of *42nd Street* when it opened in 1980 and stayed with it for most of its Broadway run. Michel Stuart, the original Greg, won a Tony Award as co-producer of *Nine,* and designed costumes for *A Day in Hollywood* and *Cloud 9.*

Several of the original cast, such as Ron Dennis, Nancy Lane, Ron Kuhlman, and Trish Garland, moved to California, where they have continued their careers in local productions. Garland directed and choreographed four California productions of *A Chorus Line,* and contributed choreography to James Kirkwood's comedy *Legends.*

Cameron Mason, after returning to *A Chorus Line* in 1976 as one of the dancers who is eliminated during the opening, left the theatre to work in his family's furnishings store. Clive Clerk, the original Larry, who later returned to the show as Zach, left performing to work in the art and design field.

A Chorus Line was intended as a show without stars, but Donna McKechnie inevitably stood out, and the grace, beauty, poignancy, and dance skills she brought to the role of Cassie have only occasionally been approached by later performers. It was both an acting and dancing triumph for her, and it earned her a Tony Award as Best Actress in a Musical.

McKechnie's career had taken many unexpected turns from the start. Intending to be a ballerina, she auditioned for Lucia Chase of Ballet Theatre when she was fifteen, but when she was asked to continue studying prior to joining the company, she took it as a personal rejection, and was unable to even watch a ballet for some time thereafter. Needing work, she auditioned for the corps at Radio City and was hired to be one of a hundred girls holding up plastic lilies as the stage rose.

After working in stock, she got her first Broadway job, dancing in the chorus of *How to Succeed in Business Without Really Trying.* After working with such top professionals as Fosse and Frank Loesser in that smash, McKechnie gained new respect for the theatre and put all her money into acting and singing classes.

MCKECHNIE: *"How to Succeed* was the only show in which I danced in the chorus. I don't know where I got the nerve to say this to myself, but I decided I was not going to be in any more choruses. There's nothing wrong with being in the chorus, but I was already excited by what you could express in a musical, what the story could tell, and I wanted to be part of that story. Even when I dance, the sense of movement doesn't thrill me as much as *why* I'm moving."

After winning the ingenue lead in the national company of *A Funny Thing Happened on the Way to the Forum,* she turned down offers from Fosse to dance in the choruses of *Sweet Charity* and *Pleasures and Palaces,* and soon reached the career crisis that was the basis for part of Cassie.

She recalled, "My marriage wasn't working out, and I called Jaime Rogers, with whom Michael and I had worked on 'Hullabaloo.' He was choreographing a show called *The Education of Hyman Kaplan,* and I told him, 'I'm in trouble. I've got to work. I've never asked for a job before, but I'll do anything, I'll get coffee, I'll teach numbers.' He said, 'You're too good, you can't do that.' All of a sudden, he created a role for me, an Irish girl in this story about Jewish immigrants."

After *Promises, Promises, Company, On the Town,* and the classics in regional theatre, *A Chorus Line* happened. For the first time, she was able to take full advantage of her acting and feel like a total performer. But playing what became the central role in the most extraordinary musical of its period proved to be a double-edged sword.

MCKECHNIE: "People identified the role of Cassie with me very strongly. They wanted to believe Cassie's story was mine, and for a while it had an adverse affect on my career. People saw me as this dramatic performer, and I was unable to get work in anything light. When I look back on it now, I realize that anything that powerful and profound in people's minds causes people to not want you to do anything else. They don't want you to take that image away from them. It took me many years to respect that.

"After the show opened, Michael and I would talk about doing something else, going on, and we both realized that *A Chorus Line* would stand apart, and that not everybody would understand that it would have to be apart from anything that we had done before or would do after."

After *A Chorus Line,* McKechnie's career included choreography for the Broadway Stephen Sondheim Tribute in 1973 and for several L.A. revues, nightclub acts on both coasts, straight acting Off-Broadway and in regional theatres, musical roles across the country, and even a stint as director and choreographer of the Los Angeles Raiders' cheerleaders. There was a short-lived marriage to Bennett, which resulted in the temporary end of their friendship, and a terrifying bout with rheumatoid arthritis that McKechnie now believes may have been partly psychosomatic. Through it all, there were no new roles on Broadway for this actress who had taken Broadway by storm.

McKechnie, brought up to believe that one does not go back and play old roles, was persuaded by Baayork Lee to play Cassie again in a summer tour that eventually took her to Japan. In September 1986, she returned to the Broadway production for nine months.

"I hadn't wanted to go back to *A Chorus Line,*" she said. "I didn't want people to come and say, 'Well, it's just a shadow of what it was, she shouldn't have done it again.' But I felt I had more to contribute to it now. . . . It was hard to enjoy it the first time around. We were like hot-house plants, I was doing interviews every day, there was a lot of personal stuff going on, and it was hard to separate myself from it. I couldn't live with the fact that I never really enjoyed it as much as I should have. I wanted to really enjoy the best show of my life, to be able to say, 'That was really good,' instead of 'It was so painful.' "

McKechnie, who had grown as a person and a performer in the intervening decade, played Cassie as a true survivor this time around, and brought greater strength, focus, and love of work to the part. It was a poignant personal triumph, which led directly to the title role in the national tour of Fosse's *Sweet Charity*. After that, McKechnie played Cassie once more, in the 1988 Paris premiere of the show.

McKechnie was ultimately Bennett's greatest instrument, because of the freedom he gave her to express herself.

"Our dancing styles were very much the same," she recalled. "He appreciated the fact that I would take his choreography, interpret it and bring a new dynamic to it that he may not have thought of. He could rely on me to justify the acting and take it somewhere else."

If her career as a performer became more low-profile than might have been expected after her initial triumph as Cassie, McKechnie's intelligence and personal strength allowed her to overcome and grow from the mixed blessings of *A Chorus Line,* as some of the other original performers were never able to do. McKechnie has received several offers to choreograph Broadway shows, and has taught musical theatre at HB Studios in New York. While she is still interested in maintaining her performing career, it seems inevitable that she will eventually choreograph, passing on as she must the legacy of which she was such an integral part.

Outsiders are often surprised to hear that being in the original cast of *A Chorus Line* was not the joyous, thrilling experience it would appear to have been. Some of this was due to Bennett's treatment of his cast, but much of the difficulty cast members have in dealing with their *Chorus Line* years relates to their subsequent careers. For some, the show was their one real moment of theatrical glory. Some were, fundamentally, chorus dancers who were not meant to be principal performers yet were made to seem special by the material they were performing. The lucky ones were ultimately able to see this experience as a once-in-a-lifetime theatrical occasion and to use that knowledge as inspiration to continue to strive for theatrical excellence in any department or on any level.

9

ITS PLACE IN HISTORY

How innovative was *A Chorus Line* and why did it become the longest-running show in Broadway history?

The show's powerful emotional effect on audiences was the result of its strong underlying thematic content. Not only was the show something with which everyone could identify but it was a musical that became a participatory event. Just as the cast was included in the development of the show, the audience was included in it: The observer becomes both Zach, judging and choosing, and a dancer on the line. The show had an uncanny ability to touch on everyone's life and to simultaneously entertain and draw one in.

Whatever the show-biz clichés or moments of sentimentality in *A Chorus Line,* audiences watching the show felt they were seeing the truth, not only about the theatre but about life. The show was able to convey a sense of honesty and truth, even after the roles were no longer being played by the performers upon whom they were based.

It seems that every generation must have its own great backstage, show-business saga, and, like *42nd Street* and *Singin' in the Rain* in their respective eras, *A Chorus Line* fulfilled that function for the Seventies.

Because its creators were writing about what they knew and concentrated specifically on the world of the dancer, they were able to make this particular backstage story work on a metaphorical level, and become about life itself.

A Chorus Line was a modern, contemporary show, using techniques pioneered in such shows as *West Side Story* and *Company,* which restored the human emotion many felt was lacking in recent state-of-the-art musical theatre. It can be considered a "concept musical" like *Company,* in that it lacks a linear plot, substitutes characters and confession for a conventional book, and is organized and held together by the concept of an audition. However, *Company* and *Follies,* two shows as brilliant as and perhaps more innovative than *A Chorus Line,* never began to achieve its popularity and this was because many observers found the characters in those shows cold and unpleasant, their lives barren and grim. *A Chorus Line* managed to use the splintered sensibility and ultramodern stage techniques of earlier concept musicals, while restoring the emotional impact of such shows as *Carousel* or *The King and I.* For the first time, audiences flocked to a concept musical in a way they never had before, and it was simply because *A Chorus Line* put back the element of humanity that many found lacking in earlier examples of the genre. It was a concept musical in which you cared about every character onstage.

Bennett's work in *A Chorus Line* was in a direct line from the work of the great choreographic innovators. Like de Mille, he used dance to convey the emotion of characters. As contemporary as it was, Cassie's dance portrayed the character's psychological state just as the dream ballet in *Oklahoma!* conveyed Laurey's. Picking up where Jerome Robbins left off, Bennett created a seamless work in which all elements were choreographed. A sequence such as the "Hello Twelve" montage took what Robbins had achieved in the area of continuous motion in *West Side Story* and carried it even further. And, like Gower Champion, Bennett still believed in razzle-dazzle, and provided a deeply ironic finale that nevertheless sent the audience into musical-comedy heaven.

A Chorus Line also has direct links with the work of Bennett's former collaborators, Prince and Sondheim. Like *Cabaret,* Bennett used mirrors symbolically in *A Chorus Line.* In both shows, the mirrors reflect the audience and make it one with the action. While the mirror in *Cabaret* implicates the audience, putting them onstage with the heedless revelers ignoring the horrors outside the Kit Kat Klub, the *Chorus Line* mirrors make us identify with the plight of the dancers and put us on the line with them.

As in *Follies*, *A Chorus Line* takes place in an empty theatre, and both deal in character revelation and the past. Both deal simultaneously on levels of reality and nonreality. In *Follies*, we are simultaneously at a reunion of showgirls and on a metaphorical plane where the central characters review their lives and attempt to come to terms with disillusionment. In *A Chorus Line*, we are at an audition, but one that becomes everybody's audition for acceptance and love.

Part of Bennett's genius was his ability to absorb and synthesize elements and techniques of Robbins, Prince, and the other great pioneers and produce a work that reached audiences more immediately than that of his predecessors. *West Side Story*, the most innovative musical-theatre piece of the Fifties, also had a strong emotional effect on the audience, but when it first opened, it was disturbing and offputting to many critics and audience members because of its nervous, often violent dance patterns and its complex scoring. Bennett managed to create a show that was as contemporary and fresh as *West Side Story* was in the late Fifties but that reached audiences as directly as the Rodgers and Hammerstein classics of the Forties.

It was also a show that left a permanent mark on the arts and on musical theatre. It brought about a new awareness of and attitude toward dancers in all media. In film, there was suddenly *The Turning Point*, *All That Jazz*, *Fame*, and *Staying Alive*, all of which explored the mystique of dancing and made audiences aware of the world of the dancer. On television, Baryshnikov danced in the *Chorus Line* finale on his special, "Baryshnikov on Broadway"; the made-for-TV movie *Legs* dealt with the plight of the Rockettes and had several themes in common with *A Chorus Line*; and Shirley MacLaine's 1976 special, "Gypsy in My Soul," became a celebration of the anonymous chorus dancer.

In the theatre, *A Chorus Line* created a new interest in dance musicals that led to such shows as *Dancin'*, *42nd Street*, and *My One and Only*, and the many companies of *A Chorus Line* created an enormous pool of talent that was employed in these later dance shows, films, and television specials. It resulted in dancers being paid as principals rather than as chorus, and this carried over to other productions to which dancers made significant contributions. Not only did the show provide employment for hundreds of performers but its graduates are still to be found in every new musical that employs dance.

Such musicals as *Runaways* and *Working* echoed *A Chorus Line* by consisting largely of confessional monologues, songs, and dances. Even *Cats* bore noticeable similarities, in that its unifying device was a competition, each cat performing a number in the hope of becoming the one that gets to go to the "heaviside layer." At the end of *Cats*, Grizabella gets a second chance just as Cassie does at the end of *A Chorus Line*.

What was most innovative about *A Chorus Line* was not the finished product but the way in which that product was created. Its greatest contribution to musical theatre was the demonstration of the value of the workshop process in creating shows. As has been noted, workshops had been used by modern theatre companies prior to *A Chorus Line* to develop pieces, but Bennett proved it was a viable device for the creation of large-scale, expensive musicals, and in so doing he introduced a new method of doing shows that temporarily saved the musical theatre.

A Chorus Line changed the way musicals were produced. Producers realized after its success that it was no longer wise to commission the writing of a show, put that show into rehearsal, take it on the road, then bring it to Broadway, all in a matter of months. Bennett had put a show into rehearsal that did not really exist, and during the months of workshop, it was written as he worked with his company. By the mid-Eighties, close to a hundred musicals had been developed in workshops, and what was once an avant-garde technique unknown to big-time Broadway was now the primary means of developing new musicals. Bennett later noted that his commandeering of this experimental technique was accidental: He knew that the material from the tapes could not be shaped in a conventional way and that more time would be necessary to develop it. Papp's offer of space and a workshop situation came along at exactly the moment when he was trying to find a way to develop the material that would allow him the time and ability to explore. This "accident" revolutionized the development of musicals.

BENNETT: "Workshops give you the opportunity to test material on actors, to try things out. They give the writers time, without being under the pressure of being in a hotel room in Boston, out of town with a deadline and $4 million on their back. Workshop allows you to be wrong, then fix it. One day you go, 'Gee, this is really pretty good, time to show it to people.' Sometimes it's never pretty good, and if you're smart you abandon it in workshop. And a workshop costs $1/100$ of what it costs to do a Broadway show. That means that anybody with an idea for a musical can really go employ a lot of out-of-work actors and can try things. It is, I think, the solution to the problem of musical theater.

"The workshop process has enabled a lot of shows that would never have gotten done because they were too risky to get on. When you go to a producer and talk about a musical that doesn't have stars in it, the tendency for producers is to be very shortsighted. They only want to do things that have elements of something that was successful already.

"Stock is gone, and that's where all young choreographers and directors used to train. You cannot do a musical unless you have grown up with them. You cannot possibly be the leader of something as complicated as a musical unless you have done a number of them before. So workshops offer new talent a place to learn their craft."

Unfortunately, *A Chorus Line*'s great legacy to the development of new musicals became bastardized through overuse. Many directors began to use workshops as glorified backers' auditions and became less interested in developing the material than in getting the show on its feet in front of those who might be able to finance a full-scale production. Others used workshops simply as extended rehearsal periods, without the constant experimentation, change, and refinement Bennett brought to his workshops. Because of union demands, workshops soon became as expensive as small productions. In earlier times, producers were not able to see what they had until going out of town, where troubled shows were often made into hits under maximum pressure. With workshops, show-business insiders and money people came to see unfinished shows, expressed doubts about them, and put a premature end to projects that might have developed into fine shows under the old system.

Bennett admitted before his death that the workshop process might have run its course and that it might be time to find a new way to create musicals. Yet at present, most new musicals employ some form of workshop in their development, and the technique that Bennett introduced to the musical will continue to be felt for decades to come.

A Chorus Line also demonstrated that the director-choreographer as most powerful member of the creative team was here to stay. Robbins, Champion, and Fosse had shown that great shows could be produced when the director-choreographer was allowed to exercise complete authority and when his contribution was allowed to dominate all others. Bennett confirmed this, while showing that the director-choreographer could allow every member of the production—from performer to designer—to contribute, in harmony with his overall conception.

The danger inherent in *A Chorus Line*'s confirmation of the importance of the director-choreographer was that there were very few capable of taking total control with the skill and talent of Robbins, Fosse, Champion, or Bennett. Many projects failed when the material was allowed to take second place to director-choreographers of lesser talent. Only Tommy Tune has succeeded in recent years in conceiving an entire production as successfully as they had.

Is *A Chorus Line,* as Bernard B. Jacobs has called it, "the finest piece of musical theatre ever"? At once so simple and so complex, so modern and so traditional, so honest and so sentimental, so daringly conceived yet so direct in its ability to reach an audience, *A Chorus Line* clearly stands as one of the finest achievements of the American musical theatre. Some would say Bennett had done work as brilliant on *Company* and *Follies,* while others maintain that in *Dreamgirls,* he would go beyond what he achieved in *A Chorus Line.* Wherever one stands on the issue, *A Chorus Line* was a brilliant synthesis of old and new, and a perfect combination of artistic achievement and popular appeal.*

. . . .

*For the story of the next fourteen years of *A Chorus Line.* 890 Broadway, and Bennett's movie deal, see Appendix A.

Above, great collaborator Bennett, surrounded by the writing team of *A Chorus Line,* 1975. Front: James Kirkwood, Bennett, Nicholas Dante. Rear: Ed Kleban, Marvin Hamlisch. [Martha Swope] Below, Bennett on the line again, but in charge, rehearsing *A Chorus Line* at the Public Theater. [Martha Swope]

Two *Chorus Line* epiphanies: above, the faceless candidates for the line at the end of the opening sequence [Martha Swope]; below, Cassie (Donna McKechnie), alone with the music and the mirror, stakes her claim to a second chance. [Martha Swope]

Two "One"'s: Zach (Robert LuPone) insists on unison dancing, which does not come easily to Cassie (Donna McKechnie), as the number is rehearsed. Below, the "One" finale: triumph or tragedy? [Martha Swope]

Donna McKechnie and Michael Bennett celebrate and ponder the phenomenal success of *A
Chorus Line.* [Ezio Petersen]

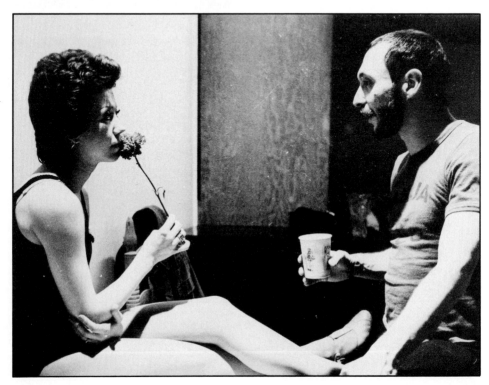

Ballroom, 1978: Dorothy Loudon as Bea, the lonely widow who finds Al (Vincent Gardenia) at the Stardust Ballroom, and dances back to life. [Martha Swope]

Above, as the Stardust Ballroom comes to life, its patrons shed their workaday existences and become young again. [Martha Swope] Below, "Some people never go dancing": The mirror ball shines down on the transfigured waltzers of the *Ballroom* finale. [Martha Swope]

Dreamgirls, 1981. Above, Michael Peters, Bennett, and Bob Avian invent choreography that must look like routines invented in Deena Jones's basement. [Martha Swope] Below, Bennett at a rehearsal with his leading ladies, Jennifer Holliday and Sheryl Lee Ralph. [Martha Swope]

Above, James Thunder Early (Cleavant Derricks), the Dreamettes, and a dancing orchestra, all swept up in the continuous movement of *Dreamgirls.* [Martha Swope] Below, corruption made palpable, as the payola-laden D.J.'s ascend to heaven in "Steppin' to the Bad Side." [Martha Swope]

Above, the Dreams make it big in Cleveland, but Effie is no longer in the middle (left to right: Jennifer Holliday, Sheryl Lee Ralph, Loretta Devine). [Martha Swope] Below, Bennett and five of his *Dreamgirls* leads were nominated for Tonys (left to right: Obba Babatunde, Sheryl Lee Ralph, Bennett, Jennifer Holliday, Ben Harney, Cleavant Derricks). Only three of them won. [Ezio Petersen]

During their triumphant engagement at the Las Vegas Hilton in the early Seventies, Deena Jones and the Dreams sing a medley of their hits, which became *Dreamgirls*'s entr'acte. This Act II opening was revised for the Los Angeles production, and later for Broadway. [Martha Swope]

At 890 Studios, Bennett rehearses his new, one-night-only version of "The Music and the Mirror" for the 3,389th performance of *A Chorus Line* on September 29, 1983. [Martha Swope] Below, the "Cassie handshake" as performed by multiple Cassies at #3,389. [Martha Swope]

Pandemonium at the Shubert: the finale of #3,389, as the audience and more than three hundred dancers become "One." [Martha Swope]

Above, Multiple Pauls (with the original, Sammy Williams, in front of the line) recite the monologue at #3,389. [Martha Swope] Below, "I have a wonderful family": Bennett takes to the stage as #3,389 ends. [Ezio Petersen]

THIS CARD ADMITS ONE

to a special black tie dress rehearsal of

MEZ H3

A CHORUS LINE

MEZ H3

celebrating its becoming
the longest running show in Broadway history.

The Shubert Theatre, 225 West 44th Street
Dress rehearsal at 2pm.   Doors open at 1:30pm.

BLACK TIE REQUIRED – No Admission Charge

Non-transferable. Sale of this card is strictly prohibited by law.

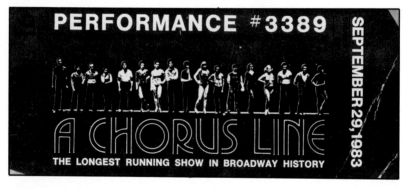

PERFORMANCE #3389

A CHORUS LINE
THE LONGEST RUNNING SHOW IN BROADWAY HISTORY

SEPTEMBER 29, 1983

Above, the hottest tickets in town on September 29, 1983: invitations to the black-tie dress rehearsal and the performance of #3,389. Below, *A Chorus Line* spoke to audiences around the world. A rehearsal of "Hello Twelve" at Vienna's Raimund Theater, 1987. [Courtesy of Raimund Theater, Vienna]

Rehearsals for *Scandal,* the Bennett musical no one ever got to see. Above and over, Bennett creates the sensuous choreography that was the best of his career. [Geoffrey Clifford/Wheeler Pictures] Below, Swoosie Kurtz borne aloft, Treat Williams extreme right, in the dazzling opening fantasy sequence. Probably only Bennett could have gotten a working turntable in a rehearsal hall. [Geoffrey Clifford/ Wheeler Pictures]

[Geoffrey Clifford/Wheeler Pictures]

PART FOUR

....

TIME TO GROW

—TIME TO GO

Martha Swope

1

BALLROOM:

OFF THE PEDESTAL

WHEN BENNETT WAS A gifted child with a reputation as an adorable bundle of talent, the Mafia approached his father about "buying" him, meaning they would have controlled him and shared in his success as they had with certain popular singers.

In 1977, Bennett believed that the Mafia was finally out to get him because he still "owed them." He claimed he had found out they were going to kill him, and he believed that everyone was in on it. He was afraid to tell his analyst, believing that even he was part of the plot. He claimed to know the exact time he was going to be killed. When that moment finally arrived and he survived, he realized he had hallucinated the whole thing. But it was in that frame of mind that he began working on his next big musical.

As a result of *A Chorus Line*, Bennett, still in his mid-thirties, had become one of the two or three most powerful forces in the musical theatre. He was keenly conscious, however, of the fact that expectations for his next show would be enormous, even unreasonable. He told Clive Hirschhorn in *Plays and Players* magazine, "There are going to be a lot more shows, and they're not going to be *Chorus Line*s. I'm going to have failures, and if I allow my whole life to be geared to what the critics and the public think, I'm going to be in for some heavy-duty painful days. I've seen too many people who've had a terrific success not do anything for the next five years because they're afraid it won't be as good as their last show."

Bennett was aware that he had to do something very different from his megahit, but he also knew that no matter what he and his team came up with, it would be compared to *A Chorus Line.* He told Robin Wagner, "Look, no matter what I do the next time out, they're going to kill me. Everybody wants *A Chorus Line II,* but I'm not going to do *A Chorus Line II.* I'll never do *A Chorus Line II.*"

The project he ultimately chose for his next musical surprised many, including those on his staff, but it was one that would ultimately prove to have much in common with *A Chorus Line* artistically and thematically. In 1975, CBS telecast an original made-for-television movie, *Queen of the Stardust Ballroom,* starring Maureen Stapleton and Charles Durning. The story of a Bronx widow who finds new happiness and fulfillment at a slightly run-down local dance palace and falls in love with a married mailman, the television film was well received by critics and audiences. It was written by Jerome Kass, with incidental music and lyrics by Billy Goldenberg and Alan and Marilyn Bergman. A year or two later, Bennett, who had been approached about directing the original teleplay, found himself working on the aborted film *Roadshow* with Kass, who was then interested in developing a stage version of his *Queen of the Stardust Ballroom* teleplay. Against his better judgment, Bennett decided to take on the stage transfer.

AVIAN: "We developed a wonderful relationship with Jerry Kass. I think because *Roadshow* didn't get made and we liked Jerry so much, Michael felt he owed him something."

LENNY: "Michael didn't see *Stardust Ballroom* as a show, but he got so close with Jerry that he finally said okay, probably in a weak moment."

Yet there was a profound personal motivation—beyond that of his friendship with Kass—for Bennett's involvement in the project. He had paid tribute in *A Chorus Line* to the gypsies who fell roughly into the twenty to thirty age category. But Bennett never forgot dancing on Broadway in the early Sixties and those with whom he had danced. By the mid-Seventies, many of those people had retired or taken nontheatrical jobs. The ever sentimental, loyal Bennett decided it was time to set them dancing again, and, in so doing, to pay tribute to an earlier generation of gypsies.

WAGNER: "When Michael told us we were doing *Ballroom,* there was a chorus of *whys.* He said, 'Because I have twenty friends over the age of 40 who will never dance on Broadway again if I don't do this show. I want to see those people on Broadway.' So it was really a labor of love."

MICHAEL VITA, dancer for Bennett in *Promises, Promises* and *Ballroom:* "*A Chorus Line* showed what young dancers could do. He wanted to do something for the older ones, because he was a part of that world. That's where he started, and it was only his genius that brought him out of that world."

The company Bennett assembled consisted of over thirty dancers in the forty to sixty age bracket who had danced in many of the classic musicals of the Forties, Fifties, and Sixties. Included were Mary Ann Niles, first wife of Bob Fosse, and Gene Kelton, who, fifteen years earlier, had danced the fireman to Bennett's rag doll in *Here's Love.* For the roles of the widow and her new love, Bennett originally envisioned Beverly Sills and Dick Van Dyke. For his heroine, he settled on a Broadway musical star who was about to join the roster of stars fired by Bennett under unpleasant circumstances.

Having experienced the workshop process on *A Chorus Line,* Bennett never considered any other way of doing his next show, and *Ballroom* became one of the first musicals to be developed in the not yet fully renovated studios at 890 Broadway. For the first of a series of workshops, Bennett hired Dolores Gray, star of such shows as *Destry Rides Again* on Broadway and *Annie Get Your Gun* in London, and a film and nightclub performer as well, to play Bea Asher. When the second workshop began a month later, the company arrived to find no leading lady.

AVIAN: "Michael just didn't see Dolores in the role. She was a little too strong. She had a voice to die over, but she's a strong personality."

JANET STEWART WHITE, a dancer in *Ballroom:* "We were all crazy about Dolores, and she's such a great singer. We were told that she had been let go because her dancing wasn't strong enough. But there wasn't that much dancing for her to do. I think her presence was too theatrical and too flamboyant. She's a stunning, dramatic-looking woman. She read well, and her singing was dynamite."

BEN BAGLEY, record producer and a friend of Gray's: "Dolores loved Michael. The pain of it was that he wined and dined her and made her fall in love with him. He made her feel like she was the greatest star in the world with the greatest voice, and he only wanted her for the role.

"She rehearsed for three weeks. One evening after rehearsal, Dolores went to dinner with Michael, then came home. At 7 A.M. the next morning, she received a call from Michael's lawyer, saying, 'Don't come to rehearsal today. He's decided he needs a trained dancer for the part, and can't use you in the show anymore.' He felt she didn't move well enough. Dolores was in a state of total shock, feeling like she had lost a good friend."

Bennett auditioned former Broadway dancers Allyn McLerie and Marc Platt for the leads, momentarily considered the original Bea, Maureen Stapleton, and Sada Thompson for his leading lady, then went to see Dorothy Loudon backstage after a performance of *Annie,* in which Loudon had won a Tony Award for her hilariously demonic Miss Hannigan.

LOUDON: "Everyone in town knew about the workshop downtown, and all the women who had been asked to work on it. I wasn't upset, but I was wondering, 'When are they going to get to me? They've had everybody else in the world down there.' I thought it was because I was still in *Annie.* But Michael came and told me he was afraid I wouldn't be able to play the part because I was a recent widow. As it turned out, that was never a problem for me, because the only thing I had in common with the character was that we were both widows. Otherwise, she was nothing like me; she was Jewish, extremely strong emotionally, had a family and children, and was very gutsy and enterprising. We were really nothing alike.

"Michael and I made an agreement that I would do the workshop for two weeks while I was still in *Annie,* and if it worked out, we would sign a contract. . . . The second day, Michael called my agent and said, 'Let's forget about the two weeks. We've got to have her.' Throughout the workshops, Michael took care of me as if I were his child. He nurtured me, because of what I had gone through in my personal life."

For leading man, Bennett chose the excellent dramatic actor Vincent Gardenia, whom Bennett had directed in *God's Favorite.*

AVIAN: "Vinny helped us find the man's character, which was very elusive. He was not a musical performer, so we had to work very hard with him and protect him."

Mandy Patinkin was also in the workshops, as Bea's son, but when the role began to shrink and one of his songs was cut, Bennett advised him to take another offer he had received. The role would eventually have no songs and few scenes.

The *Ballroom* workshops functioned differently from those of *A Chorus Line,* as the show was based on an already well-known story, and the characters were not taken from the lives of the dancers rehearsing the show. But Bennett insisted on making every dancer a character, and to do so, he employed something of his *Chorus Line* technique.

WHITE: "Michael sat us down when the workshop began and told us, 'I want each person here to tell me how you got started in this business, and what motivated you to dance.' The stories we told were not all that exciting; you couldn't have made a show out of them. But he wanted to make each character in the ballroom an individual. He tried very hard for that, but was ultimately disappointed that not everyone really became someone."

What was most exciting about the five months of workshop was seeing the dancers come alive again.

LOUDON: "When Michael hired the dancers, most of whom had been teaching or doing something other than dancing for years, they all looked like anything but dancers. As we rehearsed, they got thinner, their posture changed, and they became so good-looking. Michael would get upset when they started arriving in sleek rehearsal clothes; he would scream for them to go out and get a banana split. By the time we opened, they had to pad some of them. They were an extraordinary group."

Although the action was divided between Bea's home and junk shop and the Stardust Ballroom, *Ballroom* offered Bennett the opportunity of creating almost continuous dances, highly complex and demanding of the dancers. The fox-trots, tangos, sambas, hustles, rhumbas, lindys, cha-chas, and waltzes took endless and grueling hours for Bennett to devise.

WHITE: "We weren't in shape for Michael's demands, and it was very hard. He treated us well, but could be inconsiderate about what he demanded of our bodies. After we'd been in the workshop a couple of months, we found that we weren't recovering on our one day off, Sunday. The soreness would not go away, and we'd come in on Monday in pain. Only two of us, myself and Victor Griffin, dared complain to our Equity representative. Michael let us have half of Saturday off first, then the whole day.

"Michael had us on edge at all times. You never felt sure of any part you had in any of the dances. You felt you were auditioning every day, the whole time. He didn't mean to do that. In his mind, it was like a gigantic chess board, and he would move people around and envision new things.

"Everybody loved him, but we were afraid of him too, because he was so powerful. He kept us at a distance; he was remote. And he expected performance level of you at all times. When he said, 'Let's run through a number,' what he meant was, 'Let's do a performance of this number.'

"Michael was wonderful when he was up there dancing for us. I never saw anyone so in love with dancing as that man. He loved us as dancers, but . . . some gypsies were upset about his not gypsying around with them, because he had been one of them."

The *Ballroom* workshops were divided between 890 and the Public Theater, because Bennett, after the unparalleled artistic freedom he had enjoyed with *A Chorus Line,* wished to continue his relationship with Joseph Papp and the New York Shakespeare Festival. The Festival was originally set to co-produce *Ballroom* with Bennett, and the show work-shopped at the Public in the summer of 1978. By Labor Day, the Festival was out, and an irreparable rift had occurred between Papp and his associate producer of seventeen years, Bernard Gersten.

MERLE DEBUSKEY, the show's press representative: "As the show developed, it became apparent there was no stage space at the Public that could accommodate the physical production. Michael wanted to do the show first at some place protected, so he decided to go to Stratford, Connecticut. He wanted to hold on to his relationship with the Festival, but Joe said he couldn't put Festival money into a Broadway production that wasn't starting at the Public. Michael understood his position, and said Joe didn't have to put a nickel into it and his participation would still be the same. But Joe still refused. Bernie was very much involved with *Ballroom* from its inception, and when this schism arose, Bernie said they had an obligation to Michael, and asked if he could be responsible for *Ballroom* by himself. Joe told Bernie if he didn't sever all relationship with the show, he was finished. Bernie wouldn't accept that, and so, in Joe's opinion, he was."

Other sources indicate that Papp may have shied away from such overtly sentimental, commercial material. Papp also felt that Bennett and his organization had already, in effect, produced the show, and that it would have been inappropriate for a nonprofit organization to present a big commercial Broadway musical it had not truly developed.

The show's co-producers were ultimately Avian, Gersten, and Bennett's secretary, Susan MacNair, but its sole over-the-title producer was Bennett. This was appropriate, as Bennett had by now decided to finance the entire production himself, and had formed a new company, Quadrille Productions, to do so.

LENNY: "When Michael told me he was going to put up all the money for *Ballroom,* I said, 'You're crazy. People are dying to invest in the show.' He said, 'I have a feeling the first show I do after *A Chorus Line* is going to be a flop, and I don't want to burn up other people's money. If I'm going to gamble, I'll gamble with my own money.'"

By the time the company moved to Stratford to continue rehearsals, Bennett had begun to have serious doubts about the material and the effectiveness of the collaboration between him and the writers. While he frankly admitted that the show was his "1940's women's-picture musical," he was becoming aware that the show's plot, the simple tale of a widow who, against family opposition, finds love and learns to settle for half of her married lover's life, was dangerously thin for the elaborate production he had envisioned. Bennett and his writers had wisely decided not to have Bea die at the end as she had in the movie, but they had not come up with anything sufficently dramatic to take its place. The situation was not helped by the growing internecine conflicts.

DEBUSKEY: "Michael had great fear that it wasn't going to succeed. He knew its flaws, but he couldn't lick them. The songwriters were at odds with both Michael and the book writer. The book writer was at odds with Michael, and later maintained that he had never had sufficient time to fix it, and that the perspective of the show had changed."

Bennett had also decided on a highly unconventional use of music in the show, one that would ultimately deprive it of the full emotional impact of musicals with more conventionally structured scores. The majority of the score had been turned over to the bandstand singers in the background at the Stardust Ballroom, and only the two principal characters were permitted to express their emotions in song. By the time the show opened on Broadway, the male lead had no solo songs, and the female lead had the only six "book" or character songs in the show. While *Ballroom* was actually more about the ballroom as a metaphor for life than it was about Bea and her friends, the lack of standard theatrical numbers gave most of the score the feeling of background music.

Bennett again insisted on an invisible orchestra, and he and orchestrator Jonathan Tunick decided to place most of it in the wings on both sides of the stage, the remainder of it forming the ballroom's onstage band.

He chose the American Shakespeare Theatre in Stratford, Connecticut, for the show's tryout because its stage facilities were able to accommodate the complicated physical production, and because the theatre allowed him a month to rehearse onstage. He also felt that there would be less pressure if the show rehearsed and played away from New York. But pressure arose quickly, and Bennett was aware by the time the show reached Stratford that the collaboration was no longer functioning effectively. During the tryout, he brought in Larry Gelbart, co-author of the book of *A Funny Thing Happened on the Way to the Forum*, to add comedy and sharpen characterization, and Ron Field and Tommy Tune were invited to Connecticut to offer opinions and suggestions. Bennett was extremely close with the Shuberts at this time, and they watched closely and offered their suggestions. One major change that Bennett made, reportedly at the urging of the Shuberts, would stand as one of the most damaging miscalculations of his career.

When *Ballroom* began previews at Stratford, the curtain rose on one of the starkest openings of any musical. Loudon was alone in a drab cloth coat at her husband's grave site, and the stage was bare, with only a spotlight on Loudon. She sang an intense heartbreaking threnody entitled "Who Gave You Permission?"; this was an expansion of a brief song in the original teleplay. The number blended into the show's first dialogue scene, set in Bea's basement, which featured another beautiful song, "The Job Application," as Bea pondered her alternatives.

Before the opening in Stratford, Bennett decided that it would take the audience too long to realize the show was not about death but regeneration. He cut both scenes and numbers.

AVIAN: "We felt it was such a depressing way to start a show. It was so sad, and we felt the audience couldn't recover from that."

But cutting those songs and scenes deprived the audience of the chance to gain the necessary empathy and understanding needed for the rest of the evening. By opening night on Broadway, the show began with a dialogue scene set in Bea's junk shop, and it took the audience much longer to find sympathy for the character and her plight. The deletion of the first two numbers also eliminated probably the finest work Goldenberg and the Bergmans came up with for *Ballroom*.

LOUDON: "The original opening showed Bea's anger. It was a startling moment, and you could hear people sobbing in the middle of the song. They were destroyed, and this was supposed to be a musical. I thought the number was wonderful. At the time it was dropped, I had such faith in Michael that I talked myself into believing that he was right. But I now realize that, just because he was a genius doesn't mean he can't make a mistake. . . . The second song, 'Job Application,' was maybe my favorite in the whole show. I felt that those numbers got the audience so involved, and it was not a problem to get them back. They hadn't gone anywhere; they had come with us.

"I think anyone who saw the show originally couldn't have liked it as much after those songs were cut. At the time, I was convinced he knew what he was doing and that there was a good reason. But . . . I think even Michael might admit today that he was wrong."

By the time of the Stratford opening, Bennett had secretly lost hope and affection for the show.

LENNY: "I went up for the opening, and I loved it. After, I said to Michael, 'This show is terrific.' He said to me, 'Would it surprise you if I told you I want to close the show here?' I said, 'You'd devastate me.' He said, 'I want to close it, but the authors won't let me. The critics are going to kill me. *A Chorus Line* looks like the work of a genius. *Ballroom* looks like it could be the work of anybody."

While Bennett's judgment was grossly unfair to himself, the *Variety* review from Stratford seemed to corroborate his doubts: "It seems that Michael Bennett may have made an unfortunate choice when he decided to lavish so much talent, time and money on making a musical out of the 1975 television play, *Queen of the Stardust Ballroom,* itself a slight piece."

Yet that opinion and the bleak outlook Bennett had by this time adopted were very much at odds with the real and often thrilling achievements of the show. In spite of compromises and the inescapable slightness of the plot, Bennett had come up with a production of surpassing beauty, elegance, and thematic richness.

Tharon Musser was able to use a far more advanced lighting board than that of *A Chorus Line,* and she painted the stage in deep reds and twinkling stars. For the set, Wagner ultimately devised a mirrored paradise, a fantasy land in which the aging clientele of the Stardust became young again.

WAGNER: "The ballroom set was all done with mirrors. It looked like a crowd with very few people on stage. The whole set was based on the final scene, when the leads waltzed together. The whole thing would turn into this swirl, with thousands of stars reflected off the mirrors. Everything was built back from that moment, from that vision Michael had of these two people dancing in a constellation."

Bennett's choreography was perhaps his finest to date, featuring a breathtaking panoply of all imaginable ballroom styles, appropriately heightened for emotional effect wherever possible. He, who always liked a reason for people dancing or singing onstage, had a perfect vehicle for his prodigious creativity in *Ballroom,* but, more significantly, he used the dancing, as he had in *A Chorus Line,* for dramatic effect. The show was about renewal and self-liberation, and in the dance sequences, the characters shed their drab existences and became beautiful, just as the *Chorus Line* kids became beautiful at the ballet. The dances throughout were not strictly realistic, becoming more lyrical or frenzied where appropriate, in order to suggest the unreality these people's lives assumed when they stepped into the Stardust.

Bennett worked hard to give each dancer a personality, a few small individual quirks, a particular way of moving, or even a special way of sitting down. If there was not time in the play to develop more than a couple of the ballroom's inhabitants fully, the movement of each character was enough to tell the audience all it needed to know.

The cinematic style that was to reach its apotheosis in Bennett's next show was already in evidence throughout *Ballroom* as well. For example, when Loudon and Gardenia turned around in the ballroom to go home, they moved only a few inches. Everything around them changed instantly, and they were home.

Ballroom, in spite of its thin plot, also had thematic parallels to *A Chorus Line.*

DEBUSKEY: "The ballroom was a metaphor for life, and the people in the ballroom were beautiful. When you got to the ballroom, everything moved into an unreal world of beauty. No matter how humdrum their existence on the outside, in there everyone was a prince or princess."

Dancing gave meaning to the lives of the characters in *Ballroom,* just as it had given meaning to the *Chorus Line* gypsies.

Bennett conceived every aspect of the production with the underlying vision of a circle. There were the semicircular set, the circular dances, and even the show's original circle logo, replaced by the round mirror ball logo, all reflecting the circle of relationships and the circle of life and death that Bennett saw as the show's subject. If audiences were not as aware of the underlying metaphors of *Ballroom* as they had been of those of *A Chorus Line,* the symbolism nevertheless gave a richness to the ballroom scenes, making them rank with anything Bennett ever achieved on the stage.

By the time the box office opened in New York, the demand for tickets was such that the management was forced to open an additional box office in Shubert Alley. Many believed that *Ballroom* would have greater appeal to the mature bulk of the theatregoing public than *A Chorus Line* because it had a more developed plot, one to which mature audiences could easily relate. Nevertheless, Bennett's doubts about the material and his discomfort in the collaboration were mirrored in the show's reception when it opened on Broadway on December 14, 1978.

Several major critics were able to see beyond the slight plot and appreciate what Bennett had achieved.

WALTER KERR in *The New York Times* said: "It was Mr. Bennett's special inspiration to invent a half-fantasized world that altered itself radically and yet plausibly the moment the middle-aged lovers entered it. The moment they walked into the Stardust, they stopped walking, and started being the animated, carefree, syncopated souls they remembered themselves being before the years began going by so fast. The choreographer has somehow suggested that the dancers' own dreams buoy them up."

In *Women's Wear Daily,* HOWARD KISSEL said, "Unlike *A Chorus Line,* where the figures in the line become individuals through monologues and solo numbers as well as dance, here Bennett creates a corps full of individuals largely through dance. This is genuine theater choreography—it creates characters and drama."

Others, however, failed to comprehend or appreciate what Bennett was doing in *Ballroom,* most damagingly the daily *New York Times* critic Richard Eder, whose pan of the show may have sealed its fate more than any other element.

Bennett was devastated by the critical reception and the less-than-overwhelming reaction at the box office.

DEBUSKEY: "When it opened, Michael withdrew. He was very hurt by the experience. It was his creation, his idea, and when it didn't go over, he couldn't deal with it emotionally, and didn't want anything to do with it. Bernie Jacobs was very close and very helpful to Michael at the time, and after the show opened, the Shuberts took control of the show."

LOUDON: "We felt sort of deserted, because the creative people had all disappeared, as if they knew something we didn't. Michael was heartbroken, and I think it would have helped him if he'd shared some of that with the rest of us."

Business began to fall rapidly, and favorable word of mouth was not sufficient to stabilize it.

LOUDON: "A lot of people didn't come because they felt they'd seen it on television. Then there was a rumor around that Vinnie Gardenia and I weren't getting along. That was absolutely not the case, and it was damaging to the show. It was a love story, and people who came were saying, 'Oh, they don't really get along.' "

At the end of December, Bennett decided to proceed with an elaborate advertising campaign in an attempt to save the show and reach the audience of over-forty-year-olds for which it was intended. There was much television advertising at first, but Bennett was advised to discontinue the campaign, and he soon accepted an invitation that would take him away from Broadway for the remainder of the show's run.

WAGNER: "The Chinese had invited a delegation of 24 people for the first official American arts exchange. I went with Michael and others. While we were there, Bernie Jacobs called in with the grosses every day. The show started losing $75,000 a week, and after we were there four weeks, Bernie said, 'You have to close it.' It was partly Michael's decision, but the Shubert Organization also wanted to rent the Majestic Theatre to *I Remember Mama.*"

Ballroom closed on March 24 at a loss of about $3 million, making it one of the costliest failures in Broadway history at the time.

VITA: "When it closed, it was so sad to see all these people who had come out of their shells and become thin and independent, facing unemployment or tending bar or being a housewife again."

WAGNER: "A couple of months after the closing, I ran into one of the dancers, who said, 'That son of a bitch Michael! He goes off to China so he can close the show and not have to deal with us.' And this was one of the people he *did* the show for. The sad part was that most of these people didn't know he did the show for them, and that he took a personal loss of $3 million for them. They just felt he was a bastard for having closed it. There was no understanding and appreciation."

The show was not forgotten at Tony Award time. It received eight nominations, with Bennett and Avian sharing the prize for choreography.

In spite of its quick failure, it was a show that had a profound effect on many involved. Talking about its short life is extremely painful for cast members, and the show ranks as one of the more fondly remembered financial failures in musical history by many of those who were in it and some of those who witnessed it.

AVIAN: "There were elements we loved about it, but it wasn't big enough. It had a sweet, simple story, and a lot of the critics wouldn't let Michael get away with that. They wanted something stronger, and they wanted us to make steps in terms of writing.

"What was exciting about it was seeing those older dancers pull it back together, and seeing them back where they loved to be, on stage. The show changed their lives; by opening night, they were kids again."

MUSSER: "I loved that show and cried when it closed. We knew we had a television show to start with, and, unfortunately, we were never able to get it out of that. The plot hurt it. If any show ever proved that scenery, lights, costumes, and staging can't do the whole thing, that was it.

"Also, I will believe to my dying day that no matter what we did after *Chorus Line,* we would have had our throat cut. There is an element in our business that likes to see people fail, and I think if we had done the second coming, we still would have gotten clobbered."

For the show's star, the memory of working with Bennett is the most treasured of her career.

LOUDON: "I loved the show, and can never think of it as anything other than a hit. It was my favorite musical, and people come up to me all the time and talk about it. It was mine, and they can't take that away. I would love to do it again. I would do it on a streetcorner.

"When I think of Michael, I think of the sweetness of his face, and the confidence he would instill in me. He could somehow transmit his belief in what you were doing to you, and it was a confidence I desperately needed personally and professionally. But I don't think it was me; he did that all his life with people he worked with. In a crowded rehearsal hall, he could spot when someone was in pain or having a problem, and he would call a break, walk over to them and help. It was never manipulation. I felt he was totally honest. He had such a love of life, and he took his time and was never in a hurry. You wish now somebody had run up to him and said, 'Hurry up,' but he probably wouldn't have anyway. He loved life so much, and he knew he was going to do brilliant things."

The failure of *Ballroom* ultimately had a salutary effect on Bennett.

MUSSER: "At the opening night party for *Ballroom,* I said to Michael, 'Well, we've now done the next one. Now we can get on about our business.' "

AVIAN: "Interestingly, our personal stability seemed to come back a little bit more after *Ballroom.* Dealing with the kind of success *A Chorus Line* was was very difficult. Failure sometimes is very helpful and healthy.

It stabilizes you. The pressure was off. All right, we did another show, and it was a bomb. Now life goes on."

Bennett had fallen off the pedestal on which he was placed as a result of *A Chorus Line,* and he felt more normal as a result. He believed that one of the reasons *Ballroom* failed quickly was because it did not fulfill his definition of a "hot" musical. While the dancers in *Ballroom* were dancing for a reason, there was still a "fourth wall" between the audience and the actors that Bennett felt he had not been able to penetrate. For his next project, he would choose the "hottest" material on which he would ever work. But for those who saw *Ballroom,* the memory of sixteen couples swirling without end through a kaleidoscope of stars is likely to remain indelible.

2

· ·

DREAMGIRLS:

STATE OF THE ART

B ENNETT: "I LOVE BACKSTAGE musicals. I love *Gypsy.* I like musicals about how musicals are made. I realized they're happier when I'm doing backstage musicals, and the truth is, I am, too. It's easier. When you have characters in a play who are singers and dancers, it's easier to get them to sing and dance than it is when a dentist is the hero."

While dancing came naturally to the characters in the Stardust Ballroom, Bennett was eager to return to the backstage milieu of *A Chorus Line* and to characters who actually were performers who sang and danced. But, unlike the material of *A Chorus Line,* the idea for Bennett's next backstage musical did not originate with him.

It began this time with Tom Eyen, best known as the author of such fairly outrageous Off-Broadway plays as *The Dirtiest Show in Town, Women Behind Bars,* and *The Neon Woman.* He was also director and co-librettist of the infamous *Rachael Lily Rosenbloom* in 1973. In 1975, he wrote a musical adaptation of *Dirtiest Show,* entitled *Dirtiest Musical,* with composer Henry Krieger. Nell Carter appeared in it and delivered a show-stopping song entitled "Can You See Me?" which inspired Krieger and Eyen to collaborate on another project.

KRIEGER: "I had always had a feeling for a show with all sorts of vivid black characters. Tom had the idea of seeing the world through the eyes and experiences of back-up singers."

EYEN: "I conceived it for Nell Carter, Leata Galloway and Marion Ramsey, three girls who were roommates and friends in the early '70's. One was the difficult one, one was the beautiful one and one was the funny one."

Just as Bennett's last two Broadway musicals had begun with the Public Theater and Joseph Papp, his next one, originally entitled *Project #9,* also began at the Shakespeare Festival.

KRIEGER: "We did a first workshop of the material at the Public Theater for Joe Papp, and Nell was in it, along with Loretta Devine and Sheryl Lee Ralph. We showed it to Joe when we were finished. Nell decided she wanted to be a television star and went to Los Angeles. Joe wanted to wait for her to come back before doing it again."

Eyen and Krieger waited almost a year but were eager to get on with their project. Coincidentally, Robin Wagner, who had designed the scenery for *Rachael Lily Rosenbloom* and knew Eyen, had asked Bennett to contact Eyen about directing a workshop of a musical called *Battle of the Giants,* which Bennett and Wagner were co-producing at 890. Eyen instead decided to show Bennett, Wagner, and Avian what he and Krieger were working on.

KRIEGER: "We came in with Loretta Devine, Sheryl Lee Ralph and Ramona Brooks. Tom talked through his idea of a show about three girls who grew up together and found fame and fortune, and the various ambitions of each. At this point, there was never a mention of the group called the Supremes, although people don't want to believe that."

AVIAN: "I found the material irresistible; Michael wasn't so keen on it. Tom didn't really have a script and was having difficulty pulling it together. Michael said, 'Okay, we'll let him do a workshop, and we'll pay for it.' "

Bennett, who was becoming interested in producing projects that he would not necessarily stage, was thus not the original conceiver or director of the show that eventually came to be known as *Dreamgirls.* He decided to produce a workshop of the Eyen-Krieger project at 890 Broadway, leaving the direction to Eyen.

The first workshop, cast by Eyen and Krieger, featured Ralph, Devine, Brooks, Ben Harney, Obba Babatunde, and two young performers appearing simulataneously on Broadway in *Your Arm's Too Short to Box with*

God, Cleavant Derricks and Jennifer Holliday; all but Brooks would be in the show when it opened on Broadway more than a year later. The cast rehearsed the songs, which by the end of the first workshop included an overwhelming number called "And I Am Telling You I'm Not Going," as the script was created.

AVIAN: "There was a book, but it was only the first act, and very different from the final version."

During the first workshop, Bennett hired Michael Peters as choreographer.

PETERS: "I worked for Michael as a dancer in my first summer stock show in 1967, *West Side Story.* I was fascinated by him at the time; he was doing what I wanted to do. Although he was only the choreographer, he was running the whole show.

"In 1979, Robin Wagner asked Michael to help with the first Broadway show I choreographed, *Comin' Uptown.* Michael saw the show and sat with me for three hours. He started with the overture and went to the final curtain, giving me notes on every aspect.

"In the summer of 1980, Michael called and said, 'I'm producing a workshop. You'd be perfect for it. It's $150 a week, and you'd have to get here on your own. What are you doing for the next six to eight weeks?' I said, 'I guess I'm coming there.' "

By the time Bennett gave the okay for a second workshop, the pivotal role of Effie, played by Jennifer Holliday in the first, was being played by Jennifer Lewis.

HOLLIDAY: "I left during the first workshop. I was working at night and doing the workshop all day. I thought the material was corny, and that the workshop was going on too long."

During the second workshop, a second act was developed, in which Effie, no longer a part of the group of singers, became a nurse, employed by a Jewish woman played by Estelle Getty.

AVIAN: "At the end of the second workshop, Michael didn't think we had a show yet, but we all loved the idea."

By the time the third workshop began, the material was still not coming together in a satisfying manner, and it was at this point that a drastic change occurred: Bennett decided to assume the direction.

KRIEGER: "The idea of Michael directing the show was always something we knew could happen."

AVIAN: "It seemed like it was too much for Tom to try to write and direct it, so Michael decided to direct, which was agreeable to Tom and

Henry. It meant the show would get closer to production, and Tom could spend more time writing."

MUSSER: "We watched the workshop when Tom was directing, and Michael asked us, 'What do you think? Do you want to do this?' We said, 'Not unless you direct it.'"

PETERS: "When Michael came in, the numbers were going well, but there still wasn't a real story. There were disconnected scenes and pieces without a through line. We were all thrilled when he took over."

EYEN: "When Michael took over the direction, it was hard. I accused him of always wanting to direct the show. He had said that never in a million years was he going to direct a black show. I grew up with blacks, and that was my background.

"Without Jennifer Holliday in the second workshop, I wasn't able to write it correctly. I needed her tension."

Bennett, having taken the reins, was now to encounter difficulties with the project, which by now had changed its name from *Big Dreams* to *Dreamgirls* and featured Cheryl Barnes as Effie.

KRIEGER: "The third workshop didn't work out so well either. Michael didn't feel things were going his way as director, and didn't feel the cast was responding well to him or that he had a grasp on it. He became unhappy and disconsolate. On February 9, 1981, he said to us, 'Take the show back. It's yours. I can't go in that room again.' We said, 'Why don't you give us these last two weeks to see if we can whip it back up and give it back to you so you'll be happy again.' He said, 'Do whatever you want.' We continued the workshop, then gave a run-through. After it, Michael said we had done well, but that we should take it back anyway, but after some discussion, Michael changed his mind and decided to do it."

EYEN: "I called him a coward and said, 'You drop this show and you'll never do another.'"

But Bennett stipulated that if he was going to continue with the fourth workshop, the plot and book had to be the focus.

AVIAN: "For six weeks, we sat around a giant table and went from beginning to end with the writing. We stopped working on the staging, and just concentrated on the material. Michael and Tom were locked to the table, Henry to the piano. Michael and Tom story-boarded the plot. . . . We did it as a sit-down radio production."

PETERS: "Michael's genius was book; if A did not make sense to him, he could not go on to B. Michael took everything apart and reassembled the pieces. He knew it was not about the numbers. It was about making that book work, which he did."

For the fourth workshop, Bennett agreed to rehire Holliday for the part of Effie.

EYEN: "Henry and I wrote the show with Jennifer in mind. We wrote 'And I Am Telling You' at the end of the first workshop, and from then on, we were never happy with anyone else. Michael was always logical and didn't think Holliday was the logical choice for the role. He couldn't see this diva with Ben Harney. He knew you couldn't top the voice, but he hired Cheryl Barnes for the third workshop. . . . He finally gave in to using Holliday when I gave in to his directing the show. He also agreed to her when I gave him a full script. We had given up; we never thought we were going to have her with Michael directing. But I love divas with high-impact theatricality in my shows. Once I had Michael and Jennifer, I shut up."

But when Holliday returned, she discovered that the focus of the show had altered.

HOLLIDAY: "It was now focused on Deena, and the story had become closer to that of Diana Ross and the Supremes. That's when the first big fight between Michael and myself occurred. I felt I had been done an injustice. There was now no part for Effie in Act Two; she was only discussed. While they had not originally said that Effie would be the star, they had promised that we would have equal parts, and that was no longer the case."

The last straw for Holliday came near the end of the fourth workshop when Bennett decided to drop a song called "Faith in Myself," a very short version of which appears in the final version of the show. Holliday quit, just two days before the show was to be presented to the Shuberts, David Geffen, Metromedia, and ABC Entertainment, who Bennett hoped would finance the production.

KRIEGER: "Tom wanted to try to get her back, but Michael said, 'I'm not going to have anyone do that to me.' While Tom was right that Jennifer was extraordinary, I felt the material would get through without her, and I definitely agreed with Michael that we couldn't deal with her at that point. We got Alaina Reed, a very lovely, game woman, to do the presentation for us."

After the presentation, Bennett and others involved decided they had to have Holliday back.

HOLLIDAY: "Michael called me after several weeks and said, 'How would you like to be a star?' I laughed and said, 'I'm going to be a star. I'm going to make records and be like Aretha Franklin.' He said, 'If you come back, I'll make you a star. Why don't you fly to New York, and we'll talk about it.' He promised that the role would be built up and continue throughout the second act. . . . We realized that we had never really talked to each other before, only at each other. I now felt I could trust him. He did what he said he was going to do; not only did he beef up my role in the second act, he agreed to change my costumes, which had been designed to make me look homely."

Even without Holliday, the Shuberts, Geffen, ABC, and Metromedia agreed to finance the $3.5 million production, to be produced by Bennett, Avian, Geffen Records, and the Shubert Organization.

In contrast to the *Chorus Line* workshops, the *Dreamgirls* workshops were marked by uncertainty on Bennett's part.

BENNETT: "I was not as convinced that I ever wanted to do *Dreamgirls* as I was with *Chorus Line.* With *Chorus Line,* I don't think there was ever the feeling that that show would not one day be finished and performed. With *Dreamgirls,* there was a very real possibility that it would never be finished and performed."

The *Dreamgirls* workshops differed from the *Chorus Line* workshops in another significant way. While the personalities and suggestions of the performers were taken into consideration in the creation of the material, the characters in the play were not based on the performers' lives but were instead original creations of Eyen and his collaborators.

In common with both the *Chorus Line* and *Ballroom* workshops, Bennett pledged a percentage of his royalties to those involved in the workshops who then continued into the actual production.

Bennett was aware that he could ill afford another disappointment such as *Ballroom.* What made him, in spite of serious doubts about the material and his ability to master it, decide to take on *Dreamgirls* as his next musical? First, it was a thoroughly "show-biz," backstage piece, which allowed almost continuous natural opportunities for singing and dancing. Now that he was in charge, he made certain to keep the plot backstage, not straying off into the "real" world as it had in Eyen's workshops. On television's "Hullabaloo" in the Sixties, Bennett had danced behind girl groups, including the Supremes, just as the girls in the show began by singing behind successful stars, so Bennett had a natural affinity for the milieu and the plight of the central characters.

What may have been the strongest attraction for him was that the material in *Dreamgirls* would allow him to create his "hottest" musical yet, one in which the actors in the play were "performing" constantly, on television, in nightclubs, in recording studios, or on the concert stage. There would be no "wall" between the actors and the audience, as there had been in *Ballroom,* and the energy of the cast could be transmitted directly to the spectators.

Bennett loved big musicals, and the scope of the story of *Dreamgirls,* covering more than a decade, allowed Bennett the chance to work on a grand scale and create an epic. The production had a sweep and size beyond that of any he had done before, which was enhanced because he encouraged the writers to make the show a near-opera, with much sung "recitative" instead of dialogue, and lengthy musical sequences encompassing song, dialogue, and continuous motion.

Bennett was also attracted to the story and thematic underpinnings of *Dreamgirls.* It told the tale of three girls from Chicago who grew up together and formed a singing group, the Dreamettes. This "family," which included the brother of one of the girls, is gradually broken up— first by their ruthless manager Curtis's decision to shift the more attractive Deena into the lead spot previously occupied by Effie in order to achieve success in the white, "crossover" world. Curtis abandons Effie and shifts his romantic attention to Deena, driving Effie to a near-breakdown, which leads to her dismissal from the group. Deena eventually becomes disillusioned with Curtis, while Curtis tries to stop Effie from achieving success on her own. It was a tale of loyalty and betrayal, of a family disintegrating and reuniting, and it had profound appeal for Bennett, who always favored dealing with realistic human concerns and universal emotions.

BENNETT: "The problems that the black characters in *Dreamgirls* have are just problems about life as an American, the problems you have when you're in your 20's and you find out that happily ever after doesn't mean the things you thought . . . and that you can get everything you want and it's not what you thought it was going to be, and if you're going to survive, you have to keep wanting other things."

Bennett and his collaborators also found that the material gave them the chance to present the kind of black characters too rarely portrayed on the stage.

BENNETT: "The important thing about *Dreamgirls* for me was that I approached the material as if cultural assimilation is something that has happened in America. . . . *Dreamgirls* is not about being black, it's about being human. It's a black musical, but it's about people. It's not a black version of a white show. It's very nice for young blacks to go to the theatre and see role models who are successful and still human."

AVIAN: "We were interested in presenting the integrity of the black artist. We never saw it as a black musical; it just had black characters. It gave them a great dignity and integrity, and that was very important to us."

BERNARD B. JACOBS: "Although it's hard to perceive him like that, Michael was really a great advocate of civil rights, and he had a very strong feeling that he wanted to do a show which dealt with black people in the same way that most shows about white people deal with white people. He didn't want it to be a show that catered to race. He wanted it to be a show about blacks as people living in our society and having the same problems other people in our society have. He was very determined to do that, and to a large extent he did. One of the problems with the show was that the critics, to an extent, were unable to deal with a show about blacks the same way they would treat a show about whites."

Bennett also saw in *Dreamgirls* the most daring design possibilities of his career, and he and his team came up with a scenic concept for the show that was simultaneously dazzling in its complexity and glitz and stunning in its spare simplicity. In terms of scenery and lighting, it was the most integrated design ever created by the team, and the set even became a character in the show. Wagner created five floor-to-ceiling towers made of aluminum and Plexiglas, studded from top to bottom with stage lights. These computer-operated towers glided about in dozens of configurations, creating and defining spaces, shifting the scene from dressing room to backstage to recording studio to nightclub to television studio instantaneously, with only the addition of small pieces, such as a table or a curtain, needed to complete the environment. Bennett even found ways to use the towers, and a set of hydraulic bridges, to symbolize what was happening in the action.

BENNETT: "They're almost like a narrator. By the end of the first scene, the towers become more like a cage. They start closing in: the dressing rooms get bigger, but there are more pieces in them, and there's a feeling that these girls are trapped by their success."

The *Dreamgirls* set was a kinetic sculpture that played with spatial relationships, and, as with the *Chorus Line* set, it evolved during the workshops.

WAGNER: "The essential elements were born out of the material. We originally conceived the show as a big, lush, endless parade of places and scenes, but it got down to nothing.

"I remember getting a call from Michael at three o'clock in the morning from the Hamptons, after we had the idea of the towers. He said, 'Can

I make the towers turn?' We knew they would move on and off, creating walls and configurations, but we now devised a turning motor that moved with the unit. We also had the light bridges, which were originally intended just to sit there or move up and down to change the space. Michael decided he wanted to put actors on them, and that's where the number 'Steppin' to the Bad Side' came from.

"*Dreamgirls* could have been an elaborate show, but . . . by then, we were into functional theatre. When *Ballroom* didn't click, we all realized that we weren't very good at staged realism and creating artificial places on stage. Neither Michael nor I did that very well. Michael always said he liked me because I didn't like scenery."

AVIAN: "Robin did the most brilliant job of his life. After the show opened, Michael said, 'I want to do every show I ever do in that set.' "

The costumes of Theoni V. Aldredge played a far more important role in *Dreamgirls* than in the two previous Bennett musicals she had designed.

AVIAN: "People were not aware of what Theoni did. The men had as many costume changes as the women, 18 in all. The fabrics changed from polyester to cashmere, the cuff length from the floor changed."

PETERS: "There wasn't a realistic set, so Theoni's costumes told you where you were and what time you were in."

In his staging, Bennett came up with a concept that stressed fluidity, with scene blending into scene in a display of continuous motion never before achieved in a musical. The style Bennett chose for the show was suggested by the way in which Peters staged a later-abandoned Act Two opening sequence during the early workshops.

AVIAN: "That sequence set the style for what the whole show turned out to be. It told you what happened in the ten years that pass during the intermission, and it jumped around the stage, from girl to girl, to reporters doing interviews, using constant cutting and montage."

Bennett's cinematic style was at the heart of his *Dreamgirls* staging. Using jump cuts, crosscuts, close-ups, zooms, and wipes, Bennett did the seemingly impossible onstage, and many observers felt they were watching a film as they watched the show.

Some viewers complained that the show seemed short on actual dance numbers, and indeed, only "Steppin' to the Bad Side" exploded into a full-fledged dance sequence. Yet those who felt that Bennett and Peters were sparing with their choreography failed to realize that the entire show was choreographed, from the actors to the towers to the lights.

PETERS: "When we opened, many people said there was no choreography. But that show was staged—to death—from the moment the curtain went up. There was movement throughout, but because it was done so well, people just accepted it, without realizing what was going on up there.''

As co-choreographers, Bennett and Peters developed a very close working relationship.

PETERS: ''Michael's genius in terms of choreography was as an architect. He could take the pieces and the elements that were there, and change, form and reorder them. He'd lay out the structure or idea of a number, then he would let me play. Then he'd come in and say, 'I hate this, I love that. Change this, do that.'

''We knew early on that because it was a piece about singers, the movement had to be an extension of natural movement. The characters were drawn much more realistically than most musical comedy characters. We had to be concerned with what they had to do physically, like hold notes and harmonize. Sound had to come before movement, and our choreography had to come from a real place and be based in truth. It had its genesis in Motown routines, but it had to vaccilate between that performance quality and real movement. Michael always began with the simplest movement or gesture. The first gesture in 'Steppin' to the Bad Side' came out of the scene, then built ever so slowly: first a hand gesture, then an arm movement, then a posture, then a pose.

''The performance numbers were easier to do than the others. We did not want to vary too much in style from what groups like the Supremes actually did in the Sixties. But the performance numbers had to change in that the early ones had to look like they were choreographed by the girls in their basement, the later ones becoming more polished.

''Michael was primarily a tap dancer, and didn't have modern and ballet technique, which was my foundation. When I started to do versions of 'Steppin' to the Bad Side,' he would say, 'I'm not doing a modern dance concert. This is Broadway!' This was very intimidating at first, but we eventually developed a rapport.''

Dreamgirls was filled with explosive stage pictures and breathtaking musical sequences. Moving faster than the speed of sound, it never lost track of the human story that was its focus. The show was filled with staging highlights. There was the brilliant opening image of a group called the ''Stepp Sisters,'' backs to the audience, which immediately placed the audience backstage. In ''Steppin' to the Bad Side,'' the light bridges descended, a curtain opened, and two tiers of silhouetted figures in front of a green scrim passed records around, finally ascending to the roof of the theatre in an image of hellish corruption. This image then dissolved into the same song, performed "onstage" by Jimmy and the girls, which then dissolved into the next scene. The number "Heavy" moved from a television rehearsal to a backstage confrontation to a live performance in a San Francisco hotel, then backstage again, all without interruption. Perhaps the most cinematic moment in any Bennett staging occured at the end of Act One, at the conclusion of Effie's explosive solo "And I Am Telling You I'm Not Going," as Effie's table pulled away and moved upstage, causing her to "fade" and be "wiped" away by the girls who came on from the wings. A show curtain descended, separating them from Effie, once their "sister." At one point in Effie's song "I Am Changing" at the beginning of Act Two, the light on Effie's face narrowed to a pin-spot, and when it opened up, Effie was in a different dress, and there was an audience of enthusiastic admirers at her feet. The song "One Night Only" began as a "live" number sung by Effie, who was "wiped" away behind a tower. After a dialogue scene, Deena and the girls did a fancy, "onstage" version of the song, with cuts away to the men discussing the progress of the record. Then, like Robbins's "Tonight" sequence in *West Side Story,* "One Night Only" cut from one girl to another, focusing on the inner thoughts of each.

The electrifying force of Bennett's production was evident immediately to audiences in Boston, where *Dreamgirls* played a nine-week tryout. Much of the show was created during this time, as Bennett had had less than two complete workshops to work on the complex staging. Even after the show received rave reviews from the Boston press, Bennett continued to fine tune. During the tryout, Harold Wheeler, who had initially been asked to orchestrate only two numbers for Holliday, was asked by Bennett to re-orchestrate the entire score, while the song "One Night Only" was dropped and a different song substituted for a few performances. The fine tuning continued during New York previews, with the addition of a new ending, wherein Effie rejoined the other girls to sing the final song.

EYEN: "I think we made a mistake by bringing Effie back. In the original ending, it was just the three girls, and each had a section in which she sang about what she was going to do in the world. Then there were separate spotlights on each as they parted. It broke your heart. I was told that because we had made Effie the star character, we had to bring her back."

Bennett and Avian, who by now had come to love the show, were hurt when the New York press was far more divided about it when it opened at the Imperial Theatre on December 20, 1981. Douglas Watt in the *Daily News* was but one of several who felt that *"Dreamgirls* is all style and no substance." But others were aware of what Bennett had achieved.

John Simon in *New York* magazine said: "It is as if the entire enormous stage were a plaything in the hands of some invisible giant cooly, continuously juggling with it."

In *New Republic,* Robert Brustein stated: "Trying to criticize *Dreamgirls* is like arguing with a tank. The damn thing just rolls over your body, leaving you flat as a pancake with caterpillar tread marks on your brain. The people who put this musical together could change the social system if they wanted to."

Frank Rich of *The New York Times* said: "Mr. Bennett has long been Mr. Robbins' Broadway heir apparent, as he had demonstrated in two previous *Gypsy-*like backstage musicals, *Follies* and *A Chorus Line.* But last night the torch was passed, firmly, unquestionably, once and for all."

When Tony Award time rolled around, Bennett found himself with serious competition from his protégé, Tommy Tune. Tune's show, *Nine,* beat *Dreamgirls* as Best Musical, and Tune beat Bennett as Best Director of a Musical. While *Dreamgirls* was nominated for thirteen Tonys, it won only six, Bennett sharing the prize for choreography with Peters.

Bennett had attempted to avoid competition with the work of his erstwhile friend and collaborator Tommy Tune, and the results of the 1982 Tony race caused a permanent rift between them.

TUNE: "All through the years of his hiring me as a performer, Michael would discourage my choreographic work. He would say, 'Don't go out and choreograph that show in Podunk. Stay in New York and I'll use you in shows. You'll be a star.' But I became more interested in choreographing than performing.

"As long as I didn't have enormous success in my career, there were still times when I could get through to Michael. But when *Nine* won over *Dreamgirls,* it was a huge blow to Michael, and it made difficult all further relationship. I honestly don't think he ever forgave my winning.

"When we got the money and began rehearsals for *Nine,* it looked like we would be able to open just under the gun for Tony eligibility, although we did not plan to do that, ever. Michael called when the show was in rehearsal and said, 'Darling, you're not going to bring the show in . . . without a tryout. Don't ruin yourself trying to get in this season. You know and I know that a show can't get good without the proper out of town tryout and the proper length of previews in New York.' I couldn't believe what he was saying—it was so incredibly transparent. . . . Later, after the nominations came out, he said, 'I could take that you would win as best director over me, but I can't take that your show would win over our show, because that would mean that I'm not a good producer.' Of course, *Dreamgirls* was a big hit and a much more saleable, commercial show than *Nine*. And Michael had more Tonys than any of us. Michael walked into *Nine* once during a preview, looked at it and walked out. I don't think his ego could allow him to sit through it. I was at the first preview of *Dreamgirls,* and I loved it. I was definitely a fan of Michael's work, but I'm not sure that Michael was a fan of anybody else's."

Some observers maintain that Tony voters endorsed *Nine* in retaliation against the Shuberts, who, just two months earlier, had allowed the Morosco and Helen Hayes theatres to be destroyed to make way for the Marriott Marquis Hotel. Those in the industry knew that the Shuberts cared about *Dreamgirls,* and some voted for *Nine* as a means of getting back at them. Whatever the cause, Bennett was upset when his show did not win.

But it was not only critics and Tony voters who were divided as to the merits of the show. Some audience members found it dehumanized and accused Bennett of choreographing sets rather than people. Some saw it as an empty Las Vegas spectacle, all glitz and no substance. The emotional impact of *Dreamgirls,* with its moving story of a family that grew apart and eventually reunited, had a much harder time reaching audiences than that of *A Chorus Line,* probably because of the lightning pace and ever-in-motion staging. It required more than one viewing for some to discover the fundamental humanity of the show and to appreciate the richness of Krieger's score, which subtly shifted styles, from soul to rhythm and blues to pop and disco, in order to mirror the progress of the girls' careers.

Some of the thematic richness and emotional underpinning was Eyen's contribution, dating back to the early workshops.

KRIEGER: "There are things Tom gave the show that were really wonderful. He contributed the basic thrust and passion of the first act. So much of 'And I Am Telling You . . .' was created while Tom was director. Michael brought in the high-powered technique, know-how and multiplicity of talents so smoothly honed together of his design team. The ultimate mega-directorship he brought to it was fantastic. But the heart and guts of the conflicts were in the writing and direction of the first workshop at 890. You have to give that to Tom."

The *Dreamgirls* collaboration proved a mixed success. In the case of Peters, it was a learning experience and the beginning of a friendship that lasted for the remainder of Bennett's life.

PETERS: "Michael taught me about collaboration in the truest sense. He believed in having everybody's input, but he was the boss, the captain.

"Michael was a magician who wove spells. His beauty was that he was a man-child; he never lost that youthful innocence and exuberance. Everything was a big toy for him to play with."

For others, the experience was less happy.

AVIAN: "I loved the show and was very proud of it. But Michael was never totally satisfied with it, because there was a lot of tension and conflict. Things did not go smoothly."

DEBUSKEY: "By the end, the various creators were very unhappy with one another. It was not a love feast."

EYEN: "If you want what you want, it's always a battle. Michael and I both wanted what we wanted, and Michael was a fighter and loved to be challenged at all points. There were a lot of battles, but Michael loved battles. It was always a problem between us that Michael didn't conceive *Dreamgirls* as he had *A Chorus Line.* But I think *Dreamgirls* helped Michael get over *A Chorus Line* and go on from there."

As far as Bennett's career is concerned, *Dreamgirls* was his state-of-the-art show, a very advanced production that took musical theatre as far as it had ever gone in terms of continuous motion and speed. It moved with electrifying force, and had an enormous emotional effect on those who were reached by it. It was a show that pointed to the future, and led those who admired it to fantasize about where Bennett might take the musical next.

For its acclaimed star Jennifer Holliday, *Dreamgirls* had as overwhelming an effect as it had on its audiences. Bennett, with whom she disagreed and fought, changed Holliday's life as profoundly as he had the lives of the performers in *A Chorus Line.*

HOLLIDAY: "I had no acting experience at all, so Michael really held my hand throughout. He explained what he wanted by using emotions from our personal relationship or things we would see other places. It was like a word association game, involving things we did outside when we were not working, and it made it easier for me.

"Michael kept a close eye on the show during my year in it on Broadway. He was firm about us not overacting. He wanted to keep that first, pure thing that we all had as much as possible. A lot of things got too big and broad, and that's what he would watch for.

"I learned a great deal from Michael. The theatre was not important to me until I met him. I didn't see it through the same eyes as he did, but when I did, it became a whole different thing, because the theatre was his life. He taught me about being devoted to something you believe in, and going to whatever limits you have to go, because that's what he would do. He put up a great deal of his own money, because the other producers would say, 'No, we're over budget.'

"I found the whole show very difficult to do, very demanding, but I never got *Dreamgirls* burnout, because I was the first one to leave. They offered me more money to stay, but I didn't want to get bored. There are people who can say, 'I never saw Jennifer Holliday because when I went to 'Dreamgirls' her understudy was on,' but no one can ever say, 'I saw her and she wasn't giving 200%.'

"*Dreamgirls* had a powerful effect on audiences because Michael had that kind of effect on people. When I think about him, the word 'magic' always comes to mind. He was a kid who refused to grow up, and he loved magic. That energy stimulated everybody. The book and score were good, but his touch made it magic. He could pull rabbits out of hats."

Dreamgirls began what was to have been a lengthy national tour in Los Angeles, but two factors cut it short. Holliday withdrew after the L.A. engagement, and Bennett refused to scale down the production.

DEBUSKEY: "Michael was so insistent about doing the show the way he wanted that it became wholly impractical to tour. After L.A. and Chicago, we had to close it down. Even if you played for a long stretch, you could not amortize the cost of the move. It took over a week to get the show down in one place and up in the next."

Bennett put in several changes in the L.A. production, most notably an elaborate new opening number for Deena and the boys.

AVIAN: "We kept trying to make the show better. We never liked the original opening of Act Two, but we ran out of time."

BENNETT: "In the new opening of Act Two, I'm paying tribute to Jack Cole and what he did with Marilyn Monroe in movies. I'm doing a 1940's Jack Cole number translated to 1970, but I as a choreographer am doing it in the Eighties. That's fun to play with."

The new Act Two opening was eventually put into the New York production, as was the L.A. addition of an upstage orchestra, doubled by mirrors, in the finale.

Unhappy with the fact that the show had not reached the entire nation as *A Chorus Line* had, Bennett finally agreed to rethink the show for a bus-and-truck tour that eventually returned the show to Broadway. For many, this stripped-down version, in which the towers were smaller and moved by cast members and the hydraulic bridges were gone, allowed the show's emotional center to emerge more easily.

MUSSER: "Many thought it was better than the original, because without all the high-tech, the whole meaning of the show was clearer."

EYEN: "When Michael put together the bus-and-truck, he said, 'This is going to get better reviews for you.' And it did. They suddenly noticed the book. The show is really about a family breaking apart, a series of people leaving each other. . . . I think some of the high-tech elements were there originally because Michael was trying to top *A Chorus Line.* The pressure on him was incredible, so he made it *Star Wars Meets Gypsy.* It was dynamic, but a little overblown."

AVIAN: "Audiences were reached more by the bus-and-truck version. All the pyrotechnics, which got in the way for a lot of audiences, were eliminated. Michael once asked me, 'Do you think I overproduced the show?' I said, 'Of course you overproduced it. . . .' Ultimately, the restructuring for the bus-and-truck produced the best version: the simplest, the cleanest, and the best in terms of clarification."

When the bus-and-truck production brought *Dreamgirls* back to Broadway—at the Ambassador Theatre on June 28, 1987—the critics greeted it more enthusiastically than before. Frank Rich, always the staunchest of the show's supporters, wrote in *The New York Times,* "One is knocked out all over again by what still is the most exciting staging of a Broadway musical in this decade. Nearly all of the director's moves remain intact, and, bereft of most accoutrements, their unstoppable choreographic flow seems more impressive than ever. . . . It's not machinery or scenery but Mr. Bennett's talent for shaping stage space and propelling bodies to cinematic effect that sends the show hurtling through the night like lightning."

Unfortunately, Bennett was barely able to hear the new accolades, and would live just four days beyond *Dreamgirls*'s second Broadway opening night.

3

. . . .

#3,389

BENNETT WAS WELL AWARE that on September 29, 1983, *A Chorus Line* would be passing the record set by *Grease* to become the longest-running play or musical in Broadway history, and he had thought for some time about the best way to celebrate this event. His original conception was to bring back the entire original cast to play performance #3,389, but he realized this would do a disservice to the current Broadway company. He soon hit upon an idea that would entail the kind of organizational abilities only he possessed, an idea that would also embody the show's original message.

A Chorus Line's milestone performance (counted from the first Broadway performance on July 25, 1975) represented the first time a show broke the record while still a consistent money-maker; such record-breakers as *Hello, Dolly!, Fiddler on the Roof,* and *Grease* survived numerous unprofitable weeks in order to achieve their goal.

By 1983, with two other major musicals under his belt and at least three in development, Bennett had had a chance to put the *Chorus Line* experience—one that had changed his life as well as the lives of every participant—in perspective. The show had always been about dancers and brotherhood; what better way to embody this than to invite every performer who had ever been in *A Chorus Line,* from original cast to bus-and-truck, to participate in this gala, making it both a reunion and a celebration? He would invite the 457 alumni of all the companies and reconceive the entire show to accommodate as many as accepted.

Many dancers had been fired or left under less than happy circumstances, and this was an opportunity for Bennett to welcome back some people he may have felt he had mistreated. There were, however, two or three performers who were not invited, including one principal from the International Company who had not taken her firing at all well.

The cost of transportation, accommodation, party-giving, and the event itself came to about $500,000, more than the cost of the original Off-Broadway production of the show, and it was borne by Bennett, the Shakespeare Festival, and the Shubert Organization. The performers were offered a fifty dollar honorarium for the performance.

The term *gypsy* was not coined by chance, and it took four months to track down the performers and invite them. Some were less eager than others to participate; Robert LuPone, the original Zach, declined the invitation. Some were unable to be there, such as the original Bebe, Nancy Lane. Ultimately, 332 *Chorus Line* veterans were welcomed back on the Sunday night before the performance at a party thrown by Bennett and McKechnie at 890 Broadway.

MCKECHNIE: "When Michael called me, it was the first time I'd talked to him in a while. He was nervous about calling me, and at that point he usually didn't call me himself, so I was impressed and realized how much he wanted me to be there. I had no idea how much work and planning would go into it."

The four-day rehearsal period that began on Monday, September 26, was a stunning example of Bennett's organizational genius. He came prepared with an explicit rehearsal schedule and scripts for everyone, and he had decided to have each sequence or number performed by a different company.

TOM PORTER, stage manager: "Which company would do which part was decided according to what moments were in each section. For example, Michael knew who he wanted to do "Gimme the Ball," so the company to which that person belonged did the 'Shit Richie' section."

The finale, which would involve everyone, was rehearsed first. Then the dance captains of each company took their group to a room in 890 Broadway to rehearse the section of the show that group would be performing. Bennett worked nights on single numbers that he was restaging for the event and he began putting it together on Wednesday, with a run-through at 890. On Thursday, just hours before an invitational black-tie dress rehearsal, the entire company ran through the "new" show on the stage of the Shubert.

During rehearsal, some members of the original cast were disappointed to discover that they were not necessarily going to be performing their original number; some had arrived expecting to do the whole play, which was contrary to Bennett's democratic intention. One member of the original company was lost during the rehearsals.

BLAIR: "Michael told me that Mitzi Hamilton and I were going to do Val's number, which I thought was great—the real T & A girl and the trash mouth. But I was on a soap at the time, and the producers told Michael I could not have time off to be at all the rehearsals. Because they said no to Michael, he decided to punish me. He re-choreographed the entire number, knowing I wouldn't have enough time to learn it, and added a third girl to it. I didn't want to go on stage in that number and look ridiculous."

Rehearsals were a period of enormous emotion for those who had been there at the beginning.

MCKECHNIE: "There was no time to stop and talk to people. All you had time to do was look at each other and smile, and if you touched, that was a way of saying hello. There was a lot of non-verbal communication, making contact without having the time to sit down with people."

ROVETA: "It was incredible to see Michael put it together, but all I remember is crying the entire week. It brought back all the feelings, professional and personal, about what you had gone through when you first did the show, about the years that had gone by, and about Michael. It was exciting, but painful, like living what the show was about all over again."

The names of all 332 performers were flashed on the electronic sign on the front of the Shubert. The managements of such current hits as *La Cage aux Folles, Cats, 42nd Street, My One and Only,* and *On Your Toes* granted *Chorus Line* alumni a night off so they could participate. Don Pippin took a night off from *La Cage* to conduct the entire evening at Bennett's insistence. The stage of the Shubert was reinforced with forty-eight wooden pillars to support the weight of over three hundred people, all of whom would be onstage by the conclusion. The Shubert Organization donated the Booth Theatre—its stage, dressing rooms, and orchestra—as dressing and waiting rooms.

AVIAN: "The most amazing part of #3,389 was what happened at the Booth, where most of the cast was changing. There were giant screens set up so everyone could watch the show. As each group came off the stage, the others would scream and applaud for them; that was the most emotional part."

The result proved to be as seamless an effort as Bennett's original staging of the show. Miraculously, over three hundred people were exactly where they were supposed to be throughout the dress rehearsal, which was witnessed by a near-hysterical audience. Bennett had decided to have an invitational rehearsal because he was unable to give tickets for the evening performance to all those who had ever worked on the show. Many of those involved found this run-through more exciting than the actual performance, as the logistics of assembling the evening were so mind-boggling that no one was sure whether Bennett could pull it off. The finale was performed twice at the dress rehearsal so that it could be retaped by crews from a new NBC television show called "Live and In Person." The finale was telecast at the top of the program at 10 P.M. that evening, as if it were a live transmission from the Shubert.

After a preperformance party in Shubert Alley, the show that night began at 10:30 P.M. with a celebrity-filled audience that included Helen Hayes, Meryl Streep, Mikhail Baryshnikov, Joshua Logan, Stephen Sondheim, Francis Ford Coppola, Dorothy Loudon, Luise Rainer, and Kevin Kline. It was a virtually restaged, rethought *A Chorus Line* that just 3,200 people were fortunate enough to witness.

The performance began just as it would on any night, with the present company performing the opening sequence. But at the moment when the mirrors revolve and the company appears on line with their glossies in front of their faces, the current cast "dissolved" and the original cast, minus three, appeared, greeted by pandemonium from the audience. They performed the introductions sequence, and from that point on, cast replaced cast with a fluidity so dazzling that even those backstage could not quite figure out how Bennett had managed it.

"Nothing" was sung by Tokyo native Chikae Ishikawa. Three Vals shared that character's monologue, alternating lines and saying some in unison, then alternated between solo and unison singing in Val's song.

Cassie's number was always special, and it was treated as such that night. McKechnie gave an extremely poignant reading of her scene with

Zach, then performed "The Music and the Mirror" by herself up to the point where the mirrors descend. She was then joined by six other Cassies (Cheryl Clark, Vicki Frederick, Deborah Henry, Wanda Richert, Ann Louise Schaut, Pamela Sousa), all identically clad in the famous vermillion costume, who weaved seamlessly in and out of the rest of the rechoreographed number.

Paul's monologue was begun by its creator, Sammy Williams, who was then joined by ten other Pauls, with whom he alternated and shared lines. The Pauls finished each other's sentences and echoed each other, creating a contrapuntal effect. The use of multiple Pauls, Vals, and Cassies underlined the universality of the show's characters.

The alternatives scene was performed by members of various foreign productions in at least six languages. Throughout Priscilla Lopez's singing of "What I Did for Love," each character onstage was joined by four other actors in the same role.

If the audience had been beside itself throughout the evening, the finale Bennett had created for that night brought the house to its feet in a near-ecstatic state. First, dozens of dancers streamed onto the stage from the wings to join the nineteen who had begun the finale. At the point when the sunburst is revealed, many more ran into the aisles on the orchestra, mezzanine, and balcony levels of the theatre. Then, instead of a fade after "She's the One," the song was repeated, allowing all the dancers in the aisles to join the over one hundred already onstage in impeccable rows. At the end, each of the thirteen rows, from downstage to upstage, bowed as a unit, all rows remaining down until the last line had bowed, then all rows rising at the same instant, remaining erect as Bennett took to the stage to join the 332 identically outfitted performers.

The reaction was tumultuous. Frank Rich in *The New York Times* described it vividly: "The cast and audience had become one, united in the at least momentary conviction that *A Chorus Line* was the best thing that had ever happened to any of us. People were screaming and, when the lights slowly dimmed to black, they were sobbing. They were sobbing because they were moved, and perhaps even more so because the show was over."

Bennett gestured to the group behind him and stated in words what he had managed to convey so brilliantly in his concept for the evening: "I have a wonderful family." He called onstage virtually everyone connected with the production, and this was the only time that the usually invisible musicians had to wear clean shirts and black ties.

For the pre- and postperformance parties, Shubert Alley became a tented and carpeted mall with two bars and eight searchlights. After the show, about two thousand guests enjoyed a supper of thirty pounds of caviar and thirty-five cases of champagne, served by seventy-five waiters.

The experience meant different things to those who were a part of it. Many veteran theatregoers maintained that it was the most thrilling evening they'd ever spent in a theatre. And because of Bennett's conception, the audience had been made to feel as much a part of the event as those onstage. John Simon wrote in *New York* magazine, "Whether one had played a major part in the Broadway cast or a minor one in the bus-and-truck company, or was just a ravished spectator, one—no, *we* were all children of the greater god of the theater."

The performers had a wide variety of reactions.

MCKECHNIE: "It was incredible, the best theatre party I've ever seen in my life."

DENNIS: "It was fun to be part of, but it was bittersweet because Michael treated those of us who were never very close to him or who had never gotten much attention from him the same as always."

CILENTO: "It was so rewarding for me. Every frustration that I had doing the show came full circle. Everything I had fought in my part originally now made sense to me."

AVIAN: "A lot of them needed #3,389 to get over the *Chorus Line* experience. For many of them, that was the settling, or the ending, of that part of their lives. It freed a lot of them of it, and they needed to be freed. A lot of them who had left the show confused, disappointed, angry, finally resolved it that night, because they saw it less personally. They saw the bigger thing, that there were hundreds of dancers who had gone through this biographical experience."

For the publicity department, the event offered unlimited exploitation and widespread national coverage, and the result was a sharp rise in advance ticket sales and higher than average receipts for the performances immediately after the gala.

For Bennett, the evening was one of total triumph with a deep personal meaning. It was one of the few times in the career of this perfectionist when he was truly delighted with what he had achieved, but he also saw it as a career summation.

BENNETT: "I would settle for this being the happiest day of my life. I've had the best week rehearsing. I never graduated from high school because I went into show business, which was more important to me, so

I never had a prom or a high school reunion. But this was it: we're all back together.

"Why did I choose to re-do the show for one night? I knew I had to pay back. I wanted everyone who was part of it to share in the evening. I realized before rehearsals that what I had worked out in my head was as difficult as staging the show the first time. That's the kind of pressure that I put on myself. But I always believe in paying back for everything I get. Which maybe explains my whole career more than anything else."

Many observers felt that Bennett's genius was nowhere more evident than on this occasion. Frank Rich in the *Times* said, "It was one of those rare occasions when the theatre seemed to have gathered its past, present, and future into one house on one night. . . . The feeling in the crowd was that the artist who could make *A Chorus Line* even better—3,389 performances into its run—was an artist who could do anything. An evening that began as a celebration of past glory became a promise of grander glories to come."

Yet #3,389 would prove to be not only Bennett's crowning achievement but the last "new" Bennett staging ever to be witnessed by an audience in a theatre.

4

. . . .

PROJECTS

*D*REAMGIRLS WAS TO BE the last new musical project of Bennett's that would be seen by the general public. But he worked on at least eight other properties in his remaining years, some of which never went beyond the discussion stage, some of which reached the stage of developed scripts and scores, and one of which existed as a fully staged, almost finished musical.

Throughout his career, Bennett was known for his generosity in helping other people's shows when he was called by their directors, choreographers, producers, or writers. Few are aware of the dozens of productions he helped through his advice, guidance, and suggestion, taking no credit or pay for his assistance.

MARVIN KRAUSS: "When I was producing *Merlin,* we were in trouble. It was not Michael's kind of show, but he came and saw it, then brought in a long list of things we should do. He did this because he loved theatre; that was his life."

Bennett even helped doctor *Oh! Calcutta!,* which, because of its unorthodox playing schedule, overtook the performance record of *A Chorus Line* in 1988. Most of those helped by him express enormous gratitude for his keen observation, insight, sense of detail, and supportiveness. On one occasion, however, Bennett's attempt to help a show turned sour, and it involved the man whose production of *Nine* had deprived *Dreamgirls* of a Tony and had made him a force in musical theatre equal to any.

TUNE: "We were in previews with *My One and Only.* Baayork Lee, who was associate choreographer, Thommie Walsh, who staged and choreographed it with me, and I went to Michael's 40th birthday party at 890. He took the three of us into the men's room, closed the door, and asked us how it was going. We said, '. . . We went through hell with Peter Sellars in Boston, we're exhausted, but it's starting to work.' He said, 'I'll come look at it.' We didn't ask him to, but, when he came to see it, he thought he knew what it needed.

"He brought in his team, including Michael Peters, and they went to work, but it was very harsh work. He started taking the karma of the show and twisting it into something that had nothing to do with the period. And the other people who were involved in *My One and Only* at the time—it was being led by Mike Nichols and a myriad of producers—saw him destroying the very thing that was good about the show, which was a certain kind of naive charm. He started shooting it full of adrenaline, and losing the feeling of period.

"He did a new opening and a new 'High Hat' number. We never performed his opening because it was like something out of a music video, and we did his 'High Hat' for three performances.

"The powers that be said, 'This has to stop. We're going to tell him not to come back.' In fact, Mike Nichols, who saved the show completely—I begged him to put his name on it, but he wouldn't—stopped coming to the theatre. I was so involved in playing my role and keeping together my choreography that I had lost my perception. They said, 'Michael's choreography is ruining everything we have, and we have to let him go.' I said, 'But this man is a great choreographer. He knows musical theatre.' They said, 'Maybe he's not doing good work on purpose.' I said, 'That can't be true.' They said, 'He doesn't know that that's what he's doing.'

"Michael was drinking and drugging at the time, but there was never a time when he wasn't, so that couldn't have been the problem. It may have been his turning 40 and having lived a hard life. It had taken its toll.

"When Michael was dismissed, he called me the next day and told me not to give it a second thought. He asked only that I write a note to Michael Peters and some others who had come in to help, to thank them for their contribution. Later, he decided he should be compensated and have a percentage of the show, when in truth, not one moment of anything he did was used. He was not compensated, and that caused the final separation between us. He felt I had betrayed him."

A different version of this incident is related by drama critic Howard Kissel.

KISSEL: "Michael told me that Tune had begged him to come and work on *My One and Only*. Michael said he didn't want money unless the show went into the black, and then only for those who worked with him, not for himself. When the show started doing good business, he asked for money, and no one would cough up a cent."

During the Eighties, Bennett's projects included the staging of several elaborate fashion shows in San Francisco and New York as a favor to a close friend. For these, he brought out his team of designers and orchestrators and in a matter of days created huge productions seen only by insiders.

Bennett briefly considered directing a musical version of Quentin Crisp's *The Naked Civil Servant*, a new musical version of *Peter Pan*, and Ed Kleban's musical *Gallery*.

At 890, Bennett produced various workshops that he himself did not direct. One was a musical entitled *Battle of Giants*.

AVIAN: "We produced it on the main floor of 890 when it was still a garbage heap. *Battle of Giants* was written by Alan Menken and Steve Brown, and Michael thought it was great fun. We got Tom O'Horgan to direct it. It was about space travel, and had a certain silliness. Camille Saviola played the Queen of Outer Space in a pink bodystocking."

In April 1983, Bennett directed *Third Street*, a short, three-character play by Dartmouth sophomore Richard Colman, for the Young Playwrights Festival, sponsored by the Dramatists Guild. Bennett believed in supporting the program, and also was eager to direct a nonmusical work again.

MARTIN ZONE, a cast member: "Michael worked very closely with the writer on the play, before any of the actors came in. He had a sixth sense about how to cut it, phrase it, and work out the rhythm even before he heard actors do it.

"The play was a 30-minute one-act, very naturalistic, about three Brooklyn high school graduates, best friends for life, on the evening after graduation. They were about to go in three separate directions. Because it was about three guys, we were calling it *Dreamboys*. We thought all the critics would mention the similarity, but no one did.

"Michael enjoyed doing it . . . all he cared about was the work, not reviews or anything. He knew theatre, and was really excited about theatre, and didn't care about anything else."

Bennett received excellent reviews for his direction, which also brought him a Drama Desk nomination.

Among Bennett's projects in this period, the most bizarre were two devoted to the subject of his father.

LENNY: "Michael and his father fought like cats and dogs, but down deep Michael loved him. Michael had much more Italian in him than he had Jewish, and leaned more to the Italian side. He had the Sicilian killer instinct."

In 1983, Bennett announced that he was working on a musical with the working title of *A Chorus Line II: A Backer's Audition.*

BENNETT: "It's a very personal statement, and a story that I think is interesting. I am my father's son, and I think he's remarkable and funny and a star in his own way. My wanting to do a musical about my father has a great deal to do with turning 40.

"My father came to New York at the age of 58 and announced that he wanted to be an actor, a movie star, after years of being a machinist at Chevrolet. So I enrolled him in the American Academy of Dramatic Arts for the summer, where he took mime, fencing, speech, scene study and acting. He got an apartment in Greewich Village, started wearing dungarees, and turned into an actor. Now he's back in Buffalo, but it was an interesting summer, and that's what the show is about. It's about fathers and sons.

"I think what my father did was so incredibly romantic I can't tell you. It was a major step in reinforcing his sense of self, his ego, his sense of who he was. I think *A Chorus Line* had something to do with it."

While Bennett denied that the show would in any way be a sequel to *A Chorus Line,* the story was to be at least partially told by performers auditioning for a show the father wanted to produce, direct, write, and star in. The father in the piece was to have a son whose talent, he believed, came from him. The father believed that if the son could write, produce, and direct, then so could he. It was to have shown how the father dealt with and reacted to his son's success, and would have had a good deal of backstage truth, at which Bennett always excelled.

The book for the show was being written by Louis LaRusso II, author of two Broadway plays. At one point, the show became a film project, called *Our Father,* which would have marked Bennett's long-awaited screen directorial debut, and it was announced as a production of Francis Ford Coppola's Zoetrope Studio. His father's death in December 1983, while he was working on *Dreamgirls* in San Francisco, compelled Bennett to forge ahead, but other shows intervened and his "father project" never materialized.

Imagine Ann-Margret as Ziegfeld Follies singer Ruth Etting, enslaved in a masochistic relationship with Moe "The Gimp" Snyder, lit by Tharon Musser, gowned by Theoni Aldredge, standing on a Robin Wagner backstage set, and directed by Michael Bennett. That image came close to being a reality when Bennett became attracted to the 1955 MGM film musical *Love Me or Leave Me,* which starred Doris Day and James Cagney.

BENNETT: "Theoni Aldredge, who's a close friend of Ann-Margret's, told me Ann-Margret would like to do a Broadway show, and asked if I'd come see her act. We were sitting there with Roger Smith, her husband and manager. She was singing some standard—and she was singing it well, she's grown and has a wonderful rapport with the audience—and I was looking at Roger. I thought, 'What does this remind me of?' and I realized it was *Love Me or Leave Me.* It's another variation on my favorite theme of obsessive love and show-business triangles.

"People like it when I do backstage musicals, and I like them, too. But I don't know if I like doing star musicals. I don't do star musicals because the managers and the agents all have to earn their money, and you take their star and they don't earn money for six months while they develop a property with me."

Bennett intended to use many of the standards Etting had popularized, but he had conversations with Marvin Hamlisch and Sheldon Harnick about creating new material for the show. Harnick questioned the wisdom of writing a show about two people who don't genuinely love each other, but Bennett answered by saying that there were many ways to interpret love.

AVIAN: "Michael was very attracted to the idea. Marvin said to Michael, 'You're asking me to write a song that's a countermelody to an Irving Berlin song? Thanks a lot!' But knowing Michael and Marvin, Michael would have gotten Marvin to do it. We thought of asking David Mamet to write the script, because Michael wanted to do a very tough version of the story, very gangstery.

"Roger Smith was interested in co-producing, and Ann-Margret would have been perfect for it. One of the reasons Michael didn't keep pushing the show was the idea of doing a show with a big star. He said, 'I want to be the star. I don't want to work *for* a star.'"

No script or score was ever developed for *Love Me or Leave Me,* but a full score, book, and staging concepts were created for *A Children's Crusade,* a musical on which Bennett worked from 1983 to 1986. It told the story of a half-mythical event in the thirteenth century, when a mass of children left their families and homes in France and traveled to the Holy Land, attempting against enormous odds to save the world by spreading their faith. But Bennett's musical was to be a joyous, primitive, "event" theatre piece.

Bennett's conception of *A Children's Crusade* was inspired by seeing Luca Ronconi's *Orlando Furioso,* a theatre piece in which the audience moved from area to area, in Bryant Park in 1970, and also by his success in organizing the massive forces of the 3,389th performance of *A Chorus Line.* He decided to stage the show in a large space, either a hollowed-out Vivian Beaumont Theater, Madison Square Garden, or an armory, and intended to employ four or five hundred New York City school children. Bennett had conversations with the Department of Education about employing hundreds of out-of-school kids without summer jobs in his production, and the show would have been produced in the nonprofit sphere.

Bennett intended to put the audience onstage for at least part of the evening, creating a circuslike atmosphere in a bold and complex vision. When the show slowed down for a break when the children reached the marketplace in Marseilles, little shops were to open all over the theatre, and troubadours would sing throughout the house. The children would roam through the audience hawking various items, and the audience would come onstage, different groups witnessing different scenes here and elsewhere during the evening.

The book was the work of John Heilpern, and for the score, Bennett chose pop and country-western composer Jimmy Webb, who had achieved success with such hits as "MacArthur Park," "Up, Up and Away," "By the Time I Get to Phoenix," and "Didn't We."

WEBB: "I moved to the east coast in 1980 to work in musical theatre. In 1983, I called my friend David Geffen, and told him I'd been out here over two years and was dying. Geffen said, 'You're going to meet Michael Bennett.' I did, and after a meeting of a few hours, Michael had decided we were going to do a musical together, and I had decided I wanted to work with him in the worst way.

"Within weeks, he offered me space at 890 next to his office, and the first thing he gave me was all the material on *A Children's Crusade.* He told me that in *Chorus Line,* he had given the public a look backstage, and now. he wanted to put the audience *on* the stage.

"The show was to be broadly painted, in large strokes, as in children's theatre, with a deliberate simplicity and crudity. You weren't expected to believe the children were on a real ship; you would see people carrying it along, and there would be a huge wind machine they would go over to and crank. There was no subterfuge, and the audience was let in on everything. It was to be done more or less in the round, with the stage floor open to the audience. . . . Michael wanted the children to play the adult characters as well.

"Although we never began a workshop of it, Michael was always working on it. We did a read-through of it in the Hamptons, and Michael wanted to pay for a recording of the score to be released before the production. He especially loved the song 'Only One Life' from the show, which moved him to tears.

"The show will be done, although I don't think it will be as big as Michael had conceived it. We talked shortly before he passed away, and he told me, 'That's the best idea I ever had for a Broadway show. Finish it with my blessing.' He would have liked to think we were going ahead with it, and doing it the way he would have wanted, with great panache, vigor, wit and integrity, and lots of great dancing.

"The overpowering thing I felt in Michael's work was his insight into the human condition, and that was something everybody could share. The glitter in his work was fine, but it was really about getting inside the human condition. That's what *Children's Crusade* has to be about. . . . He loved 'Only One Life' because he believed that every human being was important and had something to say. That's what *Chorus Line* was about, and it's very important to me to carry on in my own work with that idea, to never let things stray too far from the heart, from the human being at the center of everything. Michael taught that—he was a teacher who always kept coming back to that."

Although *A Children's Crusade* was never staged by Bennett, Webb soon became involved in a musical on which Bennett worked for over four years, one that became the last fully staged Bennett production, and one that the public would never get to see.

5

. . . .

"THERE'S GOING TO BE

A *SCANDAL* ON BROADWAY"

*D*REAMGIRLS NOT ONLY PUT Bennett back on top, it placed him in a unique position in terms of his artistic freedom.

BENNETT (1983): "I as a creative artist will be able to do any kind of show I want to do. I never worry about the price tag of the show. I do the show first, and then if it's really wonderful, anybody will put up the money to do it. I'm in a unique position because I've become independent: independent of whether last season was wonderful or terrible from an investment point of view, or whatever Equity did on the last Broadway contract. I can go work in regional theatre. It's America. I'm free. I don't think everything I do has to be loved by everybody, because I wasn't doing it for everybody. I'm really doing it for me."

What Bennett announced as his new project in 1983 was a daring piece on which he had begun working in 1980, prior to *Dreamgirls,* and on which he would continue to work up to 1985.

BENNETT: "It's about sex. It's really about relationships, but when you tell people you're doing a musical about relationships, they're not interested the way they are when you say you're doing a musical about sex."

It began with Treva Silverman, a successful television writer who wrote the celebrated "Mary Tyler Moore Show." A year-long hiatus in Europe provided the inspiration for a screenplay that was brought to Bennett's attention by the lyricist of *A Chorus Line.*

SILVERMAN: "I began a screenplay for Paramount about a woman and her life and loves. I showed it to Ed Kleban, who had been meeting with Michael and looking for a project. He showed my screenplay to Michael and Bob Avian, and Michael asked me to come to New York and meet with him.

"I walked into 890. There was a magical, instant rapport. Michael felt it was time for him to deal in depth with a modern heroine, and not the kind of heroine that had been seen in a lot of musicals. Three weeks later, I moved to New York, and we began work April 1, 1980.

"We knew it was going to be about a modern woman, and what happens during a transitional time. For two months, we were looking for who this woman was and what she was doing. Then one night, Michael had dinner with Nancy Walker and her husband David Craig, who knew me from 'The Mary Tyler Moore Show.' They told him they had always wondered why I had picked up and gone to Europe. Michael had never asked me about that, but when he did, I told him about some of my experiences, and how changed I was every time I came back from Europe. He said, 'That's it! We've found the musical. We're going to write about someone seeking sexual freedom, and how difficult it is to break away from everything we've been taught. This will be an opening up for sex, and hopefully it will free people of guilt.'

"Ed was haunted by his success with *A Chorus Line.* His life stopped after it opened. Also, Michael and I would intuit each other, finishing each other's sentences. Edward's approach was much more intellectual. He didn't feel a part of our process, and felt very outside of us. There were blow-ups over his frustrations, and he was in horrible pain. It was never a question of his ability, but ultimately he decided he couldn't go through with it."

Working closely with Bennett over a five-year period, Silverman experienced the full force of his personality, and all its many sides.

SILVERMAN: "It's not so much that he encouraged you to do your best. He was able to ferret out what your best was. You got on an emotional and creative high. You would forget he was Michael Bennett; he became someone who understood how your mind worked, creatively and emotionally. When things got bad, you would work more to get approval, which was dangerous, because Michael would withold it and become manipulative. But when you were communicating on the highest level, it was hard to come down to earth afterward.

"I was stunned at how Michael was instantly able to relate deeply to me, and I was able to respond so deeply. He was able to do that with a lot of people. The sadness would come when he would move on. The love that people were in with Michael, whether they were man or woman, straight or gay, bisexual, neuter or celibate—there was always sexuality mixed into it.

"Michael was able to work on *Dreamgirls*—and when he worked on a show, it was total, 100%, which is like 1000% of anybody else—then come over to my house and work on *Scandal* for hours.

"Aside from his extraordinary gifts, his intuitive understanding of people was extraordinary. That's how he could get at you, and wound and hurt you. I was so mesmerized by Michael, and so was he. We were both talking all the time about the person we admired most, Michael.

"When people talk about Michael, they always use superlatives like, 'The most . . . that I ever met.' But even the superlatives don't get the meaning across. You have to throw in some corny word like *magic* to say that there was more than words can express. There was something about this man that if you piled all the words together, you still don't get who he was."

Bennett was not sure from the start that what Silverman was creating was a musical, and Silverman's script was so witty and strong that Bennett explored the possibility of producing it as a play with music. He thought of having an incidental score written as a pastiche of the work of various classical composers, justifying the notion by having the principal character, Claudia Miller, editing a book about classical music.

Bennett soon abandoned this notion in favor of a concept strikingly similar to that of the 1941 musical *Lady in the Dark.*

SILVERMAN: "Michael didn't want to interrupt the scenes I had written, because he loved them. He said, 'What we're going to do is, when it's real life, we're going to keep this as a play. Everytime there's a fantasy, we'll break into technicolor, song and dance.'"

BENNETT: "We will musicalize her nightmares, her daydreams, her fantasies and her projections."

In his last two hits, Bennett favored justifying singing and dancing by placing the action backstage and dealing with performers. While *Scandal* was not a show-business musical with characters who already sing and dance, the fantasy structure allowed him the same kind of freedom. In a fantasy, anyone could do anything, including singing and dancing.

When the script was finished, he decided to have a reading for his team and a few other close associates. By the time of this reading on February 2, 1984, Kleban had departed and no new composer or lyricist had been chosen, so Bennett asked Harold Wheeler to "dummy" original tunes, standards, and classical music to accompany the scenes and indicate how music would function in the fantasies. Bennett choreographed simple dance sequences to give an idea of how music and dance might be used in the play.

The two hour presentation was an enormous success, and Bennett realized that the play, which soon would come to be called *Scandal,* after such titles as *Dreamgirl* and *The American Woman* had been discussed, was something that did in fact sing and dance.

The cast for the reading included Peter Reigert as Robert Miller, the husband; Victor Garber and David Rasche in multiple roles; Fisher Stevens; and Priscilla Lopez. For the central role of Claudia Miller, Bennett and Silverman chose one of the finest young actresses around, one not previously associated with musicals.

SWOOSIE KURTZ: "Michael started telling me the wild plot of this play and about all that happens to Claudia, and asked if I would read the play. I asked what part he wanted me to do, thinking he would get Patti LuPone or another musical star for the lead. He said, 'You'd be Claudia,' and I said okay, secretly wondering who had dropped out. I had only sung and danced once, in *A History of The American Film* on Broadway, which was a play with music, but I had always wanted to do a musical.

"The script I got was a beautifully constructed, finished play. It was one of the best things I'd read in years, and I thought, 'We could open this tomorrow night.'

"The world seemed to stop as we did these two days of total immersion, intensive work in preparation for the reading. Michael's energy was such that when the two days were over, I felt like I had rehearsed, previewed and opened a show. People were in tears by the end of the reading, and that night Michael called me. He said, 'Honey, we're all sitting around here. Your reviews are in. I figure, why wait to tell you? Would you like to be the leading lady in my next Broadway musical?'"

Bennett and Silverman had discussed many possibilities for the show's composer and lyricist, including Carolyn Leigh, Ellen Fitzhugh, Peter Allen, Marvin Hamlisch, Sheldon Harnick, Burt Bacharach, Carole

Bayer Sager, Richard Maltby, Jr., and David Shire. Harold Wheeler was also under consideration following his work for the reading.

SILVERMAN: "Michael had infinite respect for Ed Kleban's talent and really felt he was the perfect person to do it. When Edward was out, the fact remained that there had never been anyone Michael respected more than Stephen Sondheim. Michael wanted Stephen to do *Scandal,* throughout the time Stephen was writing *Merrily We Roll Along* and *Sunday in the Park with George.* Michael would have waited and done anything to get him. But he never asked Stephen to be a part of *Scandal,* even though he was talked about all the time. He spoke to Stephen about the show and read him some things for his opinion. His respect for Stephen was huge; except for Robbins, I never heard him talk about anyone else that way, and Sondheim was the one person on earth it would have been too much of a blow to Michael to be rejected by. He was so afraid of Stephen refusing him anything that he never got the nerve to ask."

The show that began a series of workshops on May 1, 1984, contained perhaps the wildest, boldest, and most ribald story of any musical comedy. It was daring, hilarious, and, ultimately, profoundly moral. It concerned the marriage of Claudia and Robert Miller, which, after eight years, has fallen into a pattern of sexual staleness. Claudia has been sexually reserved with her husband, and it has begun to make a major difference not only in their marriage but in their ability to communicate with and love each other. Robert has begun seeing other women, and Claudia discovers this when Robert heroically saves several people trapped in a midtown hotel fire. Unfortunately, the woman Robert carried out of the fire, identified on television and in newspaper photos the next day as "Mrs. Miller," is not Claudia but a woman he has been seeing, and this scandal forces Claudia to file for divorce.

Following an evening at Chippendale's, courtesy of her best friend, Elaine, plus a disastrous encounter with a tennis pro, Claudia decides she's got to change her life. She makes a thoroughly un-Claudia-like decision to go to Europe, where she can be anonymous and see what sex is all about. Claudia's adventures abroad form the body of the show, with occasional cuts back to Robert, including one hilarious sequence between Robert and a psychiatrist friend, Andrew.

Silverman devised a series of encounters for Claudia of a frankness and explicitness never before encountered in a musical. However, by having Claudia constantly interrupt the most provocative situations to share her inner thoughts with the audience, Claudia remained endearing in even the most outlandish situations, and the scenes retained their humor. Claudia has an affair with a sixteen-year-old waiter in a Paris hotel, then meets a handsome shoe repairman in Rome, who brings another man with him when he arrives for his tryst with Claudia. She finds herself snowbound in a Swiss chalet with Nicole, a woman friend whom she soon realizes is a lesbian.

SILVERMAN: "She becomes more and more liberated, and realizes what a joyous experience sex can be. She realizes that her husband has been searching for that because he hasn't found it with her. She also realizes she is absolutely in love with her husband. At the end, it is clear that by going through these changes, she has become, finally, a perfect partner for him, just as he has had to go through his changes to be a partner for her. It was a love story, and within it was a woman's growth."

BENNETT: "They get back together because they deal with it, as opposed to thinking that sex is not important. I don't believe in compromise on any level. I think relationships that become compromised, where you settle, are not a good idea."

Silverman's skillful writing and Bennett's unerring taste never allowed the piece to become offensive in a manner that would have gotten in the way of what it was attempting to say.

SILVERMAN: "The subject of the show had never been done in the way we were going to do it, which was out-and-out laughing about sex and, simultaneously, being spiritual about sex. We were doing outrageous things in a way that was delicate and funny so that, if we did it right, they wouldn't know what hit them and they would be able to accept the bolder parts. Michael wanted them to leave the theatre and think, 'My God, did I really sit there and laugh and be moved by somebody in bed with two men, or fantasizing about having an affair with a lesbian?'"

KURTZ: "I was sometimes worried whether the audience would care about this woman who was going to be with everybody in sight. But I knew that Michael would never allow anything that wasn't tasteful."

Scandal had a serious moral subtext throughout.

DANNY HERMAN, the associate choreographer of *Scandal*: "It was about right and wrong, and it said that there really is no such thing. She blamed him for what he had done, but ultimately realized she couldn't judge him, and would have to understand what was behind their differences."

Auditions for the first workshop were held in Theatre 890, under construction on the ground floor of 890 Broadway, where *Scandal* would come to life.

SILVERMAN: "Michael's idea was to use very, very tall and unusually good-looking dancers. In order to make its sexuality immaculate and pristine where it needed to be, there had to be health radiating from them. And he wanted them to be tall because they were figures of Claudia's fantasy, larger than life, bigger and more beautiful than real people.

"At the auditions, I asked Bob Avian how he knew when a dancer was right. He said he knew when they were in position, but that Michael knew when they walked in. And Michael's intuition, perception and knowledge were so huge that he did."

For the role of Robert in the workshops, Bennett chose Treat Williams, a much-in-demand young star on stage, screen, and television.

SILVERMAN: "When Michael offered the role to Treat, he said, 'I want to tell you about the part. The star of the show is the woman. It's not distributed evenly between the man and the woman. She will get the reviews, and it's a tour de force for her. There are some things in your role that will be wonderful to act, but I don't want to fool you.' But Treat wanted so much to work with Michael."

Victor Garber tripled in several high-comedy roles, and David Rasche doubled as Mitch, the husband's best friend, and Andrew, the psychiatrist. Fisher Stevens played the French waiter; Priscilla Lopez was the woman Claudia met in Switzerland; Wanda Richert, then Trish Ramish, were the "other Mrs. Miller" with whom Robert was caught in the fire, and Kelly Bishop wound up playing Claudia's best friend.

BISHOP: "I had called Michael, just because I was remembering the pleasure of the creative process of *A Chorus Line.* I said if he could use me, not so much as an actress but more as an assistant director during rehearsals, I'd be happy to be there. During the first workshop, he called me. Swoosie was the only female there, so he wanted me to do all the other female parts, just for the rehearsals, which was fun, because we did a lot of improvising. Then he got it into his head that I should be in the show and play Claudia's girlfriend. He saw me as his good luck token, which was flattering but scary, too."

During the first workshop, the most crucial decision made was to have Jimmy Webb, who had been working on *A Children's Crusade* for Bennett for over a year, compose the score.

WEBB: "They were already in workshop with a script, but without a score. First, Michael said that this was a play for which he wanted me to do some incidental music and underscoring. Then all of a sudden he wanted music for two major ballets. I was writing music for the show before I wrote songs, which came later."

Together, Bennett and Webb gradually came up with a new concept for the score, that of using lengthy sequences that employed singing, dancing, and dialogue. There were several ballets and a number of songs, but most of the music in *Scandal* was combined with spoken dialogue and movement in extended, highly unconventional sequences unlike any attempted in a musical before.

The first workshop was devoted entirely to the book, although Bennett could not resist occasionally inviting some of his dancers.

KURTZ: "We rehearsed the book like a play for six weeks, no dancers, no music. During that time, Michael began testing the waters as far as my dancing was concerned. He had Danny Herman, Jerry Mitchell and Jodi Moscia come in and lift me and do some things, and Michael said, 'You can really move. You have line.'

"For the second workshop, which started in July, Michael brought in the dancers. We started doing a killer, hour-and-a-half workout every morning, part Fonda, part Herman and part Bennett. Michael tried part of it once but found some excuse to get out of it. He had me doing gymnastics, acrobatics, leaps, and I was fine.

"Then Michael would have the dancers in one room, and the actors in another. Sometimes, four different things were happening in different places. As Claudia was so central, I really couldn't take any time off.

"The songs started to come in towards the end of the second workshop. Treat got a wonderful ballad called 'They Just Don't Make Them Like You Anymore.' I began working with Cleavant Derricks, who was my vocal coach and was doing the vocal arrangements.

"We were paid $200 a week for the first workshop, $250 for the second, and $350 for the third."

During the second workshop, Bennett did something that was quintessentially Bennett, the kind of thing that only he could get done. He installed an enormous and very expensive double turntable in the rehearsal hall; it moved in two directions, functioning exactly as it would on a Broadway stage. Bennett felt this was necessary for his creation of the dazzling twenty-two-minute opening sequence, which would last sixteen minutes in its final version.

Kurtz returned from a brief trip to Italy to soak up some of the atmosphere necessary for the play, and the third workshop began at the end of September.

KURTZ: "In the third workshop, we started putting the dialogue and the musical sequences together, finding out how to get in and out of numbers and how to blend and make transitions. By October, the show started to get a real flow.

"Late in the third, I got my 'eleven o'clock number,' as Michael called it. It was a song called 'The Most Important Thing.' I think Treva was upset that the brilliant monologue she had written near the end had been turned into a song, but I spoke a lot of the original dialogue between verses of the song. It was an amazingly dramatic song in which I listed what the most important thing was not, finally concluding that it is being who you are."

WEBB: "I think Treva resented the music. Michael gave me the monologue to turn it into a song. When I played 'The Most Important Thing' for Michael and Bob, Bob cried. It was very moving, probably the best thing I wrote for that show. But there was no reaction from Treva whatsoever. She felt she couldn't give up this speech."

SILVERMAN: "I wrote Claudia's monologue in the middle of the third workshop. When I finished it, I was elated and felt almost as if Claudia herself grabbed the pen and wrote it. A few weeks later, Michael told me that in a musical, the 'eleven o'clock number' had to be a song. I was crushed and became childish and resentful when he asked Jimmy to substitute a musical sequence."

It was during the fourth workshop, which began in December, that Bennett began to show signs of severe strain.

SILVERMAN: "He was never taking any time off, and was becoming increasingly tired. But he was doing more and more coke, so he was getting more and more elated. Everyone around 890 revered Michael, but things started happening. They would tell me, 'Don't go in there. He's into his humiliation mode.' At one point, they were begging Michael to start the workshops earlier, because by the afternoon he would become crazy from the coke building up."

KURTZ: "During the last workshop, Michael announced the rehearsal date for the Broadway production. We were to have three weeks off, begin rehearsals mid-February, then open on Broadway in April. I was measured for costumes by Theoni, and around Christmas, Michael and Bob had these black sweatshirts made up which read, 'There's Going to Be a "Scandal" on Broadway.'

"About that time, Michael developed a flu that he couldn't shake. He was working like crazy, making major decisions on the scenic design, and working on several other shows at the same time. Tired as he was, he refused to quit, except for one or two days when he didn't come in. Things were getting a little tense, and Michael was getting short-tempered. The pressure was on, he was exhausted, and he still hadn't figured out a big sequence for the middle of the first act."

Once again, Bennett made use of his workshops as no other director seemed to be willing or able to do. As with *A Chorus Line* and *Dreamgirls,* Bennett insisted on using the *Scandal* workshops to develop the material, exploring every possibility, spending weeks on single sequences, and forbidding observation by many who were more than willing to invest in the production. The workshops were largely devoted to putting together the major sequences he felt were the crux of the show, so many of Webb's songs were never even rehearsed in the workshops. Unlike the workshops for *Dreamgirls, Scandal,* by Christmas 1984, was, if not totally complete, an almost completely staged production, with a working turntable, props, and additional pieces already in place. Bennett asked for and had been granted permission to do something unorthodox with the workshop schedule for *Scandal.*

SILVERMAN: "There were officially four, which was all you were allowed, but in actuality there were eight. Normally, you have a workshop, then take some time off before the next one. Michael did the first workshop on book, then instead of taking time off, he did the first workshop with his dancers. So it was: 1, book; 1-A, dance; 2, book; 2-A, dance. He got permission from Actors Equity to do this."

By the time the workshops were over, Kurtz had experienced the full force of the Bennett personality as profoundly as had all his earlier leading ladies.

KURTZ: "Michael could be a tyrant, but you always knew that he knew better than you. And forget the dance and the music—he was a great director. At one point, Michael said to me, 'You know, they expect me to pull it out of a hat.' We all depended on this brilliant leader to figure everything out, but he was human, too, and was creating out of nothing.

"People were at one time talking about Michael and I going together. Michael was a very sexual creature, to both sexes. He was a sexual being, and there was no way you could be around him and not be attracted to him, although I knew it was out of the question. It was just a fantasy, and was great fun. He said to me, 'You're the greatest physical comedienne

I've ever worked with. I don't ever want to work with anybody else.' I think he really meant it."

What Bennett had achieved over the course of eight months was work that, in several areas, surpassed that of almost anything in his career. Ranging from tap to jazz to acrobatics to ballroom to pure ballet, he had come up with what many involved maintain was the best choreography of his life. Avian was co-choreographer, and twenty-four-year-old Danny Herman was given the opportunity to be associate choreographer.

HERMAN: "I was honored to be there. Michael needed my rawness, someone who didn't have references to Fosse and other choreographers.

"Michael would say, 'In this section, Swoosie goes into a male strip joint. I want choreography that makes people's mouths drop, very sensual. Pick any song and come up with choreography.' I choreographed a number to 'Footloose' with guys on the floor. Then Jimmy saw the steps and wrote his own music and lyrics to fit. I choreographed hours of tap steps and rhythms for the Paris ballet, put them on tape, then Michael worked with Jimmy as he composed the music. What we created was character and book oriented, and had structure. Jimmy was so good that we could keep everything we had choreographed to another song. Michael could take my stuff and make it good.

"I worked with Swoosie, and she turned into quite a dancer. She can do anything she wants to do.

"It was a completely emotional state, not a physical state. We weren't working with steps, we were working with feeling. We weren't working with scripts, we were working with passion. The music wasn't so much music as sounds that made you feel things."

AVIAN: "We had a lot of choreographic invention. It was very original, and touched on things that had never been done in dance before. We also parodied certain things that had been beaten over the head in dance, bringing a satiric point of view to them. As a choreographer, I was very proud of the work. I did some of my best stuff ever, and no one got to see it, not even my mom."

SILVERMAN: "Michael was one of the funniest people I've ever met, and with this show, I felt people would learn about his humor, which ranged from out-and-out hilarity to subtle little jokes. It was all in his dances for *Scandal*. Everything he was was expressed in them."

ROBERT THOMAS: "What Michael wanted most was to prove he was a real choreographer, and *Scandal* had the best choreography he ever did. Michael and I were planning a ballet for Robert Joffrey just before

Scandal and so *Scandal* was really about Michael Bennett the choreographer."

There were two outstanding ballet sequences, one the fourteen-minute "An American Woman in Paris" ballet, in which Claudia was seen buying clothes, going to a beauty salon, meeting men and seeing the sights with them, then preparing for her first romantic night in Paris.

The dance high point of *Scandal,* and possibly of Bennett's career, was the "Menage à Trois" ballet fantasy that occurred when Claudia experienced a successful encounter with two men after an earlier disaster. She finds to her surprise that the encounter with the two strangers leads to a sense of spirituality. As she dreamily remarks on the delicate frescoes decorating the old *pensione,* the frescoes suddenly come to life. Robin Wagner devised a ceiling that would lower to reveal three dancers, angels from the ceiling, who float through a delicately erotic dance of ineffable beauty. There were several trios, along with gilded creatures suspended in the air on wires.

SILVERMAN: "As a choreographer, this dance was a source of huge, very private pride to Michael. It was the one dance in the show that he was both afraid of and looking forward to, because he knew the potential it had for him to express himself. When he finally created it, I think even he was astonished at its beauty."

WAGNER: " 'The Menage à Trois' ballet was breathtaking. It was Michael's best dancing, and it could be put on the stage of any opera house in the world."

There were at least two wildly innovative extended sequences, above all the opening fantasy, which Bennett conceived as a contemporary version of *Alice in Wonderland* crossed with James Joyce, and on which Bennett and company worked for six weeks. When completed, it had the seeming arbitrariness that the unconscious expresses in a dream.

The curtain rose on a stage in flames, Claudia's dream of the fire that revealed and symbolized Robert's infidelities. She attempts to enter the hotel, but, as in a dream, she keeps shifting back and forth in her perceptions. She believes she is either getting married or divorced in the hotel, and at the same time wants to be the Mrs. Miller in the fire. As she attempts to get past the police cordon, she is not certain whether Robert is her husband, her soon-to-be husband, or her soon-to-be ex-husband. She breaks through and wanders throughout the hotel until she finally drifts into the ballroom and hears the wedding march. The wedding ceremony turns into a divorce; the man who is giving her away is not her father but a lawyer encouraging her to take Robert for everything he's got; and the men in the procession turn into the dancers from Chippendale's. At the end of the sequence, which employed continuous movement, spoken dialogue, song, and dance, Claudia is rising into the air on her bed, trying to stop everything going on around her, as the ceiling beams collapse and the fire engulfs the stage.

There can be little doubt that this opening would have had audiences reeling from its complexity, hilarity, and sheer brilliance. Equally wonderful was the courtroom fantasy, composed in the style of Gilbert and Sullivan, in which Claudia was on trial for having a lesbian fantasy. The "Other Mrs. Miller" was the prosecuting attorney; Andrew was the defense attorney; and all of Claudia's various lovers were brought into the courtroom to join with the judge and jury in singing "She's a dyke!"

Bennett's design concepts had by now gone through a process similar to that of *A Chorus Line* and *Dreamgirls.*

WAGNER: "We always started with the real, so originally we planned to have realistic sets, with a house, a motel, a sidewalk café in Rome, a hotel in Paris, and a chalet in Switzerland. It was going to look like a Sixties musical. By the third workshop, that concept was gone. We realized that this all takes place in her mind and on the stage. We decided to go with minimal furniture pieces, with on-stage dressing rooms visible to the audience. We'd have a clear stage for ballet, and an orchestra upstage on a platform. We were going to use projections throughout, such as the fire. We were working with a cinematographer, and the dream sequences were going to look very much like film."

The Shubert Organization had been immensely helpful and supportive of Bennett throughout *A Chorus Line* and *Ballroom,* and had co-produced *Dreamgirls.* One of the many fascinating aspects of the *Scandal* period was Bennett's attempt to shut out the Shuberts.

AVIAN: "Michael didn't want any imput from the Shuberts on the show. He always had to do things to create his artistic freedom, and Michael didn't want any pressure from the Shuberts, like 'We want your show. We want you in the Imperial by such and such a date.' That's what happens. They're business men looking for product, and they loved Michael. But Michael couldn't function artistically like that, so he shut out everybody from *Scandal.* He didn't want anybody to see it because he didn't want anyone booking dates. That would have coerced and cornered him into going on with the project."

SOURCE: "Bernie felt he had a father-son relationship with Michael.

But Michael would say, 'I'm not daddy's little boy. I'm capable of doing this myself.' He wouldn't let Bernie or David Geffen in on money for the show, and was careful to keep anyone connected with them from investing. He felt that he and Bobby were the real producers, and he said he was sick and tired of giving credit to people who were not producers.''

To emphasize his temporary separation from the Shuberts, Bennett announced to the press in November 1984 that he was negotiating to buy a half-interest in the Mark Hellinger Theatre, owned by the Shubert's rival theatrical power, the Nederlander Organization. Bennett declared that *Scandal* would play the Hellinger, the theatre where he had choreographed his first Broadway show, *A Joyful Noise,* as well as *Coco,* and, ironically, where the movie of *A Chorus Line* had recently begun shooting. When a columnist reported that the name of the theatre might be changed to "The Michael Bennett," Bennett said that if he was going to rename a theatre for a director, it would be for Jerome Robbins.

WAGNER: "The Hellinger thing was a joke. He was teasing Bernie; that was called 'Bernie baiting.' Bernie and Michael were like father and son, but it was also love-hate. There was enormous respect and love, but each always felt controlled by the other. It was a very intense relationship, and Michael played a lot of games. Michael was having a great time. And then it all blew over, and he and Bernie got back together.''

The company was dismissed for its three-week break, and Kurtz, along with other members of the company, vacationed in St. Bart's. It was there they learned the news that would rock the Broadway community.

KURTZ: "Danny Herman called his service in New York, and there was a message from Marvin Krauss, the general manager, which said, '*Scandal* is postponed indefinitely. Don't turn down any jobs.' I thought there was some mix up, and that we were probably starting up a couple of weeks late. There was absolutely no warning for what happened. Usually if there are problems, you know.''

But the "indefinite postponement" ultimately turned out to be a cancellation, and on "Black Monday," over a hundred people involved in the production received their notices.

KURTZ: "We extended our stay in St. Bart's, and when I got back, Bob Herr, Michael's secretary, told me that Michael had gone off to St. Bart's. We literally passed each other in the air. After the longest three weeks of my life, Michael got back and called me. It was a painful phone call. He didn't want to know about my pain and what I'd been through. He wanted to tell me what he'd been through.''

Scandal had been scheduled to open on April 18, 1985, at the Mark Hellinger Theatre. Why was this show, which seemed to be developing into one of the most exciting projects with which Bennett had ever been associated, canceled so abruptly and so definitively?

A myriad of reasons emerged, but five seem to come up most often. The first three of these were given by Bennett to the press, in the form of hints, at various times during the next year. The fourth reason was the one that Bennett told his associates was the actual cause of the cancellation. It is still believed by many of those involved, even though Bennett ultimately admitted to some that it was untrue. The fifth reason was kept a secret from the press and from Bennett's closest associates, and, while the first three reasons all played a part in the cancellation, it was ultimately this fifth reason that put an end to *Scandal*.

Bennett first announced to the press that the workshops had demonstrated to him that *Scandal* needed more work.

AVIAN: "At the end of the fourth workshop, we were still not ready to go into Broadway rehearsals. The technical cost of the show was becoming enormous, and we got a little scared that we weren't prepared yet. It needed a little more writing, and the score wasn't finished. We made the mistake on *Ballroom* of going ahead with the show when we still weren't quite ready."

LENNY: "I think in the back of his mind, he didn't think the show was going to make it."

The second reason was not revealed to the press by Bennett until a year later.

AVIAN: "AIDS was hitting the scene, and this musical was about sexual promiscuity. We were starting to get scared. We were doing this musical teaching a woman to be sexually liberated when the pendulum had begun to swing the other way. Michael got very nervous and didn't want to take the chance."

WEBB: "When the AIDS crisis gained momentum, it became a threat to the musical. The timing was wrong for this show."

KURTZ: "Treva and I never really believed he canceled the show because of AIDS and it not being the time to do a show about promiscuity. It seemed strange that this occurred to him after working on the show for so long. Nobody ever mentioned the subject during rehearsals. I talked to Michael on the phone every night, and he shared everything with me, but he never mentioned that concern to me."

The third reason Bennett told the press relates to contractual problems with certain members of his production team and his sudden decision near the end of the fourth workshop to repeat *A Chorus Line* history and open the show Off-Broadway first.

WHEELER: "Michael got upset because some of the people who worked for him were asking for contracts that were incredibly different from their previous contracts. Everybody wanted twice as much as before, and he felt as if he was being used because of who he was and how successful he was."

THOMAS: "Michael called me and said the show was becoming unproduceable. The big shots didn't want him to be the producer of his own show. He said that everybody was asking for double what they got on the last show, and that the big shots were telling these people to charge him more, and threatening them if they didn't."

The contractual problems were aggravated when Bennett decided to inaugurate his new Theatre 890 with *Scandal,* with the intention of moving it uptown after a few months.

SILVERMAN: "Michael told the cast that the show was going to be done Off-Broadway first. I loved the idea, because it meant more time to do work. He told me later that a lot of the performers had come to him unhappy. He was angry and disappointed in their lack of support.

"Then he had a meeting with the staff. Various members of the staff said they wouldn't be making enough money Off-Broadway to survive, or that they had been counting on the Broadway money to pay off debts, or that they'd have to do another show at the same time to make ends meet. Michael decided they were all being 'greedy.' No one said they wouldn't do the show, and the announcement had been sudden, but Michael was upset. He explained to me that the financial situation was getting out of hand, and the show would be unproduceable unless everybody accepted Off-Broadway salaries first."

But to the members of his staff and his confidantes, Bennett pinned the show's cancellation on the woman who had initially conceived it. He claimed that on the Friday before "Black Monday," Silverman had had delivered to him an extensive rider to her original contract, demanding approval over the score, the casting, and other aspects of the production. Close colleagues say that Bennett, who already had doubts about the production, told them he saw this as a betrayal and as the last straw. Bennett was reportedly so incensed that, upon the delivery of the contract, he pulled the plug on the entire production.

SILVERMAN: "It stuns me that people actually believe that something

I had in my contract could have overnight caused the downfall of a musical that Michael and I had worked on intensively for five years. Michael told everybody that I'd written into the contract demands for approval over music, casting, orchestrations and all the rest. But the standard Dramatists Guild contract says that the author automatically has approval over casting, music, everything in the show. It's one of the reasons writers write plays. Michael was pretending I was asking for something extra, yet every writer who was ever produced on Broadway, from Arthur Miller to Jimmy Kirkwood, instantly and irrevocably has these approvals the moment they sign the Dramatists contract. I guess that all these people who had been professionals in the theatre for so long had been so hungry for a reason that they fell for what he said. It was all so ugly and heartbreaking; I don't think I'll ever recover.

"At the beginning of negotiations, Michael told me he was taking a point as a writer. When I said, 'That's not fair,' he said, 'That's the way it's going to be.' When my lawyer said, 'This isn't fair,' I told him, 'You have to understand. There are two things: there's fair, and there's Michael.'

"Michael told me that the two of us were to share 'conceived by' credit. Many months later, he announced that it was going to say 'conceived by Michael Bennett.' I said, 'Michael, you said we were going to share that.' He said, 'I never said anything about sharing the credit.' I said, 'Come on, Michael, you know we had that conversation.' 'I remember nothing about it,' he laughed. 'I took a lot of drugs in the Sixties.' When I kept protesting, he said, 'If you want co-credit as conceiver that much, I'll take co-credit as writer.' I didn't know what he was talking about. 'Frankly, it would be better for your career, honey, if you had 'written by' and I had 'conceived by.' But if that's what you want, let's do that. 'Conceived by Treva Silverman and Michael Bennett, Book by Treva Silverman and Michael Bennett.' I said, 'Michael, okay, okay. It will be the way you want.' Anyone who got the better of him on a contract would have gone down in history.

"Months later, around October 1985, with the help of Jimmy Webb, who served as a friendly liaison, I called Michael, and finally got through. We had a wonderful talk. He said, 'I want you to know that the contract had nothing to do with stopping the show. But it was so damned convenient. This way, it left the show immaculate, without a blemish. If I could blame it on contracts and lawyers, the show would still be intact if I wanted to do it again.' I was praying that Michael would come back and do the show, so I let him say this without saying, 'How could you have done that to me?' "

When Bennett announced the postponement, many of those involved in *Scandal* were shocked into a state of inertia, but others had become too excited about the show's prospects to take it lying down.

SILVERMAN: "When he dropped the show, I sent him telegrams and letters, asking what had happened and was there anything I could do. There was never any response. I can never look back on that period without remembering my sense of futility."

WEBB: "Treva and Michael were both funny people, and I tried to get them back together after the explosion. There was so much at stake and it seemed like such a tragedy."

KURTZ: "Michael told me Treva was the villainess, but meanwhile Treva had called me, crying, wondering what had happened. I wanted it to work out, so I called Michael and said, 'We're all sitting around in our apartments weeping and mourning. Can we try to do something about this?' I asked him if I could call Treva and tell her what he had said, and he said, 'Go ahead.' The mystery to me was that Michael said he wanted it to work out, and Treva had written to him that she would do anything. So what was the problem?"

The problem was the fifth and most fundamental reason, only revealed by Bennett to a few near the end of his life.

KURTZ: "Michael called me two weeks before he died, and told me he knew he was ill when he was in St. Bart's. That may have been the real reason; he may not have wanted it to work out. He said to me, 'I feel like I owe you one.' I needed to hear that from him for two years. 'I am so glad that you had all this success this year, with *House of Blue Leaves* and winning the Tony. If that hadn't happened, I think I would have slit my wrists.' "

SILVERMAN: "Michael phoned me from the hospital 14 days before he died, June 18, 1987. Bob Herr later told me that there were a few days at that time when he felt okay, and he called Robin, Joe Papp, Swoosie, me, and a few others. I had a huge need to hear his voice. He said, 'I think it's about time to talk as friends, which we have been.' He told me he had found out at the end of the fourth workshop that he had the AIDS virus. He said that as he was creating the 'Menage à Trois Ballet,' he saw all these beautiful people dancing, and he said to himself, 'What will the critics say about a show about sex whose director is dying of AIDS? Why would anyone want to see a show about sex when its director is dying of

AIDS?' Michael said, 'I knew you'd understand. I felt I didn't have to explain to Treva; she'd understand.' "

BISHOP: "The real reason for the cancellation must have been illness. If Michael really wanted to do something, he wouldn't have given up. It was not like him to give up."

Those involved find talking about *Scandal* and recalling the very real achievements of it painful but necessary in order to deal with the experience. No one who was there can get over the brilliance of what they alone witnessed, and the experience of working with Bennett on the show.

AVIAN: "It was particularly hard on me. I thought, 'All this work, some of it brilliant, is down the toilet.' Michael said, 'It's going to be really tough, and everybody's going to hate us, but we can't go ahead.' I said, 'You're the boss. It's your ballgame.' "

WEBB: "I can't tell you how often I dream of the night he told me would come, when we would stand in the back of the theatre together and watch our show. I couldn't wait for that night, and now it won't happen. But it's almost enough to know that he had that kind of confidence in me and my work."

KRAUSS: "The show was extraordinary and could have been a big hit. It had the best dancing he ever did."

KURTZ: "The bust-up of *Scandal* was a very painful thing to go through, but I wouldn't trade that year for anything. To work in a whole different world, with dancers and choreography and music, was an incredible experience. And I was in the best hands in the world."

SILVERMAN: "Michael said to Bobby and me mid-workshop, 'When my obituary is written, instead of saying 'Michael *(A Chorus Line)* Bennett,' it will say 'Michael *(Scandal)* Bennett.' He was so proud of his work on it.

"What was so wounding was that the show was my baby, and I found out that not only was my baby dead, but that I was being accused of killing it, and that people believed I had killed it.

"Five years of work was over in one second. Five years of some of the most intensely charged, emotional moments of my whole life. Some of the most horrible times for me now are when people say, 'It would have been so sensational, so marvelous.' I can't bear it. I still can't believe it happened; it was right there. I know it would have been funny, spiritual and beautiful. There was such fear initially that it wouldn't be good enough, and then it was."

Will *Scandal* be reactivated, and can it be?

AVIAN: "The only way it could be done now would be to set it in 1975 and do it as a period piece. That would help, but our sensibilities are now very cautious, and it wouldn't have the freedom, giddiness or silliness it needed about picking up men and having sex without guilt. In your head, you'd be thinking, 'This can't exist. People are dying out there.' "

HERMAN: "It's probably not a good time to try to do the show again. It's a shame he picked sex to talk about right and wrong, because there is now sex that *is* 'wrong.' "

KURTZ: "I would consider doing it again if it were in the right hands. I love to do good material, and it's great material, a wonderful role."

WAGNER: "If Bobby could ever put back what was there . . . I hope some day he may, but I doubt he ever will. Michael's death killed a lot of people inside."

AVIAN: "I would not consider working on a re-creation of what existed. It's too hard for me."

Silverman took advantage of the Writers Guild strike of 1988 to re-work the script of *Scandal* as a nonmusical play, now set in the more carefree Seventies. On the evening of May 19, 1988, Silverman assembled most of the performers involved in the workshops—Kurtz, Stevens, Garber, Rasche, Lopez, and Bishop—and others, and had a reading of the new version. And *Scandal* was alive again.

6

. . . .

CHESS/CHECKMATE

W HATEVER BENNETT'S FEARS ABOUT his health, he was too dynamic a personality to sit and wait for the worst to happen. He considered reactivating *Scandal* during 1985 but was persuaded by the Shuberts to take on the direction of a major new project that they would be co-producing.

The pop opera *Chess* had been released as a double album that year and had met with considerable success, including two hit singles in the United Kingdom and one in America. There was an immediate demand for a stage production of the work, and the Shuberts were planning a spring 1986 opening in London. In spite of doubts about the material, Bennett agreed to take on the project, mainly as an act of reconciliation with the Shuberts.

AVIAN: "We were handed an album, which meant that the project had a lot of built-in problems. Numbers like 'Merano' and 'The Story of Chess' were killers to stage. We never could figure out how we were going to stage 'Merano,' although we had a lot of ideas about how to keep the silly lederhosen people and the serious KGB people on stage at the same time. The merchandisers' number was another tough nut to crack.

Those numbers had no tension and no story-telling; they could have been told in two lines."

But once he agreed to take on the project, Bennett came up with a conception to unify what he saw as a sprawling story, and a scenic concept to go with it.

WAGNER: "It was going to be a real movement show. There wasn't going to be any scenery on stage other than a turntable and video monitors. He was viewing it as a show about media, as opposed to being about that story. He didn't feel the book had enough linking it all together, so the television screens were his way of telling the story. There were going to be minimal props, and we were going to use graphic screens similar to those we used in *Seesaw*."

AVIAN: "Michael wanted *Chess* to be like *Casablanca* in terms of that triangle. He liked that kind of plotting. You don't know who's guilty or innocent, but at the end each does things for reasons that help each other."

Bennett cast the entire production and had design plans fully drawn up. He met with chess experts, and journeyed to Merano to soak up the atmosphere. He flew to Holland to purchase 128 television monitors for the stage at a cost of a million pounds, in keeping with his conception of the show as a continuous media event, with many of the offstage scenes to be visible to the audience on the monitors.

Suddenly, in January 1986, just three months before performances were to begin, Bennett withdrew from the production. Trevor Nunn was rushed in to save the show, which had gone too far into production to be postponed. Nunn was saddled with a cast, concept, and design not of his own choosing, and although the show received a very mixed reception, he performed a miracle by simply getting the enormously complex show onstage.

AVIAN: "When Trevor took over, he introduced much more scenery, the mountain and the bedrooms. Michael was going to stage it pretty much like a ballet, without all those props, on a much cleaner, barer stage. We saw the Arbiter as a dance lead. We cast him to be a flamboyant creature, and they didn't know what to do with him later. He was going to have his group of punky friends, very extreme and very choreographed, running through the show."

WAGNER: "Trevor works very differently from Michael. He's behavioral, real, natural, and works from the word. Michael always worked from the gut, from impulse, from something that makes your heart beat faster. You had two different worlds that were crossing in a very strange place. Trevor wasn't comfortable with all that computer technology, and the video didn't really get used very much. Trevor is not as interested in movement, and was more interested in the story than Michael. For Michael, it was all about media."

BERNARD B. JACOBS: "Trevor saw *Chess* as being about the most important issue of our time, the relationship between East and West. Michael, no matter what it was about, was interested in making a musical of the work. Michael cast the show with the best dancers in London, which put Trevor at an enormous disadvantage, as they were precisely the sort of people that under normal circumstances Trevor would not have employed. You had the clash of two extremes: a person who believes that theatre is about a story, a book, content, and a person who believes that you balance the content with scenic effects, design and, most important of all, choreography. Michael would have told the story through choreography."

Why did Bennett depart *Chess*? The newspapers reported that he had had an attack of angina pectoris, causing palpitations and loss of breath. He told Cindy Adams in the *New York Post* in March, "It's a disease peculiar to directors. It's called stress." He told the *Washington Post*'s David Richards that May, "The doctors said I couldn't dance. They didn't know if I needed a bypass operation, and until they made that recommendation, which they still haven't made, I had to be in an absolutely stress-free situation. Well, if one wants to be stress-free, one does not direct a $7 million musical in London with a cast of 46 people and a second act that has problems."

Some papers printed rumors, denied by all parties, that Bennett was unhappy with the material or one of the stars.

The heart ailment story was the first public disclosure that Bennett was ill. But a few, such as Wagner and Jacobs who were with Bennett in London, knew the reality of the situation, while others close to Bennett began to suspect that the reports they were reading and hearing were covering up an even graver situation.

In November, Bennett gave what was to be his last public interview, to Jeremy Gerard of *The New York Times*. Bennett continued to maintain the story of the fictive illness, saying he was soon to undergo surgery for angina, but a note of truth crept in when he said of his forthcoming operation, "I've never been more scared in my life." He insisted on keeping up a brave front, however, stating, "My life is becoming simpler, and that's always good. I think I'll be able to make my comeback at 44 without a problem."

Some who were very close to Bennett soon found out the truth, although others with whom he had shared the greatest of intimacies and friendship in the past were kept in the dark for a year.

LENNY: "The minute Michael came back from London, he asked me to come over to his apartment at 40 Central Park South. We talked and talked, and then Michael got up and walked over to the piano, next to these tremendous windows that overlooked the park. He turned around and spat out the words, 'Jack, I have AIDS.' I broke down and started to cry. He said to me, 'I don't want you to worry about me. I'm the one person who can beat this. So don't worry about me. I just felt I had to tell you.' Very few knew. He said I could tell my wife, but no one else."

Bennett's decision to keep the real nature of his illness a secret, and the manner in which he chose to spend his final year, would cause considerable grief to many who felt close to him. When the illness became debilitating, he left New York, never to return. Secretary Bob Herr and close friend Gene Pruit remained with Bennett until his death.

HERR: "Gene, Michael and myself moved to East Hampton in early 1986. Michael and Bob Avian started searching the world trying to find treatments. Michael got into a program at the N.I.H. in Washington, but luckily it was the kind where you didn't have to be there all the time. So we were able to live in East Hampton and fly to Washington at least once a week. At this point, Michael was being very secretive. He didn't want anyone to know, and was using his family name in the hospital.

"Christmas of '86, we were flying out to Tucson to check on another kind of treatment we were hearing about. On the way, he became very ill and had difficulty breathing. We were supposed to stay in Tucson four days; we never came back. We were in Tucson from just before Christmas '86 to the end. The disease was now cancer hitting his lungs, and the University of Arizona's hospital had the right to use certain experimental drugs. Michael was selective about what he was willing to try, but was very experimental and willing to try anything that sounded reasonable."

Bennett bought a home in Tucson and exiled himself, not taking phone calls from anyone except a few of his closest associates, and not contacting the hundreds of people who now feared the worst and were eager to reach him.

KRAUSS: "He didn't want pity. He didn't want people calling. He wanted his privacy, and he thought this was the best way."

LIZ SMITH of the *Daily News* said: "His wish to control events and the stigma of having AIDS—in his eyes—simply didn't allow this proud fellow to become an object of pity or concern."

HERR: "He stayed pretty isolated from most of his friends; only Bob and Robin Wagner were there much. He was particularly worried about involving his mother and brother. He felt it was his fight. . . . He didn't tell his mother the nature of his illness; she found out when the *Times* printed it for the first time."

Bennett was a fighter, and because he saw himself as a winner, he may not have wanted to acknowledge the fact that his illness had reached a stage where it would inevitably prove fatal within a year. Each person, if able, is entitled to choose the manner in which he will die. Gradually, Bennett's friends came to accept the fact that this was the way he needed to do it, with dignity and grace, and to realize that it was foolhardy to question any aspect of a Michael Bennett production.

HERR: "Michael was very positive during his last months. He was demanding as always. He was often in pain, but managed it pretty well. He felt he had a good chance of hanging on, because he was willing to go wherever necessary, and had the money needed. He had the advantage of a tremendous will, and never gave up."

Bennett, who had never had his awards and prizes displayed at either his New York home or office, surrounded himself with every Tony, every citation, every certificate, in his last months in Tucson. He continued to fight against the disease, while maintaining his sense of humor and looking back on the wonders of his life.

KURTZ: "About two weeks before he died, he called me from Arizona. The moment I heard his voice, I burst into tears. I said, 'I'm sorry. This is the last thing you want to hear.' His voice was on the weak side, but as we talked it got stronger. He sounded like the old Michael, with that edge to everything he said, and the humor. He told me about the big barbecue he had thrown for all the doctors and nurses who helped him. He said there was this one nurse who he had accidentally forgotten to invite. She came to him and asked if she could come too. He said to her, 'Honey, anybody who would come to a barbecue given by an AIDS patient is more than welcome!' He told me he was buying a Rolls-Royce, the most expensive kind.

"He really thought he could lick it. He was trying every new drug from Europe. . . . But he was going through hell, with several cancers and related problems. He said he had already almost died five times."

PIPPIN: "Tharon Musser told me that when Michael knew he wouldn't last much longer, he told her, 'You know, I've really had it all. It might have been short, but I've really had it all.' "

These were the privileged few. Many others tried in vain to reach him.

LORETTA DEVINE: "Most of us tried to reach him for a long time, and there was no way to get to him. He didn't want us to see him the way he was at the end. The hardest thing was not getting a chance to say goodbye to him."

STEVE BOOCKVOR: "It bothered me that I was not able to talk to him, hold his hand, and kiss him goodbye. He didn't allow that, and at first I was angry about that. But then I understood that that's the way he had to go. I'm sure the way he went was unacceptable to him; it lacked style, although he gave it as much style as he could."

After many months of rumor and speculation, the truth finally came out in the press in May. Bennett had sold the building he bought at 890 Broadway, and Marvin Schulman, his former business manager, was suing for 5 percent of the profits from the sale of the building. The *New York Post* reported: "What Broadway knew was made official yesterday—the fact that Michael Bennett, 44, won't be back. The sad word came in Manhattan Supreme Court, where the choreographer is being sued by Marvin Schulman. . . . Bennett's secretary, Robert Herr, submitted an affidavit saying the showman hasn't been properly served because he moved to Tucson, Arizona, last December. He has since put his apartment and East Hampton house up for sale. Herr says Bennett 'has been and is now under extensive medical treatment for a life-threatening disease.' "

Knowing that he could not attend the *Dreamgirls* reopening on Broadway on June 28, Bennett threw his own opening-night bash in Tucson, inviting every nurse, orderly, intern, and doctor who had helped him and cared for him to his home for the evening.

Michael Peters flew out to Tucson after the *Dreamgirls* reopening to take Bennett the reviews.

PETERS: "Michael had called me a few weeks before and said, 'Hi. Is this Mikey Peters? Well, I miss you and I want to see you. I need to laugh. I want you to come out here.' That's why I went. I know that he knew I was there and that we had opened. I didn't read the reviews to him, but I told him that they loved the show again and loved him. And he heard that and knew it."

When Robin Wagner asked Bennett, days before his death, whether he could make any sense of his illness, he replied, "I'm tap dancing my way to heaven."

Just as many in the Broadway community were preparing to leave for an extended holiday weekend, the news came: Bennett died Thursday, July 2, at 6:50 A.M. at his home in Tucson, the official cause being lymphoma, an AIDS-related cancer.

Bennett's Broadway shows would, of course, go on. *Dreamgirls* was at the beginning of its successful return engagement, and the performance that night and for the rest of the week was dedicated to Bennett. There was an even more emotional scene at the Shubert Theatre.

TOM PORTER, stage manager: "What happened that night was almost more of a memorial to Michael than even the real memorial was. They called me from Tucson that morning, and I had the assistants call the company. That night, Joe Papp, all the designers, the Shuberts, and others arrived with the company at 6:30. It just sort of happened—the only ones who were called at 6:30 were the cast. We all met inside the house. It was like all these people needed to be together at that time. A few people spoke. No one really said a whole lot or needed to—they just needed to be with each other. Joe asked the cast to sing 'One'—they tried, but they didn't do very well. We talked about what to do that night, and decided not to do anything. We didn't even make the announcement about the taking of photographs before the show. We dimmed the lights, and there was at least a minute of applause in the dark. And then we just did the show. The kids had asked if they could do the last chorus of the finale changing the word 'she' to 'he' in 'One.' That was the only change we made. It was a highly charged emotional evening, and the audience knew without anybody saying anything."

From that night on, performing *A Chorus Line* was what the company did for love of Bennett. The show was now his permanent tribute and monument.

The lights on Broadway dimmed at 8 P.M. on July 2 in tribute to Bennett, and the verbal tributes began to pour in.

BERNARD B. JACOBS: "I think Michael contributed more to the American theatre in his short life than other artists who lived far longer."

PAPP: "He was not a literary-type person. He was a street person. But when it came to the stage, he was a supreme being. Michael's ability was to take rough, raw material and shape it into something that became exquisite. It's a great loss to the culture of this country, it's not just a loss to show business."

HAMLISCH: "Most people will miss the fact that they won't be able to audition for a Michael Bennett show anymore. And I will miss him because I won't have him for a friend anymore."

Bennett's death came at a time when the public and the media were becoming increasingly aware of the horrendous toll AIDS was taking in the arts community. Such figures as playwright-director-actor Charles Ludlam, pianist Paul Jacobs, dancer Charles Ward, Broadway hair stylist Ted Azar, and fashion designer Perry Ellis had all been claimed by the disease in recent months.

On August 10, *A Chorus Line* celebrated its 5,000th performance, and it was, of course, dedicated to Bennett. All involved knew it would be foolish to attempt to emulate the 3,389th celebration, which was still fresh in the minds of most observers as the theatrical experience of a lifetime. For the 5,000th, it was decided to invite anyone who had ever appeared in an American production of the show in stock, community theatres, or colleges to enter a "Chance to Dance" contest, which would allow nineteen winners, one for each role, to perform onstage at the Shubert. The winners were flown to New York, where they were taught the original choreography by Tom Porter and the show's dance captain. The nervous group joined the cast during "What I Did for Love," then reappeared to dance the finale, forming the front row of a double line. After the performance, a five-foot cake in the form of a finale hat was wheeled out, and Papp paid tribute to Bennett.

Later that month, the details of Bennett's will were made public. He bequeathed 15 percent of his estate to organizations "which are involved in the research of or the cure or treatment of patients afflicted with the disease known as AIDS." He directed Avian and his lawyer, John Breglio, to establish a trust for the commercial development of the original tapes that were the basis for *A Chorus Line,* Avian and Breglio each to receive one-quarter of the profits from that enterprise, the balance to be split equally among the people who participated in the tapes. He left personal effects to Avian, Herr, and Pruit; a share in the estate to Avian, Breglio, Pruit, and Wagner; and a solid-silver top hat inscribed by the original cast of *A Chorus Line* to Bernard B. Jacobs and his wife. Chief beneficiaries of the estate, which was estimated at $25 million, were Bennett's mother, brother, and half-brother.

Plans were immediately underfoot for the memorial service, but before it could take place, T. Michael Reed, an important figure in the history of *A Chorus Line,* was also claimed by AIDS. Then on September 23, Bob

Fosse died of a heart attack while working on a tour of *Sweet Charity* starring Donna McKechnie.

In March 1988, the original cast of *A Chorus Line* reassembled once more, at an AIDS benefit entitled "Hollywood's Salute to Broadway" at the Dorothy Chandler Pavilion in Los Angeles. As a huge photo of Bennett smiled down on them, the company recreated several numbers from the show, then closed the evening with "One," ending, as always, with everyone kicking in unison as darkness overtakes them.

On the 1988 Tony Awards telecast three months later, McKechnie and the original "Dreamgirls" paid tribute to Bennett, a salute that ended with a single top-hatted dancer in spotlight, striking a pose from the finale.

The line would continue.

Broadway seemed to be dead. With Champion, Fosse, and Bennett gone, and de Mille, Robbins,* and Kidd inactive in the theatre, the musical theatre that Bennett dreamed of as a child in Buffalo was no more. Those who had worked with him or seen his shows found it impossible to express their feeling of loss, of the gap created by his death. Having seen how far he had taken the musical, all felt deprived of the next twenty-five years of dazzling Bennett productions, and the new directions Bennett's work might have taken. While talented directors such as Tommy Tune had emerged in recent years, there did not immediately seem to be anyone to continue the tradition that connected the innovative work of de Mille, Robbins, and Bennett. There was an underlying panic in the theatrical community that those who knew how to do it, how to make it happen, were gone.

The musical theatre had by now become dominated by the British, by spectacles often lacking in the emotional truth central to Bennett's work and by musicals without real people at their center. While Bennett had himself been working in his last years at sustaining longer and longer musical sequences, the operatic, serious turn musicals had taken in recent seasons veered away from his Broadway vernacular and devotion to recognizable human truth.

The Broadway community he joined in the early Sixties was a thrilling place, in which he sensed a real commitment to and love for the work.

. . . .

*Robbins returned to Broadway in 1989 with a triumphant retrospective of his work, *Jerome Robbins' Broadway*.

There were now fewer shows, more performers who were using Broadway as a stepping-stone to television, and producers who were afraid to give new talent a chance and felt the need to make every show an "event." The effectiveness of the workshop system Bennett had pioneered had broken down, and many felt that Broadway, with the exception of the occasional megahit imported from London, had ceased to exist.

But Bennett knew better.

BENNETT: "I grew up this kid who fell in love with the Broadway theatre. I had that luxury of going into the theatre and doing exactly what I wanted to do. I've been allowed to be an artist. Isn't that what everyone dreams of?

"Broadway has died about three times since I came here. They've been asking me the same questions all these years, the future of the theatre . . . why isn't the musical theatre fun anymore, blah, blah, blah. But I really believe this: the one thing you don't have to worry about in the world is the theatre. Religions die quicker than theatre."

Michael Bennett created dazzling entertainment and indelible images of truth, while profoundly affecting the lives of everyone with whom he came in contact.

He was many things: a leader and manipulator of people; a conceptual artist; a perfectionist who made everyone strive to do his or her best; an incomparable stager of plays; a collaborator; a street kid who created stage poetry; a theatrical genius who had an incalculable impact on the lives of hundreds of people and on the theatre itself; a magician; and a tap-dancing kid who never grew up.

EPILOGUE

. . . .

REMEMBERING

THE MAN

M OST OF THOSE INTERVIEWED for this book invoked the word *genius* when discussing Bennett, and not in idle "show-biz" fashion. To his collaborators and performers, he was a true theatrical phenomenon unlike any other with whom they worked. Many spoke of his extraordinary leadership qualities, and his ability to inspire by trust.

TUNICK: "He was a great leader of people. He would have made a great political leader or general or king. He had large conceptions and the ability to inspire people to follow him in carrying out these conceptions.

"Michael inspired people to do their own work well. He allowed everybody to do their own work, the composers to compose, the designers to design, without stifling them. Once you had his trust and confidence, he respected your ability. . . . A lot of directors are so intent on putting their own personal stamp on the work that the people who work with them become more like secretaries than actual artists. But Michael never did that. He demanded great work, and he allowed it to happen. He got the best work out of so many of us."

PIPPIN: "Michael's genius was always being able to tell people what to do and sometimes how to do it. He always gave people the raw materials to make it happen, and he always got people around him who could do what was needed. He had a genius for knowing how to put people together whom he could control, but he was controlling them for their own good."

STEVENS: "With actors, Michael's technique was to leave them alone, not to say, 'Do this' or 'Do that.' He'd talk to them about the scene or the song, allow them to feel confident, then start editing. First he cast the right people, then he trusted them, nurtured them and protected them. And they grew bigger and bigger, and took risks."

One of the keys to his ability to lead was his hard-earned awareness of the necessity of total control.

BENNETT: "I never like to feel that I'm working for anyone. I'm an Aries, a control freak, and I have to be the boss."

KRAUSS: "Michael was a perfectionist, and we always tried to keep a step ahead of him and anticipate his needs. We all pulled in the same direction, and his ability to get that was part of his success. I saw him get upset and have his tantrums—what genius doesn't? He could be tough. But whatever he did, there was a purpose to it, and it was a means to an end. He always knew what he wanted to accomplish."

Several performers and writers have mentioned, however, that in order to get from them what he wanted, he would woo them on a personal level.

DANTE: "Michael believed he had to manipulate you to get the work out of you, and he romanced everybody. Many directors do that, in their way, but Michael really did it on a personal level. It annoyed me that Michael got me and others to fall in love with him to get the work he wanted, which wasn't necessary. It's one thing to manipulate your talent; it's a whole other thing to manipulate your personal emotions to get to the talent."

BISHOP: "He was so charismatic that he had a tendency to make people feel they were the most important person in the production, and they got to believe that. He was capable of making people fall in love with him, and he didn't miss that, and used that, too."

Stylistically, Bennett never repeated himself.

BENNETT: "I hate being typecast. I never like to do a show that's anything like the show I did before. . . . I also resisted being categorized. I didn't want to be just a choreographer, just a director, or just a great stager of musicals."

TUNE: "Michael once said to me, 'I want to be so good that if you saw a show of mine and my name wasn't on it, you wouldn't know who did it. I want to serve each show so completely that I won't have just one style.'"

He was also steeped in show-business tradition but was able to use that tradition for dramatic effect.

SONDHEIM: "What Bennett had is a sense of the tradition of the musical theatre combined with a dramatic imagination, that is to say, a way to use the tradition of the musical theatre. I've spoken to people who know a lot more about dance than I do who say that his vocabulary was very limited. But within that vocabulary, which was very specifically oriented in musical comedy tradition, he was very imaginative, particularly about how to use stage space. The only person I know that had it more than he was Jerry Robbins, and it's not coincidental that Michael always looked up to Jerry with great admiration. Michael knew how to use that tradition for something more than flash, although Michael was dangerously attracted to flash and big hands, which is not always a good idea.

"We talked about doing shows together occasionally, and he always wanted to do shows that had some kind of show business reference, and that, I think, was why we never did another one together. I would occasionally discuss an idea with him, and he would immediately think of it in a show-biz framework. He was a little too much into show-biz."

The dancing in his shows was always *about* something, and always had underlying concepts and ideas. It was always reflective of character and it advanced the action and made character points. He would go into a rehearsal hall well prepared, knowing exactly what he wanted his dances to convey.

ROVETA: "Michael's concepts and ideas were more important than individual steps and combinations. He worked in terms of ideas, and he would get the overall feeling and picture for a number, then go back and work on specific steps. What was important was whether the idea was coming across, and whether it had the right feeling. In *A Chorus Line,* it wasn't the choreography, it was how it all fit together, what it expressed, and the feeling it conveyed that made that show."

HERMAN: "Michael's vision was unlimited. When he thought of a step for a number, he took into account who would be doing it, the audience, the cost, the theatre it would be playing in, the time when it would be seen, and how it would hold up ten years later."

Bennett's craftsmanship and ability to shape all the elements of theatre may have been his most unique feature.

WAGNER: "With every show we ever did, there was always more at first than later on. He started off with prose, and ended with poetry. He was always distilling down, getting down to a minimal essence of something. He used workshops to get close to the truth or the dynamic of the moment. He was always looking for some little bit of life that could come forward and take your imagination to another place."

STEVENS: "Michael oberved, then orchestrated. He didn't fall in love with his work, and was an objective being among all this craziness that we would go through. He could work on something for a long time, look at it, and if it didn't work, it was gone, no matter how good it was. It had to work for the show."

DANIELE: "Michael made every moment work, which is very hard in the theatre. There was not one moment he skipped and said, 'Let's go on to the next one.' "

Bennett used most of the best dancers in the business, dancers who were also in demand by such other top choreographers as Fosse and Champion. Those who worked with Bennett and Fosse draw interesting comparisons between these two giants.

STEVENS: "When you did a Fosse show, you were always doing Fosse. Everyone on stage was Fosse. . . . You acclimatized your talent to Bob, and then, if you're a star like Chita or Gwen or Ann Reinking, you come through. But you're still doing Fosse, no matter who you are. Michael always served the piece. There's not a Bennett style, other than his objectivity about what worked and his wonderful cinematic sense. As a dancer, you were doing what Michael created for the piece, not what he did with his body.

"Fosse and Champion always had to be in control; they demanded it. When I worked with Michael, he was more the boy-next-door; everybody respected him, but he was a little more personable, more tangible, closer to the actors than the other two. Fosse and Champion were a little older, while Michael was working with his peers."

CILENTO: "Fosse choreographed every single step himself. He imposed his style on you more than Michael. Michael incorporated the style of what his *show* was within the dancing, but it was basically us, the way we danced. Our style took over his material and its overall look. With Fosse, it was Fosse first, then our style."

DEBUSKEY: "Michael's knowledge of the musical stage was beyond that of anyone else. He was not the greatest choreographer; Fosse was a better choreographer. But in terms of the totality of the staging, Michael was a much greater conceptual person. He was bottomless and never seemed to dry up.''

DANIELE: "Fosse and Bennett were both masters. They both had a very clear vision of what they wanted when they started, and as perfectionists, they were difficult to please and demanded a lot. Bob was moodier, but they both respected dancers more than anything, and were in awe of them, having been dancers themselves and known the discipline it takes. Once they had the people they needed around them, they trusted them as individuals. They took what we did best and molded it. That's why the same dancers would be fantastic in a show with Michael or Bob, and not so fantastic in other shows."

STEVENS: "As a kid in love with show business, Michael did not always perceive reality the way the rest of us did. But his heart was in the right place. He loved us, and so did Fosse. For all the manipulation and the bad stuff, these men got their life source from us. They recognized that, and they appreciated it and loved it."

Perhaps the key to Bennett's uniqueness lay in his ability to collaborate. While every worker in musical theatre is well aware of the need to be open to one's fellow creators, Bennett went beyond anyone in his talent for and need of collaboration.

BENNETT: "The hardest thing about musicals is that they're about collaboration. The mistake I made in my earliest musicals is I was so ambitious that my work showed up a lot of other work in the show. And you know what happened? Those shows closed in a week, because I showed off and made the rest of the stuff look weak, as opposed to pulling everything to the same level. People should sit back and watch and not know where one contribution ends and the next takes over.

"I have a great team because I hate to be alone. I never work alone. If you're in the room with me, it's because I know how talented you are. You're not there to prove you're talented every second. You're there to work on the play, so you're allowed to be wrong."

Bennett's ability to work with others was most evident in his work with his design team: Wagner, Musser, and Aldredge.

AVIAN: "It was fantastic. There was such open discussion and respect among the team. Michael placed heavy importance on us all being together anytime there was a meeting. Everyone sat together over the set models for hours. It was a total, mutual respect team, and he would never have considered doing a show without them."

DEBUSKEY: "They developed an ideal creative circumstance. They did not contribute individually to a project as with most shows. It was an integrated unit. Each bounced off the other and helped the other creatively, but it was all because of Michael."

WAGNER: "He involved us all because he saw a show as a visual piece. He was visually attuned to every moment, and loved all the elements of design. He said to me before we did *Scandal,* 'You direct this one, and I'll design it.' "

MUSSER: "Michael realized the importance of design more than most directors do, and really believed that every element was important. Theatricality just oozed out of his pores.

"It was wonderful to be there and involved from the birth of the idea. . . . You don't get the same results when you're handed a ground plan and a script and the director says a few words to you. I've never worked with anyone where the collaboration was so extended and we were so involved. That's the way he liked to work, and he fed off of us the same way we fed off of him. For most people, designers are what they need to present the show, and they're not looking for their involvement. With Michael, we were always throwing out ideas.

"Elia Kazan, with whom I worked when I was a baby, was a lot like Michael. They both got what was good that you had to give, and that much more. But it spoils you for a lot of other work. I know Michael was a once-in-a-lifetime as far as I'm concerned, and it makes it very difficult doing shows without him. Even though we all did shows with other people while we were working with Michael, it's very difficult knowing that it ain't there anymore."

Perhaps even more unparalleled than the collaboration between Bennett and his designers was that between Bennett and Avian.

BENNETT: "We balance each other extremely well. Our personalities are very different. He has wonderful ballet technique, and his style of dancing is very different from mine. His perspective on dancing makes us that much more a well-rounded choreographer."

TUNICK: "Bob was a very stable person, and he lent Michael's professional life a certain amount of stability and solidness that he needed and recognized."

MCKECHNIE: "I would give Bob a 50% share of everything Michael did. That's what their life was, so I think it's fair to say. Bob was his real support system, and contributed a lot of dance vocabulary. Bob was perhaps more responsible for the steps, but they worked so closely together and complemented each other so well that it's hard to distinguish. Michael may have had more of the concepts, but Bob had a say in everything, be it writing or lighting."

DANIELE: "Many times I wondered, and I said this to Michael, if he would have gone as far as he did without Bob around. There was a marriage, a total trust between them that is so necessary to a choreographer. We have to turn around to somebody we trust completely and say, 'What do you think?' That's what Bob was all his life. And then there's Bob's gentleness and beauty of soul and heart. Sometimes Michael could be tough, or get a little upset. Like most great geniuses, he wanted perfection and he was impatient for it. And it was always Bob who would smooth the edges."

AVIAN: "We were best friends, roommates, and I knew him since he was 17. When he asked me to work for him, it was never about being employed by someone. I was just his pal sitting next to him, saying, 'I like that,' or 'I don't like that.' It always had that kind of honesty to it. We relied on each other, and I felt my greatest talent for him was being his editor.

"We had a basic, best-friend attitude toward each other and relied upon each other. We'd come home from work and be on the phone all night long.

"He made my life so wonderful. I never left him because the grass was never greener anywhere else. I shared his incredible career, and it was thrilling for me. It was totally honest and straightforward. There was never tension between us that would last longer than 24 hours.

"He needed to be the star, I needed my privacy. I used to kid him that I was a 'stage mother,' and I often was. I protected him, insulated him, and was the liaison in many situations. All I wanted to do was get him into the room to work.

"My strongest recollection of him is of his generosity. He was such a great friend to me. He took care of me, protected me, and gave me a career."

In April 1986, Bennett was inducted into the Theater Hall of Fame at the Gershwin Theatre. While it was entirely fitting, those who were lucky enough to experience collaborating with Bennett needed no such accolade to remind them of the experience.

KRAUSS: "Those who did not have the opportunity of working with

Michael should feel cheated. They will never know what they missed. It was an experience that can never be repeated in my lifetime. It was his energy, his ability to draw from people, and his love."

AVIAN: "I had such respect for his work, watching him grow and develop year by year and get smarter and smarter. He got smarter by doing, and by heavy analysis, which he felt was very key to his work. He felt the analysis gave him an intellectual approach and a way of understanding.

"But Michael wasn't intellectual. He was a gut artist, a heart-felt artist. He couldn't cry, didn't ever cry, but he judged his later shows by whether or not he made the audience cry. That was very key to him. He wanted to make the audience shed that tear, whether it be for happiness, joy or pain. It was something he couldn't do himself, but he strived to make that the payoff for his work. His work came from a basically sentimental place, even though he worked as a tough man. Above all, it was about his heart."

As a person, Bennett was a sharply contradictory figure. Many of those interviewed stress his kindness and generosity, then mention his neuroticism or occasional cruelty. Those close to him for a period of time inevitably experienced a "roller-coaster effect," whereby, sooner or later, they would be hurt by him. Yet the hurtful things done by him were accepted by most as part of his genius, and in no way prevented those who experienced them from adoring him. The irony of his existence is that he was never able to integrate the many facets of his personality as well as he was able to integrate the elements of a musical.

Those in the audience who were aware that the characters in *A Chorus Line* were, to an extent, based on the show's performers, naturally wondered whether Zach, the director-choreographer in charge of the audition, was based on Bennett. While there were elements of Bennett in other characters in the show, and while he said he would never run an audition the way Zach does, there are definite similarities between him and Zach. Both were driven people, obsessed with work above all else. Both had difficulty with relationships because they placed work first, and both had relationships with performers in their productions that caused strain.

Bennett's enormous ambition and drive brought him to the top of his field, but many felt it ultimately separated him from his true self and did not bring him genuine happiness.

JOE CALVAN, stage manager of Bennett's *West Side Story* tour, *Subways Are for Sleeping,* and *A Chorus Line* in 1976: "Success like *Chorus Line* breeds great assurance. Michael became tremendously powerful. But I don't think he ever found peace, happiness or contentment. He had all the wealth in the world, but never seemed to get any great pleasure out of it. He would rather have been with a bunch of gypsies at a saloon somewhere. He missed that, and when he became so successful, he couldn't enjoy that anymore, because he knew most people were looking for something or wanted something from him."

MCKECHNIE: "Everyone looked up to Michael and put him on a pedestal, but he really wanted to be one of us. Baayork always said that one of her regrets is that Michael was never on the line in *Chorus Line.* There was a bond between all of us, something we experienced as a group. He gave us that, but he never got the rich experience of that himself. . . . He loved the show, it was his life, but it got in his way and he resented it. All the power people gave him was sometimes a monkey on his back."

Bennett's life changed irrevocably after *A Chorus Line* opened. He went from a talented "hot" young director-choreographer to "Michael Bennett," an institution, an industry, and one of the most powerful figures in the theatre. He found it difficult to adjust to the show's success, and began to grow weary of the responsibility of supervising company after company of it.

To some observers, the show changed Bennett's personality, and not for the better.

TUNE: "Michael was a mentor to me, until it all changed with his success with *A Chorus Line.* His personality changed, and suddenly he had no more time. A lot of that was just the pressure of the work, but he changed forever. Those of us who were his closest and dearest were no more. The success of it drove him up in the air into an ivory tower, and suddenly you could not get through to him. The phone number one had always called was gone. He became totally protected. . . . He didn't distinguish between those of us who were really close to him and the ones who were after him to get him to do something. In his rise, he had to cut off everyone."

Bennett was constantly in analysis, five times a week in 1976. He found that success didn't dispel his personal ghosts, and that, having achieved everything about which he had fantasized, he needed new goals and something new for which to strive.

He was essentially a private person with a very limited circle of friends, always headed by Avian, but he tended to see himself as gregarious.

TUNICK: "He was a distant person. He liked to play the role of big brother and father confessor, and would like to have been a very warm and compassionate person. But he fell in and out of that style. His really close friends were very few. Many people became disappointed or disillusioned with him. Michael liked to think himself a caring person, yet he was really rather isolated. From time to time, he would disappoint people who thought they had a deep relationship with him, which turned out not to be so deep."

DANTE: "Michael had a certain group of friends that remained constant. Around that nucleus of close friends were the people he was working with. After each show, he'd go on to the next group of people he was working with, and then the next. He would woo you, and then you'd get hurt when you were out of the picture."

His manipulative tendencies are referred to frequently by those who knew him, and they seem to go beyond the natural need of any director to manipulate his workers to fulfill his vision.

PIPPIN: "Michael liked to play games that could be a little tough on some people, and then he could be this wonderful, warm, generous person. He had this strange dual personality. I saw both sides and was a recipient of both sides. I loved him dearly, I'd do anything for him, and I wanted to kill him sometimes."

DANTE: "Michael knew the human condition very well, which is why he was so good at getting you to do what he wanted. His understanding of it was extraordinary, and I'm only sorry that he couldn't live within those parameters. I felt Michael always felt he had to live outside those parameters. He viewed the human condition as if it were happening outside, understood it, but kept himself apart from it, above it."

AVIAN: "In spite of the things in Michael's personality that many had trouble with, I felt he was so talented, so bright. It takes that extreme personality to have all those gifts within him. He was a volcano. I felt, to bring that artistry out, let him do whatever he wants. But it was hard on a lot of people."

All of the negative aspects of Bennett's personality can to a degree be explained by the fact that the only thing that mattered to him was the work.

BENNETT: "My parents were very poor, and money was such an issue that the one thing I wanted out of life was never to worry about money. I am obsessive in that I do not care what's in the bank account. I am overextended all the time, and I have no attachment to things. The most important thing to me in life is to want to get up and go to work every day. I'm afraid of the day that I don't want to go to work."

He cared only about the freedom to work on projects that excited him, and he tended to put on weight and sink into depression between shows. His life revolved around the theatre, and success to him meant being allowed to do the work he wanted to do, without having to worry about its acceptance or rejection by the public.

TUNE: "Michael was a man of enormous dreams. I remember years ago his talking about an office high in the sky that would control all the dancing that happened on Broadway. If you wanted dancing on Broadway, you would have to come to him. He, Bobby, myself, we would all have offices high in the sky, and if you needed dancing, you would come to us."

Many of those interviewed for this book wept openly when recalling Bennett's enormous kindness to them and others.

SONDHEIM: "He was very generous, and I'm not talking about money. I'm talking about enthusiasm and praise, even for his rivals when he felt they deserved it. He had a lot of charm and enthusiasm. When I think of Michael, my first association is the friendliness of his voice when he answered the phone. I never saw any dark side to him."

WAGNER: "He was one of the most loyal people I've ever known in terms of his commitment to 'his people.' He gave everything to anyone who ever asked him, and he was always there if you needed anything. He knew everybody's name on the crew, who their kids were, their birthdays. . . . He was into a big, overwhelming kind of 'family' thing. He was the center of it, but he never used that. You couldn't know this guy and not love him."

BISHOP: "Because he hurt a lot of feelings, people sometimes forget how loyal he was. He liked going through the years with all his people."

AVIAN: "He was the most generous person I ever met in my life, and the most giving. He used to get so upset when he saw that people were upset with him. He'd say, 'Haven't I given them everything? I give them money, I give them parts. Why do they hate me?' It was because of what he did to their lives."

Nowhere was a dichotomy more evident in Bennett than in his sexuality.

BISHOP: "He was a very sexy man, and being bisexual, he could genuinely respond to both men and women. His seduction really got people; they believed it."

CALVAN: "Michael always had a strong inclination to be with a woman, but physically he was attracted to males. There was a constant collision of emotional things in him; he was always fighting a battle. Even though there was a lot more freedom in the theatre, being homosexual was not always accepted outside. And coming from an Italian background, the guilt about maybe being homosexual was a tremendous thing to bear."

Throughout his life, he had numerous affairs with men, including a director with whom he worked in summer stock, the leading man in the national company of a musical he choreographed, a designer in San Francisco, an artist, and at least two principal male performers in *A Chorus Line*. He admitted to bisexuality and homosexuality.

BENNETT: "I was very frightened when I was a kid that I was going to be a homosexual. I was accused of being one long before I'd ever done anything, because I was a boy dancer. I was plagued by the question, 'Am I a homosexual?' So I had a nice homosexual affair to find out if I was. And I found out, 'Yes, if I like a person, I'm a homosexual.' I decided that was nice—if I really like someone, then I can feel for them and sex is just an extension of that feeling, whether it's a man or a woman. So I don't exclude or limit any relationships in my life."*

Yet Bennett seemed to feel the need of maintaining a heterosexual image to the public. In the Sixties, he lived with a female dancer from his *West Side Story* tour. In December 1976, in Paris, he wed Donna McKechnie, but the marriage soon broke up, ending officially in divorce in 1978. The failure of the marriage caused a severe rupture in the lifelong friendship and alliance of the two, which was not restored until the *Chorus Line* reunion in 1983. There are those who believe that he married McKechnie to fulfill his vision of himself and McKechnie as another Bob Fosse-Gwen Verdon partnership, while others maintain that he got married under the advisement of powerful theatrical forces who made him believe that he could never have a "superstar" career like Fosse's, which included theatre, film, and television, if he were not married.

In attendance at the Bennett-McKechnie wedding were French actor Jean-Pierre Cassel and his wife, Sabine. By 1978, Cassel and his wife had separated, and Bennett began living with Sabine, a relationship that lasted several years.

. . . .

*To W. Stephen Gilbert, "Stepping Out of *Line*," *London Gay News*, August 1976.

Were Bennett's relationships with women covers to deceive the public? No. Bennett genuinely loved the women with whom he lived, even if, to a degree, he was forcing himself to relate to women in order to avoid the other side of his nature. Bennett admitted his habit of falling in love with his leading ladies throughout his career, and developed very strong friendships with Alexis Smith, Dorothy Loudon, and Swoosie Kurtz, in addition to a fascinating love-hate relationship with Jennifer Holliday.

There was an underlying reason for his desire to be with women, and that was his very strong wish to have a child.

PIPPIN: "Michael wanted so much to fit into the world at large, the so-called 'normal' world. He wanted so much to be a father, and tried to have a child with Sabine. It was a great frustration to him that all the money he had couldn't give him that. He wanted to be part of society, rather than this wealthy, odd-ball gypsy. He wanted to be an ordinary person."

BOOCKVOR: "Michael always envied me having a wife and children. But I told him his shows were his children."

Bennett had strong feelings of resentment for his father that he was never able to resolve, and one of the most interesting relationships in his life was that between him and the Shuberts, particularly Bernard B. Jacobs, president of the Shubert Organization.

JACOBS: "He would come to me to ask my opinion about things, and sometimes my help. He looked for guidance from everybody, but was always his own person and always made his own decisions.

"As time went on, Michael perceived that I was a kind of father figure in his life, and, more and more, he would rely upon me for my advice, help and counsel.

"Michael had a tempestuous Italian temper, and, from time to time, he would go off on his own. There were periods of time when we didn't talk to each other for months. But if the phone rang between 2 and 4 A.M., it was always Michael."

He would arrive at rehearsal sporting a red baseball cap and announce, "The kid is here." The key to Bennett's psyche may be the fact that he was essentially a boy, a street kid never fully comfortable with the adult world into which he was thrust.

WAGNER: "He always identified strongly with kids, and always felt he was still the tap-dancing kid his father sent out in the snow to tap-dance for money."

PIPPIN: "He was a street person. Everything he had was on a basic, primal level, but it worked. He was never a mature adult, ever. . . . Whether he liked it or not, he was thrown into this tremendous adult world after *Chorus Line,* which was painful for him."

BENNETT: "Now I'm the Establishment. I'm proud of the fact that I've matured. But I always thought the character of Peter Pan was fabulous. I grew up playing Let's Pretend as a boy. That boy I keep very much alive. Out of him comes musicals."*

*To Scott Haller, "Broadway's #1 Bash," *People* magazine, October 1983.

APPENDIX A

. . . .

THE

CHORUS LINE

YEARS

1

THE MOVE TO BROADWAY

B ERNARD B. JACOBS RECALLS, *"A Chorus Line* came at a time when everybody was predicting the Broadway theatre was dead and would never come back again. Along came *A Chorus Line* and everyone changed their opinion about Broadway. There was a new wave of enthusiasm and hope, and the show played an important part in the theatrical revival of the next decade."

There is irony in the fact that, while the show "saved" Broadway by giving it an excitement that had been absent in the previous couple of seasons, the show itself was, metaphorically, about the demise of Broadway. *A Chorus Line* made it clear that there were fewer jobs available and no security whatsoever, but it gave many of those involved in it the kind of secure berth almost unknown in the theatre.

The other irony of *A Chorus Line*'s arrival on Broadway was, of course, that a show that had been created by methods wholly antithetical to standard Broadway practice became a bigger success than any show manufactured in the time-honored Broadway manner.

Unlike many other hit musicals that have played as many as four different Broadway houses over a long run, *A Chorus Line* had a permanent home—at least as of this writing—at the Shubert Theatre, where Bennett had danced in *Bajour* and *Here's Love* and choreographed *Promises, Promises.* It had not been immediately available for the move, however.

JACOBS: "Michael said, 'We must have the Shubert Theatre. The show belongs there.' I told him we couldn't give it to him because David Merrick had a contract with us to present a new play by Tennessee Williams called *The Red Devil Battery Sign* at the Shubert.

"We looked at the Winter Garden, where Michael contemplated doing it in an arena-type staging, which would have meant eliminating many seats. We went to the Barrymore and the Broadhurst. We then had a meeting at which Michael said, 'If you can't give me the Shubert, I'm going to have to look elsewhere.' I called David Merrick and explained the situation, and after two weeks of negotiation with him, he agreed to put *Red Devil* in the Broadhurst. *Red Devil* ultimately closed in Boston, so those negotiations could have been avoided."

A dispute between Equity and Bennett arose at the time of the move to Broadway over the fact that, at the Public Theater, the entire cast had been hired on "white," principal contracts. Equity asked that the seven dancers who were dismissed at the beginning, the understudies, be put on "pink," or chorus contracts when the show moved to Broadway. Bennett maintained that they all were equal and should be treated as such. Ultimately, it was decided that the seven would be permitted to remain on white contracts, but that replacements on Broadway and actors in future companies in those roles would be hired on pink contracts.

Certain changes were necessitated by the Broadway move. Off-Broadway, the orchestra played off-stage right, while on Broadway, the musicians played in the pit. But Bennett insisted on keeping them invisible, and decided to cover the pit at the Shubert with black netting to maintain the feel of an audition. Some felt the size of the orchestra should be augmented for Broadway, but musical director Pippin strongly objected, and it remained at sixteen.

At the Public, the seven extra mirrors for Cassie's dance were rolled in by seven performers, just as the mirrors in *Seesaw* had been brought on.

ROBERT KAMLOT, the show's general manager when it moved to Broadway: "On Broadway, they flew in, they came down. That was decided in consultation with Local One, which wouldn't allow the actors to push the mirrors on. We would have had to employ seven stagehands, one for each mirror, to push them on. So we flew them on, and the effect was fabulous, more elegant."

Cast salaries rose to $650 a week for the nineteen principals, $425 a week for the others, and the top ticket price rose to $15, with a potential gross of $140,000 a week. All tickets sold at lower prices at the Public were honored when the show moved to Broadway sooner than expected. The size of the cast changed as well: there were twenty-six in all at the Public, but on Broadway, there were twenty-eight, and that number rose to thirty-two in later years as double and triple understudies were hired. The workshops and the production at the Public had cost about $550,000. The move to Broadway cost even more, coming in at about $590,000.

Lighting was always one of the key elements in the success of *A Chorus Line,* and, while the lighting looked the same on Broadway, the methodology behind it was radically altered. First, Musser insisted on the installation of a light bridge, suspended from the ceiling of the Shubert at a cost of $43,000.

MUSSER: "I had to have a position similar to what we had downtown. When the line is all the way upstage and a number like 'Ballet' is going on downstage, you don't want the follow-spots to hit the line upstage. That angle was crucial, and when they told me they didn't know if they could fit the bridge in, I said, 'If it comes out in the Shubert offices or Alex Cohen's office, too bad.' "

But more importantly, *A Chorus Line* introduced to Broadway a new device, the computerized lighting board.

MUSSER: "At the Public, we did the show with a pre-set board, and I brought in an extra 'six pack,' because, with all the 'thought lights,' I needed more control. When we were going to move, the Shuberts said I could have anything I wanted, and I said, 'Look out. Let's jump right into the memory boards.' The computer board was called Sam, and it lasted until 1987 when we finally had to switch boards because, if you sneezed, Sam went out to lunch.

"The difference in the show's lighting from the Public to Broadway was next to nothing. But the computerized board made it much easier to run the show. It offered a consistency of show you could not get any other way, and I'm vehement about shows always looking as good as they did originally.

"The design of the lighting on the floor was very important, and at the Public, everyone was able to look down at the floor. One of the reasons why we wanted the Shubert so badly was that it was the only Broadway house with a rake comparable to what we had downtown."

Many feared that *A Chorus Line* would lose something in intimacy, impact or excitement when it moved from a 299-seat theatre to a house of almost 1,500 seats. This proved not to be the case; *A Chorus Line* was able to reach audiences just as powerfully in the larger house, and in some ways the show gained in force. A Broadway theatre proved to be an even more appropriate venue, because the type of audition portrayed in the show would most likely have been held in such a theatre.

MCKECHNIE: "It was more intimate downtown, but I didn't feel much of a loss, because we were always supposed to be looking out into the black and talking to a void; it was still an audition. In some ways, the larger theatre made me feel even smaller and more vulnerable. The finale was even better in a real Broadway theatre."

CILENTO: "Downtown, the show had a rawer quality. When we got to Broadway, it became more slick. Just the fact that we were in a hit changed the show."

KAMLOT: "There were two major concerns. One was that by moving uptown, we would lose the intimacy of the show. The second was that the show was by now so wildly heralded that everyone concerned was afraid it would be a letdown on Broadway. But the fact is it played better in the bigger theatre, and the pre-hoopla did not affect it adversely."

A Chorus Line finished its run at the Public on July 13, 1975, and began performances at the Shubert Theatre on July 25, yet it did not have its second official opening night until October 19.

In later years, plays that moved from Off-Broadway with as little alteration as *A Chorus Line* were not rereviewed by most critics. This was not the case in 1975, however, and the management of *A Chorus Line* was eager for the show to be rereviewed. Thus they decided to let the show play, to sellout houses, for two months and have a gala Broadway opening on September 25, by which time the critics would have had time to listen to the original cast album, which had been released just before the show moved to Broadway, and read the many analytic pieces about the show's development that were appearing as cover stories in national magazines.

An unforeseen event occurred at this point, one that not only forced the show to postpone its opening until October but to close down temporarily. A strike of Broadway pit musicians was called on September 18, and every Broadway musical was shut down through October 13. *A*

Chorus Line had to wait until the first Sunday after the settlement for its second opening night. The new reviews were, if anything, more enthusiastic than the first set. Walter Kerr said, "Everything is even better," and Martin Gottfried described it as "more thrilling than ever." A lavish party at the Public Theater was attended by nine hundred people, and such luminaries as Ethel Merman, Senator Jacob Javits, Bella Abzug, Jule Styne, Bette Midler, and John Lindsay rode in chartered buses from the Shubert to the show's birthplace. It was a show about Broadway itself, and it was now, and for many years thereafter, where it was meant to be.

2

. . . .

THE FIRST YEAR

F OR SOME MEMBERS OF the cast, performing the emotionally cathartic show eight times a week soon became taxing.

DANTE: "The cast had extraordinary pressure on them as the creators of the show. Some started getting ugly just after we opened, and continued in that vein from there on in. Things got divisive and tense, with fights and bad attitude. It just happens from that kind of success."

BLAIR: "I was never able to enjoy doing the show the first year on Broadway. It was very competitive backstage, a very difficult atmosphere. Michael created that atmosphere of intense competition over a period of months. He knew what he was doing, and did it on purpose. . . . He used to say that he was doing that to create the required tension for the show."

SCHWEID: "Many of the cast had never said two words on stage before, and now they were supposed to be actors, and some of them really weren't. There was a lot of angst, a lot of nervous energy, but that fed the show and added to it."

Money became an issue. A few cast members felt they deserved higher salaries, particularly after awards had been handed out. And other money-related issues led to disenchantment on the part of some.

DENNIS: "There was a dispute over the merchandising of the logo, which was a photo of the original line. That photo was used on everything—mugs, towels, T-shirts—and we received no money from any of that. We were never told that that photo was going to be used for profit in the merchandising market; we had approved its use only for ads. One of us contacted a lawyer, but, one by one, the powers that be came down to browbeat us out of it. To appease us, they gave us each a towel with our face on it and a Bloomingdale's credit card."

Bennett became very upset when the threat of a lawsuit arose, brought by Cy Coleman, with whom he had worked on *Seesaw,* and James Lipton, who wrote the book and lyrics of *Nowhere to Go but Up.* Coleman alleged that in 1973 he had shown Bennett two projects on which he was working. One was a movie about the life of chorus dancers, the other a musical, *Beautiful People,* written with Lipton, which dealt with a group encounter session and a line of people who stepped forward to tell about their lives. *Beautiful People* was optioned for stage and screen productions, and Coleman asserted that Bennett had meetings about the stage version before declining to direct it. Although the show was ultimately dropped, the similarities between it and the recently opened *A Chorus Line* were obvious.

LENNY: "Cy claimed that Michael got a script through me, but that was not so. Cy sent me a script for another client of mine who decided not to do it. Michael never had the script, and to my knowledge never had any idea of what the show was about. The case was dropped because they never would have won.

"At the same time, a guy in Toronto sued Papp and the authors for $100 million, claiming he had sent a script based on the same idea to Papp. Joe said he never saw it, and the case was thrown out, but it cost us a lot of money."

DANTE: "Michael claimed he never read Cy's script, but I think he did, because he was so nervous about the case. I didn't see why, because the material in the show came from the tapes and the other interviews, and Jimmy and I never saw Cy's script."

The awards began to pour in. The show took the Best Musical prize from the New York Drama Critics Circle in May 1975, the Tony Award in April 1976, and the Pulitzer Prize the following month, on the night of the first performance of *A Chorus Line* outside of New York City—the international company's debut in Toronto. Only three other musicals in

Broadway history, *South Pacific, Fiorello!,* and *How to Succeed in Business Without Really Trying,* had ever captured this triple crown. But the award that may have meant the most to Bennett was a prize for outstanding contribution in the field from *Dance Magazine;* pictures from that magazine had adorned the walls of Bennett's childhood room and were his inspiration for coming to New York.

No single show ever dominated a Tony Awards ceremony as did *A Chorus Line* on the unseasonably hot evening of April 18, 1976. The telecast, live from the Shubert Theatre, began with the slightly trimmed opening of *A Chorus Line,* beautifully photographed and providing glimpses of individual cast members impossible to get in the theatre. While the first two musical prizes of the evening, for costumes and sets, went to Florence Klotz and Boris Aronson for *Pacific Overtures,* and Wagner's *Chorus Line* design did not even receive a nomination, Musser won (against herself for *Pacific Overtures*) for best lighting, and every musical award thereafter went to *A Chorus Line.* Williams won a Tony as Paul over LuPone's Zach. Bishop was pitted against dressing roommate and friend Lopez, and the winner was the actress who was rejected at the end of the show each night. In her acceptance speech, Bishop, alluding to such ensemble stints at the Shubert as *Promises, Promises* and *Golden Rainbow,* said, "I've played this theatre several times in the chorus, and I am again. But this is one of those dreams, and it's come true. I have to accept this along with the rest of the cast, because it's impossible without. I'll keep it at my house, though."

Bennett and Avian shared the award for Best Choreography, and Bennett, reacting to the fact that Avian had never before been nominated along with him, told the audience, "I have not worked as a choreographer or a director one day of my life without Bob Avian. Michael Bennett *is* Bob Avian and me, and I'm so glad that you get to see us together and that we get to share one for real."

When Bennett accepted his award for direction, he said, "I really wanted this, and so many people did so much to help me get this. I only wanted one thing: to be a Broadway director. And I am. And I wanted one moment, and I have it."

Upon winning as Best Actress in a Musical, McKechnie described the show to the audience as "a theatrical experience I cannot describe here, it's so personal, and a personal experience that taught me so much about performing and about people and humanity."

Hamlisch and Kleban won over Sondheim, John Kander, Fred Ebb, and none other than Hamlisch's *The Sting* collaborator, the sixty-years-dead Scott Joplin, who was nominated for his opera *Treemonisha.* Dante thanked his "fellow N.S.A. members for teaching me to believe in people again" when he won his award; and Kirkwood contrasted the "hurtful experience" of the failure of *P.S. Your Cat Is Dead* with his *Chorus Line* triumph as he accepted his.

When Eddie Albert appeared to present the Best Musical prize, his reading of the nominees was greeted with laughter, so clear-cut was the decision by that time. *A Chorus Line* beat *Bubbling Brown Sugar, Chicago,* and *Pacific Overtures,* and the telecast closed with the end of the show's finale.

It was a particularly sweet victory for Bennett, as his creation had trounced Fosse's *Chicago,* a hit that took not a single Tony, as well as former collaborators Prince and Sondheim's *Pacific Overtures.* While Bennett would go on to win other Tonys, several of these prizes would prove to be mixed blessings to the other recipients, who were unable in the next years to follow them up.

Those at the tape sessions had sold their stories to Bennett for one dollar, and he was under no obligation to pay anyone anything further for the use of that material in the show's book and lyrics. But before the show had even opened on Broadway, Bennett decided that those who had contributed their lives to the show deserved a bonus, and on the first day of 1976, he drew up a precedent-setting contract with thirty-seven of those involved. The contract allowed the thirty-seven to receive a portion of Bennett's author's royalties: "an aggregate amount equal to one-half of 1% of the gross weekly box office receipts, and a pro rata portion of the subsidiary rights income in the same proportion as one-half of 1% bears to the maximum total percentage of gross weekly box office receipts payable to all of the authors of the play."

He divided the thirty-seven into three groups. Those in Group A received two shares of this fund, while those in Groups B and C one. Those in Groups A and B would receive their shares for as long as they lived, while those in C received payment only as long as they stayed in the show. When those in Group C gradually dropped out, the number of shares was reduced and the others received more money.

Bennett's division of the thirty-seven into these groups was based on the size of the individual's contribution to the show's material, although the members of each group do not necessarily share the same degree of involvement in the show. For example, Group A includes Michon Peacock and Mitzi Hamilton, who were at the tapes but not in the workshops or original show; Candy Brown, at the tapes and one workshop but not in the show; and Robert LuPone, in the workshops and show but not at the tapes; along with McKechnie, Lopez, Bishop, and others who were at the tapes, in the workshops, and in the show. Group C consisted of the show's understudies and those principals who were not at the tapes. Everyone who had been at the tapes was included in one of the categories, but performers such as Jane Robertson and Barry Bostwick, who either left or were dismissed during the workshops, were not included.

STEVENS: "Michael didn't have to do any of this, but . . . he was a good person deep down, and a kid in love with show business."

DENNIS: "As much as people want to glorify the royalty payments, it was only ½ of 1% of Michael's writer's royalty, which was not that much money. . . . Those of us in Group C contributed to the show, even though our life stories weren't in it. After we left the show, we started to miss those checks. People who Michael didn't think could sing and dance the parts well enough got money always because their stories were used."

Bennett's generosity in this case led to a new agreement between Actors Equity and producers, whereby performers in a workshop can be paid as little as $150 a week but must share in a percentage of the receipts when the show goes to a full production, that percentage depending on the extent of their participation in the workshop. Within five years, the *Chorus Line* dancers split a pool of $750,000.

3

NEW COMPANIES

A COUPLE OF YEARS AFTER *A Chorus Line* opened, Bennett told Tommy Tune, "The last thing in the world I want to do is make another hit show. . . . It means you have this company and that company and that company, and you eat and live and breathe it. You have to balance them all and keep them all up. It's a terrible responsibility."

But the country and the world were demanding to see *A Chorus Line,* and Bennett began thinking about new companies as soon as the show reached Broadway. By March 1976, Bennett had assembled three new companies, one for Broadway, one for Los Angeles, and one, the International Company, for London. Nothing in the development of *A Chorus Line* was ever conventional, and Bennett again tried something without precedent by rehearsing all three companies simultaneously in the basement of New York's City Center, just steps away from his Fifty-fifth Street apartment. In a huge mirrored rehearsal hall, more than sixty dancers worked together for two weeks, learning the big numbers, such as the opening, the montage, and "One," under the guidance of Bennett, Avian, and Lee. Then they split into three separate companies, working closely with Bennett on the scenes, each group watching the others perform the same sequences. Equity would not permit Bennett his original concept of rehearsing everyone without designating in advance which actors would be in which company. A very supportive atmosphere pervaded the hall, and a sense of healthy competition contributed to the ultimate performances.

Tears flowed freely on stage the night of the last performance of the original cast on Broadway, April 24, 1976. Everyone in the original company had been offered the opportunity to go to the West Coast with the show, and all but five of the original nineteen principals left New York to form the National Company. The five who stayed were Bishop, Cilento, Walsh, Mason, and Clerk, and they were joined by a talented new group, several of whom had auditioned for the workshop almost two years before, and several of whom had worked for Fosse in *Pippin*.

Bennett was not sure of the fourteen newcomers at the Shubert, so they were signed to "conversion contracts," which gave management the option, after the fifth performance, to convert the performer to a run-of-the-play contract or to leave them on a standard minimum contract whereby they could be fired on two weeks' notice. The new Val was soon let go, as was Barbara Luna, a friend of Bennett's and an actress of some repute who had been hired as the new Diana Morales. According to members of the company, she lacked energy, was vocally weak, and was not used to ensemble dancing, and she was gone by the end of the first week of performances.

For his new Broadway Cassie, Bennett chose Ann Reinking, a more established performer than most *Chorus Line* players.

REINKING: "Michael told me, 'I know you can dance and act it. I just want the song to be right in your register.' They lowered it a lot for me, as Donna is a soprano and I'm a tenor.

"Michael was very helpful and understanding, and I was allowed to change a few steps, adding more jumps, jetes, extensions and backbends. I dance differently from Donna, and Michael wanted that. He wanted who I was, as he did with all the other Cassies, and he utilized who they were. He had a very set way about how he wanted the dialogue delivered, but after a while he allowed my personality to come in."

There were certain problems of adjustment for the new performers, who were working with several others who were present at the show's inception.

JUSTIN ROSS, the new Greg: "For the most part, everyone got along well. A few who had attitude served it. The originals who stayed had to adjust to us, and we had to adjust to them.''

BISHOP: ''It was horrible for us who stayed. We were inundated with a bunch of people who really hadn't been rehearsed properly. I thought rehearsing multiple companies together was counterproductive, if economical. The competition got so intense so early that you started reaching a performance level before you'd done the work. It wasn't so much fun for me with the new company.''

The original cast was so closely identified with the show that some of the show's fans felt let down seeing it for the first time without the originals. *New York Post* critic Martin Gottfried was particularly unhappy when he rereviewed it: "*A Chorus Line* is not what it was . . . a severe drop in its energy level has left the show less compelling. . . . Instead of being selected for appropriateness to a part, replacements seem to be chosen in an effort to physically duplicate the original cast member. . . . Right now it plays like a road company.''

But audiences who had not seen the originals had no difficulty enjoying the show with the new cast, who continued in the show for eighteen months, some switching places with originals in Los Angeles after six. Reinking in particular managed to give a striking performance and make the role her own.

One memorable incident during the run of the first Broadway replacement cast was the night Kelly Bishop walked off.

ROSS: ''She was very upset because she had asked for something in her new contract. It was nothing unreasonable; she had been doing the show a long time and just wanted a perk. They refused her, and she became preoccupied with it. She stepped forward to begin her monologue, and suddenly said, 'Zach, I have to leave. I can't talk to you any longer. I'm sorry.' Joe Bennett, who was playing Zach, said, 'Sheila, if the light's bothering you, we can change it,' to try to get her back into the lines. She paused at the proscenium and said, 'I have to go. I'm sorry,' and exited. Thommie Walsh, who was close to Kelly on and offstage, said, 'Zach, I think I better check on Sheila,' which left two gaping holes next to each other on the line. No one had any idea that this was going to happen, including Kelly. Zach cut to Kristine, skipping 'At the Ballet,' and you could hear pages flipping wildly in the pit. After that, Sheila didn't exist, and some of her lines were given to other people.''

WAYNE CILENTO later recalled: 'I decided to stay in the New York production instead of going to L.A. because I didn't believe anything was really going to happen to those who went." His theory would prove to be correct.

Just as many predicted that the show was too intimate, special, and "in" for Broadway, there were now those who predicted that *A Chorus Line* was too "New York," too "Broadway," and that no one outside of the largest cities would care about the plight of Broadway dancers, even though that was not the real subject of the show.

The National Company of *A Chorus Line* opened in May 1976, in San Francisco, then moved in July to the Shubert Theatre in Los Angeles, where it opened to the largest advance sale in L.A. history and remained through January 1978. The company then played a year in Chicago, during which time several members of the International Company joined, and then began a road tour that concluded in September 1980 in Montreal. As it wended its way across the country, *A Chorus Line* reopened long-dark theatres and revived long-moribund subscription series.

Two fully operative sets, based on the original New York designs, were built for the tour, so that the show could be set up in the next city as it completed its engagement in the one before.

The National Company initially consisted of the original Broadway cast with five replacements on the line, as well as other new faces among the understudies and swings. Some of the originals had reportedly become greedy when it came time to sign contracts for the road, and some perks were given to those with larger roles. Some of those who had been on the original line felt that playing the show in L.A. was never quite the same as playing it on Broadway.

BLAIR: "I didn't enjoy doing the show in L.A., because I didn't have Michael to do it for anymore. I did it for him. I think we all did. When he wasn't there every night, it just didn't mean as much. I loved it when he stood in the wings watching."

DENNIS: "We were all treated like stars in New York, but that feeling didn't carry over to Los Angeles. The Shubert Theatre in L.A. is much bigger, and while the audiences loved the show, they didn't really get into what it was about.

"It was difficult for us to get considered for TV work, because *A Chorus Line* was considered a 'New York show.' It was good for the town, because they could invite you to their parties with all the stars, and you'd come in and be practically ignored.

"I did the show in L.A. for a year and eight months, and by that time there was no strong morale booster. The people in charge on the road still·saw us as chorus dancers who they could treat any way they wanted to. It was not pleasant to see other people doing a bad imitation of Michael Bennett."

During the Los Angeles run, Bennett finally persuaded Leland Palmer to play Cassie.

PALMER: "After the show opened, Michael called me very often about the companies that were forming. Finally, out of loyalty to him, I did it in 1977. But I soon knew it was not a good decision for me. In rehearsal, it didn't feel right. Baayork put me in, because Michael was in London. When Michael came in toward the end of my rehearsal time, he didn't adjust it that much for me, which might have made it more comfortable. I opened in it, but stopped after just a few performances."

The International Company opened in Toronto in May 1976, moved in July to London for six months, and continued touring in Baltimore in 1977, staying out through August 1983 when it closed, where it had begun, in Toronto. While this company was to have gone to Australia and other foreign countries, its only overseas stop proved to be London, and it never became truly "international."

It was a company of dazzling young dancers, including Mitzi Hamilton, whose story at the tape sessions was partially the basis for the role of Val, which she was then playing; Eivind Harum, who would continue to play Zach on and off for the next decade; Troy Garza, who would become the show's dance captain on Broadway; and T. Michael Reed, who would soon become one of those in charge of maintaining all the companies of the show.

HARUM: "Our company was the strongest dance company of the show ever, almost like a ballet company. Everybody was so competitive. It was always who would jump the highest and be the most spectacular."

For the role of Cassie, Bennett eventually chose Sandy Roveta, with whom he had worked in three shows in the early Sixties.

ROVETA: "I was in L.A. when *A Chorus Line* was created. I was splitting with my husband, and Michael now told me, 'You can audition for the show. I have two major companies forming.' I needed something because of the breakup of my marriage, and that desperateness was right for the show and the role. I really related to the need to get to something you really wanted to do that was your very own. Then there was the parallel between Cassie and Zach and my relationship with Michael, an old friend I had been close to and hadn't seen in a while, to whom I was now saying, 'Help.' It really wasn't much of a stretch as an actress.

"The Cassie dance was Donna's; she had worked on it, honed it, and had found so many little things of her own that no one really knew exactly how to break it down and teach it now. Baayork taught it to us with Michael, but they had to keep going back to Donna."

Bennett was generous in allowing his new actors to find the roles themselves.

HARUM: "Michael never tried to make the actors in our company fit the pattern established by the originals. He directed from honesty. He chose the actor to play the part, and he wanted that actor to be that part. He would say, 'You're lying. I want to see *you*. Don't be afraid to be yourself. That's why I hired you.' If he saw someone 'acting,' he'd say, 'No, just talk to me. . . . That's the character.' "

The International Company, which, as we shall see, would go on to great success in London, was probably hardest hit by the devastation of AIDS in the Eighties. Five of the original men who rehearsed at City Center—Bennett; Andy Keyser, the original Greg; Timothy Scott, the original Mark; T. Michael Reed, the original Larry and dance captain; and Martin Herzer, the stage manager—were gone by the International Company's 1988 reunion.

By now, a team had been assembled to maintain the three companies of *A Chorus Line,* soon to be joined by another touring company and many foreign productions. Baayork Lee; Jeff Hamlin, the show's production stage manager; Otts Munderloh, who supervised the show's sound across the country; Fran Liebergall; Robert Thomas; and Bernard Gersten, along with Bennett and Avian, were all involved in auditioning actors across the country and supervising the companies. Soon, T. Michael Reed and Joseph Nelson, who had danced for Bennett in *Follies,* became supervisors of the three major companies, in charge of casting and maintaining the show's staging and choreography around the country. Lee would continue to stage the show internationally throughout the Eighties.

Much switching of actors from company to company occurred, as did much moving up of actors, whereby an understudy would become Mark, then later move up to Mike or Larry, while a Don would become Zach. An enormous chart in the office of the Shubert in New York helped Reed, Nelson, and Tom Porter, who joined the show as stage manager in Chicago and soon moved to Broadway, where he would remain as stage manager, keep track of each role and those who were playing and understudying it across the country. The logistics of maintaining the show were complex, but everyone was caught up in the whirlwind of its success.

London awaited the arrival of *A Chorus Line* as it had not awaited a musical since *My Fair Lady,* and it arrived at London's enormous and beautiful Theatre Royal, Drury Lane, as the most expensive musical production in England's history, largely because of the outlay for the technology involved in the show's lights, sound, and engineering.

The International Company arrived in London with great anticipation, to be greeted by a stage with a rake of sixteen inches, which almost caused several of the dancers to fall into the pit or crash into the proscenium during the opening combinations. A few months after the July opening, the company began to suffer from the raw British weather, requiring the addition of legwarmers and sweaters to costumes and the installation of hot-air blowers in the wings. Injuries were frequent as the dancers had to stand in line, sweating after the opening, on the enormous frigid stage.

Nevertheless, the members of the International Company, who were permitted by Equity to stay only six months, look back on performing the show in London as one of the most joyous experiences of their lives. Some feared that the reserve of British audiences might be a problem for a show dealing largely in frank confession and painful revelation, but audiences responded enthusiastically. While they may have missed some of the references and failed to comprehend one or two idiomatic expressions (some of which had been altered for London), their response at the conclusion was often more enthusiastic than that of American audiences.

The first-night audience included Andrew Lloyd Webber, Tom Stoppard, Michael Crawford, and Kenneth Tynan, and the reviews, while far more divided than in America, were generally strong. Michael Billington in *The Guardian* said: "Anyone who regards the musical as a serious theatrical art form should rejoice in this superb production. It has a resonance that spreads far beyond its immediate context."

Michael Coveney of *Financial Times* reported: "The bally-hoo was justified. The entire production rings a poignant death knell for 'the musical' as well as existing in its own right as a triumphant re-birth of the genre. This is something that the great American musicals have always done, from *Oklahoma!* through to *My Fair Lady, West Side Story* and *Company.*"

Among the negative reviews was that of John Lahr in *Plays and Players:* "What Bennett creates is an often dazzling spectacle that looks like a departure from its predecessors, but whose message of pluck 'n luck is as tried and true as the buck 'n wing. Like all tinsel, *A Chorus Line* is shiny, irresistible and soft."

The score was far better received than it had been in New York, the show became a quick sellout and was awarded the London Evening Standard Award for Best Musical.

Eight hundred British performers auditioned to be in the company that would replace the Americans in London in January; Bennett found it so difficult to find dancers who could meet the very high standards of his three American companies that it was announced in the press in September that the show might close because of a lack of suitable British replacements. But Bennett did manage to weed out a company of performers, most of whom already had more experience in musicals than the majority of the performers in all three of the American companies. Such British actors as Diane Langton, Geraldine Gardner, Michael Staniforth, Michael Howe, and Jeff Shankley already had several principal roles to their credit, and would go on to be featured in numerous West End musicals in later years. The one non-British member of the new company was Jean-Pierre Cassel, a well-known film and stage actor in France, who was making his English stage debut. He was signed to play Zach for six months, after which he was to produce *A Chorus Line* in Paris (he did not, and the show did not receive its Paris premiere until 1988). Cassel was a curious choice, as he was not really a dancer, had a thick accent, and was older than most Zachs. Bennett even told the British press that the role of Zach was based on Cassel, a claim that seems most unlikely because neither Cassel nor his native country had ever had much association with American musicals.

It was Bennett's choice for the role of Cassie in the new British company that precipitated one of the biggest scandals in which he and *A Chorus Line* would ever be involved.

Elizabeth Seal had performed such dance parts as Carol Haney's in *The Pajama Game* and Gwen Verdon's in *Damn Yankees* in London, but she was best remembered for the title role in *Irma La Douce* in London and on Broadway, where she won a Tony Award as Best Musical Actress of 1961 over Julie Andrews, Carol Channing, and Nancy Walker. Her career had not lived up to these early successes, but, at age forty-two, she had gotten back into shape and decided to actively seek work again.

Seal, whom Bennett had seen in *Irma* in the early Sixties in New York, auditioned eight times for the role of Cassie, side by side with Petra Siniawski, a much younger dancer also under consideration for the role. When Bennett chose Seal and retained Siniawski as understudy, the news was greeted with delighted announcements about old-favorite Seal making a comeback in a part about the comeback of a near-star.

After weeks of rehearsals supervised by Baayork Lee and T. Michael Reed, during which everything seemed to be going smoothly, Bennett returned to London about ten days before the scheduled first night of the British cast. He watched Seal rehearse, and fired her on the spot. Bennett told the press, "She's very talented and I wanted to see her a big star again. But it became a show about Elizabeth Seal coming back on the stage, not Cassie. It's my mistake, I'm the villain." When pushed, he also admitted that she was too old for the role.

The London press was eager to hear Seal's side, and she told it. She said Bennett suggested she tell the press she had broken an ankle but that she had insisted that Bennett tell the truth and announce to the press that he had fired her. Seal threatened a massive lawsuit, saying, "I will show these people how to survive in real-life showbiz. It is all about survival, and I will survive. I will demand compensation for my time and for the possible damage to my reputation. I still can't believe that after all the tests, auditions and talks, he could simply have made the wrong choice. There was no discussion—he had changed his mind and that was that. I think the rest of the company must now feel that they are on trial every minute they are on stage." When asked about the reasons for her firing, she added, "I think it's just that he will never be happy with anyone other than Donna for the part." The papers reported that Bennett had made other British dancers audition fifteen times, only to reject them, and Seal became the topic of newspaper editorials and photo layouts showing the gallant star back in dance class after being dismissed.

But even greater trouble was to ensue when Bennett made the next move. Who would now play Cassie? Understudy Siniawski seemed the logical choice, but Bennett felt she would not be ready in time for the opening. Coincidentally, McKechnie, now married to Bennett, had flown in the day after Seal's firing to help with rehearsals. Bennett asked British Equity to allow McKechnie to perform the role of Cassie temporarily. The press had a field day with the idea that Bennett had fired a British favorite to put his wife in the show, and accused Bennett and McKechnie of contriving the dismissal so that McKechnie, who had earned a reputation in London in *Promises, Promises* and *Company,* could play her part before British audiences.

MCKECHNIE: "Michael and I walked right into a whole political thing without being briefed. The truth is I was not happy to have to go there; I was happy starring in New York again after L.A., and I had only gone over to help Michael rehearse the new company. Michael told Equity that I would play Cassie until the understudy was ready, and that the show would not be re-reviewed until she was in it. But the press made Michael into a monster. There were death threats for both of us, especially me. They said, 'If she steps one step on that stage, we'll be up in the balcony and we'll get her whenever she appears. All she has to do is walk on stage and she's dead.' "

On January 17, Equity made the following announcement: "It is unacceptable for an American to come in in the circumstances. Miss Seal was engaged after eight auditions over a period of six months and was then sacked in the most regrettable circumstances. We believe British artists who have already been closely involved in the rehearsals are able to play the role."

The next day, Equity reversed this decision and granted permission to McKechnie to play Cassie for four weeks, but only after Bennett and British producer Michael White warned that the show might have to close down for two weeks. While it is difficult to believe that Siniawski still did not know the role well enough to assume it at this point, Equity did not want to risk the jobs of so many.

Two days later, and four days before the new cast was scheduled to go on, members of the casts of West End shows demonstrated at the offices of Equity, then marched to Drury Lane. Complaints poured in; an emergency meeting of Equity's council was called; and, after a three-and-a-half-hour session, the decision was reversed yet again. The role was now Siniawski's, but the opening was postponed five days to give her more time.

The sacking of Seal and the constant reversals by Equity had made headlines for ten days.

MCKECHNIE: "When President Carter was inaugurated, he was on the fifth page, but I was on the front page. They used the same picture every day, with the caption 'Donna will go on' one day, then 'Donna nixed' the next."

McKechnie returned to New York and the Broadway company exhausted, and Bennett told London reporter Tom Sutcliffe, "I hope very much this country now finds something else to talk about. There's an Australian company of the show going into rehearsal in March which I will have nothing to do with. There's a staff now trained to do the show. But I've had it. In America, if an actress is let go from a part there are two lines in *Variety*. I think this whole thing is a much bigger issue. We're being used as a pretext. It's about British Equity, American Equity, and the state of English theatre. I don't understand this country."

In March, Seal received a settlement of four thousand pounds.

MCKECHNIE: "I knew how hurt she was, to be fired after all the publicity about her comeback. It was a terrible humiliation for her. But I believed Michael when he told me that it would have been worse if she had done it."

The reviews of the new cast were sharply divided, some declaring it "a magnificent new company," others saying they were not as good as their American predecessors. All agreed that Cassel was woefully out of place. Robert Cushman in *The Observer* asked, "In view of British Equity's bewildering vacillations over the proposed secondment to the British company of Donna McKechnie from New York, what is a Frenchman doing in the role of Zach? A French actor, too, who barely holds his own in the dance numbers, where his predecessor, the magnetic Eivind Harum, was their guiding force." Cassel withdrew soon after, but the London production continued to play through March 1979.

The National Company closed in Montreal on September 14, 1980, and, four days later, re-opened as a bus-and-truck tour, playing one-week and shorter stands for two years throughout the United States and Canada. Bennett and his designers rethought the show so that it could be easily set up.

ROBIN WAGNER: "It would take too long to put up the periaktoids, so we used three drops, a mirror drop, a black drop, and a final drop. The black was in front of the others, and when it went up, you had the mirrors. The mirrors bolted together, and folded in half and fit in a box. We rolled out a soft vinyl floor which already had the line on it, and the whole show went up in four hours."

CHARLES WILLARD, company manager of the bus-and-truck: "Everyone was signed for six months, because burn out could set in and they didn't want to be obligated to people who weren't cutting it anymore.

Before the end of each six-month period, Joe Nelson and T. Michael Reed would come out and decide who they wanted to keep in the bus-and-truck, who they wanted to move to New York or the international company, and who they wanted to get rid of.

"Performers were hired as understudies for the bus-and-truck, would learn three roles, and would be put into the show in different combinations. It was very competitive, and Joe and Tom had tremendous power. The promise was always that if you behaved yourself and were good on the road, you would get to go into the Broadway company. There was constant tension about the big corporate enterprise the show had by now become. A great deal of introspection was spent on your future with *A Chorus Line,* like your future with a big corporation.

"The cast was very young, median age about 19, and for most it was their first job. Their youth was an advantage in that they were able to travel well in all conditions, but they were really too young to play these parts. When they got to the alternatives scene, they were just mouthing lines they didn't understand.

"The biggest problem this company had was a kind of dance company mentality, where actors felt they were interchangeable and never felt that they owned their roles. Because of this, they thought nothing of being out of the show, and we had several understudies on every night."

During the first five years of the show's Broadway run, the program listed the show's time as "now," but it was changed thereafter to 1975, as the dates of birth of the characters and many of the references no longer coincided with young dancers in the Eighties. When the bus-and-truck began, it was decided to use a contemporary setting.

DANNY HERMAN, who began his association with the show on the bus-and-truck tour and went on to play Mark, Mike, and Larry on Broadway: "For the bus-and-truck, they changed periods and made it contemporary, 1980. They updated the costumes to what people would wear at rehearsal then, and they changed the birthdays of those on the line. That lasted over a year, and then they went back to the original period."

When the bus-and-truck tour ended in Pittsburgh on October 3, 1982, it was the end of the original chain of national companies of *A Chorus Line.* While foreign productions were still proliferating and stock productions would begin to flourish in a few years, there was now only the Broadway company to maintain.

People had said that the show spoke to a limited audience and would never make it on Broadway. Then they said it would never appeal to audiences outside of New York City. Now it demonstrated its universality by taking over the world. In 1977, *A Chorus Line* opened in Sydney, Australia. The show reached Berlin in 1980, Mexico City in 1982, Brazil in 1983, Paris and Vienna in 1988. Lee went on to direct the show in Sweden, Hawaii, Japan, and Paris. It was also seen in Norway, Spain, Puerto Rico, and Argentina, and original cast albums of the Norwegian, Japanese, and Austrian casts were released.

A Chorus Line did not have quite the worldwide success of such later musicals as *Cats* or *Les Misérables,* probably because it was often not as well performed by foreign dancers, and because it reflected values that were alien to some foreign audiences. Yet it was an international success on a grand scale.

Donna McKechnie recalls playing Cassie, in English, to a Japanese audience in 1986.

MCKECHNIE: "The show had already been done there in Japanese, and broken the long-run record. The Japanese audiences have a polite way of watching and not applauding or reacting until it's all over, which made it hard to do because the show needs a lot of energy from the audience. . . . But the audiences loved it. The adolescent boys and girls would come backstage filled with emotion, in contrast to the way the audience behaved during the performance. It's a basically repressed society, with young people not encouraged to show their feelings, but these kids would be shaking with feeling because they weren't used to experiencing things."

In 1983, the management of *A Chorus Line* declined a $1 million advance from Samuel French for the stock and amateur rights to the show, believing that the value would increase as the run continued. But in 1985, a $2 million advance from Tams-Witmark was accepted, a figure nearly six times that of the previous record, set by *Annie.* While the authors and producers wanted to withhold the show as long as possible from stock and amateur companies when it was still running on Broadway, the offer was accepted at that time because they wanted it to get in one summer of stock productions before the release of the film version in December 1985.

Stock productions were widespread immediately, and in the next years, the authors tended to earn more income from stock than from the fluctuating grosses of the Broadway version.

Many stock productions have been directed and choreographed by one of the hundreds of performers who has played in *A Chorus Line* in one of the companies, and thus the original staging has been handed down to so many performers by now that it will probably never disappear entirely from stagings of the show. In a major summer tour that led to the Japanese engagement, McKechnie played Cassie and co-author Nicholas Dante played Paul, pouring out his own story night after night to a new generation of audiences.

4

. . . .

STAGE BUG

A CHORUS LINE HAD BEEN optioned by an Israeli producer, and, in late 1980, he or an associate called the management of the show in America to inform them of a new Israeli musical entitled *Haydak Bama (Stage Bug)* that was in rehearsal. Bennett called co-author Kirkwood and asked whether he would fly to Israel to investigate reports that the show was too close to *A Chorus Line* for anyone's comfort. A lawyer, Daniel Mirkin, had been hired to represent the creators of *A Chorus Line* in Israel, and, after Mirkin translated the script of *Stage Bug,* the similarities became shockingly apparent.

Kirkwood took a videotape of *A Chorus Line* done at the Public Theater to Israel to show to a judge, and went off to a dress rehearsal of *Stage Bug.* Kirkwood described the performance in an article in *The Dramatists Guild Quarterly* in 1981.

"The opening sequence was stunningly like the opening sequence of *A Chorus Line.* The director-choreographer was putting a cast of 12 candidates through their paces at a final audition. There were grey-beige panels upstage, fronted by a ballet-bar; no other scenery or props, except a stool for the director to sit upon. The orchestra was offstage left, as was ours when we first started down at the Public Theater. At the end of a set of vigorously performed dance combinations, all the dancers marched downstage to form a line, holding up in front of their faces, not eight-by-ten photographs of themselves as in *A Chorus Line,* but large blow-ups of newspapers that supposedly ran the ad announcing the auditions for *Stage Bug.* There was a homosexual who told his story in a touching manner; there was the ex-wife of the choreographer who was there seeking a job in the show and was asked, as is Cassie in our show, 'What are you doing here?' Her reply was: 'I need a job.' At the end of the evening, the director-choreographer made his choice of four out of 12 candidates as opposed to our eight out of a final 16.''

When Kirkwood peeked behind the upstage panels and found mirrors on the other side, he was informed that the mirrors were not in use yet but would be revolving in due time. It was decided to proceed with the case.

Shuki Wagner, a former actor who authored the book and composed the songs of *Stage Bug,* told *Variety,* "I have seen Michael Bennett's show several times. I know it by heart and I'm one of Bennett's greatest admirers, but it would be foolish to copy his production." Wagner maintained that such films as *All That Jazz* and *Fame* had also borrowed elements from *A Chorus Line,* but Kirkwood countered by maintaining that, whereas an audition was only one element in those films, it was the entire show in both *A Chorus Line* and *Stage Bug.*

An injunction to prevent *Stage Bug* from beginning performances was denied, while major changes were made in it to decrease the similarity. The judge in the case saw *Stage Bug,* and then he and lawyers for both sides flew to New York to see *A Chorus Line* in the flesh, the videotape having been deemed of insufficient quality. Bennett and Kirkwood testified before the judge in New York, and, three weeks later, *Stage Bug* was closed down in previews, without ever officially opening.

KIRKWOOD: "It took a lot of time, energy and money on our part. I think it cost us something like $46,000. It was a shame, because you don't want to put anybody out of work, but if you let it happen in one country, it happens in others.''

5

THE *CHORUS LINE* INDUSTRY

A CHORUS LINE BECAME A financial phenomenon that rescued an entire industry. In addition to employing over four hundred performers and over nine hundred musicians, stagehands, managers, and other related staff, the profits by 1983 were higher than those of such comparable blockbusters as *My Fair Lady* and *Fiddler on the Roof.*

The first public disclosure of figures came in 1979, when *Variety* reported that the profit was then $22 million. By 1983, it had risen to $37 million, with a worldwide gross of $260 million. It had by that time played in 184 U.S. cities, 10 Canadian cities, and 8 countries, and had had at least three return engagements in 24 cities.

Seventy-five percent of the profits went to the New York Shakespeare Festival, and 25 percent to Bennett as co-producer. By 1983, the profit structure had been revised so that the royalty participants, Bennett, Avian, Kirkwood, Dante, Kleban, and Hamlisch, split the weekly operating profits with the producers—the Shakespeare Festival and Bennett—on a 60–40 basis. This new setup allowed the show to break even at a gross of $150,000 a week or lower, an extremely low figure for a Broadway musical.

Joseph Papp had allowed commercial producers to move the musical *Hair,* which had inaugurated the Public Theater, to Broadway and the world, but by 1975, he had moved several Shakespeare Festival productions to Broadway, and he clung tightly to *A Chorus Line.*

The millions that the Shakespeare Festival, a nonprofit organization, took in from *A Chorus Line* formed the basis of an endowment, and the Festival was able to use only the interest from this endowment for operating funds during the show's heyday. The Shakespeare Festival used this money to present dozens of new productions at the Public and Delacorte theatres, and Papp readily admitted that without *A Chorus Line,* the Festival might not have been around into the mid-Eighties, and certainly would not have been able to expand its programs. Papp compared the use of the Festival's *Chorus Line* income to the subsidies received by theatres and other arts institutions in Europe.

The windfall from 25 percent of the profits plus royalties as stager and writer changed Bennett from a director-choreographer into an industry. As Plum Productions, he had been co-producing since the time of *Twigs,* realizing that total control necessitated this extra step.

BENNETT: "I like producing because it takes care of me artistically. There's not a producer to say, 'You can't have that.' Artistically, I'm the producer and I take responsibility for the show, which I did as the director anyway, so I might as well have real responsibility without having one other person who's worried about whether I'm making the right decision every time. No one makes the right decision all the time."

But, by the late Seventies, co-producing *A Chorus Line* had brought him wealth beyond that of any creative talent in the theatre. Bennett had begun the *Chorus Line* workshops in debt, and sank further into arrears during the workshop period when he was earning one hundred dollars a week. Now he was able to purchase a vintage white Rolls-Royce and a $3 million house in the Hamptons, and *Variety* reported that, by 1977, the various companies of the show were earning him $90,000 a week gross income.

But, like that of the Shakespeare Festival, most of Bennett's *Chorus Line* money was soon poured back into the theatre, although Bennett was to put his specifically toward the development of musical theatre. In 1978, Bennett stumbled on to a loft building on Broadway between Nineteenth and Twentieth streets, a department store at the turn of the century, which he would turn into his gift to the industry he loved.

BENNETT: "It was an accident. Eliot Feld and I are very close; I replaced him as Baby John in *West Side Story,* and he had found this building and was renting the eighth floor. The building has no pillars, it has a center steel support system down the middle, which means you can knock out 10,000 square feet on each floor on each side of the steel, and you can put football fields in here. When you're a dancer, you spend your life in little dance studios dancing around pillars. But not here.

"I was looking for new office space and I'd always wanted rehearsal studios. The idea for this building is Hal Prince's, which is really based on a small movie studio, where you have everything in one building, the costume shop, the designers, the production office, rooms for writers, your business offices, so that you're not running around town all day. Nor are your performers spending two hours getting across town to go for a shoe fitting.

"When the fourth floor became available, I tried to rent it, and in the process of negotiating the lease, I bought the building. As leases in the building expired, I either gave them to other people who were working in the musical theatre or converted them to more rehearsal studios."

The building at 890 Broadway that Bennett purchased for $750,000 in 1978 would become, within five years, a haven for much of the creative talent in the musical theatre and dance worlds, a place where writers, designers, choreographers, singers, and dancers could work and develop projects away from the standard Broadway system.

Bennett was seeking to re-create the experience that had enabled him and his writers and performers to create *A Chorus Line,* and he initially envisioned 890 as a place to produce four yearly workshop productions developed along the lines of the *Chorus Line* workshops. In the late Sixties, Jerome Robbins, with a similar vision, had begun his American Theatre Laboratory only a few blocks away from 890 Broadway, but he was a part of the tradition that needed a book and score before creating a show, and Robbins abandoned the project after less than two years, with no production emerging from it. Bennett was also a part of that tradition, but, having experienced with *A Chorus Line* a new creative process that was at least partly his invention, he was ready for 890 Broadway.

Most of Bennett's income from *A Chorus Line* went into renovating and maintaining the eight-story building as a rehearsal and workshop space for the arts community of the city. He created a spacious suite of offices for himself, first on the fourth and later on the seventh floor, which ultimately encompassed a kitchen, sleeping loft, gym, meeting room, and lounge. He created enormous rehearsal spaces, plus showers, lockers, greenrooms, and kitchens, comforts unheard of in earlier rehearsal situations. The building soon included the offices of the Eliot Feld Ballet, American Ballet Theatre, set designer Wagner, costume designer Aldredge, and Barbara Matera's costume shop.

As if all this wasn't enough, in 1983 construction began on a three-hundred-seat theatre on the first floor of the building, one modeled along the lines of the Public's Newman Theater, where *A Chorus Line* began, but with a full orchestra pit and fly space. This space opened for commercial presentations in 1985 as Theatre 890; it had been used for auditions and run-throughs by Bennett for his own shows in the previous two years.

Some observers believed that Bennett would profit substantially from renting out space to all the new musicals that could secure it, but, in truth, he did not charge his ballet tenants sufficient rent, and he eventually subsidized much of what went on in the building.

BENNETT: "I don't like to think of myself as the landlord, but I own the building. In 1983, the building and the rehearsal studios broke even for the first time. I've spent all my *Chorus Line* money renovating and rebuilding. It's not about money. Nothing has been about money.

"The studios are not called 'Michael Bennett Studios,' although everyone refers to this building as 'Michael's.' It's 890 Broadway or 890 Studios, and my name is not on my door or on the front of the building.

"When I'm working, I use some of the studios, and when I'm not, I rent out to everybody else. What I want to do is encourage theatre. I believe in the musical theatre. I hate it when I spend evenings with my friends and they're sitting there bitching about not working. It's wonderful to work in this building because you go into a room, you have problems with your writers, problems with your actors, and you know that across the hall, Hal Prince is having problems with somebody else, and everybody's doing the same thing. There's much more a feeling of community, that it's not so special what we do.

"There was one thing I loved about the theatre the way it used to be: everybody did three shows a year. There wasn't such a heavy artistic or economic trip laid on all of us. I believe very few people do great work under pressure. If you evolve as a human being, you get better about knowing that it is not strictly out of neurosis that talent comes. So anything that takes the pressure off helps the creation of something."

Near the end of his life, Bennett was forced to negotiate the sale of the building to businessmen. That sale was prevented, however, when the

Feld Ballet and ABT came up with money to match the sale price and take on the responsibility of maintaining the building. The ballet companies preserved 890 Broadway as a building devoted to the arts and as a monument to Bennett. Today, one has only to enter the building, take the elevator to any floor, and glimpse the creativity that is everywhere to realize the significance of 890 Broadway in Bennett's life. The building still deserves the appellation "Michael Bennett Studios."

In 1989, Bennett's idol, Jerome Robbins, made his return to the commercial theatre with a retrospective called *Jerome Robbins' Broadway*. Naturally, Robbins rehearsed it at 890.

6
. . . .

THE LONG RUN

A SHOW AS SPECIAL AS *A Chorus Line* naturally became host to world leaders and special events. President Gerald Ford attended in 1977 with wife Betty, who was seeing it for a second time. The Broadway company entertained at the first official White House dinner of the Reagan administration. And when the Iranian hostages were released in early 1981, *A Chorus Line* was one of their two Broadway stops.

BOB MACDONALD, general manager and later company manager: "The city asked us if we would be willing to give 100 tickets to the hostages on a Friday night, and we said yes. They were attending *Sugar Babies* the night before. At the beginning of the week, everyone at the Festival said, 'We're not going to do anything special.' We knew *Sugar Babies* would take advantage of the event, and we intended to be more tasteful about it. But after the coverage *Sugar Babies* got on Friday morning, Michael called and said, 'I need a 40-foot flag for the back of the stage tonight.' . . . During the finale, the flag came down in place of the appearance of the sunburst. Michael brought all the hostages on stage, and they looked like they wanted to be out of there."

An ambitious and much-publicized attempt at an East-West cultural exchange involving *A Chorus Line* failed spectacularly.

ROBERT KAMLOT: "Joe Papp went over to Russia and tried to effect a cultural exchange, whereby the Festival would bring over the Moscow Art Theatre in three plays and play Boston, Washington and New York, and we would bring *A Chorus Line* to Russia and play Kiev, Leningrad and Moscow. I went over to look at theatres and see if I could negotiate the deal with the Ministry of Culture.

"But the Russians at that time had become involved in the Afghanistan situation, and the climate for raising money for this project in America was very bad. Our relationship with the Soviet Union deteriorated very badly, and we were ultimately unable to raise any money at all. Only Jessica Tandy and Hume Cronyn, who had played *The Gin Game* in Russia and believed strongly in this type of cultural exchange, offered $25,000. It would have cost us about $1.5 million. I think the Moscow Art Theatre would have been very hard to sell over here, whereas *A Chorus Line* would have been a blockbuster over there."

While Bennett always maintained that the show was the star, cast changes do affect the quality of any show, and when a show runs as long as *A Chorus Line,* there are bound to be hundreds of such changes. Some performers have shifted from role to role, while some have played the same role for the better part of a decade. The steps of Cassie's dance may change slightly for different performers, while some Mikes, such as Don Correia and Danny Herman, have added extra acrobatics to "I Can Do That." Dancing ability must be considered before vocal strength in hiring replacements, so the show has not always been as well sung as it was originally. If later cast members could not bring the immediacy to the material that the original cast—most of whom were models for the characters—brought to it, the show still seems to work for audiences.

As noted, original cast members have returned to the production throughout the run, and their return has always been a special event.

HERMAN: "You want them to like you, because they understand the play, and it's good to see that they respect it so much that they want to come back to it. After working with them a little while, you find they're a lot like you. They're dancers, gypsies, and have the same insecurities out there as you do."

BISHOP: "I thought I'd never put that leotard on again, but I went back twice. It was a challenge, but I think I actually pulled the company together."

A Chorus Line offers cast members something that only a few other Broadway musicals, such as *Cats* and *Les Misérables,* can offer.

MACDONALD: *"A Chorus Line* pays very low salaries compared to most Broadway musicals. Cassie, Zach and sometimes Sheila and Paul get a little more money than the others, but only a small amount. The union minimums have gotten so high that they now border on the cast salaries. But we have always taken a hard line on that, because it's one of the ways we have been able to keep the show running. We've never gone for gimmicks, like bringing in a star who would have to be paid $10,000 a week. And while the salaries are low, we offer something to the cast that most shows can't: year-round employment. They know if they come and work for us, they're not going to be out of work in six months. They'll still be here."

From the years of road tours, *A Chorus Line* developed an enormous pool of performers on which to draw for replacements in the Broadway company, and the show became a giant university, in which a skilled team found the talent, trained it, and moved performers up from understudy to small role to larger role, and from tour to Broadway.

Until his death, Bennett went in and rehearsed the show every four or five months, and would go in whenever Tom Porter felt his presence was needed.

PORTER: "Michael standing in the wings for ten seconds could do more than anybody else could do in three hours."

As with any dance show, injuries are frequent, and most of those in *A Chorus Line* occur during the opening.

EIVIND HARUM: "It's because of having to stand on the line so much. You're sweating like a pig after the first ten minutes, then you come to a dead stop, and you stand there, sweating and cold. Then you have to move again, then come back and stand in line. Injuries occur because of the hot and cold muscles."

All thirty-two performers in the company receive two weeks of vacation annually, which means that there is always someone on vacation, although only one man and one woman are allowed to go at the same time.

Porter now does preliminary auditions with Troy Garza and Fran Liebergall, and the ones they select are seen by Avian. At present, an attempt is being made to hire people who have not appeared in the show before.

PORTER: "It became clear that, if we were to maintain any sort of freshness at all, it would be best to hire people who hadn't done it. We had an enormous number of people to draw on from the road companies, but once a performer has played a role somewhere else, whoever directed them gave them certain habits we don't want."

Maintaining any long run has its problems, particularly when it's a show that portrays a tense situation. Cast members who have been in the show a long time find it difficult to keep up the sense of urgency required in the opening, and to maintain the feeling of being at an audition throughout the performance; many find it helpful to go to auditions while they're in the show and draw upon that experience in their performances.

PORTER: "Because the whole show is choreographed, everybody has to be in a certain place at a certain time. There's no leeway, so it's easier to keep up than some shows I've worked on. But it is the hardest thing in the world to keep a feeling of tension up there. I try to think of new ways of giving the same notes, and I use anything I can think of to get their blood going, like anybody being in the audience. Michael's presence always made a difference."

MACDONALD: "Michael would show up after the show had started, and sneak into the stage-left wings. There's a point in the opening where everyone turns to the left, and suddenly they'd see Michael. The stage managers would sneak into the back of the house to watch the cast's reaction when they saw him there. The energy level would change totally."

There comes a point when no performer can maintain the proper sense of stress and pressure required by the material, and the staff is always on the lookout for *"Chorus Line* burnout." Even members of the original company experienced this, particularly those who got rejected at the end night after night and soon found it difficult to do the show week after week. Performing *A Chorus Line,* while not necessarily more physically exhausting than other dance musicals, is emotionally draining, and some cast members find it difficult to shake the experience, even after the rousing finale.

MACDONALD: "Michael always knew when a performer's time had come, and when they had burned up their energy for the show. When the stage manager and dance captain and vocal people had done what they could, Michael would take them in the office and say, 'I want you to leave. I'll use you again some place else, but you're hurting the show, and it's time for you to leave.' "

Now that there is only the Broadway company to maintain and Bennett is gone, everything goes through Avian.

AVIAN: "Every person is approved by me. In 1980, Equity changed their rules about letting people go after Martin Charnin went back to see *Annie,* was dissatisfied with what he saw, and fired loads of people. There are now strict 'just cause' provisions, so I bring in every new person on a 3-month contract, and I let it terminate if they're not good. But there are some carry overs, people who have been there five years or more, who are on different contracts, and Equity has made it difficult to fire them. But they are tired and should be gone. I had to let six go in December, 1987."

LIEBERGALL: "The quality and standard of the show are of the utmost importance to us, and we're not going to settle. Unfortunately, it took Michael's death to reinforce that."

In the early Eighties, there was a Christmas party for the Shakespeare Festival in the lobby of the Public Theater to which many of those involved in *A Chorus Line* went dressed as elderly versions of the show's characters. MacDonald went as Zach, using a walker to move, while the actress playing Judy at the time wore her costume but with added breasts that sagged to her knees and padding for cellulite. Indeed, it appears the show may continue to run long enough for the characters of 1975 to become senior citizens.

Bennett had envisioned moving the show—when it had finally run out of steam at the Shubert—downtown to the theatre in 890, which was built to resemble the original *Chorus Line* theatre. This now seems unlikely, as the fate of that theatre is uncertain at present. Whether it continues at the Shubert or moves to another Broadway house,* it appears likely that audiences will continue to react to *A Chorus Line* as strongly as always. Trish Ramish, a recent member of the cast and one of the last performers ever to be rehearsed by Bennett, said, "Maintaining the show is the only way we have to show that he's still alive, and that we're thankful to him for what he gave us."

. . . .

*Reports published just as this book was going to press have indicated that *A Chorus Line* might close before the end of 1989.

7

. . . .

BENNETT AND *A CHORUS LINE*

GO TO THE MOVIES

O NE OF THE KEYS to Bennett's work was his use of cinematic techniques, so it was inevitable that he would be paged by Hollywood and that he would be receptive to its overtures. And, as is the case with almost all great Broadway successes, the movies wanted *A Chorus Line.* In 1975, Universal Studios purchased the film rights to the show for a record $5.5 million, and at the same time offered Bennett a lucrative contract to produce and direct the *Chorus Line* film and three other movies of his choosing during the subsequent five years.

Bennett had contributed very limited choreography to the 1968 Universal comedy *What's So Bad About Feeling Good?,* a limp urban satire that featured several performers, such as John McMartin and George Furth, with whom Bennett was to work later in his career. But he felt that he was destined to do major work in the film world.

Bennett took palatial Park Avenue offices at MCA, the parent company of Universal, and decided to get at least one film under his belt before tackling *A Chorus Line.* He and Avian went out to Hollywood to observe the filmmaking process—under the supervision of Verna Fields—and soon announced plans for four projects. One was the musical *Pin-Ups,* the show Bennett might have done instead of *A Chorus Line* had he not been told it would be too expensive to mount. It was now to be a backstage saga about the creation of a revue during World War II. He planned a film version of "Bobbitt," a short story from Thomas Tryon's *Crowned Heads* about a child star's later years. He was also interested in Joyce Carol Oates's "Wonderland" as a possible property.

The project in which he was most interested, however, was *Roadshow,* which he had conceived as a movie about a bus-and-truck tour of the musical *Seesaw.* Jerome Kass, who would later write the book of *Ballroom,* developed a screenplay that would allow a certain amount of the *Seesaw* material to be used but that would also focus on the performers in the company, in particular a young actress who is paged to replace the original leading lady.

What seemed like a natural for Bennett's film debut ground to a halt because of a dispute with the studio over casting. Bennett's choices of Robert Redford as leading man and Tommy Tune from the original *Seesaw* were accepted, but he had conceived the film with Bette Midler in mind as the new leading lady. Midler had not yet made her successful film debut in *The Rose,* and Universal insisted that the only way the film would work was if Bennett used Barbra Streisand, Liza Minnelli, or Goldie Hawn in the female lead. Bennett refused, and the film, which had been budgeted at $6 million, was never made.

Bennett quickly soured on Hollywood and asked to be released from his contract. He was a man of the theatre and was uncomfortable in the very different world of the movies. He realized that the artistic freedom he had found in the theatre could not be his at a Hollywood studio.

LENNY: "Michael said to me, 'There isn't anyone at a movie studio who isn't frightened of somebody, from the very top down. There's always somebody they're worried about.' "

AVIAN: "In New York, with his production team, Michael was king of the mountain. All of a sudden at Universal, people were telling him no, and he didn't like it. And he had an attitude that made them nervous. One day, he said to me, 'I've had enough. How about you?' I said, 'Sure.' When it was time to go, he left a note on his desk which said, 'Gone fishing.' We went to the hotel, packed our clothes, and left for New York.

"My personal feeling was we belonged in the movies; I thought it was an inevitable destiny to go there. But when the time came, we went to the wrong studio, and Michael was so successful in New York that it didn't click in. It was sad. I think Michael would have been great at film, and the actors would have adored him."

BENNETT: "I'm not eager to lose one eye and look through the camera. There's something about doing that that leaves a part of life out. I respect film and I'm very cinematic in the way I work in the theatre, but when it actually came to making a movie, it wasn't as interesting as I thought it would be, because you do things in pieces. When you make something happen in the theatre, it happens live. Then you make it happen again and again and again. You don't just capture it once. I don't know why that excites me, but it does. I know how to get things done in the theatre, but I don't know how to get things done in the movies."

Bennett might have made a marvelous film director, and could perhaps have revitalized the screen musical. But the theatre was where he lived, and Bennett was unable to work in an atmosphere that was alien to him.

BENNETT: "I don't care about going down in history. I like it that theatre lives only in the memory."

Giving up his contract meant, of course, relinquishing the opportunity to bring *A Chorus Line* to the screen, but, surprisingly, Bennett felt few qualms about doing so because of the fundamental difference between the way he conceived the movie and what Universal had in mind. Having bought the show and its director, Universal expected Bennett to transfer the show to film more or less intact, but Bennett was in no way interested in doing that. By the time he was supposed to have commenced work on the *Chorus Line* film in 1979, he had cast, staged, and maintained all the show's companies, and he now felt he could not spend another two or three years of his life on the film if it was to be no more than a literal transcription. More importantly, he had his own concept for the *Chorus Line* movie.

AVIAN: "Michael wanted to structure the movie as an audition for the movie version of *A Chorus Line,* to give it the same reality as the show. Instead of having Mike do his sequence, he would have four kids who played it, from Broadway and the road companies, all wanting the movie version. It would have had the same documentary reality in movie terms. . . . But Michael never even told Universal the idea, because they never would have bought it. They bought the show, and you couldn't tell them you were doing something so different. But it would have been a better movie, because it would have been truth."

LENNY: "Michael said, 'I'm the only one who could put *A Chorus Line* on the screen, but I don't want to do it. I'll tell you what will happen when it's made into a movie. If it's a hit, they'll say I'm a genius because I created the show. If it's a flop, they'll say it's a flop because Michael Bennett didn't do it.' "

The latter words would prove all too prophetic when the film version finally appeared.

When Universal realized that they had Bennett's show but not Bennett, they contacted several major directors and screenwriters, some of whom attempted the project before abandoning it. Mike Nichols, James Bridges, and Sidney Lumet were all announced to direct it at one time or another, while Bo Goldman and Joel Schumacher both wrote screen treatments of the material. Ann-Margret was announced for the lead in 1977, while John Travolta, a big fan of the show, was also mentioned for a role in the screen version.

Eventually, Universal gave up on the project, selling the rights to Broadway and film producers Cy Feuer and Ernest Martin, who had tried to take an option on the film rights after the show's second Public Theater preview. The film was ultimately an Embassy Films and Polygram Pictures presentation of a Feuer and Martin production, released through Columbia.

The direction of the film was placed in the hands of British director Richard Attenborough, who had recently won an Oscar for *Gandhi* and had made one previous screen musical, *Oh! What a Lovely War.* The choice of an Englishman not associated with musicals to direct this quintessentially American show-biz musical raised many eyebrows, but at least Attenborough was willing to tackle a project before which so many others had thrown up their hands.

It was now 1984, and Attenborough decided to give the material a contemporary look by casting primarily young and attractive dancers in their teens and early twenties, and hiring Jeffrey Hornaday, choreographer of the hit film *Flashdance,* to reflect contemporary styles in the choreography. Attenborough spent months watching the show at the Shubert and seeing hundreds of performers who were eager to appear in the film. He chose three, Justin Ross, Pam Klinger, and Matt West, to play in the film the roles they were currently performing on Broadway. His choice for Cassie, Alyson Reed, had played that role and Val on tour, while his Sheila, Vicki Frederick, had played Cassie on Broadway and on tour. Most members of the original cast auditioned for the film but were considered too old to blend with the California youngsters Hornaday brought with him; not a single member of the original cast got to appear in the film.

After eight weeks of rehearsal, sixteen weeks of shooting began in October at the Mark Hellinger Theater. Months of editing and dubbing followed, and the film premiered at Radio City Music Hall a few weeks before Christmas 1985. It was not greeted favorably by most critics or by those involved in the original show.

Vincent Canby of *The New York Times* said: "They said *A Chorus Line* couldn't be done [on screen]—and this time they were right."

KIRKWOOD: "I saw it at a screening that Feuer and Martin gave for everyone. When it was over, we all lied, then went to Joe Allen's. We started calmly, saying, 'Well, maybe if you didn't see the show and you weren't that close to it,' but by the end of the evening, we were saying, 'Murderers! Baby killers!' "

While the film did receive a few good notices and better ones in Europe, it was immediately perceived as less than a success, and Embassy Films, which was in the process of folding at the time of the film's release, was unable to put much in the way of advertising dollars behind it. It failed quickly and had a relatively rapid release in the home video market. Any fears that the film would be a threat to the continued existence of the show proved completely unfounded, and the Broadway production was actually helped by the film's reception.

In spite of many changes in lines, numbers, and characters, Attenborough had made a sincere attempt to be faithful to the original material. He and his staff, however, made several mistakes that effectively sabotaged his desire to remain close to the original. First, believing that the material needed a unifying element, it was decided to build up the Cassie-Zach relationship. Suddenly, Cassie's part became much larger and Attenborough cut away from the stage to scenes of Cassie wandering in the wings, dressing rooms, and throughout the theatre, and to flashbacks of the Zach-Cassie romance in happier times. While this gave filmgoers a central love story for which to root, the relationship became shallow and clichéd when blown up; the show's creators were careful not to let this element dominate, realizing that this was not really what the show was about. The increase in the size of Zach's role was not aided by Michael Douglas's relentlessly grim and tortured performance.

Attenborough made two damaging changes in the musical numbers.

Substituting a disco-style number called "Surprise" in place of "Hello Twelve" deprived the audience of all the exposition and character detail contained in the original number. More crucially, he gave "What I Did for Love" to Cassie, making it a solo about her relationship with Zach, and thus depriving the others of their climactic emotional statement.

Aside from these mistakes, Attenborough was unable to solve the fundamental problem that probably no director could have solved—that of the difference between the two media. In the theatre, *A Chorus Line* was performed in a black, sometimes mirrored box with a white line painted on the floor. It was never allowed to be merely a "real" audition; rather, it used the audition metaphorically. The movie lost all the metaphorical richness by creating a far more realistic audition and cutting away from it to scenes all over a realistic-looking theatre. In the show, the lack of realistic theatre signposts (such as dressing rooms or a stage doorman's booth) made the audition into a symbolic landscape in which the dancers became representatives of people in all walks of life. And the nonstop tension, unrelieved by an intermission, forced every audience member onstage with the dancers. In the film, the material was vastly diminished in scope and resonance, and the audience was no longer at an audition for life.

Could another director have made a richer film of *A Chorus Line?* One has only to see the opening minutes of Bob Fosse's *All That Jazz,* released several years before the *Chorus Line* film, to see the work of a director who had found exciting cinematic equivalents for stage techniques.

8

A CHORUS LINE

IN RETROSPECT

As WE HAVE SEEN, *A Chorus Line* gave many of its performers an experience that took years to assimilate and come to terms with. As far as the show's writers are concerned, *A Chorus Line* proved an unalloyed blessing for two and a very mixed one for the others.

Marvin Hamlisch did his finest work to date for the theatre in *A Chorus Line.* His subsequent theatrical contributions include one hit, *They're Playing Our Song,* and two failures, *Jean Seberg* at the National Theatre in London, and *Smile* on Broadway. There are those who are quick to point out that only Bennett got the best work out of Hamlisch. Hamlisch looks back on *A Chorus Line* with enormous admiration for what was accomplished.

HAMLISCH: "The most important thing that came out of *A Chorus Line* was that it showed that if you're willing to have an open view of Broadway, and if you're willing to collaborate, and if you're not too scared to be daring, then not only can you have a show that you like, but you can have a show that the people will like because you're not underestimating their intelligence. . . . What was beautiful about *Chorus Line* was we didn't worry too much about 'them'; we were worried about what we felt, what we thought was good. We put it up there, and we thought, if we love it, chances are they'll love it.

"The beauty of the show was that it was a total collaboration. I wasn't just the music department, Ed wasn't just lyrics. Michael wasn't just choreographer and director. Everybody had a say in everything, which is the healthiest way to write.

"I'm thrilled that my first show became a hit and the longest-running show. I just hope a show I write in the future beats it."

When asked why the show turned out so well, James Kirkwood replies: "We were all so wild about doing it. It was our lives, and I would have walked across hot coals for that show. . . . It was the only time I've ever been associated with anything in the theatre where there weren't major battles. A couple of years afterward, we all started drifting apart, and we didn't work together again, which was unfortunate."

Kirkwood's only regret is that the text of the show has never been published.

"I was certain that we would publish the script, in a picture-book format. We had a couple of publishing deals, but Michael somehow blocked them. Some people said that was because Michael's name would not have been on it as author, so it was less important to him. Then there was the threatened litigation from Cy Coleman. Nicholas and I did a lot of work on the script for publication, because the script distributed to actors is rather slim. For publication, it had to be more descriptive, and it was. . . . It really should have come out a year or two after it opened as a big Christmas book.

"I recently saw an all-black production of the show at Kennedy King College in Milwaukee, with Equity members playing Cassie, Zach and Paul, and the rest students. It worked brilliantly, and I told Joe Papp, Marvin, Ed and Nicholas what a fantastic idea I thought it was. Michael was too sick at the time. If we did it on Broadway with an all-black cast, I bet we'd sell out for about two years. A lot of people would come back.

"When I look back on *A Chorus Line,* I look back on it like high school—I want to be back in high school again."

Kirkwood has not had another genuine theatrical success since *A Chorus Line,* although his comedy *Legends,* starring Mary Martin and Carol Channing, toured America for a year and was a financial hit. He was already an established writer before *A Chorus Line* and is currently working on several books, so he has no reason to see it as a phantom hanging over him.

The other two offical authors of *A Chorus Line* found it a burden and a source of pain; one of them has now grown to accept it, while the other was.unable during his short lifetime to come to terms with his success.

Ed Kleban's work for *A Chorus Line* forms one of the most beautifully integrated, skillful, and witty sets of lyrics of any modern musical. Hamlisch is unstinting in his praise of Kleban's contribution to the show.

HAMLISCH: "I always felt Ed was the great unsung hero of the show. That beautiful fusion between book and lyrics which is what great theatre lyricists are all about was something that he cared so deeply about.

"The first time I heard the line in 'At the Ballet,' 'Every prince has got to have his swan,' I said to him. 'No matter what you write in your life, you have touched me in a way that I cannot be touched again.' I will always be indebted to Ed because he cared about the revisions, and wouldn't let me get away with murder. When a melody was good but not as good as he wanted it to be, he said, 'You can do better.'"

Kleban had worked on several musicals before *A Chorus Line,* and attempts were made to reactivate two of these after the *Chorus Line* success. Papp presented a workshop of Kleban's *Gallery,* directed by Richard Maltby, Jr., in July 1981 at the Public Theater, but Papp would later say that while the songs were gorgeous, the show's problems proved insoluble. Peter Stone asked Kleban to pick up *Subject to Change* again but was told by Kleban that he had "retired." Kleban worked with Paul Rudnick on a show called *Musical Comedy,* and in the last year of his life on an autobiographical musical, *Light on My Feet.*

Kleban seemed to have a deep-rooted fear of trying to equal his first produced show and he was not able to conquer it during his lifetime. During most of the run of *A Chorus Line,* he spent New Year's Eve checking out the latest cast; but he was unable to see the December 31, 1987, performance, as he died of cancer just three days before.

Kleban the perfectionist had not even been completely happy with his great hit.

KLEBAN: "Thank God they didn't leave it to me whether or not to open it. I would never have opened it. I only like about 65% of it now, so it's fortunate it was not left to me."

He left explicit instructions for his memorial service: anyone could sing or play music, "with the exception of the composition 'What I Did for Love,' which I do not wish to be performed." He directed that his remains be placed in the wedgewood urn he received when *A Chorus Line* won the London Musical of the Year Award, and that the urn be present at his memorial. At that service, Composer David Shire spoke of "the painful irony of Ed's career: that the artistic soul of the distinguished lyricist of Broadway's longest-running musical was to a great extent most characteristically embodied in a large number of songs, for which he wrote both words and music, that never really went public."

Yet Kleban left a very definite legacy in the musical theatre aside from *A Chorus Line*. A member of the BMI Musical Theatre Workshop for seventeen years and one of seven composers and lyricists who ran it after the death of its founder, Lehman Engel, Kleban taught and inspired such writers of today's musical theatre as Shire, Maltby, Maury Yeston, Alan Menken, and Howard Ashman. Kleban's entire week centered around Friday afternoons at four when he went to the workshop that meant so much to him. Ultimately, his greatest contribution to the musical theatre was not *A Chorus Line* but his guidance of young talent and his recognition of excellence in others. It is probably the BMI workshop, rather than the show at the Shubert, that stands as Kleban's memorial.

Co-author Nicholas Dante has written for theatre and film since *A Chorus Line* but without great success. His rise from despair to self-awareness is one of *A Chorus Line*'s most fascinating personal sagas.

DANTE: "I never really wrote the Paul monologue. I said it at the tapes, and what came out that night was used in the show almost exactly. For that reason, I tended to dismiss that speech and my contribution to the show. I always felt like the fag dancer that tagged along on everybody's coattails. I've been treated that way, and I've treated myself that way. I dismissed the monologue because it was the most obvious thing I contributed, and because I never went on as a writer, although I tried to. . . . Now, I think the whole show hangs on that monologue and I'm thrilled with it. I think now it paved the way for *Torch Song Trilogy* and other gay material that reached Broadway.

"I've just done a few years of intense therapy. I had a lot of anger and never quite understood why. I finally realized that that big a success is wonderful, but it can also be a terrible albatross. It crippled me on many levels, but mainly because my collaborators and producers dismissed me. They were all so busy trying to take the credit or survive that success on their own terms. I was treated so rudely and so unimportantly by my producers, so how could I take myself seriously? Joe Papp is always talking about discovering new playwrights. After *A Chorus Line,* I sent him a movie script that I wrote, and he never read it. Michael said he was going to take care of me and manage me, even though I hadn't asked him to. But he wasn't helpful after *A Chorus Line,* and I hid in this Buddhist organization so I wouldn't freak out.

"Michael could be wonderful, but there was that other side of him. In 1985, I was asked to play myself, Paul, for the first time in the show in the Donna McKechnie company that was touring and later went to Japan. Baayork, who put the tour together, asked me, and I said, 'I'd love to.' Then Baayork called and said, 'Nick, I'm really sorry, but Michael found out and wants you out. He told me if I use you, I'll never work for him again or do the show again.' I called Michael and said, 'What is your big problem? I'm not fat, I'm not ridiculous, and I'm not going to embarrass myself.' He said, 'You all think it's so easy.' It was the manipulation, the power, making me know who's boss. It was also jealousy, because he would have loved to play Zach, but he couldn't because of who he was and his position. I was going out and doing something he would have loved to do, to be out there with Donna and Baayork, but when you have that kind of ego about mystique and position, you don't do that.

"When Donna and I did interviews on the tour, everyone asked, 'What have you done since *A Chorus Line?*' People make you feel you have to go out and do it again and again. There's something very wrong with that value, and it weighed Donna down, too.

"I was in the tour as a dancer, not as the author, but when we were rehearsing in Asbury Park, we hit a line that was no longer working because we were doing the show in the round. I wanted to change it, but the actress who had the line questioned me, and so did Donna and Baayork, in front of the company. Even they were dismissing me; if it had been Jimmy Kirkwood, he would not have been dismissed the way I was. I realized that all these people had dismissed me all of these years, and they were now doing it to my face, so I quit.

"I didn't want anyone else's credit for the show. I just wanted the credit due me. Because so many people have taken more credit than they deserve, who did what has gotten lost. In order for me to get the credit I deserve, I have to write another play.

"I have to accept the fact that my writing career since *A Chorus Line* has thus far failed, but it's not over. If you do something good, people should recognize it, and if you never do it again, that should be okay. I was so afraid of seeming like a failure, a flash in the pan. And if I am, well, that's okay, too. It was a great flash. I'm not afraid of the truth anymore. I wrote this great thing—what am I apologizing for?"

Can *A Chorus Line* stay on Broadway forever?

MACDONALD: "In recent years, the show's business has fallen into a pattern, and this year's figures are almost totally consistent with last year's. January has become a killer for the show, but it always picks up in the spring.

"The royalty structure has been revised twice, and we have one of the lowest breakevens of any musical.

"But the financial problems continue to escalate, costs rise, and the musicians, stagehands and other unions are not willing to make concessions. They say, 'You've made a lot of money out of it. Why should we take less at this point?' For about ten years, I've been saying, 'It's good for two more years.' The Shuberts are very committed to keeping the show running as a landmark."

One hopes that, whatever the fluctuations of business, *A Chorus Line* can remain on Broadway as the most fitting monument to the chorus dancer who created it.

APPENDIX B

. . . .

MICHAEL BENNETT

ON VIDEO

O THER THAN CONTRIBUTING VERY brief sequences to *What's So Bad About Feeling Good,* Michael Bennett never made a film. But we are fortunate that a great deal of his work exists on videotape, much of which can be seen in museums and libraries. The following is a list of some of the most valuable documents of Bennett's career that exist on videotape, with indications of where these items can be viewed. Some of the tapes of complete live performances of shows are unavailable for viewing at this writing.

"Hullabaloo": Bennett and McKechnie can be seen dancing on episodes of this Sixties television series.

Henry, Sweet Henry: Alice Playten and company performed the number "Poor Little Person" on "The Ed Sullivan Show."

How Now, Dow Jones: Anthony Roberts and company performed the number "Step to the Rear," which is at least partially Bennett's work, on the 1968 Tony Awards. All Tony Awards telecasts are in the Theatre on Film and Tape Collection at the Library and Museum of the Performing Arts, the New York Public Library at Lincoln Center.

Promises, Promises: Jerry Orbach performed "She Likes Basketball" and McKechnie and company performed "Turkey Lurkey Time," a key number in the early Bennett career, on the 1969 Tony Awards.

Pinocchio: Bennett choreographed this Hallmark Hall of Fame original television musical, which aired December 8, 1968. It can be seen at the Museum of Broadcasting in New York.

Coco: Katharine Hepburn, George Rose, Gale Dixon, and David Holliday appear in scenes and the "Always Mademoiselle" number on the 1970 Tony Awards, probably the longest sequence from one musical ever featured on a Tony telecast.

Company: A complete performance of *Company* with the original staging (minus the moving elevators) was taped at the end of the national tour on May 20, 1972, at Washington's National Theatre. The black-and-white tape, featuring McKechnie in her original role, Gary Krawford as Robert, Julie Wilson as Joanne, and Tandy Cronyn, Jane A. Johnston, Louisa Flaningham, Joy Franz, J. T. Cromwell, and others, preserves Bennett's thrilling opening sequence, the "Side by Side" number and "Tick Tock," with McKechnie particularly electrifying in the latter. It can be seen in the Theatre on Film and Tape Collection.

Follies: One of the most legendary productions in theatrical history, there are three short videotapes in existence that preserve portions of the original Prince-Bennett staging. The Theatre on Film and Tape Collection has two half hours, one silent and one with sound, shot in Los Angeles. The sound tape was shot during a rehearsal, while the silent tape is edited and combines footage shot from the wings and above the stage with footage shot from the orchestra. Los Angeles replacements Janet Blair and Ed Winter are in the silent half hour. There is also a fifteen-minute compilation of sequences from the show shot at the Winter Garden Theatre during the final New York performance. This tape is in private collections. All three tapes are video transfers of material shot on film. Alexis Smith performed "The Story of Lucy and Jessie" on the 1975 Tony Awards, but this version features only traces of Bennett's original choreography.

Seesaw: Michele Lee performed "I'm Way Ahead" on the 1974 Tony Awards telecast.

A Chorus Line: The original New York Shakespeare Festival production was videotaped at the Public/Newman Theater in 1975. The black-and-white tape is of mediocre quality but is nevertheless an invaluable document. It is in the Theatre on Film and Tape Collection. The original cast can best be seen on the 1976 Tony Awards telecast in the opening sequence (slightly cut) and the final section of the finale. The Theatre on Film and Tape Collection also has a one-hour dialogue with Bennett and Avian from 1977, which covers the genesis of

A Chorus Line from workshop to Broadway. Also in the collection is a tape of the #3,389th Gala Performance. The finale of that performance was telecast on the NBC program "Live and in Person," and there was an enormous amount of television coverage of the performance and celebration, most of which is available in the Theatre on Film and Tape Collection. Various casts of the show can be seen in the finale on the Kennedy Center Honors and "Baryshnikov on Broadway." McKechnie can be seen in some of the "Music and the Mirror" choreography on the 1980 HBO special "Showstoppers," and on the salute to Bennett on the 1988 Tony Awards.

Ballroom: Dorothy Loudon performed "Fifty Percent" on the 1979 Tony Awards.

Dreamgirls: A complete performance of the show, taped near the end of the original Broadway run in August 1985 at the Imperial Theatre, is in the Theatre on Film and Tape Collection. The final scene of Act One, somewhat cut, was performed by the original cast on the 1982 Tony Awards. Various casts performed the title song on several network television programs.

INDEX